Irish Civilization

Irish Civilization provides the perfect background and introduction to both the history of Ireland until 1921 and the development of Ireland and Northern Ireland since 1921. This book illustrates how these societies have developed in common but also those elements where there have been, and continue to be, substantial differences.

It includes a focus on certain central structural aspects, such as:

- the physical geography
- the people
- political and governmental structures
- cultural contexts
- economic and social institutions
- education and media.

Irish Civilization is a vital introduction to the complex history of both parts of the island and discusses the present state of the relationship between them. It is an essential resource for students of Irish Studies and general readers alike.

Arthur Aughey is Professor of Politics at the University of Ulster and Fellow of the Royal Society of Arts. He is also a Senior Fellow at the Centre for British Politics at the University of Hull. His previous publications include *Politics of Northern Ireland: Beyond the Belfast Agreement* (2005), *Nationalism, Devolution and the Challenge to the United Kingdom State* (2001) and *Northern Ireland Politics*, edited with Duncan Morrow (1996).

John Oakland was a Senior Lecturer in English at the Norwegian University of Science and Technology. His previous publications include *British Civilization* (2010), *American Civilization* co-authored with David C. Mauk (2009), *British Civilization: A Student's Dictionary* (2003) and *Contemporary Britain: A Survey With Texts* (2001).

Irish Civilization

An Introduction

Arthur Aughey and John Oakland

Routledge
Taylor & Francis Group
LONDON AND NEW YORK

First published 2013
by Routledge
2 Park Square, Milton Park, Abingdon, Oxon OX14 4RN

Simultaneously published in the USA and Canada
by Routledge
711 Third Avenue, New York, NY 10017

Routledge is an imprint of the Taylor & Francis Group, an informa business

British Library Cataloguing in Publication Data

A catalogue record for this book is available from the British Library

Library of Congress Cataloging in Publication Data
Aughey, Arthur.
    Irish civilization : an introduction / Arthur Aughey and John Oakland.
        p. cm
    Includes bibliographical references and index.
    1. Ireland—Civilization. 2. Ireland—History.
    I. Oakland, John. II. Title.
    DA925.A94 2012
    941.5—dc23   2012013191

ISBN: 978-0-415-34667-2 (hbk)
ISBN: 978-0-415-34668-9 (pbk)
ISBN: 978-0-203-62453-1 (ebk)

Typeset in Berling and Futura
by Keystroke, Station Road, Codsall, Wolverhampton

Printed and bound in Great Britain by
TJ International Ltd, Padstow, Cornwall

Contents

12 The media   **309**

Plates

Figures

Tables

Preface and acknowledgements

This book examines central features of Irish civilization, such as geography, cultural contexts, peoples, politics, government, international relations, law, economy, social services, media, education and religion, in an attempt to illustrate the island's diverse societies and identities.

Methodologically, the book combines descriptive, factual and analytical approaches within a historical context. Most chapters have a historical perspective and also provide information on debates and recent developments in Ireland and Northern Ireland. The book is designed to allow students (particularly those from overseas) to organize their own responses to Irish history and to encourage discussion. Essay and term exercises at the end of each chapter may be initially approached from material contained in the text. In-depth information may be found on the suggested websites and in the Further reading sections.

Additional material may also be accessed online from Northern Ireland newspapers such as *The Belfast Telegraph*, *News Letter*, *Irish Republican News*, *Irish News*, *Ulster Examiner* (Unionist) and *NewsHound* (with links to other media). Newspapers in Ireland are the *Irish Independent*, *Irish Times* (chargeable), *Irish Examiner* and *Sunday Business Post*. Online news may be obtained from BBC News, BBC Northern Ireland, ITN News, Radio Telefis Éireann (RTE) and Teletext News (Northern Ireland).

A book of this type is indebted to many sources (too numerous to mention individually here) for most of its facts, ideas, theories, debates and statistics, to which a general acknowledgement is made (see also Further reading and websites). Particular thanks are due to opinion poll organizations such as *Eurobarometer*, *TNS/MRBI*, *Northern Ireland Life and Times Survey*, *TASC*, *CAIN*, *ARK*, *Ipsos/ MORI*, *Gallup*, independent websites and the official websites of the Irish and Northern Irish governments and their agencies.

The authors would like to thank the following colleagues for their help in reading chapters at draft stage. Many errors of omission and commission were avoided, but we remain responsible for any that remain: Colin Armstrong, Paul Bew, Derek Birrell, Ruth Fee, Hala Gormley-Heenan, Charles Kenny, Alan McCully, Tracey McRoberts, James Stinson and Michael Taylor.

Chronology of significant dates in Irish history

ca. 1.5m– ca. 20000:	Old Stone Age (Palaeolithic): ice ages with periods of higher temperatures and rising sea levels. No proven evidence of human habitation in Ireland
ca. 10000:	Middle Stone Age (Mesolithic) hunter-gatherers travelled to east and north coasts
ca. 4000:	New Stone Age (Neolithic) people arrived; built megalithic tombs
ca. 2000–1800:	Early Bronze Age metalworkers in tin, copper, gold and bronze arrived
ca. 1000 and 400–100:	Inhabited circular enclosure at Navan fort near Armagh constructed
ca. 600–300:	Celtic groups arrived, with Iron Age manufacturing expertise
ca. 100:	Gaels travelled to Ireland

1–500:	Building of fortified lake islands and hill forts
ca. 200:	High Kingship of Tara initiated
300:	Possible arrival of first Christians
431:	Palladius sent from Rome by Pope Celestine as first bishop to Irish Christians
432:	Contested date for arrival of St Patrick. Conversion of pagan Irish kings to Christianity
ca. 445–53:	O'Neill (Uí Néill) dynasty reputedly created by Niall Noígiallach
ca. 490:	St Éndae founded earliest Irish monastery at Aran
493:	Traditional date for death of St Patrick (17 March); 461 also suggested

Sixth century

520:           Irish missionaries spread Christianity through Britain and Europe
546:           Monastery founded at Londonderry/Derry by St Columba (Colum Cille/Colmcille)
563:           St Columba's mission to Isle of Iona, Scotland; founded monastery
590:           St Columbanus (Colmán) began Irish mission on Continent; founded monasteries
ca. 597:   Death of St Columba

Seventh century

600–800:   Golden Age of early Christian Ireland (illuminated manuscripts, treatises, art)
615:           Death of St Columbanus
635–51:   St Aidan's mission from Iona to Northumbria; founded Lindisfarne
ca. 650–750:   Metal manufacture; stone sculpture and high crosses; Brehon law
664:           Synod of Whitby (Yorkshire); Roman Church's Easter date generally accepted
ca. 668–730:   Transition from tribal social structures to dynastic politics
670– ca. 690: Growth of ecclesiastical authority (centred on Armagh)

Eighth century

710–725:   Irish canon (church) law sources compiled
720–728:   Irish missionaries in Switzerland and Germany; monasteries founded
ca. 740:   Compilation of *Senchas Már* (legal corpus)
ca. 770– ca. 840: Ascetic Culdee (Céile Dé) reform group in Irish Church
795:           First Viking raids on Dublin coast (Lambay Island)

Ninth century

802 and 806:   Iona raided by Vikings
807–813:   Vikings attacked western coast
837–876:   Scattered Viking settlement in Ireland
841:           Permanent Viking camps at Annagassen, Co. Louth. Dublin founded
852:           Vikings occupied Dublin and Waterford
876–916:   Decline in Viking attacks on Ireland

Tenth century

900– ca. 911: Irish and Viking infiltration into England
914:           Viking fleet based at Waterford

916–937:	Renewed Viking activity in Ireland
922:	Foundation of Viking town of Limerick
978:	Brian Boru (Brian Borúma mac Cennétig, 940–1014) became King of Munster
980:	Máel Sechnaill II defeated King of Dublin and Vikings; became High King

Eleventh century

1000:	Brian Boru captured Dublin from Máel Sechnaill
1002:	Máel Sechnaill II acknowledged Brian Boru as High King
1005:	Brian Boru visited Armagh; religious importance of Armagh established
1014:	Brian Boru killed while defeating Vikings and Irish allies at Battle of Clontarf
1028:	Sitric Silkbeard, King of Dublin, and Fannacán, King of Brega, on pilgrimage to Rome
ca. 1028–1036:	Christ Church Cathedral founded by Sitric and Dúnán, first Bishop of Dublin

Twelfth century

1100–1172:	Reform of the Irish Church initiated by St Malachy
1101:	First Synod of Cashel, Co. Tipperary (royal and ecclesiastical centre)
1111:	Synod of Ráith Bressail: change from monastic to diocesan organization of Irish Church
1124:	Round tower at Clonmacnoise monastic centre completed
1132:	St Malachy consecrated Archbishop of Armagh
1142:	First Irish Cistercian religious house founded at Mellifont
1152:	Synod of Kells/Mellifont. Diocesan organization of Irish Church
1155–1156:	Reputed approval by Pope Adrian IV for conquest of Ireland by Henry II
1162:	Synod of Clain; Armagh ecclesiastical primacy confirmed
1166:	Rory O'Connor (Ruaidrí Ua Conchobair, 1166–1175, last High King of Ireland) drove Dermot MacMurrough (Diarmait Mac Murchada, 1134–1171), King of Leinster, from Ireland
1167:	MacMurrough recovered kingdom of Leinster with Norman support
1169:	Normans landed at Bannow Bay, captured Wexford. Henry II claimed Ireland
1170:	Normans and Richard de Clare/Fitz Gilbert ('Strongbow') arrived at Baginbun, Co. Wexford; Waterford captured. Dublin seized by Macmurrough and Norman allies
1171:	Macmurrough succeeded by 'Strongbow' as King of Leinster. Henry II landed near Waterford; submission of Irish kings
1171–1172:	Second Synod of Cashel; Henry II granted charter to Dublin
1172:	Pope Alexander III granted Ireland to Henry II
1177:	John de Courcy invaded Ulster. Henry II created his son Prince John Lord of Ireland

Thirteenth century

1204:	Dublin Castle established as centre of royal administration
1207:	First Irish national coinage, with symbol of the harp
1210:	King John landed at Waterford; created Anglo-Irish government; Irish kings submitted
1216:	Magna Carta applied to Ireland
1224:	First Irish Dominican religious houses at Dublin and Drogheda
ca. 1224–1230:	First Irish Franciscan religious houses at Youghal and Cork
1235:	Conquest of Connaught by Richard de Burgo; Anglo-Norman castles built
1258:	Galloglasses (Hebridean mercenary soldiers) arrived in Ulster to support Irish kings
1262–1263:	Irish kings offered High Kingship to Haakon IV of Norway, in return for military help
1264:	First Parliament in Ireland at Castledermot, Co. Kildare
1280:	Irish claimed English law should apply to them
1297:	Parliament in Dublin; lordships and counties represented
1299:	Parliament in Dublin; towns represented

Fourteenth century

1310:	Parliament at Kilkenny; Irish barred from Anglo-Irish religious houses
1311:	Papal permission for establishment of university in Dublin
1315–1318:	Edward Bruce of Scotland invaded Ireland; killed at Battle of Faughart (1318)
1320:	Dublin Parliament approved establishment of university in Dublin
1331:	English law applicable to Irish and Anglo-Irish, except for serfs
1348–1349:	Black Death at Howth and Drogheda
1366:	Parliament at Kilkenny; statutes of Kilkenny against gaelicization of Anglo-Irish

Fifteenth century

1435:	Irish poets and musicians barred from Anglo-Irish areas in Ireland
1455–1485:	English War of the Roses (Yorkists against Lancastrians) reflected conflicts of Irish lords against Anglo-Irish
1460:	Irish parliamentary independence declared at Drogheda Parliament
1461:	Henry VI deposed; Yorkist Edward IV succeeded. Lancastrians defeated at Towton
1463:	Thomas Fitzgerald, Earl of Desmond, appointed Lord Deputy by Edward IV
1468:	Tiptoft (Chief Governor); Drogheda Parliament; rebels crushed; Desmond executed
1478–1513:	Gerald, Earl of Kildare (Garret Fitzgerald), Governor of Ireland under five kings
1485:	Battle of Bosworth; Richard III killed; Lancastrian Henry VII succeeded

1494:	Drogheda Parliament; Poynings' Law gave control of Irish Parliament to English king
1495:	First mention of the term 'Pale' to denote Anglo-Irish controlled area around Dublin

Sixteenth century

1504:	Battle of Knockdoe (Cnoc Tuagh); Kildare and Anglo-Irish defeated Irish lords
1509:	Accession of Henry VIII
1513–1534:	'Garret Oge', Earl of Kildare, served three periods as Lord Deputy
1515:	Anarchy in Ireland
1520:	Henry VIII sent Thomas Howard, Lord Lieutenant, to Ireland to subdue Irish lords
1534–1535:	Failure of Kildare rebellion
1536–1537:	First Protestant Reformation Parliament in Dublin; royal supremacy enforced
1537:	Papal authority rejected; gradual suppression of monasteries
1539:	Dissolution of monasteries. Defeat of Irish leaders O'Neill and O'Donnell
1541:	Henry VIII crushed Irish uprisings; declared himself King of England and Ireland
1547:	Death of Henry VIII
1547–1553:	Edwardian (Edward VI) Protestant Reformation in Ireland
1549:	First English Act of Uniformity; Book of Common Prayer imposed in Ireland
1550–1557:	English settler plantations in Laois and Offaly
1552:	Second English Act of Uniformity imposed second Book of Common Prayer
1553–1558:	Accession of (Catholic) Mary I: restoration of papal authority
1555:	Pope Paul IV made Ireland a kingdom
1558:	Accession of (Protestant) Elizabeth I. Protestant Reformation not accepted in Ireland
1560:	Reformation Parliament, Dublin; royal supremacy and Elizabethan Church Settlement
1562–1603:	Elizabethan wars in Ireland
1562–1567:	Conflict between Irish O'Neills, O'Donnells and MacDonnells
1569–1570:	Parliament under Lord Deputy Sidney attempted to subdue Ireland
1570:	Pope Pius V excommunicated Elizabeth I
1573–1576:	Earl of Essex attempted to establish plantations in Antrim
1579–1583:	Munster rebellions against government suppressed
1580:	Revolt in Leinster against government
1585:	Composition of Connaught; tax agreements between Crown, lords and commons
1585–6:	Lord Deputy Perrot's plans for land confiscation and composition failed
1586:	Plantation of Munster
1588:	Twenty-five ships of Spanish Armada wrecked off Irish coast
1592:	Foundation of Trinity College, Dublin
1594–1603:	Rebellion of Hugh O'Neill and Red Hugh O'Donnell
1598:	O'Neill defeated government forces at Battle of the Yellow Ford in Ulster

1599: Government defeated (Deputy's Pass, Wicklow and Curlew Mountains, Roscommon)

Seventeenth century

1601: O'Neill and O'Donnell defeated by Lord Deputy Mountjoy at Battle of Kinsale

1603: Death of Elizabeth I; accession of James I. Conquest of Ireland; English law enforced

1606: Scots settled in Ards peninsula

1607: O'Neill and O'Donnell rejected English rule and fled into exile (Flight of the Earls)

1607–1610: Ulster plantation policy; English and Scottish immigrants settled on forfeited land

1612: Creation of new boroughs (many in Ulster)

1613: Charter granted to London companies established Derry as city of Londonderry

1613–15: James I's Parliament

1625: Death of James I; accession of Charles I

1626: Charles I offered concessions to Irish in return for grants (funds)

1639–1641: Charles I's second Irish Parliament; the last with Catholics (except for 1689)

1641: Ulster Rising; Irish and Old English demanded return of lands; massacre of Protestants at Portadown; government defeated at Julianstown Bridge, Drogheda. Fifty-nine per cent of Irish land held by Catholics. Conflicts between Catholics and Protestants

1642: Scottish army under Robert Munro landed at Carrickfergus to crush rising; first Scottish presbytery by army chaplains; Owen Roe O'Neill (Catholic) arrived in Ulster to reverse plantation policy; Civil War in England (royalist forces against Parliamentarian armies) started and continued until Parliamentarian victory in 1651

1642–1649: Catholic Confederation (assembly) of Kilkenny; conflicts with absolute monarchy

1643: Hostilities halted between Royalists and Confederate Catholics

1646: Lord Lieutenant Ormond peace with Confederates; Munro defeated at Battle of Benburb; Confederates rejected Ormond peace

1647: Ormond surrendered Dublin to parliamentary forces under Col. Michael Jones; Jones defeated Confederates at Dungan's Hill, near Trim

1648: Second Civil War in England; Scots defeated by Cromwell at Preston, Lancashire

1649: Second Ormond peace with Confederates. Execution of Charles I. Jones defeated Ormond at Rathmines. Cromwell captured Drogheda (massacre), Wexford and New Ross

1650: Cromwellian conquest; deportations; Catholic landowners exiled to Connaught

1652–1653: Cromwellian land settlement; land taken from opposition and given to supporters

1654: Parliament in London; Ireland had 30 representatives

1658: Death of Cromwell

1660:	Restoration of monarchy in England and accession of Charles II. Navigation Act controlled England's external trade. England and Ireland became one economic unit
1660–1665:	Restoration land settlement restricted; Catholics possessed 22 per cent of Irish land
1661–1666:	Charles II's Irish Parliament
1663:	England restricted Irish trade with colonies and importation of Irish cattle into England
1666:	Act of Uniformity established Protestant liturgy in Ireland and Britain
1671:	Navigation Act excluded direct imports of sugar and tobacco from colonies to Ireland
1673:	English Test Act excluded Catholics and Protestant dissenters from public office
1678–1681:	Popish plot (alleged English Catholic conspiracy to assassinate Charles II)
1685:	Death of Charles II and accession of James II
1688:	James II deposed in England; Londonderry/Derry and Enniskillen opposed his forces
1689:	James II arrived at Kinsale; siege and relief of Londonderry/Derry. James II's Irish Parliament. Defenders of Enniskillen defeated James's forces at Newtonbutler, Co. Fermanagh
1689:	The Irish Patriot Parliament; 224 MPs were Catholic (of whom two-thirds were Old English). Its proceedings were annulled in 1695 under William III
1690:	William of Orange (William III) landed at Carrickfergus and defeated James II at Battle of the Boyne (11 July); flight of James to France (died 1701). First siege of Limerick
1691:	William defeated Catholic forces at Aughrim. Second siege of Limerick; Treaty of Limerick. English Test Act excluded Catholics (1692–1829) from public office in Ireland
1691–1703:	William's land confiscation; 14 per cent of land in Ireland held by Catholics
1695:	Penal laws against Catholics limit civil rights (1695–1709)
1698:	William Molyneux pamphlet opposed England's right to make laws for Ireland
1699:	England restricted export of Irish woollens

Eighteenth century

1700:	Louis Crommelin established linen industry in Lisburn, Co. Antrim
1702:	William III died; accession of Queen Anne
1705:	Direct export of Irish linen to American colonies allowed
1707:	Union of English and Scottish Parliaments
1710–1720s:	Westminster control over Ireland; Penal Laws restricted access to jobs, schools and religion for Catholic majority and reduced Catholic land-ownership to 7 per cent by 1714
1713:	Jonathan Swift installed as Dean of St Patrick's Cathedral, Dublin
1714:	Queen Anne died; accession of George I
1718:	Emigration of Ulster Presbyterian Scots to American colonies
1719:	Toleration Act removed many restrictions from Protestant Dissenters
1720:	Declaratory Act; right of British Parliament to legislate for Ireland and rejection of appeal jurisdiction of Irish House of Lords

1720:	Jonathan Swift wrote anonymous *Proposal for the Universal Use of Irish Manufacture;* advocated boycott of English goods
1726:	Non-subscribing Presbyterians formed separate presbytery of Antrim
1727:	George I died; accession of George II
1728:	Catholics lost the vote until 1793
1729:	New Parliament building at College Green, Dublin; first Parliament meeting in 1731
1737:	*Belfast Newsletter* founded by Francis Joy as first newspaper in Ulster
1739:	British removed duties on import of Irish woollen yarn into Britain
1739–1741:	Bad harvests, fever and famine in Ireland
1758:	Import of salted beef, pork and butter from Ireland into Britain permitted
1759:	Restrictions removed on import of Irish cattle into Britain
1760:	The Catholic Committee formed in Dublin; George II died; accession of George III
1761:	Agrarian protest in Munster
1763:	Rural disturbances in Ulster. First number of *Freeman's Journal* (last number 1924)
1766:	Tumultuous Risings Act
1769:	Agrarian disturbances in Ulster
1772:	Catholic relief reform began with Bogland Act; allowed Catholics to take bog leases
1774:	Act enabling Catholics to acknowledge allegiance to the king
1775–1783:	War for American Independence
1775:	Henry Grattan led Patriot Party and the opposition in Parliament
1776:	American Declaration of Independence
1778:	Organization of the Irish Volunteers in Belfast. Gardiner's Catholic Relief Act gave landownership to Catholics (leases for 999 years and inheritance rights)
1780:	Ireland allowed to trade with British colonies on equal terms with Britain. Grattan campaigned for Irish legislative independence. Repeal of Test Act for Protestant dissenters
1782–1800:	Grattan's Parliament; Habeus Corpus Act; struggle for Irish legislative and judicial independence and relaxation of Penal Laws; Gardiner's second Catholic Relief Act (Catholics could acquire specific land; some Penal Laws removed); Bank of Ireland founded; Gardiner's third Catholic Relief Act allowed Catholics to act as teachers and guardians
1783:	Renunciation Act gave Irish Parliament right to legislate for Ireland, independence of the judiciary, and exclusive jurisdiction to Irish courts. William Pitt, Prime Minister of Britain
1784:	Foster's Corn Law (regulating corn trade; lasted until 1846)
1784–1785:	First meeting of Irish Academy (later Royal Irish Academy)
1786:	Belfast Academy (later Belfast Royal Academy) opened
1789:	Whig Club formed in Dublin
1790:	Northern Whig Club formed in Belfast. Wolfe Tone became Secretary to the Catholic Committee. Edmund Burke's *Reflections on the Revolution in France* published
1791:	Thomas Paine's *Rights of Man* (Part 1) published. Demonstrations in Dublin and Belfast commemorated fall of the Bastille (14 July 1789). Wolfe Tone's *Argument on Behalf of the Catholics of Ireland.* The Society of United Irishmen founded in Belfast by Tone and others

1792:	Langrishe's Catholic Relief Act; Catholics able to practise as solicitors and barristers and ban on Protestant/Catholic intermarriage repealed
1793:	France declared war on Britain. Hobart's Catholic Relief Act gave Catholics the vote and repealed some disabilities. Convention Act prohibited any assembly, except Parliament. St Patrick's College, Carlow, opened, first Catholic higher education college in Ireland
1794:	United Irishmen's parliamentary reform plan published; Dublin branch suppressed
1795:	Battle of the Diamond near Loughgall, Co. Armagh led to foundation of Orange Order
1796:	United Irishmen planned rebellion; Ireland under martial law; Habeas Corpus Suspension Act; French fleet (with Wolfe Tone) in Bantry Bay attempted invasion of Ireland
1797:	Bank of Ireland suspended gold payments. Ulster disarmed. French invasion attempt
1798:	United Irishmen risings in Leinster and Ulster failed. French surrendered fleet; Tone convicted of treason and sentenced to death; died after attempted suicide
1799:	William Pitt encouraged parliamentary union of Britain and Ireland; legislation introduced; Orange Order protested against Union

Nineteenth century

1800:	Act of Union (Great Britain and Ireland) passed
1803:	Habeas Corpus suspended, Robert Emmet's rising in Dublin failed; Emmet executed
1807:	Daniel O'Connell as Catholic leader. Christian Brothers (lay teaching order) founded
1813:	Catholic Relief Bill defeated at Westminster
1814:	(Royal) Belfast Academical Institution opened. Apprentice Boys (Londonderry) formed
1815:	Napoleon defeated at Waterloo; war with France ended
1816–1817:	Failure of potato crop; famine; typhus epidemic
1817:	British and Irish tax systems merged
1821:	Failure of potato crop; famine and fever in west of Ireland
1823:	O'Connell's Catholic Association founded; campaigned for Catholic emancipation
1825:	Catholic Association and Orange Order banned. Ireland and Britain as a free trade area
1826:	Irish and British currencies joined. Collapse of textile industry
1828:	O'Connell elected MP for Clare in by-election
1829:	Catholic Relief Act passed removing most remaining restrictions on Catholics
1830s:	O'Connell led movement to repeal all Penal Laws
1830:	George IV died; accession of William IV
1831:	Tithe war began; primary education (National Schools) instituted
1832:	Parliamentary Reform Act; 1.2 per cent increase in Irish seats and electorate
1833:	Tithe Arrears Act

1834:	O'Connell initiated Repeal of Union debates at Westminster. Opening of first railway in Ireland from Dublin to Kingstown
1836:	Grand Orange Lodge of Ireland dissolved. Royal Irish Constabulary formed from 1867
1837:	Death of William IV; accession of Queen Victoria
1838:	Poor Relief Act extended English poor law and workhouse system to Ireland. Tithe system converted into a rent charge
1840:	O'Connell's Repeal (of Union) Association founded. General Assembly of the Presbyterian Church of Ireland formed. Municipal Reform Act
1841:	Whigs defeated; Sir Robert Peel as Prime Minister. O'Connell elected Lord Mayor of Dublin
1842–1848:	Young Ireland movement. *Nation* newspaper founded. Total abstinence movement
1843:	Repeal of the Union debates and meetings; failure of O'Connell's movement
1844:	O'Connell and others found guilty of conspiracy (1843); reversed by House of Lords
1845–1851:	An Gorta Mor (the Great Hunger) and potato blight in Ireland; population eventually halved by starvation and emigration
1845:	The Queen's Colleges founded. Peel ordered corn from USA for Ireland; government relief committee appointed to relieve public need
1846:	Repeal of Navigation and Corn Laws by Peel; Peel replaced as Prime Minister by Lord John Russell. Breach between O'Connell and Young Ireland over use of force. Potato crop failed
1847:	O'Connell died
1848:	Cholera; Poor Relief Act; welfare moved to local rates and outdoor relief. Repeal of Union linked to land reform. Young Ireland rising in Munster; James Stephens fled to France
1849:	Potato blight reappeared. Queen's Colleges at Belfast, Cork and Galway opened
1850:	Tenant League formed in Dublin. Queen's University of Ireland founded
1851:	Catholic Defence Association of Great Britain and Ireland formed
1852:	Election; 40 MPs supported Tenant League
1853:	Assembly's College, Belfast, opened for theological training of Presbyterian clergy. Opening of shipbuilding yard in Belfast (later Harland and Wolff)
1854:	Provision for National Gallery in Dublin. Catholic University of Ireland opened
1856:	James Stephens returned from France; Phoenix Society formed at Skibbereen
1857:	Sectarian rioting in Belfast
1858:	Stephens founded Irish Republican Brotherhood (IRB) in Dublin; parallel body (Fenian Brotherhood) founded in America (1859)
1859:	*The Irish Times* published. Breakup of Tenant League. Evangelical revival in Ulster
1860–1864:	Cold and wet seasons; droughts; agricultural depression; Land Acts; evictions
1861–1865:	American Civil War
1862:	Poor Relief Act extended outdoor relief
1863:	Newspaper *Irish People* founded
1864:	James Stephens declared 1865 as date for Fenian insurrection

1865:	Dublin International Exhibition. Magee College, Londonderry/Derry, founded as arts and Presbyterian theological college. Stephens' arrest and escape from Richmond Jail, Dublin
1866:	Habeas Corpus suspended (until 1869); Stephens abandoned Fenian Rising; removed as head of IRB. Archbishop Cullen created first Irish cardinal
1867:	Failed Fenian raids and risings; execution of Fenian Manchester Martyrs; Clerkenwell bomb explosion by Fenians
1868:	Irish Parliamentary Reform Act liberalized franchise. Election; Liberal victory with Gladstone as Prime Minister for first time
1869:	Church of Ireland disestablished (effective 1871)
1870:	Home Government Association (Home Rule) founded by Isaac Butt; Gladstone's first Land Act; Charles Stuart Parnell led Home Rule Party and the Land League movement
1871:	Westmeath Act provided detention without trial for agrarian offences
1872:	Ballot Act introduced secret voting; sectarian rioting in Belfast
1873:	Home Rule Confederation of Great Britain founded under Butt; Home Rule League
1874:	Election returned 60 Home Rule MPs; Gladstone resigned; Conservative government under Disraeli succeeded; Butt's motion on Home Rule defeated at Westminster
1875:	Parnell (MP/Meath). Catholic bishops condemned Queen's Colleges/Trinity College
1876:	Support for Irish Republicans from USA and Australia; IRB withdrew support for Home Rule; Home Rule motion defeated at Westminster
1877:	Parnell as President of Home Rule Confederation; bad harvest and agricultural depression (repeated 1878–1879)
1878:	Intermediate Education Act
1879:	Famine and economic crisis; evictions; land agitation; National Land League (Parnell as President) founded
1879–1882:	The Land War
1880:	Parnell's affair with Mrs O'Shea; campaigned in USA on land question. Election; gains for Parnell and Land League; Gladstone as Prime Minister; Parnell as Chairman of Irish Party; Parnell's Galway speech; trial of Parnell and others for conspiracy
1881:	Gladstone's second Land Act; Parnell and others imprisoned; no-rent manifesto; Land League suppressed
1882:	Parnell and others released from prison. Phoenix Park murders of Lord Frederick Cavendish and Thomas Henry Burke. Trial and execution of Invincibles. Irish National League replaced Land League. Royal University of Ireland founded, but later failed
1884:	Fenian dynamite campaign in Great Britain. Gaelic Athletic Association founded at Thurles. Franchise Act gave votes to householders; large increase in Irish rural electorate
1885:	Defeat of Gladsone's second ministry; Salisbury (Conservative) as Prime Minister; Ashbourne Act provided state assistance for land purchase; Labourers' Act
1886:	Election; Salisbury defeated; Gladstone formed third administration; Parnell held balance between Liberals and Conservatives; Gladstone's conversion to Home Rule; introduced first Home Rule bill; riots in Belfast; formation of Ulster Anti-Repeal Committee; Home Rule bill defeated. Election; Gladstone defeated; Salisbury as Prime Minister

1887:	*The Times* published letters implicating Parnell in Phoenix Park murders. New Coercion Act; Mitchelstown riot; Nationalist demonstrations in London
1889:	Parnell letters exposed as forgeries; Parnell and Gladstone discussed Home Rule; O'Shea filed for divorce, naming Parnell as co-respondent
1890:	Opening of Science and Art Museum and National Library of Ireland. Verdict against Mrs O'Shea and Parnell in divorce case; Parnell deposed as leader of Irish Party
1891:	Anti-Parnell Irish National Federation formed in Dublin; Irish Labour League formed; Parnell died; John Redmond as leader of Irish Party
1892:	Ulster convention rejected Home Rule cooperation. Election; fourth Gladstone ministry. Belfast Labour Party formed (first Labour party in Ireland). Gaelic League founded
1893:	Gladstone introduced second Home Rule bill; defeated in Lords; Belfast disturbances
1894:	Resignation of Gladstone; Rosebery as Prime Minister. Irish Trade Union Congress formed
1895:	Election; Rosebery defeated; Salisbury as Prime Minister
1896:	Irish Socialist Republican Party formed by James Connolly
1898:	United Irish League formed; creation of elected county and district councils. First number of Connolly's *Workers' Republic*
1899:	Irish Literary Theatre founded. Arthur Griffith established newspapers *United Irishman* and *Sinn Féin*; first number of *An Claidheamh Soluis* (journal of Gaelic League)

Twentieth century

1900–1901:	John Redmond chairman of reunited Irish Party; Salisbury's fourth administration
1901:	Death of Queen Victoria; accession of Edward VII
1903:	Wyndham's Land Act settled agrarian question; Independent Orange Order formed
1904:	Abbey Theatre succeeded Irish Literary Theatre
1905:	Sinn Féin founded by Griffith and Hobson; Ulster Unionist Council created
1906:	Liberals won election under Campbell-Bannerman (Asquith 1908)
1907:	*Ne Temere* promulgated by Pope Pius X (children of marriages between Catholics and non-Catholics must be raised in the Catholic faith)
1908:	Queen's University, Belfast, and National University founded. Strikes in Dublin docks
1909:	Land Purchase Act
1910:	Irish Party held balance between Conservatives and Liberals. Death of Edward VII; accession of George V; Edward Carson elected leader of Irish Unionists
1911:	Anti-Home Rule demonstration in Belfast
1912:	Third Home Rule bill; Solemn League and Covenant in Ulster; Ulster Unionists resist Home Rule; sinking of *Titanic* (built in Belfast)
1913:	Ulster Volunteer Force, Irish Citizen Army and Irish National Volunteers founded
1914:	The Curragh mutiny. Third Home Rule bill received royal assent but not

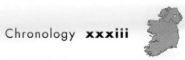

	implemented due to First World War 1914–1918. Larne and Howth gun-running
1916:	Easter Rising (Dublin) suppressed; execution of 17 leaders. Battle of the Somme; heavy Irish losses especially by the 36th Ulster Division. British government proposed exclusion of six Ulster counties from Home Rule. Formation of Lloyd George coalition
1917:	Sinn Féin won Roscommon by-election. Prisoners from Easter Rising released; de Valera won East Clare; Irish Convention met; no solution to issue of Irish self-government
1918:	First World War ended; British General Election returned 73 Sinn Féiners who did not sit at Westminster; victory over Irish Party in Ireland; last all-island vote
1919:	Sinn Féin Westminster MPs formed Dáil Éireann in Dublin, declared independence and proclaimed an Irish Republic; Anglo-Irish War, 1919–1921
1920:	Auxiliaries and Black and Tans of Royal Irish Constabulary arrived; 24 executions by June 1921. Government of Ireland Act partitioned Ireland by creation of Irish Free State (26 counties) and Northern Ireland (6 counties). Auxiliaries burnt Cork
1921:	George V opened Northern Ireland Parliament in Belfast with Sir James Craig (later Lord Craigavon) as Prime Minister; truce between Sinn Féin and Britain; Anglo-Irish Treaty signed in London; repealed Act of Union; creation of the Irish Free State within the Empire
1922:	Treaty ratified in Dáil Éireann; opposed by anti-Treaty IRA; election in Ireland gave pro-Treaty majority; Civil War over Treaty; deaths of Griffith and Collins; Free State (Saorstát Éireann) established in December; Royal Ulster Constabulary (RUC) formed
1923:	End of Irish Civil War
1926:	De Valera founded Fianna Fáil
1927:	Election in Free State; De Valera and Fianna Fáil enter Dáil
1931:	IRA declared an illegal organization in the Free State
1932:	Free State election; Fianna Fáil victory; de Valera as Prime Minister. Economic war with Britain over Land Annuities; Parliament buildings at Stormont, Belfast, opened
1933:	United Irish Party (later Fine Gael) formed; Special Powers Act in Northern Ireland
1935:	Shooting and bombing campaign by Loyalists and Republicans; increased sectarianism
1936:	Public Order Act in Northern Ireland; death of George V; abdication of Edward VIII; accession of George VI
1937:	Irish Free State becomes Éire/Ireland in Constitution of Ireland (Bunreacht na h Éireann); articles 2 and 3 claimed sovereignty over the whole island of Ireland
1938:	Economic war ended; Britain ceded military and naval rights in Treaty ports
1939:	IRA bombing campaign in Britain and raids in Ireland. Second World War; Ireland neutral; Northern Ireland in British/Allied war effort
1941:	German air raids on Belfast; 3,000 people killed or wounded
1942:	US troops landed in Northern Ireland in preparation for Allied invasion of Europe
1943:	Sir Basil Brooke became Prime Minister of Northern Ireland

1945:	End of Second World War. Labour Government elected in Britain (no Nationalist representation in Northern Ireland); Sean O'Kelly as President of Ireland
1947:	Education Act provided universal secondary education in Northern Ireland
1948:	Election in Ireland; defeat of Fianna Fáil and de Valera. National Health Service (NHS) created in Northern Ireland
1949:	Republic of Ireland declared; accepted by Britain with guarantee of support for Northern Ireland (Ireland Act); Republic left Commonwealth
1950s:	IRA Border Campaign
1951:	Collapse of Ireland Mother and Child public health plan due to Catholic Church opposition; Conservatives elected in Britain
1952:	Death of George VI; accession of Elizabeth II
1954:	IRA raid on Gough Military Barracks, Armagh, and attack on Omagh Barracks. Flags and Emblems Act in Northern Ireland used against the flying of Ireland's tricolour
1955:	Ireland admitted to United Nations; Conservatives elected in Britain
1956–1962:	IRA campaigns in North; internment used north and south of the border
1959:	De Valera elected President of Ireland; Sean Lemass became Taoiseach; Conservatives elected in Britain
1961:	Radio Telefís Éireann (RTE) started television broadcasts in Ireland
1962:	End of IRA border campaign
1963:	US President Kennedy visited Ireland. Terence O'Neill as Prime Minister in Northern Ireland
1964:	Campaign for Social Justice formed in Northern Ireland. Labour elected in Britain
1965:	O'Neill–Lemass talks; Anglo-Irish free trade agreement signed.
1966:	Jack Lynch as Taoiseach; fiftieth anniversary of 1916 Easter Rising. Ulster Volunteer Force (UVF) formed to oppose Republicans; declared illegal. Labour elected in Britain
1967:	Northern Ireland Civil Rights Association founded in Londonderry/Derry
1968:	Londonderry/Derry clashes between civil rights marchers and RUC
1969:	Belfast to Londonderry/Derry civil rights march attacked. O'Neill resigned; Chichester Clark as Prime Minister. Breakdown of law and order; British troops sent to Londonderry/Derry; IRA campaign; Scarman Tribunal into disturbances. Downing Street Declaration by British and Northern Ireland (NI) governments affirmed NI's position within the UK. Split within IRA
1970:	Dublin Arms Trial. Provisional IRA (PIRA) and Official IRA formed; Alliance Party and Social Democratic and Labour Party (SDLP) formed; Conservatives elected in Britain
1971:	First British soldier killed by PIRA in Belfast. Chichester Clark resigned; Faulkner as Prime Minister. Internment without trial introduced; 342 arrested; total interned 1,576. Democratic Unionist Party (DUP) formed
1972:	Bloody Sunday, Londonderry/Derry, 30 January; 13 civil rights marchers shot by British soldiers; direct rule; NI Parliament suspended. PIRA bombing in Belfast, 21 July, killed 11; worst year in Troubles (472 deaths). Official IRA suspended military operations
1973:	Ireland and UK joined the EEC (EU). Referendum on Northern Ireland's membership of UK (57.5 per cent voted for). PIRA bombings in London; Emergency Provisions Act provided for single judge trials of terrorist suspects (Diplock courts) in NI. Sunningdale Agreement; Assembly elected with power-sharing executive

1974:   Ulster Workers' Council strike; collapse of Assembly; direct rule re-imposed. Labour elected; anti-power-sharing Unionists gained 11 of 12 NI seats; phasing out of internment; Prevention of Terrorism Act; Loyalist bombs in Dublin/Monaghan killed 33 civilians

1975:   Northern Ireland Constitutional Convention formed to discuss future of NI. Éamon de Valera died. Detention without trial in Northern Ireland ended; PIRA ceasefire

1976:   Northern Ireland Convention dissolved. UK Ambassador to Ireland killed by PIRA. Republican prisoners in NI claimed political prisoner status; denied

1978:   PIRA prepared for long war. Amnesty International alleged prisoner and legal rights abuse in NI; European Court ruled prisoner interrogations in NI inhumane and degrading

1979:   European Monetary System instituted; Ireland a member, UK not. Member states of EEC voted for MEPs in first direct elections to European Parliament. Pope John Paul II visited Ireland. Conservatives elected in Britain; Margaret Thatcher as Prime Minister

1980:   Meetings between Thatcher and Charles Haughey (Taoiseach) on British/Irish relations. Republican prisoners in NI prisons began hunger strikes

1981:   Ten hunger strikers died; dying hunger striker Bobby Sands won UK parliamentary seat; strikes called off. Election in Ireland; Garret Fitzgerald as Taoiseach; meeting with Thatcher

1982:   Election in Ireland; Haughey as Taoiseach. James Prior announced rolling devolution for NI. PIRA exploded bombs in Hyde and Regent's Parks, London, killing 10 servicemen. Election for NI Assembly (Sinn Féin won 10 per cent of vote); election in Ireland; Fitzgerald as Taoiseach. Bomb at Droppin Well Inn, Ballykelly, Co. Londonderry/Derry killed 11 British soldiers and 5 civilians; Irish National Liberation Army (INLA) claimed responsibility

1983:   Politicians from Ireland and NI in first session of New Ireland Forum. Referendum on Ireland's constitution rejected laws permitting abortion. Conservatives elected in Britain; Thatcher as Prime Minister. PIRA escape from Maze Prison, Belfast

1984:   US President Ronald Reagan visited Ireland. European Parliament election. Grand Hotel, Brighton, bombed during British Conservative Party Conference (four killed)

1985:   Anglo-Irish Agreement by Fitzgerald and Thatcher (London and Dublin to consult formally on NI); Unionist protest in Belfast against Agreement. Progressive Democrat Party formed. Rioting in Portadown over Orange Order march

1986:   Referendum in Ireland; ban on divorce confirmed. Republican Sinn Féin founded by R. Ó Brádaigh and D. Ó Conaill. Northern Ireland Assembly dissolved

1987:   Election in Ireland; Haughey as Taoiseach. SAS killed eight PIRA members at Loughall, Co. Armagh. Referendum in Ireland on Single European Act. PIRA bomb killed 11 and injured 63 at Remembrance Day Service in Enniskillen, NI. Conservatives elected in Britain; Thatcher as PM. Unionist leaders ended boycott of British government ministers

1988:   SAS killed three PIRA members in Gibraltar. European Court ruled against seven-day detention rule in NI. SDLP entered talks with Sinn Féin

1989:   European Parliament election; election in Ireland; Haughey as Taoisach. University of Limerick opened. Guildford Four released

1990:   Northern Ireland Fair Employment Act. Mary Robinson elected President of Ireland. John Major succeeded Thatcher as Conservative Party leader and Prime Minister.

1991:   Mortar bomb attack by PIRA on 10 Downing Street, London. Release of Birmingham Six with convictions quashed. Talks between NI parties and British and Irish governments

1992:   Haughey resigned; succeeded by Albert Reynolds. Conservatives win British election; John Major as Prime Minister. Referendum in Ireland on Maastricht Treaty. Ulster Defence Association (UDA) banned in NI Referendums in Ireland on rights to life, travel and information. Talks between NI parties resumed. Ulster Unionist Party delegation visited Dublin (first since 1922); talks collapsed

1993:   Reynolds elected Taoisach; Downing Street Declaration signed by Reynolds and Major (principle of consent in NI). Meetings between John Hume of SDLP and Gerry Adams of Sinn Féin

1994:   Amnesty International Report on 'political killings' in NI published. European Parliament elections. PIRA and loyalist paramilitaries began a ceasefire. Forum for Peace and Reconciliation opened in Dublin. Meetings between British officials and Sinn Féin on participation in future political talks (dependent upon IRA decommissioning of weapons)

1995:   John Bruton (Taoisach); British and Irish governments published *Frameworks for the Future*. David Trimble became UUP leader. Referendum permitting divorce in Ireland passed. US President Bill Clinton visited Belfast, Londonderry/Derry and Dublin. Senator George Mitchell headed Commission to resolve problems of decommissioning and entry to talks

1996:   Mitchell Report committed participants in all-party talks on NI to principle of non-violence and decommissioning. PIRA ended ceasefire with bomb at Canary Wharf, London. Multi-party talks began without Sinn Féin. Disorder at Drumcree Orange Order march

1997:   Labour won election in Britain; Tony Blair as Prime Minister. Election in Ireland; Bertie Ahern as Taoisach. PIRA ceasefire; Sinn Féin (but not PIRA) subscribed to Mitchell principles and admitted to all-party talks. Independent Commission on Decommissioning appointed; Mary McAleese elected President in Republic. Adams and Martin McGuinness visited Downing Street

1998:   Judicial inquiry (Saville) into Bloody Sunday began. Good Friday (Belfast) Agreement (signed by eight NI parties – except DUP – and the Irish and British governments) (10 April); agreement endorsed in referendums in north and south. Elections to NI Assemby. Amsterdam Treaty endorsed by referendum in Republic. Real IRA killed 29 people in a bomb attack in Omagh, Co.Tyrone. John Hume and David Trimble awarded Nobel Peace Prize. President McAleese and Queen Elizabeth II commemorated Irish First World War dead at Messines

1999:   Euro launched in Ireland but not UK. Privatization of Telecom Éireann. Devolved government in NI, with David Trimble (UUP) as First Minister and Seamus Mallon (SDLP) as Deputy First Minister. Ireland government replaced articles 2 and 3 of the 1937 Constitution; British government repealed Government of Ireland Act 1920. PIRA met decommissioning body. Review of Good Friday (Belfast) Agreement by George Mitchell

Twenty-first century

2000:   Direct rule in NI and suspension of Assembly due to PIRA's failure to decommission its weapons. Loyalist feuding; dissident Real IRA rocket attack on M16 headquarters in London

2001:   Labour won General Election in Britain; Tony Blair as Prime Minister; increased support for DUP; Sinn Féin became largest Nationalist party in NI. Ireland electorate rejected Nice Treaty in referendum. Increased Loyalist paramilitary activity. NI Assembly suspended twice. After 9/11 attack on the USA, PIRA started decommissioning. Police Service of Northern Ireland (PSNI) replaced RUC with a 50/50 (Catholic/Protestant) recruitment policy. Population in Ireland reached 3.84 million; immigration and increased birth rate contributed to growth

2002:   Dissident Loyalist and Republican violence continued in NI. Assembly suspended due to allegations of PIRA spy ring operating in Assembly. Direct rule from London

2003:   Talks between Taoiseach, British Prime Minister and Northern Irish politicians at Hillsborough Castle, Co. Down attempted to restart devolved government. Assembly elections; gains for DUP and Sinn Féin; Assembly not restored

2004:   EU Parliament elections (Sinn Féin MEPs elected from NI and Ireland). Review of Good Friday Agreement. Mary McAleese returned unopposed as President of Ireland

2005:   NI Assembly remained suspended. Labour won election in Britain; UUP lost all but one seat; Sinn Féin and DUP increased seats and were the dominant parties in NI. PIRA ordered members to cease 'military operations'; decommissioning body reported that PIRA weapons had been 'put beyond use'; some Unionist paramilitaries moved to disarm

2006:   Prime Minister Tony Blair and Taoiseach Bertie Ahern reopened talks with NI parties; November deadline for resumption of NI Assembly not met; new attempts to re-establish devolution by 26 March 2007 and overcome Sinn Fein's attitude to policing in NI. Independent Monitoring Commission reported that PIRA had ceased its paramilitary activities

2007:   NI Assembly election (March); DUP with 36 seats and Sinn Fein with 28 were largest parties; power-sharing between DUP and Sinn Fein in restored Assembly and Executive (May); Ian Paisley as First Minister and Martin McGuiness as Deputy. High Court in London ruled that Londonderry must keep the name (not Derry) given to it by Royal Charter by Charles II in 1662. Gordon Brown succeeded Tony Blair as Prime Minister. Fianna Fáil-led coalition won election in Ireland; UVF and UDA announced end of armed resistance. Sinn Féin accepted PSNI and security arrangements in NI. Credit and banking crisis in NI and Ireland

2008:   Peter Robinson succeeded Ian Paisley as DUP First Minister in NI Assembly; Brian Cowen succeeded Bertie Ahern as Taoiseach in Republic. Irish voters rejected Lisbon Treaty in a referendum. End of 10-year Celtic Tiger economic growth in Ireland as economy suffered downturn and entered recession; unemployment rate was highest for 10 years; Northern Ireland unemployment rate was highest for 28 years

2009:   Ireland government invested finance in Allied Irish Bank and Bank of Ireland. Attack by Real IRA on army base in Co. Antrim; two soldiers killed (the first since 1997) and four civilians injured: PSNI policeman killed by the Continuity IRA; first murder of a policeman in NI since 1998. Loyalist UVF and UDA formally announced that they had placed their 'arms beyond use'. Ireland accepted Lisbon Treaty in repeat referendum

2010: Most policing and criminal justice powers devolved from Westminster to Stormont; appointment of NI Justice Minister. INLA decommissioned its weapons. Saville Report on Bloody Sunday concluded that the killing of 14 people was 'unjustified and unjustifiable'. Sporadic car bombs, pipe bombs, mortar attacks, rioting and sectarian violence continued in NI; Catholic Church hierarchy faced criticism and claims of cover-ups over clerical sex abuse of children. Irish government injected funds into banking sector with possibility of nationalization; severe spending cuts. Women challenged Ireland's abortion laws in EU court. Londonderry/Derry chosen as UK City of Culture. British General Election resulted in coalition government between Conservatives and Lib Dems, with David Cameron as Prime Minister

2011: Fianna Fáil heavily defeated on economic record in Ireland election; Fine Gael formed a coalition government with Labour; Enda Kenny as Taoiseach. The DUP (38 seats) and Sinn Féin (29 seats) won most seats in the NI Assembly election, with Peter Robinson as First Minister and Martin McGuinness as Deputy: serious sectarian violence erupted in East Belfast (June), allegedly by Loyalist paramilitary groups against Catholics. In Ireland, debt and unemployment increased. The housing market, consumer spending and job creation were weak, but exports grew and the economy was forecast to return to growth by 2012. Taoiseach Enda Kenny criticized the Vatican for its alleged undermining of efforts to report suspected clerical child sex abusers to the police. Michael D. Higgins elected as President of Ireland

1

The Irish context

- Prehistory: 10000/8000 BC–AD 400
- Early Christian Ireland: 400–795
- The Viking era: 795–1166
- Anglo-Norman Ireland: 1167–1536
- Reformation, sectarianism and revolt: 1536–1641
- The Protestant ascendancy: 1641–1801
- Union with Great Britain: 1801–1921
- Opposition: Home Rule and the repeal of the Union
- Partition and aftermath: 1921–
- Contemporary attitudes
- *Exercises*
- *Further reading*
- *Websites*

Many names have historically been given to the island of Ireland. The English term 'Ireland' has in modern times often referred to the second largest of a group of islands lying off the north-west coast of the European mainland. Its nearest large neighbour to the east is the island of Great Britain (Scotland, Wales and England), with which it has long been involved.

It is argued that 'Ireland' is a combination of modern Irish 'Éire', Old Irish 'Ériú' and the Germanic word 'land'. 'Ériu' seems to be an early native form, which may have been derived from Old Celtic 'Iveriu' and later became 'Éire' and 'Éirinn'. Other names originated outside the island, such as the Greek 'Ierne' around the first century. The Greek geographer, Ptolemy, initially referred to Ireland in the second century as Mikra Brettania (Lesser Britain) in contrast to Megale Brettania (Great Britain). He later identified Great Britain as Albion and Ireland as Iouernia (or Latin Ivernia), which may have been derived from existing indigenous names for a part or the whole of the island. It is said that the Romans later wrongly Latinized Iouernia as Hibernia or Scotia. By the nineteenth century, the Irish term 'Éirinn' was Anglicized as 'Erin', together with other symbolic personifications of the nation.

In this book, 'Ireland' describes the island before 1921. 'Irish Free State' is sometimes used for the independent state from 1921 to 1937, but the later constitutional title 'Ireland' is preferred for the whole period from 1921 to the present. The north-eastern part of the island from 1921 is referred to as Northern Ireland.

Ireland has had a long history, which is usually divided into generally accepted defining periods. However, commentators often give their own interpretations of what supposedly happened at particular times as they revise earlier theories or respond to new information.

The island has attracted international interest, especially since the start of the Troubles in Northern Ireland in the late 1960s. Discourses on Irish colonial occupation, economic crises, social deprivation, political conflict and sectarian violence have produced many popular and academic studies with very varying theories and interpretations. These reflect complicated constitutional, political, social, religious and cultural developments over the centuries, which are indicated in the following historical outlines.

Prehistory: 10000/8000 BC–AD 400

Palaeolithic (Old Stone Age) Ireland was probably uninhabited before 10000 BC and archaeological evidence suggests that the first people arrived in the island between 10000 and 8000 BC with the retreat of existing glaciers. They were initially nomadic Mesolithic (Middle Stone Age) hunter-gatherers who travelled from Britain and Europe to the east and north coasts. From about 4000 BC, they were joined by Neolithic (New Stone Age) immigrants, who lived in more permanent communities and began to farm and cultivate the land. These people were followed around 2000 BC by Bronze Age metalworkers in copper, tin and zinc.

Between 600 and 100 BC, Celtic groups came to the country, who, together with Gaels from around 100 BC, formed the basis of a Celtic/Gaelic Irish society. They are believed to have travelled to Ireland sometimes through Great Britain but also from southern France and northern Spain. A number of kingdoms or independent tribes developed prior to the beginning of the Christian era and gradually became the provinces of Ulster, Leinster, Munster and Connaught, which were later based on ecclesiastical structures. Debate continues about who the Celts actually were; where their origins lay; when they came to Ireland; and whether their arrival was a large-scale military invasion. It is suggested that small, rather than large, numbers settled in Ireland, assimilated with the indigenous peoples, and shared linguistic and cultural similarities with other Celtic groups throughout Europe.

Early Christian Ireland: 400–795

Ireland, unlike much of Western Europe and England (55 BC–AD 410), had not been occupied by the Romans, although artefacts discovered south of Dublin in 2005 may be the remains of Roman trading stations, which might indicate a small Roman administrative presence. Ireland was largely unaffected by the prevailing foreign invasions of Europe after Roman withdrawal and experienced a peaceful early medieval period.

It is traditionally claimed that St Patrick and other monks introduced Christianity to pagan Ireland by 500–600 AD, although there is some evidence of a Christian presence on the island in at least the third century. Christianity was to play a dominant role in Ireland's history, culture and conflicts, and the sixth and seventh centuries saw an expansion of Irish cultural life. The monastic model, rather than European diocesan structures, shaped the early Irish Church and society. Irish monks established monasteries and centres of learning in many parts of Britain and Europe in the post-Roman period between 410 and 800 AD.

Although there were cultural similarities between the various inhabitants of Ireland, the country was not united politically or militarily. Power was divided between different tribes headed by warring kings, who accepted the authority of regional overlords. Over these were the kings of the four main provinces. Tara in a smaller fifth province of Meath was the seat of the Ard Righ or High King. The High King was supposed to promote unity among the kings and to lead resistance to invaders. However, the High Kingship did not function well and the tribal system resulted in conflict rather than solidarity and common action.

The Viking era: 795–1166

The disunited country could not initially overcome regular Viking (Danish and Norwegian) attacks which started in 795 AD and continued in the ninth and tenth centuries. National weakness was illustrated by shifting alliances between Irish kings and Vikings to gain protection, power and possessions. The Vikings raided the country, its monasteries and the Christian culture. They founded Dublin, which served as a military base and later became a centre of commerce and government. The Vikings conquered significant parts of the island, but were overcome in the Battle of Tara in 980 and a rising by Dublin Viking and Irish forces was defeated in 1014 at Clontarf by the High King of Ireland, Brian Boru, and his allies.

Before and after this defeat Vikings settled in Ireland and assimilated with the indigenous population. They were an influential social, political and military presence; helped the growth of Ireland as merchants and traders; and built other

PLATE 1.1 Dublin Castle has been central to Irish history since the Vikings built a fort here in 841–2. The castle dates from ca. 1228 and was the seat of British rule in Ireland until 1921. The Norman Record Tower is the oldest intact part of the castle. In the foreground is the Garda Memorial Garden opened in 2010.

market towns and ports such as Waterford, Wexford and Cork. Dublin replaced Tara as the capital and the Lord of Dublin effectively became the King of Ireland.

Anglo-Norman Ireland: 1169–1536

There had been some limited, if unsatisfactory, progress towards a united Ireland under a High King in the eleventh and early twelfth centuries, but this was broken in 1169 by the arrival of Anglo-Normans, who had earlier (1066) conquered England and Wales. When King MacMurrough of Leinster was deposed in 1166, he asked Henry II of England and Anglo-Norman nobles to help him regain his throne and repaid them with land in Ireland. The Anglo-Normans conquered Dublin and parts of Ireland in 1169 and in 1170 under Richard de Clare/Fitz Gilbert ('Strongbow'). A period of significant political and religious change was then launched.

Ireland was under the political authority of Henry II, but he feared that Anglo-Norman landowners in Ireland would establish an independent state, which could be a threat to his power. Supported by Popes Adrian IV and Alexander III, he conquered Ireland in 1171 in what has been seen as the first colonization of the island. Henry proclaimed himself overlord of Ireland, was confirmed as Lord of Ireland by the Pope and recognized by church leaders.

PLATE 1.2 Carrickfergus Castle, Northern Ireland. The Norman castle lies on the North Antrim Coast Road by the shore of Belfast Lough. It was founded in 1177 by John de Courcy and completed by Hugh de Lacy in 1205. William III landed here in 1690 before travelling to Belfast and later to the Battle of the Boyne. © David Lyons/Alamy

Henry received permission from Pope Adrian IV to reform the Irish/Celtic Church whose beliefs were in conflict with the structures/theology of the Roman Church in Europe. Disputes between the two Churches had continued since the Synod of Whitby (664), which had been called to reconcile differences between them. A church administration based on monasteries was slowly replaced by one organized in dioceses, whose boundaries matched some existing kingdoms and provinces. Church structures were strengthened; the island was absorbed into the Angevin Empire; and the Catholic faith was to dominate Ireland in future centuries.

But the Anglo-Normans had not conquered the whole country and were restricted to the Pale. This term was first used in Ireland in 1495 by Edward Poynings to describe the fortified lowland region around Dublin ruled by the Anglo-Normans. Their language, customs, social hierarchy, agriculture, legal system and government were based on those of England. The Pale was defended militarily from the 1470s until the mid-1530s against attacks by the Irish.

The Anglo-Norman settlers were an important presence in Ireland for the next 400 years. They ended the power of Viking-influenced Ireland and introduced a new ruling class. Their descendants assimilated and married into Irish culture, and became known as Anglo-Irish or the Old English.

Powerful Anglo-Irish earls, such as Ormond, Desmond and Kildare, ruled lands beyond the Pale. Although they often acted as deputies for the English monarch, they were largely independent of the Crown. They conquered about two-thirds of the island, continued to fight among themselves and formed shifting alliances. The authority of English kings was restricted to Dublin and the Pale by the fifteenth century, and English power in Ireland seemed in danger owing to Irish expansionism and the cultural Gaelicization of Anglo-Norman settlers.

Reformation, sectarianism and revolt: 1536–1641

In 1500, Ireland was still a rural and agricultural country, although some towns were expanding. It had an identity, language and culture independent of England, whose rule was based in Anglo-Norman Dublin. This situation changed in the sixteenth and seventeenth centuries as a result of political and religious developments in Tudor England and Europe.

These periods saw the introduction of Protestantism into Ireland (begun in England by Henry VIII and culminating in the Protestant Settlement of Elizabeth I); the growth of sectarianism between Catholic and Protestant; the Catholic Counter Reformation against Protestantism; the plantation of Ireland (particularly Ulster) by Protestant settlers from England and Scotland; the decline of the Irish political order; and the significance of Ireland as a site for potential European military invasions. These events conditioned Irish history, but also strengthened English power in Ireland.

The Reformation and Counter Reformation affected English and Irish religious identities. By the 1560s, European countries such as England were Protestant, while Italy, Spain, France and Ireland remained Catholic. Conflicts between Churches led to civil and spiritual change in some countries, and territorial disputes and political ambitions among nations and monarchs.

Catholic Ireland was seen as strategically important in the European power struggle; a menace to Protestant England's security; and a base for English dissidents, Irish rebels or foreign enemies. Europe was moving from feudalism and advances in military technology encouraged European expansionism. Henry VIII countered these threats and opposed the growing power and militancy of Irish chieftains.

Such pressure led to rebellion against English rule in areas around the Pale by Thomas Fitzgerald, Earl of Kildare and other Irish nobles in 1534 and 1539. Henry subdued the revolts, placed Ireland under direct rule, strengthened English rule in the Pale, was declared Head of the Church in Ireland in 1536 and in 1541 became King of Ireland. Religious change and Henry's break with Rome in 1534 had a major impact in Ireland, but most Irish people and the descendants of the original Anglo-Norman settlers (Old English) did not accept the Protestant Reformation or the establishment of an Anglican Church of Ireland.

Edward VI continued the Reformation in Ireland until the brief restoration of Catholicism under Mary I. But Henry VIII's younger daughter, Elizabeth I, secured Protestantism with her Church Settlement (1559) and created deputies to rule in Ireland on behalf of the monarch. After anti-English, anti-Protestant revolts were crushed in Connaught and Munster, England controlled three-quarters of Ireland and only Ulster remained rebellious. However, England's war with Catholic Spain in the 1580s encouraged Irish rebels to form alliances with Spain.

The Flight of the Earls

In Catholic Ulster, two Irish chieftains, O'Neill and O'Donnell, gave grudging allegiance to the English Crown and were created Earls of Tyrone and Tyrconnell. But they rebelled and an anti-English alliance between them and Catholic countries was formed, which led to landings at Kinsale in 1601 by Spain. The alliance was defeated in 1603 by Mountjoy, Elizabeth I's deputy, and many people were either killed or starved. Tyrone and Tyrconnell did not surrender, but later fled into exile (1607) and the Crown had to organize a defeated Ulster.

Plantation policy (Ulster 1607)

The difficulties and costs of managing six Ulster counties of Armagh, Fermanagh, Londonderry/Derry, Cavan, Tyrone and Donegal were removed when Scottish and English Protestant settlers were 'planted' on land taken from Irish Catholics by the state. Landlords were given land and they contracted with and protected colonists, who received tenancies to work the fields. Land was also granted to soldiers who had served the Crown.

The plantation policy aimed to destroy Irish political culture; create a Protestant ascendancy loyal to the English state; take over native Irish land; and ultimately to expel the Irish from Ulster. But large-scale physical expulsion proved impossible. The Catholic Irish lost their land and were forced into basic subsistence living. They reacted by periodically attacking the Protestant settlements. Between 1603 and 1640, some 30,000 to 40,000 Scottish and English Protestants were planted in Ulster. A religious and political division was created in which a Gaelic Catholic culture was subservient to a settler or planter culture.

Sectarianism

European political conflicts in the sixteenth and seventeenth centuries were heavily conditioned by religion as anti-Catholicism and anti-Protestantism increased. In Ireland, religion was apparent in the political division between dispossessed Irish Catholics and English and Scottish Protestant settlers, although economic considerations were often arguably more important than the religious. In England, anti-Catholicism was encouraged by alleged Popish plots, which united the English against a common enemy in the Catholic Irish (and Catholic France and Spain). Englishness was partly defined by this opposition, which profoundly influenced the identity and nation building of the English Protestant state.

The Protestant ascendancy: 1641–1801

Sectarian division became more open, polarized and violent during this period, which culminated in the suppression of Ireland by Oliver Cromwell following the 1641 Irish rebellion, the imposition of a restrictive Penal Code upon the Catholic Irish and an increase in Protestant power.

The 1641 rebellion

In 1640 Charles I quarrelled with the English Parliament and tried to rule without its consent (divine right). This conflict and the Ulster plantation policy encouraged Irish Catholics to challenge English Protestant authority and resulted in the 1641 Irish rebellion, which began in Dungannon, Charlmont and Newry. Protestants were massacred by Catholics who then suffered violent revenge from Protestants. Religious, political and economic factors fuelled the rebellion and led to long-lasting hatred and suspicion. The 1642 to 1649 period was confused, with divided loyalties and anger in Ireland and civil war in England. After the defeat and execution of Charles I (1649), the English Parliament sent Oliver Cromwell to subdue the rebels and Ireland (1649–1650).

PLATE 1.3 Battle of the (River) Boyne, 11 July 1690, near Drogheda, where the Protestant English King William III defeated the Jacobite forces of deposed King James II. Courtesy of the Council of the National Army Museum, London.

Cromwell arrived in Dublin and overcame Ireland quickly in nine months. The campaign began with the sacking of Drogheda with a great loss of military and civilian life (allegedly as revenge for the 1641 rising), followed by the destruction of Wexford. Many landlords and most Catholic landowners lost their property, which was given to those who had fought with Cromwell, financed his campaign or were English settlers. It is estimated that out of a population of 1,448,000, one-third died from war and famine, had emigrated or been deported. Cromwell was demonized in Ireland, but there is still disagreement about his campaign, his motives and the details of the bloodshed.

The English now owned two-thirds of Irish land, but many lived in England as absentee landlords. Cromwell's conquest of Ireland established a colony with Protestant upper and settler/planter classes in a country of Irish Catholics. A struggle for supremacy between the two sides began. The Catholic James II (1685–1688) tried to return rights and land to the Irish, but was prevented by the Protestant William III of Orange, and fled to France. James returned to Ireland, but his army was defeated by William at the Battle of the Boyne in 1690 and finally at the Battle of Aughrim in 1691.

King and state were associated with Protestant settlers, and the established Anglican Church of Ireland (one-tenth of the population) held much political power and land. By 1691 a Protestant ascendancy was achieved. Old English and

Irish Catholics were weakened and many of their members (the Wild Geese) left Ireland for better prospects overseas and to escape persecution.

In 1695, new penal laws disenfranchised Irish Catholics (and some Protestant dissenters) by restricting their religious, political and economic rights. The impact and efficiency of the penal laws are questioned, but most Catholics had a separate, unequal status and the political nation was the Protestant nation.

The eighteenth century

Britain started to build a global, influential empire after the Union of England, Wales and Scotland in 1707 to form Great Britain, and Ireland was its food supplier. The Irish economy expanded in the eighteenth century as the Ulster linen industry grew, and wool, beef, butter and pork became valuable exports. An Irish parliamentary tradition developed, although the Dublin Parliament excluded Catholics and was subordinate to Westminster. Irish Protestants also fought for reduced English control over Irish affairs and there was increased emigration, as discriminated Catholics and Ulster Presbyterians left for North America.

British eighteenth-century empire building led to global revolts against colonialism and the growth of independence movements. During the American War of Independence (1775–1783), the withdrawal of British troops from Ireland was seen as an opportunity for a French invasion. Attempts were made to prevent the threat by restoring some rights to the Catholic population. Anti-Catholic laws were relaxed in 1781 and some Catholics were given the right to vote in elections and to take lower level government jobs in 1793. Poynings' Law was repealed in 1782, creating de facto Irish parliamentary independence. But the conflict between Britain and the American colonies and the philosophical influence of the French Revolution encouraged radicalism and nationalism. This political atmosphere led to the creation of the Society of United Irishmen and a pro-independence paramilitary force, the Irish Volunteers.

Fears about a French invasion of Ireland grew when revolutionary wars between England and France began in 1793. Wolfe Tone of the United Irishmen appealed for French help and there were two failed French landings. The United Irishmen rebelled in 1798 and aimed to establish an independent Irish republic. The rebellion was put down but problems continued, and Prime Minister William Pitt proposed unification of the Irish and Westminster Parliaments (with a hint of Catholic emancipation). Protestants opposed this solution, but a fierce campaign led to the Act of Union between Great Britain and Ireland in 1800 (effective in 1801), which created a parliamentary union. Failed Irish attempts to rebel against British rule in the late eighteenth century had thus resulted in Union, the disestablishment of the Irish Parliament in Dublin and the central-ization of political power at Westminster.

Union with Great Britain: 1801–1921

The period 1800 to 1921 began with the Act of Union and ended with the partition of Ireland and quasi independence for Southern Ireland. There were conflicts about the status of the Union; the growth of Irish nationalism; the Famine of 1845 with its economic, social and political consequences; the growth of modern Ireland; agrarianism (anti-landlordism and redistribution of landed property); Land War agitation from 1879 to 1903 about the transfer of ownership of tenanted land from landlord to tenant; an Irish cultural revival; the Home Rule movement and Unionist reaction; the 1916 Easter Rising; and the War of Independence.

The Act of Union was partly a reaction to the 1798 revolts and violence. British politicians believed that the Act would solve historical Irish problems and reduce administrative costs for the government. Ireland was incorporated with Great Britain to form the United Kingdom (UK). The Irish Parliament was dissolved and 100 MPs and 28 life peers were transferred to the Westminster Parliament. The Churches of England and Ireland were united (with four Irish bishops serving in the Westminster House of Lords) and a customs union joined Ireland and Great Britain. Ireland was the last UK nation to join the Union, but was the first to leave, impelled by the nineteenth- and twentieth-century campaign

PLATE 1.4 Opponents of the Act of Union, 1801, drown their sorrows after the Act was passed by the British Parliament with the alleged use of bribery, corruption, patronage and intimidation. *The Union Club, 1801* (colour engraving), James Gillray (1757–1815)/Private Collection/The Bridgeman Art Library

for Irish Home Rule, which demanded devolved self-rule for the Irish in an Irish Parliament in Dublin.

The Act of Union lasted for 120 years, but was arguably flawed from the beginning, since the union with Ireland differed from that between other component parts of the UK. William Pitt seemed to promise Catholic emancipation (full civil and religious rights), but this was opposed by the Protestant George III and only granted in 1829. The Catholicism of the Irish majority was minimized and the Anglican Church of Ireland was dominant in Ireland. Opponents argued that the Union was not between Britain and Ireland but between Britain and an Irish Protestant elite. Most Catholics and some Protestants supported the cause of Irish nationalism in the nineteenth century.

Ireland lost its parliament but paradoxically there was an Irish administration in Dublin and a Privy Council with judges and law officers. It thus had an executive and judiciary but no legislature. It was argued that Ireland was subordinate to Britain and the Union represented centralized political power in London. There were deep tensions and the potential for fragmentation and collapse. In Ireland, cultural differences and conflicts remained; religion was represented by a weak Catholic majority and a powerful Protestant minority; small peasant farmers suffered and often had to leave unproductive land; and emigration increased.

Meanwhile, Britain rapidly industrialized and urbanized in the nineteenth century, while Ireland, except for Ulster, did not. Ireland had an agrarian rural economy and the country's growing population was dependent on the potato as a staple crop. At the beginning of the nineteenth century, Ireland had 5.3 million inhabitants (reaching 8 million in 1841), most of whom lived in the countryside. Much of the land was owned by British landlords living mainly in Britain and leased to Irish small farmers. Poverty was considerable; jobs were scarce; people lived in poor conditions; and many were obliged to emigrate.

In 1845, potato blight caused harvest failure and food supplies declined. In the late 1840s, the potato crop failed over a two-year period, famine resulted, and Ireland's economy and people were decimated. One million people died of starvation and disease, and a million emigrated to Britain and America. Between 1846 and 1856, the population fell from 8 million to 6 million, and further to 4.5 million in 1920 as emigration increased, while that of Britain trebled in size by 1900. Population figures have not recovered since 1845 and the estimated populations of Ireland and Northern Ireland are 4.6 million (2011) and 1.8 million (2010) respectively.

Opposition: Home Rule and the repeal of the Union

Conflict over the handling of the Famine and the Act of Union grew in Ireland. Although the Famine is still subject to different interpretations, British government policies, lack of adequate relief programmes and absentee landlords were blamed for the disaster. Many, if not all, in the Protestant community defended the Union while a majority of Catholic opinion could not accept it and demanded national freedom. These opposed views led to increased sectarian tension between Catholic and Protestant (and between Nationalist and Unionist).

Those opposed to the Union called for an independent self-governing Ireland (Home Rule) and the repeal of the Union. In 1858, the Irish Republican Brotherhood (IRB) was formed out of the Fenian Movement, which protested about the Famine, as did Irish-American Fenians (Warriors). The Home Rule campaign was linked to agrarian and land reform, and landlords were under political and economic pressure. Unrest led to legislation in the early twentieth century which forced landlords to sell land to their tenants, who were given loans to buy their holdings.

However, the Home Rule question was not initially settled despite efforts by Daniel O'Connell and Isaac Butt in the 1840s and 1870s. However, under the leadership of Charles Stewart Parnell, the Irish Parliamentary Party (the Irish Party) forced Home Rule on to the British political agenda. In 1886, the Liberal Party under W.E. Gladstone supported limited self-government for Ireland after much internal conflict.

Meanwhile, pro-Unionist feeling grew in mainly Protestant Ulster where the British had invested in textiles, shipbuilding and other industries and the North had progressed. But Ireland was economically, socially and religiously divided between the North and the South. Many northern Unionists opposed Home Rule and separation from Britain, which would leave them as a minority in an independent and self-governing Ireland. A main force opposed to Home Rule was the Orange Order (founded in memory of William of Orange). Prior to the First World War, the paramilitary Ulster Volunteer Force (UVF) was established and was prepared to defend Ulster by force. Unionists and their supporters in England argued that Home Rule would lead to the collapse of the Union and possibly the Empire.

In Southern Ireland, the Home Rule movement became stronger and Britain was obliged to remove some restrictions against Catholics. The Anglican Church lost its monopoly, Catholics were able to sit in Parliament and Catholic children gained their own school education. Home Rule emphasized the national unity of the Irish people and their Gaelic history, culture and language. Leading figures in the national cultural revival were authors J.M. Synge and W.B. Yeats, who linked Ireland to a literary past.

In 1905, Sinn Féin ('ourselves alone') was founded and supported an independent Ireland. Opposed paramilitary organizations such as the Unionist Ulster Volunteer Force and the Nationalist Irish Volunteers mobilized. Conflict was avoided by the outbreak of the First World War in 1914 and the postponement of the Home Rule bill at Westminster. The Irish Volunteers armed; began a rebellion in Dublin (the Easter Rising) in 1916; seized the General Post Office; and proclaimed an Irish Republic. The rising lacked support and was quickly put

PLATE 1.5 The General Post Office on O'Connell Street, Dublin, after the failed Easter Rising, 24–29 April 1916, organized by the Irish Republican Brotherhood (IRB) and the Irish Volunteers. Archives Charmet/The Bridgeman Art Library

down by British troops. However, the execution of 15 participants caused public anger and long-lasting defiance of British rule. Sinn Féin supporters were successful in the General Election of 1918, when they defeated the Irish Party, which had supported Home Rule.

A majority of Sinn Fèin members did not take their seats at Westminster and founded the first Dáil (government) in Dublin in 1919. They unilaterally declared

Ireland to be a revolutionary state known as the 'Irish Republic'. The Irish War of Independence (1919–1921) broke out, influenced by Sinn Féin and the Irish Republican Army's (IRA's) campaign against British troops. This ended in a truce, and the Anglo-Irish Treaty in 1921 led to 26 counties or five-sixths (83 per cent) of the island in the south and west with their 95 per cent Catholic majority forming the Irish Free State (IFS) or Saorstát Éireann. It possessed significant domestic independence; had dominion status within the British Commonwealth; swore allegiance to the British Crown; accepted a Governor-General; and allowed appeals to the British Privy Council. The Articles of Agreement were signed by representatives of the British and Dáil governments on 6 December 1921.

The creation of the IFS led to civil war (June 1922 to May 1923) between Free State supporters of the Treaty and those who rejected partition and wanted an independent Irish republic. The former won, but the war was a divisive political event and repeal of the Union did not formally take place until 1962. Meanwhile, six counties in north-east Ulster had been given their own Northern Ireland Parliament by the Government of Ireland Act, 1920 and remained within the UK.

Partition and aftermath: 1921–

The Treaty and the 1920 Act were fiercely opposed by the various political factions, and partition of the island after 1921 has not generally been accepted as a solution to the island's problems. Different forms of self-government were adopted by the two parts of the country over the next 90 years, but these were based on the facts of division, conflict, and divergent political, cultural and economic priorities. New geographical and constitutional terms were introduced to deal with the shifting realities of partition; the two parts began to distance themselves from each other; and the Irish Free State moved further away from Britain.

W.T. Cosgrave of the Cumann na nGaedheal party (later Fine Gael) led the first IFS government. He was followed by Éamon de Valera, who founded Fianna Fáil and was periodically Head of Government from 1932 to 1959 and President of Ireland from 1959 to 1973. Coalition governments became a necessary part of political life as either of these two main political parties governed with the Labour Party, Democratic Left, Progressive Democrats or others.

Constitutional links between Britain and the IFS gradually weakened; a new 1937 Constitution (Bunreacht nah Éireann) replaced that of 1922; and the Irish Free State became Éire/Ireland. The constitution claimed that Éire/Ireland was 'a sovereign, independent, democratic state' with Éire as the official Irish-language name of the state and Ireland as its English-language translation. Article 2 of the constitution defined 'the national territory' as 'the whole island of Ireland, its islands, and territorial seas'. However, Article 3 stated that, 'pending integration of the national territory' (i.e. the North and South of the island), jurisdiction was limited to the 26 counties of the former Irish Free State. Ireland remained neutral after partition and during the Second World War (despite German bombing raids on Dublin and pressure from the USA to support the Allied cause).

After the war, the Republic of Ireland Act, 1949 declared Éire/Ireland to be an independent republic. The Act was passed by an interparty government in an attempt to clarify Ireland's international position and its name. The Republic of Ireland (Poblacht na Éireann) is the official description of the state in the Act, although not its constitutional name as defined in the 1937 Constitution. The Act did not change the status of Éire/Ireland and there is no reference to a republic in that constitution. Arguably, the 1949 Act was intended to emphasize that the ideal 'island-wide' state was a republic and not a monarchical model.

Some critics maintain that Éire/Ireland may misleadingly be seen to refer to the whole island. 'Republic of Ireland' is constitutionally inaccurate, since 'Éire/Ireland' are the constitutional names and the Constitution is the basis of the Irish legal system. The inclusion of 'republic' in the 1937 Constitution was recommended in its 1967 review, but was not implemented. The term 'Republic of Ireland' is widely accepted (and used officially) as descriptive of the independent Southern state; arguably distinguishes it from Northern Ireland; and has a legal status by virtue of the Republic of Ireland Act, 1949.

Éire/Ireland is the name usually employed for official purposes, such as international diplomacy, treaties, government, legal documents and membership of global bodies. After Irish was named as the European Union's twenty-first official language in 2007, the Southern state is referred to in both official languages (Irish and English) as 'Éire/Ireland'.

Since the 1960s, Ireland has seen some industrialization, but the country remains largely rural. The Catholic Church has a significant (although declining) influence on schools, health, education and social life. Irish is used in everyday speech in parts of the west and some urban centres, but is studied by all school children together with English. Ireland was admitted to the United Nations in 1955, and its membership since 1973 of what became the European Union (EU) has had significant effects.

Although Ireland has experienced major modernizing and entrepreneurial changes in its political, social, economic and cultural life, the economy stagnated in the 1970s and early 1980s, due to a world oil crisis, global competition and the lack of domestic diversification. However, a young workforce, new technology, adjustment to the new economic world order and development funds from the then European Community created a lively economy in the 1990s, particularly in the technology, financial, media and agricultural sectors. But this 'Celtic Tiger' economy declined in the 1990s and early twenty-first century, and suffered badly as a result of the credit crunch and global recession from 2007 to 2008.

At the end of the twentieth century, there was debate about reforming Ireland's social laws, which were influenced by the Catholic Church and considered (particularly after revelations in the 1990s and 2000s of clerical sexual abuse of children and resultant cover-ups) to be oppressive. Many people wanted a more open and progressive society. A 1995 referendum narrowly approved the legalization of divorce. Ireland has not legalized abortion and a foetus's right to life from conception is upheld, although termination is possible under restricted conditions if the mother's life is in danger and women cannot be prevented from travelling abroad for abortions. Contraception is restricted, although advice and prescriptions are provided by GPs, voluntary organizations and private family planning clinics.

Northern Ireland became a self-governing (devolved) country within the UK from 1921. It occupies six counties in the north-east or one-sixth (17 per cent) of the island and is also known as Ulster or (for some Nationalists) the Six Counties, the North of Ireland or the North. Its first Prime Minister was Sir James Craig, and, with its 60 per cent Protestant majority at partition, it has been a region (province) of the United Kingdom for over 90 years.

It is argued that the Unionist-dominated Northern Ireland Parliament from 1920 discriminated against the Nationalist minority in areas such as political representation, housing, employment, social benefits and education. Town and city boundaries and voting arrangements were manipulated, so that local government elections ensured Unionist control of local councils. The province experienced periods of relative economic growth and sectarian violence until devolved power-sharing government between Unionists and Nationalists was achieved in 1998.

The Troubles (Northern Ireland)

The politics and life of the island were influenced for much of the late twentieth century by conflict between opposing forces in Northern Ireland. In the 1960s, attempts to reform the political system in the province were hindered by opposition from hardline politicians and trade unionists. Pressure from Nationalists for political change and from Unionists for a 'No Surrender' policy to Nationalist demands resulted in deadlock and an alternative non-sectarian civil rights movement was formed by community leaders such as John Hume and Austin Currie. In 1968, riots and communal violence broke out in Belfast and Londonderry/ Derry after clashes between civil rights marchers and the largely Protestant Royal Ulster Constabulary (RUC). The British Army was sent to Northern Ireland to preserve order and was initially welcomed by all groups, but eventually faced opposition and suspicion from many quarters. The killing of 13 civilians in the Bogside area of Londonderry/Derry by British paratroopers on Bloody Sunday (30 January 1972) further inflamed the situation. The Saville Inquiry, established by the British government, found in its Report in June 2010 that the shootings were 'unjustified and unjustifiable'.

Escalating violence led to the appearance of the Provisional IRA (PIRA), a breakaway grouping from the Official IRA, and loyalist paramilitary groups like

PLATE 1.6 Republican/Nationalist mural painting in the Bogside, Londonderry/Derry, Northern Ireland. The Bogside lies beneath Londonderry's walls and was the scene of Bloody Sunday, 30 January 1972. © Rex Features

the Ulster Defence Association (UDA), which further inflamed the situation in Northern Ireland. The Nationalists were aided by the PIRA, who in 1974 carried out attacks in England, where bombs exploded in London and Birmingham. In the 1970s, the Unionist Vanguard Movement argued for a political response, but the UDA wanted to confront the PIRA with force. In the 1970s to 1990s, extremists on both sides carried out acts of murder, kidnapping, torture, bombing and arson often involving and targeting civilians. The most notorious outrages included the Le Mon, Enniskillen and Omagh bombings by Republican groups in attempts to force political change.

Many views were proposed about how to improve the situation in Northern Ireland. Early attempts were made to unite Unionists and Nationalists, such as the Civil Rights Movement initiated by Bernadette Devlin on a socialist, secular platform to unite the working class. In 1976, Protestant and Catholic women demonstrated together for peace in Ulster. None of these attempted solutions was successful. Some British and Irish politicians proposed British withdrawal from Northern Ireland, but Irish governments were opposed. They argued that chaos would follow withdrawal, with Nationalists moving to western Northern Ireland and Unionists to the east. A civil war could envelop Northern Ireland, the Republic and Scotland.

Faced with a deteriorating situation, the British government, under the Government of Ireland Act, 1920, introduced direct rule with law and order powers in 1972; prorogued the Parliament at Stormont; and the province was governed from London through a Northern Ireland Office and Secretary of State in the province. A number of attempts failed to return political power to Northern Ireland in the next 20 years, including power-sharing under the Sunningdale Agreement, rolling devolution and the Anglo-Irish Agreement, 1985, which allowed Ireland some cooperation with Britain in governing the province.

Meanwhile, demographic patterns in Northern Ireland were slowly changing. The 2001 census showed that people with a Protestant background formed a majority of 53.1 per cent of the population, while those with a Catholic background formed 43.8 per cent. Although Protestants had traditionally dominated the labour and housing markets, Catholics gradually improved their economic, employment and social positions. But tribal cultures continued and both sides demonstrate their loyalties with flags, murals, graffiti and marches.

The Good Friday (Belfast) Agreement, 1998

By the 1990s, most people in Northern Ireland seemed weary of violence and intolerance. The PIRA had not won the military battle, achieved mass political support or British withdrawal. Unionist parties were in entrenched positions; and Sinn Féin was struggling for a viable, non-violent political strategy. There seemed to be no consensus for progress.

However, politicians in Dublin (Albert Reynolds, Fianna Fáil)), London (John Major, Conservative) and Ulster (David Trimble of the Ulster Unionists) provided momentum to a peace movement and a resolution of some of the old problems. Contacts between Gerry Adams (Sinn Fèin) and John Hume of the Social Democratic and Labour Party (SDLP) led to all-party negotiations that eventually (and tortuously) produced the 1998 Good Friday (Belfast) Agreement. It is generally recognized that the driving forces behind the Agreement's final acceptance, despite many tactical difficulties, were the British Prime Minister (Tony Blair) and Ireland's Taoiseach (Bertie Ahern).

The Agreement between the political parties in Northern Ireland led to referendums of the people in Northern Ireland and Ireland. A majority of both communities in Northern Ireland approved the Agreement (71.1 per cent), as did 94.3 per cent of voters in Ireland. They accepted the creation of a devolved, power-sharing Northern Ireland Assembly and Executive which, following elections, began operating in 1998.

On 2 December 1999, the government of Ireland changed articles 2 and 3 of the 1937 Constitution which, following the partition of Ireland in 1921, had claimed possession of the six counties of Northern Ireland and sought sovereignty over the whole of the island. The Constitution was amended by recognizing Northern Ireland's right to exist, while also acknowledging the Nationalist desire for a united Ireland. An arrangement was made whereby all people born in the island can claim Irish nationality, subject to some initial restrictions.

The British government declared that it had no strategic interest in Northern Ireland and restated its position that any future unification of Ireland could only be effected with the consent of the majority of the population of Northern Ireland. This principle of consent was also agreed by the Irish government and arguably satisfied the Unionist community, which had long felt that cross-border cooperation would lead inevitably to control by Dublin.

Three cross-border bodies (the North–South Ministerial Council, the British–Irish Council and the British–Irish Intergovernmental Conference) were created. These developments, while preserving the partition of the island, seemed to indicate hope for the future, a positive partnership between the Irish and British governments, a power-sharing peace in Northern Ireland between Unionists and Nationalists, and greater cooperation between the North and South of the island and between administrative and political structures of the UK and Ireland.

Under the Agreement, each party that reaches a specific level of support in Northern Ireland elections has the right to name a member of its party to government and a ministry. The Ulster Unionists, SDLP, Sinn Féin and the Democratic Unionist Party (DUP) each had ministers in the new power-sharing Assembly and Executive, with the Ulster Unionist David Trimble as First Minister and Seamus Mallon of the SDLP as Deputy First Minister. However, these bodies were suspended in 2002 due to the PIRA's delay in implementing its agreement to decommission its weapons. Direct rule from Westminster was imposed again and the province was run by the Secretary of State for Northern Ireland and a British ministerial team. Implementation of the Good Friday (Belfast) Agreement was delayed.

An attempt to restart the Assembly was made in May 2006 by the British and Irish governments, with a deadline of November 2006. This deadline was not met, but negotiations continued with the aim of re-establishing devolution by March 2007. By the end of 2006 Sinn Féin had accepted the principles of a new Police Service of Northern Ireland (PSNI) and security arrangements. Following Assembly elections in March 2007, the Unionist DUP and Nationalist Sinn Fèin gained most seats and agreed (May) to a restored power-sharing devolved Assembly and Executive. Ian Paisley of the DUP (replaced by Peter Robinson in 2008) became the new First Minister and Martin McGuinness of Sinn Fèin became Deputy First Minister. The devolution process also moved forward when policing and justice powers were eventually transferred from Westminster to the Assembly in 2010.

The current situation in Northern Ireland swings between pessimism and optimism, with some people questioning the success of the Good Friday (Belfast) Agreement and the new political institutions. Although the worst violence has subsided and daily life has improved, old tribal distrust and criminality continue. Bomb attacks and shootings by Republican and Loyalist splinter groups and rioting during the July marching season increased in 2009 to 2011 throughout the province. Recent incidents in Northern Ireland have involved car bombs, anti-personnel devices and booby-traps which have targeted individuals, such as police officers. The threat level for Irish attacks on Britain was raised in September 2010 from 'moderate' to 'substantial', indicating that an attack from dissident groups was a strong and real possibility.

However, following centuries of hostility between Nationalists (many, if not all of whom have traditionally wanted reunification with the Republic) and Unionists (who mostly wish to preserve the union with Britain), some cooperation and an acknowledgement of a shared history and common interests have grown in recent years between the two parts of the island and between them and Britain.

Contemporary attitudes

Northern Ireland

The people of Northern Ireland have varied attitudes to their society. These range from everyday concerns to questions about the present and future of Northern Ireland, and may sometimes reveal departures from stereotypical images of the province.

According to the *Northern Ireland Life and Times Survey* ARK 2009, the political parties to which respondents felt closest were the DUP (21 per cent), Sinn Féin (13 per cent), UUP (18 per cent), SDLP (19 per cent) and the Alliance (7 per cent), while, very significantly, a relatively large 21 per cent chose no political party. In terms of alleged tribal attitudes in Northern Ireland, 37 per cent of respondents regarded themselves as Unionists, 19 per cent as Nationalists and a substantial 43 per cent as neither. However, in practical terms, it is the DUP and Sinn Féin which have gained most seats in recent Assembly elections.

When asked what the long-term policy for the province should be, a small 17 per cent considered that it should remain part of the UK with direct rule from Westminster; 53 per cent thought that it should remain part of the UK with devolved government; 18 per cent felt that it should reunify with the rest of Ireland; and 6 per cent maintained that it should be an independent state. These statistics suggest that a considerable 70 per cent of all communities wanted to preserve the UK link. But if in the future a majority of people in Northern Ireland voted in favour of a united Ireland, 14 per cent of respondents who had voted against reunification would find unification virtually impossible to accept. However, although 44 per cent would not like the situation, they could accept it if necessary; and 40 per cent would happily accept the wishes of the majority. Some 84 per cent were therefore less extreme in their views on possible Irish reunification than traditional attitudes would suggest.

Like people in other countries, 50 per cent of Northern Irish respondents did not have much trust in politicians in general; 29 per cent did not have any trust at all; 19 per cent had a fair amount; and 1 per cent a great deal. More specifically, 37 per cent were very dissatisfied with the way members of the Northern Ireland Legislative Assembly (MLAs) were doing their job; 30 per cent were fairly dissatisfied; 18 per cent were neither satisfied nor dissatisfied; and 1 per cent were very satisfied. Opinions were also lukewarm on the performance of political institutions. Although 27 per cent of respondents said that the Assembly was giving ordinary people more say in how Northern Ireland is governed, 9 per cent thought it was giving less, and 61 per cent considered that it was making no difference. Overall, 7 per cent thought that the Assembly had achieved a great deal since its establishment; 49 per cent a little; 23 per cent nothing at all; and 18 per cent felt that it was too early to tell.

However, when considering the effects of political changes in Northern Ireland on ordinary people since the Good Friday (Belfast) Agreement, 1998, opinions seemed to be reasonably balanced. For example, 2 per cent of respondents thought that Protestants had benefited a lot more than Catholics; 2 per cent thought that Protestants had benefited a little more than Catholics; 14 per cent thought that Catholics had benefited a little more than Protestants; while a majority 51 per cent thought that Protestants and Catholics had benefited equally and 8 per cent thought that neither side had benefited. These figures show more balance than some polls, which show decided bias against either Catholics or Protestants.

In terms of aims for the country over the 10 years from 2009, attitudes reflected recent history in Northern Ireland. Some 32 per cent of respondents thought that priority should be given to maintaining order in the region; 28 per cent felt that people should be given more say in important government decisions; 32 per cent argued that rising prices should be combated; and 8 per cent emphasized protection of freedom of speech. Like voters in other countries, concerns about employment, the economy, crime, pensions, taxation, welfare and other basic 'bread-and-butter' issues were at the forefront of other opinion polls in 2009 to 2010.

Ireland

Opinion polls in Ireland in 2009 (Eurobarometer and TNS/MRBI) were dominated by economic and employment matters, owing to the steep downturn in the Celtic Tiger economy in the 1990s and the global recession of 2007 to 2008. Respondents felt that the two most important issues facing the country were unemployment (58 per cent) and the economic situation (48 per cent). These figures were higher than the EU27 average due to the higher starting point in the Irish economy and the corresponding steeper fall of the recession.

But respondents also had concerns about rising prices/inflation (12 per cent), healthcare (29 per cent), immigration (4 per cent), pensions (3 per cent), taxation (6 per cent) and education (6 per cent). These views were similar to those of the UK in 2010, but 10 per cent of Irish respondents felt that the employment situation would improve in 2010.

The performances of economic and political institutions, such as the European Union and Irish organizations, were inevitably important in the distressed financial climate of the early twenty-first century. Although Eurobarometer polls reported in 2009 that Irish respondents felt that in the global crisis it was better to be part (71 per cent) of the EU than not (18 per cent), this first figure marked a drop of 9 per cent over a previous poll, suggesting a declining faith in the EU and uncertainty about its performance.

A Eurobarometer poll in September 2009 also reported that 59 per cent of Irish respondents thought that Ireland itself was going in the wrong direction, which was nevertheless an improvement from 74 per cent earlier in the year. However, Irish respondents had only a 20 per cent trust in their national government and 19 per cent in their political parties. Given the reactions to the global economic recession, the Irish people were also vigorous in their views about Irish political and economic institutions. According to TNS/MRBI polls in 2009, respondents were dissatisfied with their government (80 per cent) as against 15 per cent satisfied; but thought that the private and public sectors were sharing the pain of recovery equally. However, in considering how the situation should be improved, 57 per cent thought that taxes should not be increased (with 35 per cent for); 36 supported the Labour Party's proposal to nationalize the banks (with 38 per cent against); 70 per cent thought that the government should cut public spending rather than increasing taxes (14 per cent for); the public pay bill should be reduced by salary cuts (58 per cent) rather than redundancies (26 per cent for); and social welfare should not be cut (75 per cent), with 21 per cent saying it should be cut. These figures were very similar to those in the United Kingdom in 2010 when respondents there were asked how they would cope with spending cuts and taxes in any attempt to reduce budget deficits.

Exercises

Explain and examine the following terms:

Northern Ireland Assembly	SDLP	Anglo-Normans
direct rule	Meath	the 1641 rebellion
Sinn Féin	Clontarf	the Bogside
the Pale	sectarianism	Fianna Fáil
Battle of the Boyne	Drogheda	Nationalist
Oliver Cromwell	Neolithic	Unionist
the English Reformation	Celts	plantation policy
Wolfe Tone	PIRA	sectarianism
Act of Union	Tara	DUP
Taoiseach	RUC	Good Friday (Belfast) Agreement
Home Rule	landlords	Orange Order

Church of Ireland   the Famine   Easter Rising (Rebellion)
Bertie Ahern   High King   Mesolithic

Write short essays on the following topics:

1   Discuss the links between politics and religion in Ireland and Northern Ireland.

2   How valid is the term 'colonialism' when applied to Irish history?

3   Evaluate whether partition must be a permanent feature of Irish life.

4   Examine the opinion poll results on Ireland and Northern Ireland in this chapter. What do they tell us about the two societies and their people?

Further reading

Bew, P. (2007) *The Politics of Enmity 1789–2006* Oxford: Oxford University Press

Brown, T. (2004) *Ireland: A Social and Cultural History 1922–2002* London: Harper Perennial

Connolly, C. (ed.) (2003) *Theorizing Ireland* Basingstoke: Palgrave Macmillan

Connolly, S.J. (ed.) (2007) *The Oxford Companion to Irish History* Oxford: Oxford University Press

Coohill, J. (2000) *Ireland: A Short History* Oxford: Oneworld Publications

Elliott, M. (ed.) (2002) *The Long Road to Peace in Northern Ireland* Liverpool: Liverpool University Press

English, R. (2004) *Armed Struggle: The History of the IRA* London: Pan Books

Foster, R. (1990) *Modern Ireland, 1600–1972* London: Penguin

Foster, R. (2008) *Luck and the Irish: A Brief History of Change 1970–2008* London: Allen Lane

Hennessey, T. (1997) *A History of Northern Ireland 1920–96* Basingstoke: Palgrave

Kee, R. (2000) *The Green Flag: A History of Irish Nationalism* London: Penguin

Kinealy, C. (1999) *A Disunited Kingdom: England, Ireland, Scotland and Wales 1800–1949* Cambridge: Cambridge University Press

Lalor, B. (ed.) (2003) *The Encyclopedia of Ireland* Dublin: Gill and Macmillan

Litton, H. (2003) *The Irish Famine: An Illustrated History* Dublin: Wolfhound Press

McGarry, J. and O'Leary, B. (2004) *The Northern Ireland Conflict: Consociational Engagements* Oxford: Oxford University Press

McKittrick, D. and McVea, D. (2001) *Making Sense of the Troubles* London: Penguin

Moody, T.W. and Martin, F.X. (2001) *The Course of Irish History* Cork: Mercier Press

Powell, J. (2008) *Great Hatred, Little Room: Making Peace in Northern Ireland* London: The Bodley Head

Ranelagh, J. O'B. (2005) *A Short History of Ireland* Cambridge: Cambridge University Press

Taylor, P. (1998) *The Provos: The IRA and Sinn Féin* London: Bloomsbury Publishing

Taylor, P. (2000) *Loyalists* London: Bloomsbury Publishing

Taylor, P. (2002) *Brits: The War Against the IRA* London: Bloomsbury Publishing

Tonge, J. (2005) *The New Northern Ireland Politics?* Basingstoke: Palgrave Macmillan

Websites

Northern Ireland government: www.nidirect.gov
Northern Ireland business: Nibusinessinfo.co.uk
belfasttelegraph.co.uk
BBC: bbc.co.uk/northernireland/
www.culturenorthernireland.org/
www.direct.gov.uk/en/Governmentcitizensandrights/UK
Identities: http://alt-usage-english.org/ireland.html
Ireland government: www.irlgov.ie
TASC think-tank: www.tascnet.ie
Conflicts, politics and society, Northern Ireland, CAIN: http://cain.ulst.ac.uk

2

The country

Ireland has 83 per cent (five-sixths) of the total land area of the island and Northern Ireland has 17 per cent (one-sixth). They have some geographical features in common, while others are different and a few can be very distinctive. The Ireland population was estimated at 4.6 million in 2011 and was 1.8 million for Northern Ireland in 2011.The island is divided into counties, each with its county town, and is sparsely populated outside the urban centres. The counties are still used as a basis of local government in Ireland, but no longer have a political or administrative function in Northern Ireland.

Geographical features

Ireland experienced two prehistoric ice ages (glaciations). The first covered most of the country and the second reached a line between Limerick and Dublin by 10000 BC. Ireland and Great Britain were once part of the Eurasian land mass, but both were eventually separated from the mainland and from each other by rising sea levels caused by melting glaciers.

The island lies to the west of Great Britain and is the most western part of an archipelago (group of islands) situated off the north-western European coast. These islands are sometimes geographically and collectively known (incorrectly for some people) as the British Isles, but are also described as 'Great Britain and Ireland' or the 'Atlantic Archipelago'.

Ireland and Northern Ireland occupy a temperate zone between latitude 51 and 55° N and longitude 5.5 and 10° W; lie on the raised European Continental Shelf; are influenced climatically by the North Atlantic Current (a north-eastern extension of the Gulf Stream); and are surrounded by seas that are generally less than 656 feet (200 m) deep. The greatest distance from north to south is 302 miles (486 km); from east to west it is 174 miles (280 km); and the coastline measures 1,971 miles (3,172 km). Malin Head (latitude 55° 27′ N) and Mizen Head (latitude 51° 27′ N) are respectively the most northerly and southerly points of the island, and the most eastern and western extremities lie on longitudes 5° 25′ W and 10° 30′ W.

Ireland and Northern Ireland comprise the second largest island of the archipelago after Great Britain. It has a total area of 32,575 square miles (84,369 sq km), with Ireland having 27,108 square miles (70,209 sq km) and Northern Ireland occupying 5,467 square miles (14,160 sq km). Ireland with its capital and largest city Dublin (population 1,045,769 for the Dublin Urban Area in 2006) is separated from Great Britain to the east by the Irish Sea and North Channel, and

FIGURE 2.1 Ireland and Northern Ireland: counties and county towns

to the south-east by St George's Channel at distances varying up to 120 miles (193 km). The west and south coasts face the North Atlantic Ocean. Northern Ireland with its capital and largest city Belfast (population 483,418 for the Belfast Urban Area in 2006) lies in the north-east of the island and is separated from Scotland by the North Channel (13 miles/21 km wide at its narrowest point). Northern Ireland and Ireland share a land border of 224 miles (360 km) between Lough Foyle in the north-west and Carlingford Lough on the east coast.

Physical relief

Geologically, lowland areas of the island generally comprise limestone and glacial deposits of clay and sand. The varied landscape (soils, rocks, mounds, hills, mountains and valleys) was formed by glacial movements and weathering agents, such as wind, rain and water. Some older rocks, such as quartzites, granites and shales, have weathered into poor soils. Other rocks have been overlaid by glacial

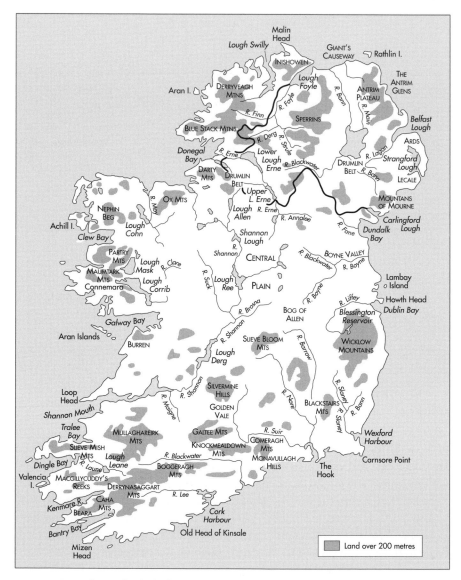

FIGURE 2.2 Physical relief of Ireland and Northern Ireland

waste (drift) carried on the bottom of glaciers, which has resulted in good soils over parts of the island, such as the western limestone areas.

Ancient bogs and peat areas are mostly post-glacial, wet, red-brown areas, which take different forms and are scattered widely around the Irish countryside. They initially hindered exploitation of the land, but have historically been used as fuel and building material, and have in some areas become productive land after drainage.

The physical topography of the island has been described as basin- or saucer-shaped. Its main features are central lowlands in Ireland and Northern Ireland with relatively low mountain ranges on many coasts. The extensive lowland regions comprise low hills, peat bogs, rivers and lakes, and the principal rivers flow from the central and east plains.

The mountain regions of the south are formed of old red sandstone separated by limestone river valleys. Granite is common in other areas, except in the north-east which is covered by a basalt plateau. The east coast is mainly regular and has few deep inlets. However, the west coast looks to the 2,000 mile (3,129 km) wide Atlantic Ocean and consists of drowned or submerged valleys, sharp, steep cliffs and small islands, which have become separated from the mainland by the weathering agents of the Atlantic Ocean and the climate.

Ireland

Ireland has a broad, central, limestone plain with low coastal highlands. Granite mountains lie in the west, north-west and east with Old Red Sandstone ridges in the south, where the folded mountain areas are separated by limestone river valleys.

The main mountain ranges are the Blue Stack Mountains of Donegal in the north-west; the Wicklow Mountains south of Dublin in the east rising to more than 3,000 feet (915 m) above sea level; Macgillycuddy's Reeks in Kerry (with Carrantuohil at 3,415 feet (1,041 m) being the highest point in the island in the south-western highlands); the Knockmealdown and Comeragh Mountains in Waterford; and the Twelve Pins (Bens) in Connemara in the west.

Smaller ranges are the Derryveagh Mountains of Donegal in the north-west; the Mamturk Mountains and the Nephin Beg Range containing Mount Nephin (2,359 feet (719 m)) in the west; the Caha Mountains (2,300 feet (700 m)) in the south-west, containing Mount Knockboy (2,321 feet (707 m)); the mountains of Donegal in the north-west, containing Errigal Mountain (2,466 feet (752 m)); and the Boggeragh Mountains in the south (2,100 feet (640 m)).

Breaks in the coastal mountain rim enable low plains to stretch to the coast in several areas, such as the eastern coast north of Dublin. Most of the central plain lies 200 to 300 feet (60 to 90 m) above sea level. It includes lakes and swampy, bog areas, as well as fertile agricultural land. Scattered hills between 600 and 1,000 feet (183–305 m) rise above the flat plain, but only some 15 per cent of Ireland is above 700 feet (200 m).

PLATE 2.1 Carrantuohil, the highest and most rugged mountain in Ireland, at 1,041m (3,415 ft), Black Valley, Co. Kerry. © Rex Features

The west and south-west coasts are broken by steep cliffs where the mountains of Donegal, Mayo and Kerry reach the Atlantic and are separated by deep, wide-mouthed bays (or inlets), some of which, like Bantry Bay and Dingle Bay in the south, Galway Bay in the centre and Donegal Bay in the north, are submerged river valleys. Bantry Bay, which is 20 miles (32 km) long and between 3 and 5 miles (5–8 km) wide, is an important deep-sea anchorage. Hundreds of small islands are scattered along the western coast, such as Achill Island and the Aran Islands.

The east coast is more regular with few high breaks, and most of Ireland's trade uses its ports because of their proximity to British and continental markets. Substanial inlets are Dundalk Bay and Dublin Bay, with Cork Harbour being the largest harbour in the south.

Ireland has many loughs (lakes) and rivers. Loughs include Ree and Derg on the Shannon and Mask, Corrib and Conn in the west. The three small Lakes of Killarney lie in the south-west mountains and the highest waterfall is Powerscourt (398 feet (121 m)) at Enniskerry in the foothills of the Co. Wicklow Mountains, south of Dublin.

The main rivers are the Erne and the Shannon, which are effectively loughs joined by stretches of river. The Shannon is the longest navigable river in Ireland at 240 miles (386 km). It rises in the north-west plateau country near Sligo Bay and travels south and west for 161 miles (259 km), reaching tidal levels at Limerick through a wide estuary before flowing into the Atlantic Ocean. Half the length of the Shannon is made up of Loughs Allen, Ree and Derg. The northern and southern parts of the central plain are drained by the Erne and the Shannon respectively.

The rivers that rise on the seaward side of coastal mountain fringes, such as the Liffey and the Boyne in the east and the Lee in the south-west, are short and quick-running, draining the mountains and hills near the sea. The inland streams, however, are longer and flow slowly, often through marshes and lakes, and enter the sea by waterfalls and rapids. Other major inland streams (with salmon fisheries) are the Slaney in the east; the Nore, Barrow and Suir which drain the south-eastern part of Ireland; the Blackwater, Lee and Bandon in the south; and the Clare and the Moy in the west.

The porous limestone rocks have formed underground drainage systems, which service rivers and lakes. Drainage schemes have curbed flooding, provided cultivatable land by improving water flow in rivers, lowered lake levels and renewed wasteland.

Northern Ireland

Northern Ireland's physical area includes 242 square miles (628 sq km) of inland water. The distance from north to south is 85 miles (137 km) and from east to west it is 110 miles (177 km). The province is defined in the north and north-east by the North Channel, on the south-east by the Irish Sea, and on the south and west by the border with Ireland.

It has a low-lying central plain with highland rims on the coasts and Lough Neagh (153 square miles (396 sq km)) in the middle. Five of the six former counties (Antrim, Down, Armagh, Tyrone and Londonderry/Derry) meet at the lough, which is the largest freshwater lake in the island and the UK. Upper and Lower Lough Erne, in Fermanagh, are also substantial freshwater lakes, and Belfast Lough, Carlingford Lough, Strangford Lough and Lough Foyle are the biggest sea inlets.

PLATE 2.2 Lough Neagh, the largest and oldest freshwater lake in Northern Ireland (and the UK) at 148 square miles (383 sq km). © Paul Lindsay/Alamy

To the north and east, the Antrim Mountains/plateau and the Glens of Antrim tilt upward towards the coast. They are 1,817 feet (554 metres) high at Trostan, with the plateau culminating in a cliff coastline of basalts and chalk that is broken by a series of glaciated valleys or glens, which face towards Scotland. The northern coast has the Giant's Causeway (basalt columns created by the cooling of lava flows). Other highland ranges are the Mourne Mountains (2,000 feet: 600 m) to the south-east; the Sperrin Mountains in the north-west, containing Sawel Mountain (2,240 feet (693 m)); and the uplands of south Armagh to the south. The region's coastline consists of wide, sandy beaches, broken by steep cliffs in the north, north-east and south-east. Rathlin Island and smaller islands lie off the northern coast.

The rounded south-east landscape of drumlins (mounds left by melting ice in the last ice age) is interrupted by Slieve Croob (1,745 feet (532 m)) and ends in the Mourne Mountains, which rise to Northern Ireland's highest mountain Slieve Donard (2,789 feet (850 m)) within two miles of the sea in Co. Down. This area of granite peaks is bounded by Carlingford Lough to the south.

The land to the south of Lough Neagh is gentler and rises to 1,886 feet (575 m) at Slieve Gullion near the border with Ireland. West of Lough Neagh the land rises gradually to the more rounded Sperrin Mountains where some hills are over 2,000 feet (610 m) high. Co. Fermanagh in the south-west of the province contains Lough Erne and hills above 1,000 feet (300 m) high.

PLATE 2.3 The Giant's Causeway, near Portrush, on the north coast of Co. Antrim, Northern Ireland, was formed from cooling volcanic basaltic lava, which created the characteristic columns of the area. © Kuttig – Travel – 2/Alamy

PLATE 2.4 Slieve Donard, Mountains of Mourne, Co. Down, the highest mountain in Northern Ireland, at 3,600 feet (1,100 m). The region is designated as an area of outstanding natural beauty. © Michael Walters 2/Alamy

Much of the Northern Ireland landscape is undulating, and many low-lying areas are covered with glacial drumlins, which have caused local drainage difficulties and formed characteristic marshy hollows. Glaciation also created the province's main river valleys, which have been important travel routes and run from the central plain to the sea.

The main river is the Bann, which rises in the Mourne Mountains, travels northward through Lough Neagh and is a wide, navigable waterway with a canal system, draining to the Atlantic Ocean in the north. Lough Neagh is also drained by the River Blackwater to the south-west and the River Lagan to the east. The River Foyle flows north to the sea at the port of Londonderry/Derry, forming the border with Ireland for part of its length. The Lagan flows north-east to the sea at Belfast.

Climate

The island's climate is classified as western maritime and does not have extremes of weather. The main influences are the Atlantic Ocean and other surrounding water since nowhere in the country is more than 70 miles (110 km) from the sea. The prevailing mild and moist south-westerly winds and the warm North Atlantic Current contribute to the moderate, temperate climate of the island. There is concern that the Current may collapse or alter its course under the effects of climate change and the melting of Arctic ice.

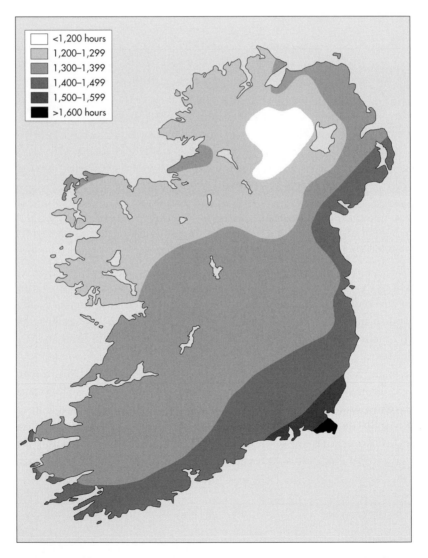

	<1,200 hours
	1,200–1,299
	1,300–1,399
	1,400–1,499
	1,500–1,599
	>1,600 hours

FIGURE 2.3 Average hours of sunshine in Ireland and Northern Ireland

Much of the weather is influenced by south-westerly low-pressure systems, which carry rain and clouds. The north is near the central track of such lows and often experiences high winds. Westerly gales occur in the north and on the east coast; the central lowlands are open to the wind and storms; and above 800 feet (245 m) trees suffer from the weather conditions. Opinions differ on whether the island is being affected by global warming and if there will be higher summer temperatures and more severe and wetter winter storms. The weather can occasionally be humid and overcast because of relatively high rainfall and cool to mild annual temperatures, and Ireland remains green for most of the year. The sunniest months are May and June, when there is sunshine and good light for an average of 5.5 and 6.5 hours a day, and the south-east generally has more sunshine.

Temperatures are mostly uniform throughout the island with winters being relatively mild and summers cool. January and February are the coldest months, with mean winter temperatures ranging from 40 to 45 °F (4 to 7 °C), but are still some 25 °F (14 °C) higher than other places at the same latitude in Central Europe or on the east coast of North America. July and August are the warmest months and mean summer temperatures range from 59 to 62 °F (15 to 17 °C). However, although higher readings are sometimes recorded in the summer, the mean is about 7 °F (4 °C) lower than other locations at the same latitudes.

Inland areas are warmer in summer and colder in winter, and some 40 days of the year inland are below freezing at 32 °F (0 °C) compared with 10 days on the coast. The island can experience short heatwaves, as in 1995, 2003 and 2006, but in 2009–2010 it had the coldest and longest winter for 30 years with continuous low temperatures and heavy snow. However, snow is infrequent except in the mountains, and severe snowstorms are rare.

Daily conditions in Northern Ireland can be changeable, but there are no extremes and little fluctuation in the mean annual temperature. January temperatures range from 38 °F (3.3 °C) on the north coast to 35 °F (1.7 °C) in the east; in July, temperatures of 65 °F (18.3 °C) are usual. In late spring and early summer the east has lower temperatures, with coastal fogs.

Temperatures in Ireland are about 41 °F (5 °C) in winter and may occasionally reach about 84 °F (29 °C) in summer. The southern and western parts of Ireland have a longer growing season than the rest of the island owing to their mild climate and rainfall. In many areas, pasture or grazing land for animals can be used for the whole year.

Rain in the island also occurs throughout the year but is relatively light on average, although more frequent and heavy in the west than in the east. The west is also more subject to snow and hail, with storms and high winds from the Atlantic in the late autumn and winter months. Annual rainfall averages 40 inches (1,000 mm), but is lighter in the east. Munster in the south has the least snow and Ulster in the north experiences more snow.

Northern Ireland has a relatively dry spring, a wet summer and a wetter winter. Annual rainfall decreases from west to east from some 80 inches (2,000

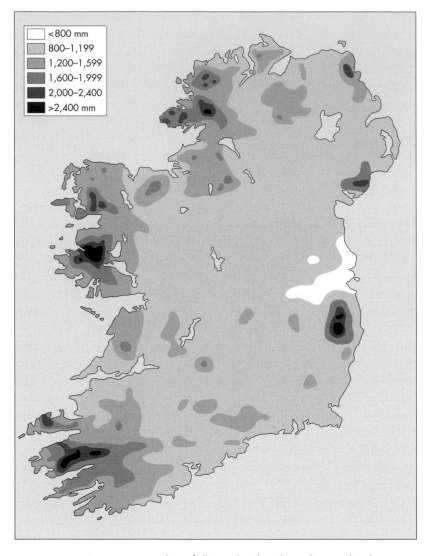

FIGURE 2.4 Average annual rainfall in Ireland and Northern Ireland

mm) in the west to 32.5 inches (825 mm) at Lough Neagh and the south-east. The rainfall and the equable climate sustain the grasslands, which are vital for the province's large livestock population.

Ireland has a mild, wet climate. Average annual rainfall is about 30 inches (750 mm) in the east and at least 100 inches (2,000 mm) in the western and south-western highlands, which are exposed to the Atlantic rain clouds. There may be up to 275 days of rain annually in some areas and flooding can occur in parts of the country during rainy periods.

Plant and animal life

Some two-thirds of Ireland was covered by ice during the last ice age and only relatively small numbers of indigenous plants and animals survived on the island. Much of the contemporary flora and fauna has therefore migrated from other parts of the world at a later date.

Flora (flowers, plants) derived from seeds driven by wind mainly from north-western areas of the European Continent and Britain after the ice melted, although some may have come from the Mediterranean or from North America through Greenland and Iceland. Sturdy species, such as sedges, rushes, ferns and grasses, are the main plants but more delicate types, such as Irish spurge (from North America), the Irish orchid (of Mediterranean origin), foxglove, sundew, rhododendrons and fuchsia are also present on the island.

Ireland's extensive grasslands give the landscape its characteristic green colouring. Prior to the seventeenth century there were thick forests in central Ireland, but woodlands and trees have been cut down or disappeared as most of the land has been ploughed, drained and cultivated over the centuries. Large areas of peat bog are found throughout the island and were originally a main source of domestic heating. However, most homes were connected to electricity networks by the 1980s, and peat production has declined. Rough pastures are grazed above cultivation limits and beyond them is tough mountain vegetation.

Irish fauna (animals) are similar to those of England or France. Some mammal species are native to Ireland, such as the red fox, the Irish stoat, hedgehog, otter, badger, the Irish hare, red deer and pine marten. The tough and adaptable native Connemara pony has been used by Irish farmers since prehistoric times. But there are only two kinds of mice; the great Irish deer and the great auk (garefowl) were eliminated centuries ago; and the bear, wolf, wildcat, beaver, native cattle and other species of animals have also been lost.

Other survivors are field, garden and shore birds such as waterfowl and different types of gull. Bird species that breed in Iceland and Greenland in the summer months winter in Ireland or stop over on their migratory journeys. Other birds come from Scandinavia, the Baltic, the Arctic and Canada. The western coasts attract breeding seabirds, and the lakes, estuaries and wetlands have visiting waterfowl, geese and ducks. Northern Ireland's wild bird population is estimated to have increased by 17 per cent in the 10 years up to 2010.

Existing plant and animal life has remained relatively unchanged owing to restricted building projects; low human population density; and strong conservation movements. There are, for example, some 40 nature reserves and several bird sanctuaries controlled by the Ulster Trust for Nature Conservation and by the Department of the Environment. Coastal regions in Northern Ireland such as Lough Foyle and Strangford Lough are important for waterfowl and waders, while upland areas and bogs are significant for plant life and insects. There are five National Parks of scientific importance in Ireland (Glenveagh, Killarney,

PLATE 2.5 The Connemara pony is an ancient native breed of wild horse, originally used by prehistoric farmers. © Foto Grebler/Alamy

Connemara, The Burren and the Wicklow Mountains), 12 forest reserve parks managed by the Irish Forestry Board for public use and recreation, and 71 National Nature Reserves covering woodlands, boglands, grasslands, sand-dunes, bird sanctuaries, coastal heathlands and marine areas.

Agriculture

Although extensive peat deposits cover the island, a mild climate and regular rainfall give generally fertile soils, grasslands and plant growth. Much of the land is suitable for grazing animals throughout the year and a lesser amount is used for arable and cultivated land.

Ireland

Traditionally, most Irish people made a living from farming the land and agriculture was the main element in the national economy. It is still important and most farms today are working family farms, where hired workers comprise only a small percentage of agricultural employment. Mixed farming is practised by most farmers, although specialization and large agribusinesses have also developed.

Difficult export markets after the Second World War hindered the growth of Irish agriculture. In the 1960s, Ireland developed industrial policies, promoted

PLATE 2.6 Neolithic field walls and farmland excavated from peat beds in Co. Mayo, above sheer cliffs on the west coast of Ireland. Dating from ca. 3,700–3,200 BC, the Céide Fields are the oldest enclosed farm landscape in Europe and mark the transition from hunter-gatherer to farmer/agriculturalist. © David Lyons/Alamy

manufacturing and expanded the service sector, with which agriculture could not compete. But in 1973, Ireland joined the European Economic Community (EEC), now the European Union (EU), which provided a large market for agricultural products, protected farmers and paid them subsidies. Although the situation improved, farm incomes and employment in the late 1970s began to decline again owing to rising production costs, despite Irish government aid and regulation. After a two-decade decline, farm incomes began to rise in the 1990s. In 2010 to 2011, agriculture employed 5.6 per cent of the workforce and accounted for 3 per cent of GDP (8 per cent for the agri-food sector). However, although Ireland's economy experienced a period of vigorous economic growth and rapid social change in the 1990s, it suffered a severe economic recession from 2007 to 2009, in which agriculture was also affected.

Ireland's main natural resource is its lowland soils, which produce rich grasslands over much of the country. They are used as pasture for grazing animals during most of the year or for growing hay. Raising livestock is the chief agricultural activity and there are large livestock herds. The production of beef cattle is prioritized in the midland regions, with dairy farming in the south. Sheep-raising is widespread on the hills and mountain slopes throughout the country and especially in western areas.

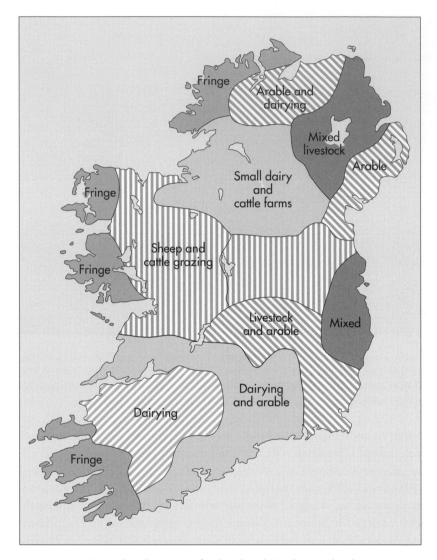

FIGURE 2.5 Agricultural regions of Ireland and Northern Ireland

The most fertile soils and cultivatable arable farmlands are located in the east and south-east and produce cereal and root crops. The main cereal crops are wheat, barley and oats, with other products like potatoes, hay, turnips, sugar beet, poultry, eggs and wool. Farmhouse cheese production has expanded in recent years and specialized food, such as organic items, has increased, although GM (genetically modified) farming has not been widely supported.

Most agricultural production consists of livestock and livestock items. Cattle are the biggest item, followed by milk and pigs; meat and meat products are important exports; and the trade in live animals, such as horses, and dairy products is also significant. The bloodstock (thoroughbred) industry is a vital part of the agricultural economy, and Irish horses and breeders have international reputations.

Northern Ireland

Soils vary in scope and quality, and areas below 700 feet (215 m) have been affected by glacial waste and underlying rock. Brown arable soils are extensive in the north-east, with peaty soils and bogs in the Sperrins and acid brown soil in the south-west. Although protected, some peat is still cut and used for electricity generation and horticultural compost.

Despite the varied quality of the soils, Northern Ireland has significant agricultural resources, which historically have been a major part of its economy. But agriculture declined in the twentieth century and the number of farms decreased. However, new technologies, better equipment, modernization and mergers resulted in larger and more productive farms or agribusinesses, with a better livelihood for fewer farmers. In 2010 to 2011, agriculture accounted for 5 per cent of the workforce and was less labour-intensive. Nevertheless, about two-thirds of farmers are working owners who own the freehold of their land and property, although some agricultural land is let on leases for varying periods of time.

About three-quarters of the land area was used for agriculture, forestry and livestock. British entry into the EU in 1973 has had mixed results for Northern Irish farmers with criticism about the workings of the Common Agricultural Policy (CAP). Farming subsidies have helped considerably, but agriculture is subject to government and EU regulation, which can reduce productivity as land use is diverted to other areas such as leisure activities.

Northern Ireland's regular rainfall, periodic high humidity and wet harvests to some extent can restrict arable farming, although local conditions do produce good grass and rich pasture. Mixed farming was traditionally employed, but there is now more specialization. About half the farms concentrate on sheep and beef, and about one-fifth specialize in dairying. Principal field crops include potatoes, barley, wheat and oats, and turnips are grown to feed livestock. The production of grass seed and seed potato for export is also important. There is a rich orchard and horticultural region to the south of Lough Neagh, with apple growing and market gardening.

Fisheries

Ireland and Northern Ireland (UK) have faced fishing problems and restrictions since the 1970s. Since both are members of the EU, their fishermen and annual fish catches are subject to regulations and quotas established by the EU's Common

Fisheries Policy (CFP), which limit the amount of fish caught and the time spent at sea. Overfishing by fishing nations in European waters has depleted the number of fish at sea and the reduction of some breeding grounds and species. This situation has resulted in reduced fish catches, fewer fishermen and decreasing numbers of associated fish production businesses.

Ireland

The fishing industry has been underdeveloped in Ireland, especially on the west coast, despite large resources offshore. Domestic consumption of fish is low, as is Ireland's overall landing of fish caught in Irish waters. Sea fishing and aquaculture resources have been expanded since the late twentieth century, but the industry has encountered international competition and must develop more efficient and diversified operations. However, it does contribute about €380 million annually to the Irish economy and plays a significant role in the socio-economic life of coastal communities.

Some 15,000 people are employed in the sea-fishing industry, with 6,100 in the fishing fleet and the rest in processing factories, services and the aquaculture industry. The fleet comprises 1,400 vessels of which 90 per cent are family businesses, 400 make up the offshore fleet and the rest are the part-time or seasonal inshore fleet.

Deep-sea catches have traditionally included herring, cod, mackerel, hake, whiting and plaice, but cod, for example, is a threatened species. Crustaceans like crabs, lobsters, crayfish, scallops and prawns, and molluscs such as oysters and periwinkles in coastal waters make up most of the country's seafood exports.

Inland rivers and lakes provide very good commercial and sport fishing for salmon, trout, eel and different types of coarse fish such as perch and pike. Fresh- and saltwater fish farming is increasingly more important as natural sea catches drop.

Northern Ireland

The sea-fishing industry in Northern Ireland amounted to 654 fishermen in 2009 with 147 deep-sea vessels and 204 inshore vessels. Deep-sea fishing is usually confined to the northern Irish Sea and involves trawlers that operate mainly from the Co. Down ports of Kilkeel, Ardglass and Portavogie. Shellfish, such as prawns, are the biggest catch from these ports, followed by mackerel and herring, and the more expensive and declining cod and whiting. There has been increasing development of marine farming, particularly for oysters. It is argued that the sea-fishing industry needs newer vessels, modernization, diversification and sustainable fishing.

The province's inland rivers and lakes have abundant fish, such as pike, perch, trout, eel, salmon, and a whitefish (the pollan) found in Lough Neagh.

Forestry

Thick woodlands covered the island until the 1600s. Today, after centuries of uncontrolled felling, it is the most deforested region in the EU. The latter has an average 24 per cent tree cover of its total land area comprising 27 member states.

Ireland

In 1921, woodlands in Ireland amounted to less than 1 per cent of the land area. By 2005, forests had increased and occupied 10 per cent of the country's land area, which produced commercial timber of 88 million cubic feet (2.5 million cubic metres). However, much of the forest consists of non-indigenous species, although some native woodland remains in areas such as the Killarney National Park. The forests need growth and protection from deer and sheep in order to regenerate the woodland stock.

The Irish government has used state replanting and reforestation programmes to increase tree acreage; to reduce the country's dependence on timber imports; and to provide raw material for paper-mills and timber industries. Private afforestation also grew in the late twentieth century, and a company (Coillte) was established in 1988 to manage commercial forestry and natural resources. It owns some 445,000 hectares (1.1 million acres) of land, which is 7 per cent of the land cover of Ireland. However, most state-owned forests are in the east and the development of privately owned forests on the upland areas of the west is required.

Northern Ireland

Most original forests in Northern Ireland were cleared by the end of the nineteenth century and some 1 per cent of the land was forested at the beginning of the twentieth century. The importance of forestry was gradually realized and reforestation and plantations were encouraged. A State Forestry Commission was established in 1919 to develop planting policies. By the end of the twentieth century, some 200,000 acres (81,000 hectares) were planted, with three-quarters of the woodland administered by the State Forest Service. However, timber production is still limited; it accounts for a small percentage of employment and gross domestic product (GDP) on state-owned lands, and only about 5 per cent of the land is now under forest.

There is a need for private planting to supplement the state forests and encourage timber industries. The State Forest Service became an Executive Agency of the Department of Agriculture and Rural Development in 1998 and implements UK forestry policy in Northern Ireland. Legislation in 2010 was intended to promote afforestation, sustainable forestry and recreational use of the forests. In 2011, the Forest Service and Coillte in Ireland announced further cooperation in forestry issues, which may improve forests on the island as a whole.

Energy and mineral resources

Energy networks in Ireland and Northern Ireland were organized separately following partition in 1921. However, there are now connections between North and South and through Great Britain to mainland Europe. Secondary (electricity) energy resources are derived from oil, gas, solid fuels, renewable and other sources (such as solar energy, hydro and thermal power stations), and are mainly dependent upon oil, gas and coal imports from the UK and abroad. Demand for electricity from large and small consumers increased from the 1990s and coal was replaced as the main generating fuel by oil and gas. The share of renewable sources, such as solar and wind power, has increased by relatively small amounts.

EU directives in 2000 opened up the electricity market in the island to competition and larger customers were able to choose their own electricity supplier. The retail market opened to full (including domestic) competition in 2005, and in 2007 a Single Electricity Market (SEM) became operative for wholesale electricity on an all-island basis.

From 2011, energy suppliers in Ireland were free to set their own tariffs. The electricity transmission system is known as the national grid (EirGrid), which distributes electricity to wholesale transformer stations. Electricity suppliers are licensed by the Commission for Energy Regulation (CER) to supply electricity to retail customers. CER regulates the electricity market and deals with complaints. It is argued that there is a lack of competition in domestic markets, concerns about high energy prices and insufficient supplies.

Following the creation of the SEM in 2007, all customers in Northern Ireland can contract with one of the electricity supply companies licensed to provide electricity in Northern Ireland and which purchase wholesale electricity from generating companies. Customers can switch companies to find the best tariff rate. Suppliers are regulated by the Northern Ireland Authority for Utility Regulation (NIAUR), but complaints about prices and lack of competition in the market continue. Northern Ireland Electricity (NIE) operates the Northern Ireland electricity network but does not itself generate or supply electricity.

Gas supplies in Ireland and Northern Ireland follow similar operating, supply and regulatory structures to electricity. Suppliers, such as Phoenix Gas and Firmus Gas in Northern Ireland, buy from the wholesale markets and supply customers direct. The gas distribution network is also now all-island, with a pipeline linking North and South, and interconnectors between Scotland and the island. Most gas imports are from Norway and the UK. Decreasing supplies come from Kinsale Gas Field off the Co. Cork coast, and the Corrib Gas Field off the coast of Co. Mayo has faced problems and opposition.

There have been recent efforts in the island to use renewable energy such as wind power. Onshore turbines have been constructed in coastal counties such as Donegal, Mayo and Antrim and there have been attempts to create offshore farms off the west coast. It is predicted that wind power could generate 13 per cent of the island's power needs. However, this is a relatively small income for the capital required to start up wind projects: the construction of wind farms has been delayed or cancelled through local opposition; the viability of wind has been queried; and there is a lack of commercial infrastructure. Renewable resources may prove helpful in the future as supplements, but at present they do not contribute significantly to the total demand for energy.

Although discoveries of silver, lead, zinc, gypsum, barite and dolomite from the 1960s were successfully developed and Europe's largest lead and zinc mines opened at Navan in 1977, Ireland is not rich in mineral resources. In the 1980s, offshore oil and gas wells began production in the Atlantic Ocean and the Celtic Sea south of Co. Cork. But extraction was limited and a pipeline from Britain had to be constructed in the 1990s to provide alternative supplies. The island depends heavily on energy and mineral imports. Mining plays a relatively minor role in Ireland's economy, although it is an important exporter of lead and zinc.

Ancient peat bogs covered much of the land and peat was used as the main domestic fuel. Since the 1980s, most rural households are connected to the national electricity network. Although peat production was mechanized and industrialized in the twentieth century, its exploitation is now restricted under EU law. However, it is still used for some limited domestic and industrial processes.

Northern Ireland is not rich in mineral resources, mining contributes little to the economy and less than 1 per cent of workers are employed in mining. Among the minerals extracted are basalt, limestone, chalk, clay, salt and shale, and there is some iron ore, bauxite and coal. Most coal was historically imported from Great Britain, although local chalk, clays, limestones and gravels are used to produce lime, bricks and cement.

Roads, railways and waterways

Ireland

Ireland ideally needs a large road system to service its scattered population. Generally, local roads are reasonably well surfaced and main roads have been modernized. Ireland has received funds from the EU since 1973 to improve its transportation infrastructure and a motorway network now radiates from Dublin to the rest of the country. The paved road system amounts to some 59,488 miles (95,736 km). However, more road construction is needed to meet transport demand and the Irish government initiated a major investment plan in road building from 2006 until 2015.

The Irish transport system (Córas Iompair Éireann) has financial control over three autonomous operating companies in charge of transport services. The Irish Transport Company (Iarnród Éireann) manages long-distance passenger trains, which connect most major towns and cities. The main bus company is Irish Bus

(Bus Éireann), which offers extensive passenger services outside Dublin, and Dublin Bus (Átha Cliath) specifically serves the Greater Dublin area. The Dublin Area Rapid Transit (DART) system links the city centre with coastal towns and is operated by Iarnród Éireann. An electrified commuter rail system opened in Dublin in 1984 and a street-level light-rail (tram) system, the Luas, run by Veolia, opened in 2004 and serves passengers in the central and western suburbs. There are 1,160 miles (1,870 km) of rail services between the principal cities and towns linking Cork, Limerick, Galway and a number of other points to Dublin (including a link with Northern Ireland Railways via Belfast). In addition, the Irish Peat Board operates over 800 miles (1,300 km) of narrow-gauge railway in the countryside. Several more Luas lines are planned as well as a Dublin Metro. However, many branch lines are uneconomical and have been replaced by road services for passengers and goods, although the Cork to Midleton line was reopened in 2009.

The River Shannon is navigable for most of its length, but the rest of inland navigation largely depends on a canal system built in the eighteenth and nineteenth centuries to provide transport and communications. Parts of this system have been restored, including the Royal and Grand canals that link Dublin and the North Sea to the Shannon. The rebuilt Ballinamore–Ballyconnell Canal, originally opened in 1860, connects the Shannon and Erne and led to the restoration of other waterways in Ireland and Northern Ireland. There are some 270 miles (435 m) of navigable waterways but these are used mostly by recreational boats. It is argued that the canal infrastructure should be upgraded and used for commercial freight traffic in order to reduce pressure on the road and rail systems.

Smaller ports are important to the local business communities, but most of the seaborne trade is conducted through the main east and south coast ports, such as Dublin, Waterford, Rosslare and Cork. The ports in Limerick and Galway serve western Ireland. Dún Laoghaire, Dublin, Rosslare and Cork are used by cross-channel passenger, motor vehicle and freight services to Britain, and there are also some ferry services to the Continent. Ferry services via the Irish Sea include routes from Dublin to Holyhead, Swansea to Cork, Fishguard and Pembroke to Rosslare and Holyhead to Dún Laoghaire, and have significantly increased the amount of overseas car traffic. Irish ports annually transport 3.6 million travellers across the sea to Britain, and Rosslare and Cork also operate ferries to France.

The trend towards larger vessels and container ships has adversely affected the smaller Irish ports and privately owned shipping companies. Only a small part of foreign trade between Ireland and continental ports is carried by the Irish merchant fleet. The emphasis now is on big container ships, operating from a small number of container ports, and a reduction of shipping companies and manpower. But most heavy goods trade is still done by sea and Irish ports handle 7.6 megatons of trade with Britain annually.

Northern Ireland

Northern Ireland has a network of minor roads that connects all parts of the province. But the motorway system radiating out of Belfast covers only a small part of the province, although public road transport outside the Belfast municipal service was nationalized in 1935.

Since 1968, the Northern Ireland Transport Holding Company has controlled the railways, bus companies and Belfast International Airport. The railways declined from 824 miles (1,326 km) to about a quarter of that figure in the economic reorganization following nationalization in 1935. All rail services are provided by Northern Ireland Railways. The railway system connects Bangor, Larne, Coleraine, Londonderry/Derry and Dublin with each other, although critics argue that rail links outside the main urban centres are inadequate. Services in Northern Ireland are sparse in comparison with the rest of Ireland or Britain, and the railway network was heavily reduced in the 1950s and 1960s. The main bus company in Northern Ireland is Ulsterbus, which offers extensive passenger services, and Metro operates services within the greater Belfast area.

Inland waterways have almost disappeared, although some commercial traffic still uses the Lower Bann Navigation to Coleraine and there is recreational and tourist sailing.

Northern Ireland is well connected to the other regions of the United Kingdom by sea. Belfast is one of the major ports in Britain and Ireland, and has several miles of quays with modern container facilities. Larne (also a container port) and Londonderry/Derry are the other large ports. Coleraine and Warrenpoint handle some freight and Larne and Belfast handle passenger transport. Northern Irish ports together organize 10 megatons of heavy goods trade with Britain annually. The ports also handle car ferries, such as those from Belfast and Larne to ports in Scotland and between Liverpool and Belfast via the Isle of Man.

Air transport

Ireland

Ireland's major international airports are located at Dublin, Shannon, Cork and Knock. Dublin Airport is the busiest of these, carrying over 22 million passengers a year, and is forecast to increase numbers with a new terminal and runway. There are several smaller regional airports, mostly in the west, such as Sligo, Galway, Kerry, Donegal and Waterford. Aer Rianta, a public limited-liability company, has responsibility for the operation, management and development of Dublin, Shannon and Cork airports. Shannon was for many years an important (and famous) refuelling point for transatlantic routes and the world's first duty-free airport. Substantial tax breaks and other commercial advantages are offered to manufacturing and warehousing concerns which intend to establish plants within the Shannon (midwestern) region. It has recently opened a pre-screening service allowing passengers to pass through US immigration services before departing from Ireland. The principal airlines are Aer Lingus (the former national airline), the low-budget carrier Ryanair, Aer Arann and CityJet. Air services are dominated by routes to the United Kingdom, mainland Europe, within the island and by transatlantic flights to North America from Dublin and Shannon.

Northern Ireland

Belfast International Airport has regular air services to major cities in Britain and Europe and transatlantic routes to North America. The smaller George Best Belfast City Airport was built in central Belfast in 1938 (with a new terminal in 2001) and has become popular with passengers travelling to Britain, within the island and Europe, despite disputes and delays over a proposed extended runway, which created protests from residents on environmental grounds and caused Ryanair to cease operating in Belfast. Nevertheless, scheduled, charter and low-cost airlines fly out of the airport, such as Flybe, bmi, Easy Jet and Aer Arann. Londonderry (City of Derry) Airport has also established itself in the British and Irish markets.

Attitudes to the environment

The Environment Protection Agency-EPA (Ireland) and the Environment Agency (Northern Ireland) analyse concerns about the island's environment, ecosystems and biodiversity, such as climate change; tree loss; invasion by non-native species; inappropriate agricultural practices; loss of wildlife areas and hedgerows; tourism; housing development; litter; pollution; use of peat bogs; nuclear systems; and the depletion of fauna and flora.

EPA research (2004 and 2007) suggested that Scandinavian and 'Germanic' countries and the Netherlands are more environmentally aware than Southern and Eastern European countries. Britain, Northern Ireland and Ireland arguably have an intermediate position, with less pro-environmental concern than Northern Europeans and weaker performance in the recycling of household waste and car usage.

Ireland

Environmental protection in the early twentieth century was not significant for Ireland as it pursued economic growth and consumption. However, worries about air, water and agricultural pollution; waste disposal, landfills and recycling; global warming; genetic modification of crops (GM); and nuclear power gradually grew. But, as in other countries, support for the environment does not always include accepting increased costs or taking personal action to protect the environment. The following opinion polls on the environment often reveal conflicting or contradictory attitudes.

A BITCI/Ipsos/MORI survey in Ireland in 2009 suggested that companies should take corporate responsibility for the environment because they play a significant part in producing carbon emissions. Eighty-one per cent of respondents to the survey agreed that climate change is affecting them. Large majorities said that they always or sometimes act to make an impact on climate change, such as recycling (92 per cent); turning off lights when not in use (92 per cent); buying green products and services (86 per cent); purchasing locally produced goods (78 per cent); adjusting thermostats to use less energy (69 per cent); and using/buying energy-efficient appliances (66 per cent).

However, despite such findings and good intentions, people differ about how much they, companies, the government, local authorities, the EU or the United Nations should be responsible for the environment. They debate whether environmental action should be paid for by taxes or charges and whether they should give up their cars even if public transport is inadequate. The rates of household waste recycling have increased since the late 1990s, but still lag behind other European averages; practice varies because individual local authorities have different priorities on how to deal with recycling; the use of incineration centres is opposed; and landfill sites are still widely used. Respondents may say that they are in favour of environmentalism, but their levels of active involvement vary considerably.

Nevertheless, the EPA reported in 2005 that in Ireland 22.7 per cent of total household waste, 34.6 per cent of municipal waste, 59.9 per cent of packaging waste and 86.9 per cent of construction and demolition waste was recycled, with the remainder going to landfill. Increased targets were set and Ireland was the first country to introduce a plastic bag levy. Consumers paid 15 cents for a bag, which led to a 90 per cent decrease in circulation. Electric and electronic equipment retailers are obliged to take back old equipment and Ireland is the leading country in Europe for electronic recycling. The Central Statistics Office reported in 2007 that 90 per cent of households recycled *some* of their household waste, compared with 48 per cent in 1999.

A 2007 report by Safefood and the Food Safety Authority of Ireland linked the environment to food safety with 57 per cent of respondents believing that safety had improved over the previous 10 years. Sixty-four per cent felt that the level of food regulation was adequate, although there were concerns about food processing and additives/antibiotics. Seventy-five per cent agreed that hygiene standards were rising in Ireland and there was less concern about cleanliness in food outlets, such as take-aways, restaurants, local butchers, cafés, sandwich bars and supermarkets. However, a poll by Safetrack 6 in 2007 found that 67 per cent of respondents worried about food safety generally and 54 per cent were concerned about food produced on Irish farms.

According to EPA and National Development Plan research in 2003, a large majority of respondents in Ireland considered that nuclear power and fuel reprocessing stations, water pollution, air pollution generated by cars, aviation and industry, the 'greenhouse effect' and the use of pesticides and chemical use in farming negatively affected the environment. There was a preference to pay higher prices (53 per cent) rather than higher taxes (34 per cent) to sustain the environment. Half of the respondents were optimistic about the effectiveness of their individual efforts and half were more pessimistic. Environmental groups (with university research centres in the lead) were most trusted to give solid information about environmental issues. Government departments were less trusted (50 per cent) and industry and business were the least trusted source at less than 10 per cent of respondents.

A large majority of respondents agreed with paying 'more to recycle waste' but believed that manufacturers should be responsible for recycling their own products. Despite fierce campaigns against the building of incinerators in Ireland, 40 per cent of respondents said that 'using incinerators is the best way to dispose of waste'. However, 43 per cent in fact agreed that 'new landfill sites should be developed to dispose of waste'.

In terms of people's behaviour, three-quarters of respondents claimed that, where recycling facilities were available, they *sometimes* sorted the different types of household waste. However, while half of the respondents believed that car pollution was dangerous, few were willing to cut back on their car use for environmental reasons. The majority of car users reported that they have never cut back on using a car, and one-third said that they had sometimes done so. Similarly, few were prepared to cut down on air travel for environmental reasons.

The research suggested that few people in Ireland were actively involved in more direct social and political forms of environmental activity. Only 4 per cent of respondents were members of an environmental group and 5 per cent claim to have protested about an environmental issue. However, there did seem to be increasing support for more active campaigners and environmentalism. A quarter of respondents had signed a petition, one-fifth had given money to an environmental group and some 40 per cent had done both.

Northern Ireland

The 2011 Northern Ireland Environmental Statistics Report (NIESR) for the Northern Ireland Executive reported that in 2009 the province's population was 16 per cent greater than in 1971 and the number of households had increased by 61 per cent between 1971 and 2008. Air travel had grown by 64 per cent from 4.6 million passengers in 2000 to 7.5 million in 2009. But numbers had fallen by 9 per cent from 2008 to 2009 from 8.2 million to 7.5 million, arguably due to the economic recession. Car travel remained high and accounted for 70 per cent of all journeys made over a five-year period. But journeys made by walking had dropped to only 17 per cent of total journeys, and public transport increased to 6.0 per cent of all journeys between 2007 and 2009. The average temperature in Northern Ireland has increased since the start of the twentieth century and there have also been changes in the seasonal distribution of rainfall as annual winter rainfall has increased and summer rainfall has decreased.

These features can increase environmental pressures. The Northern Ireland Statistics and Research Agency (NISRA) *Continuous Household Survey* in 2009 to 2010 said that 18 per cent of respondents were very concerned, and 58 per cent were fairly concerned about the environment. This was a reduction of 6 per cent from 2008 to 2009 for the two categories. The main worries were climate change (38 per cent), household waste disposal (36 per cent), pollution in rivers (31 per cent) and traffic congestion (30 per cent). Concern about climate change had grown since 2003–2004, while that for waste disposal and pollution in rivers had increased since 2008. Other concerns in descending order were traffic exhaust fumes and urban smog (a reduction since 2003–2004), pollution in bathing waters and on beaches, ozone layer depletion, loss of plants, animals, trees and hedgerows, and use of pesticides and fertilizers.

Respondents to the survey reported that they had taken individual action to protect the environment by using energy-saving light bulbs (64 per cent), reducing the amount of energy used in the home (44 per cent), recycling paper and glass (31 per cent), safeguarding wildlife (30 per cent), reducing the amount of water used in the home (29 per cent), buying organic food (20 per cent) and not buying packaged goods (14 per cent). But only 20 per cent had reduced car usage and 18 per cent had used public transport for environmental reasons. There had been decreases in recycling paper and glass, using energy-saving light bulbs, water reduction at home and not buying packaged goods.

However, the survey suggests that Northern Ireland performed relatively well overall. The amount of municipal waste produced has remained constant since 2004–2005, but there has been a significant increase in the proportion that is recycled or composted: from 18 to 32 per cent. Households in 2009 were recycling more total waste (39 per cent) and exceeding targets. The remaining 61 per cent of household waste was sent to landfill sites, although attempts are being made to reduce landfill and the carbon emissions associated with it.

Air quality has shown some improvement in recent years and greenhouse gas emissions have decreased since 1990 with an 11 per cent fall achieved in 2008. The three main contributors to these emissions were transport, agriculture and energy supply, amounting to 68 per cent of Northern Ireland's total emissions. Most sectors have shown a decrease on 1990 levels, with the exception of transport. The Programme for Government has a target of a 25 per cent decrease in greenhouse gas emissions by 2025. The target for output from renewable sources of energy such as wind farms was 12 per cent of all electricity by 2012 and the figure reached in 2009–2010 was 9.3 per cent.

In 2009, there were 2,152 water-pollution incidents, of which 1,248 were substantiated and 16 per cent of these were of high or medium severity. The quality of river water is generally good, while the quality of lakes is variable. Groundwater is of high quality; drinking water is at the highest quality level since 2004; discharges from commercial activities and water companies have improved. Beaches, with 2 out of 24 failing, met EU standards.

Soil quality decreased in 2008–2009 with over-enrichment of 39 per cent of some soils. However, areas of special scientific interest were in good condition. Although the wild bird population had increased by 21 per cent in the 10 years to 2008, wetland birds had decreased by 17 per cent during the same period. The overall status of priority habitats and species has remained unchanged between 2005 and 2008.

Exercises

Explain and examine the significance of the following terms, names or expressions:

glaciation	Shannon	basalt
Carrantuohil	Lough Neagh	Mayo
Bantry Bay	Aran Islands	Powerscourt
EU	overfishing	peat
pike	afforestation	the Luas
ozone layer	horticulture	fossil fuels
Gulf Stream	Slieve Donard	Lough Erne
Bann	archipelago	Continental Shelf
St George's Channel	western maritime	Coillte
Common Fisheries Policy	reforestation	glacial waste/drift
subsidies	shellfish	waterways

Write short essays on the following topics:

1   Describe in outline the main physical relief of Ireland and Northern Ireland.

2   Briefly examine the available energy resources in Ireland and Northern Ireland.

3   Compare attitudes to environmentalism in Ireland and Northern Ireland.

Further reading

Connolly, S.J. (2007) *Oxford Companion to Irish History* Oxford: Oxford University Press

Coyne, J.S. and Bartlett, W.H. (1841) *The Scenery and Antiquities of Ireland* London: George Virtue: Digital Books

Graham, B.J. (ed.) (1997) *In Search of Ireland: A Cultural Geography* London: Routledge

Graham, B.J. and Proudfoot, L.G. (1993) *A Historical Geography of Ireland* London: Academic Press

Grierson, G. (1726) *A Natural History of Ireland in Three Parts* Dublin: Digital Books

Kelly, M., Kennedy, F., Faughnan, P. and Tovery, H. (2003) *Cultural Sources of Support on which Environmental Attitudes and Behaviours Draw. Second Report of National Survey Data* Co. Wexford: Environmental Protection Agency

Kelly, M., Kennedy, F., Faughnan, P. and Tovey, H. (2004) *Environmental Attitudes and Behaviours: Ireland in Comparative European Perspective. Third Report of National Survey Data* Co. Wexford: Environmental Protection Agency

Kelly, M., Tovey, H. and Faughnan (2007) *Environmental RTDI Programme 2000–06, Environmental Attitudes, Values and Behaviour in Ireland (Synthesis Report)* Co. Wexford: Environmental Protection Agency

Lalor, B. (ed.) (2003) *The Encyclopaedia of Ireland* Dublin: Gill and Macmillan

Mitchell, F. and Ryan, M. (1998) *Reading the Irish Landscape* Dublin: Town House

Polley, D. (1999) *Home Ground: A Geography of Northern Ireland* Northern Ireland: Colourpoint Books

Strategic Policy Research Unit (2006) *Public Perceptions, Attitudes and Values on the Environment – A National Survey* Co. Wexford: Environmental Protection Agency

Whittow, J.B. (1974) *Geography and Scenery in Ireland* London: Penguin Books

Woodcock, N.H. (2000) *Geological History of Britain and Ireland* Oxford: Blackwell

Websites

Central Statistics Office, Ireland: http://www.cso.ie

Central Survey Unit, Northern Ireland: http://www.csu.nisra.gov.uk

Commission for Energy Regulation, Ireland: http://www.energycustomers.ie

Consumer Council, Northern Ireland: www.consumercouncil.org.uk

Department of Agriculture, Ireland: http://www.agriculture.gov.ie

Department of Agriculture and Rural Development, Northern Ireland: http://www.dardni.gov.uk

Energy regulator in Northern Ireland (Ofreg): http://www.reckon.co.uk/tags/ofreg

Environment Protection Agency, Ireland: http://www.epa.ie/

Northern Ireland Environment Agency: http://www.ni-environment.gov.uk/

Northern Ireland Executive: http://www.northernireland.gov.uk

3

The people

- Prehistoric settlement
- Celtic/Gaelic Ireland
- Christianity
- Viking invasions
- Anglo-Norman invasions and settlement
- Colonialism, Protestantism and Catholicism
- Emigration and immigration
- Attitudes to national identity
- *Exercises*
- *Further reading*
- *Websites*

This chapter describes human entry into Ireland from prehistoric times until the seventeenth century, when settlement and modern identities became more fixed. Thereafter, allegiances were influenced by politics, religion, famine, landowner-ship, Home Rule, Nationalism, Unionism and partition of the island. Modern immigration and emigration movements in and out of the country and the establishment of ethnic/cultural minority groups are also examined.

The current populations of Ireland and Northern Ireland are descendants of people (both peaceful and warlike) who travelled to the island over many centuries from Europe, Great Britain and elsewhere. They included categories such as Mesolithic, Neolithic and Bronze Age groups who arrived from around 8000 BC; Iron-Age Celtic tribes from Continental Europe who came between 500 and 100 BC; Danes, Norwegians, Normans, English, Welsh, Scots and Bretons who were associated with invasions and colonization in later centuries from AD 795; and more recent immigrants, such as political refugees and economic migrants. Celtic peoples introduced pre-Christian Celtic/Gaelic cultures as their diverse clans spread throughout Ireland. It is argued that they eventually achieved dominance because their societies assimilated prehistoric groups and later arrivals. The Irish population is considered to be mainly of Celtic/Gaelic descent, but with an admixture of other ancestries.

Geneticists have varying theories about the origins of humans in Ireland. Some argue that most of the current Irish male population have Y-chromosomes similar to other Western Europeans and that 80 per cent of contemporary European men have Y-chromosomes derived from Palaeolithic Stone Age hunters, who first settled in Europe about 40,000 years ago. Other theories in 2009 speculated that male European populations derive from the agricultural Neolithic rather than the Palaeolithic era and suggested that prehistoric and Celtic arrivals in Ireland had originated in Atlantic Spain and southern France. However, research in 2011 queried the agricultural ancestry and inclined towards the Palaeolithic origin model.

Although genetics is a young science, these analyses do suggest a common genetic origin for most Western European peoples; but this root has been overlaid by ethnic variety, which is determined by cultural and evolutionary adaptive factors. It seems that there was human diversity over long periods of time in Ireland and the scattered population may have had considerable cultural differ-ences. It may be that indigenous groups were not overwhelmed by immigrants but lived alongside new arrivals, who gradually assimilated with and modified existing cultures. Both arguably influenced each other in many ways such as art, tech-nology, architecture, industrial production and language.

Prehistoric settlement

The first arrivals

Although full information about Ireland's inhabitants before the fourth century AD or their relationships to each other is lacking, conclusions about the composition of the people have been made. The presumed absence of early human settlement in Ireland was arguably due to the northern ice ages and the island may have been the last part of Europe to be occupied between 10000 and 8000 BC. There are theories (but no concrete evidence) that Old Stone Age (Palaeolithic) nomads may have travelled before 10000 BC to ice-free areas in Munster via a land or ice bridge linking Scotland to Ireland, which was later submerged by rising sea levels. Palaeolithic groups were characterized by their use of very basic stone implements, and hunted wild animals and fished in the sea and rivers, depending on climatic conditions.

The north-eastern sea channel between Scotland and Ireland (12 miles (19.2 km) at its narrowest point) has encouraged the movement of people and ideas in both directions. Geography and history have linked the peoples of Scotland and Ireland and gave parts of the old kingdom of Ulster a Scottish identity. Scots have helped to develop the region and shared its periods of conflict, while the Irish in their turn colonized western Scotland.

The Mesolithic

The ice-cap covering Northern Europe until 10000 BC had probably receded before migrants arrived in Ireland. The climate warmed and Europe entered a post-glacial age. The initial newcomers were nomadic hunter-gatherers and fishers of the Middle Stone Age (Mesolithic) period, who began to settle near river banks. There are few facts about when and from where the migrants came. They possibly arrived around 8000 BC by boat from western Britain or Scotland and Atlantic France/Spain. Small groups spread widely over the island and some evidence of their presence is preserved in domestic sites, burial practices and monuments.

A Mesolithic settlement at Mount Sandel on the eastern bank of the River Bann near Coleraine, Co. Londonderry/Derry has been carbon dated to between 7000 and 6600 BC and is arguably the oldest immigrant site on the island. Groups may have moved briefly to isolated settlements from such a base and hunted in a warm and forested environment. Cultural evidence, like flint tools or microliths, has been found in Co. Offaly, Co. Cork, Scotland and southern Britain. It is thought that several thousand people were living in Ireland by 4000 BC and that this figure suggests a significant population relative to the rest of Europe.

PLATE 3.1 Mount Sandel Fort. Arguably the site of the earliest Mesolithic arrivals in Ireland on an escarpment overlooking the River Bann estuary near Coleraine on the north coast of Co. Londonderry/Derry, Northern Ireland. © Design Pics Inc. – RM Content/Alamy

The Neolithic

Agriculture originated in the Near East and was probably brought to Ireland around 3900 to 4500 BC in the New Stone Age (Neolithic), which slowly succeeded the Mesolithic and ended with the transition to the Bronze Age in about 2000 BC. This period illustrated a human evolution from hunter-gatherer to agriculturalist. Neolithic groups possibly came from Brittany, settled at the mouth of the River Boyne in Co. Meath and arguably were the first large immigrant groups in Irish history. They spread along the Irish and British coasts of the Irish Sea and as far west in Ireland as Co. Sligo, Co. Mayo and Co. Tyrone.

Later Neolithic groups came from the Baltic and settled in eastern Ireland about 2000 BC. They moved south down both sides of the Irish Sea to what are now Dublin, Waterford and Wicklow, and to Pembrokeshire (Wales) and Cornwall (England). They spread into the inland valleys of the island and completed the first substantial colonization of Ireland.

The Neolithic Age introduced changes in food production, settlement patterns, burial practices, monument building, pottery, stone utensils and knives. The settlers cleared forests, planted crops and raised imported cattle and sheep. Houses were built and remains of the first farmhouses have been found in

Ballyglass, Co. Mayo and Ballynagilly, Co. Tyrone. These domestic sites have revealed pits used for cooking and refuse, pottery and stone implements.

Evidence of Neolithic peoples is also found in megalithic tombs, which were the sites of communal burial rites and are covered with either earth (barrow) or stone (cairn). The four main tomb types were built about 3000 BC and are of differing sizes. There were court tombs in the north of the country, which often had a court area at one end and were derived from Western European graves; circular passage tombs, like Newgrange, Co. Meath with parallels in western Britain, Scotland, Brittany, Spain and southern Scandinavia; small portal tombs in the north; and wedge tombs in the south and west.

Pottery, flint tools, spiral carvings and (arguably) wall writings decorate the burial sites. Megalithic tombs suggest high levels of engineering, organizational skills and artistic proficiency. The variety of tombs may indicate increasing social stratification and complexity in Neolithic society, and customs and influences from many European sources.

Tomb locations and personal decoration suggest that the settlers had a semi-urban lifestyle within a localized collectivist structure. However, the many burial sites indicate that Mesolithic and Neolithic peoples were not centralized, but rather isolated groups which could be culturally and geographically distinctive, albeit with family or ethnic resemblances. This scattered lifestyle and population size might suggest that indigenous prehistoric peoples were not overwhelmed and quickly replaced by new groups.

PLATE 3.2 Entrance stone of Newgrange Neolithic passage tomb burial chamber, Boyne Valley, Co. Meath, Ireland, built ca. 3000 BC. © Holmes Garden Photos/Alamy

Ireland's Neolithic prehistory lasted 2,000 years and witnessed significant change. Metalworkers and farmers laid the foundations of a future nation. Neolithic settlers changed the Irish landscape considerably and there was a relatively large estimated population of 50,000 to 100,000 in the island by 2500 BC.

A transitional group between the late Neolithic and early Bronze Age was the Beaker Folk (about 2400 to 1800 BC), who probably arrived from southern England and possibly the Baltic. They worked with tin, copper, bronze and gold and were buried in single (rather than group) graves, which contained their distinctive pot beakers (drinking cups). Burial remains under round mounds in the east show Baltic-like pottery similar to that of the portal tomb people. This might indicate contact with relations and Indo-European groups in the Baltic and down the River Elbe. Another group of metallurgists and cattle farmers emigrated from north-west France into Ireland's south-west and spread along the west coast and into Co. Clare.

The Bronze Age (ca. 2000 to 500 BC)

Ireland's prehistoric culture continued into the Bronze Age proper as new production methods added to existing artwork and monuments. Metal tools and weapons replaced stone implements or co-existed with them, and new products were exported widely within Europe.

Bronze Age burial structures were not elaborate (like in the Neolithic) and the dead were often buried in pits, stone boxes and single graves. Social prestige or status was probably reflected in the actual possession or ownership of bronze and copper artefacts, rather than their use as functional objects, and wealth was represented by early Bronze Age gold objects.

Technological advances, increased production of ornaments and weapons and a more organized society suggest that Ireland developed a complex and rich social structure after 1000 BC. Nordic metalworkers travelled around the Irish Sea, spread knowledge of Irish copper and gold, increased trade links and helped to industrialize the farming economy. Bronze weapons and luxury goods were exported to the Baltic and other markets. New immigrants entered eastern Ireland to exploit the trade and introduced advanced technology. Gold artefacts reflected trade with Scotland. From about 1200 BC, more bronze implements and wood-working tools were produced; log roads were built into the bogs; new axes, swords and shields were introduced about 700 BC; and large gold hoards were deposited.

Mesolithic, Neolithic and Bronze Age civilizations had been created over many centuries. They were mainly concentrated in the northern third of the island along the east and north coasts and along the north-west coast in Sligo and the south-west. Inland settlement was initially established beside larger rivers such as the Bann, the Boyne and the Shannon. Migrants came from Atlantic France and Spain; the north via the Irish Sea; the Baltic, the Elbe and the Rhine; Scandinavia and Central European countries; Scotland; and southern and western England

and Wales. Prehistoric settlers from many places had therefore lived in Ireland for 7,000 years before the arrival of the Celts and their total numbers may have been relatively large in terms of existing European populations. But it is still debated whether these immigrant groups continued to be a basic element in the Irish population, whether they gradually assimilated with the Celts or whether they were quickly eliminated.

Celtic/Gaelic Ireland

Descendants of Mesolithic, Neolithic and Bronze Age groups were probably living in Ireland in the late Bronze Age when Celts began to arrive around 500 BC. Ireland had continued to use bronze, but the cheaper, superior and technologically simpler iron was used in Europe in what became the Iron Age. It is traditionally maintained that iron was introduced into Ireland by the Celts between 500 and 100 BC, but it is also argued that Celtic/Gaelic groups arrived in the British Isles and Ireland before the Iron Age proper.

The term 'Celt' refers to disparate peoples with similar cultures from mainland Europe. They spread along the Rhine and Danube, and inhabited Bavaria, Austria, Switzerland, Hungary and Bohemia. They expanded west to Spain and France, south to Italy, east to Asia Minor and north to Britain and Ireland, before being overcome by the Romans. Firm evidence is lacking for their numbers, landing sites, arrival dates in Ireland and their precise homelands. But it is argued that they moved into Ireland in two ways: one directly from northern Spain and south-western France; and the other through Great Britain (where they had already settled).

The last of these newcomers, the Gaels, arrived about 100 BC and are said to have founded Gaelic Ireland. 'Gael' derives from the generic Welsh word *gwyddell* ('raider') and was allegedly taken over by the Irish. The Gaels' language (Gaelic/Irish) was spoken by most people in Ireland until about 1850 and is preserved today by Irish speakers on the west coast (the Gaeltacht) and elsewhere. The Celts/Gaels intermingled with others, arguably dominated Ireland numerically and survived challenges against them until the Flight of the Earls in 1607.

Traditional history suggests that Celtic/Gaelic warriors overwhelmed the indigenous peoples and assimilated them into a Gaelic culture and language, so that little survived of the earlier hunters, farmers, metalworkers and herdsmen, apart from their monuments. This interpretation assumes large military forces, an abrupt transition from old to new societies, and the disappearance of earlier lifestyles and peoples. Alternative theories suggest that prehistoric groups survived the Celtic migrations. They were gradually Gaelicized by AD 450, although elements of the indigenous culture were probably incorporated into Gaelic lifestyles. There are no reliable population estimates for the existing population or the incoming groups, although the latter are believed to have been relatively small.

It seems that the Celtic peoples were linked linguistically by variants of a common language and culturally by similar characteristics in appearance, dress and way of life. They were known as Keltoi or Celts by the Greeks and as Galli or Gauls by the Romans. It is argued that the terms Celt, Gaul and Gael are primarily linguistic labels denoting one group of Indo-European languages with several branches, which in Ireland developed into Gaelic/Irish. The linguistic name was apparently linked to the people who spoke the various languages and became descriptive of the group. It seems that there were different groups, different forms of the language, different origins and differing customs, belief patterns and histories.

The Romans did not conquer Ireland, left Britain in AD 410, and the Roman alphabet and writing were unknown in Ireland. There is therefore little written documentation about the island before the arrival of Christianity. It was apparently a disunited country composed of independent tribal kingdoms or clans, who lived by agriculture and fighting each other for cattle and land. They formed shifting alliances in order to survive. The epic stories of the Celtic heroic age were probably written centuries later, but may contain some accurate echoes and images of life in pre-Christian Ireland.

A partly mythic Gaelic land was described in tales such as the Táin, which is the main story of the Ulster Cycle and was possibly written in the monastery of Bangor in AD 600. Ireland was divided into four major kingdoms or provinces (Connaught, Ulster, Leinster and Munster), which were constantly at war with each other. The tales include legendary figures such as Cú Chulainn (defender of the north) and the king of the Connaught ruling family, Niall of the Nine Hostages, who founded the powerful dynasty, the Uí Néill. All these rulers were concerned to win more land and power. For example, the Ulaidh (a dynastic group later representative of Ulster) was overthrown by the Connaught clan in AD 400 and restricted to land east of the Bann. In AD 500, they expanded their north-eastern kingdom by colonizing Argyll in Scotland, whose rulers became kings of Scotland. The Romans called Scottish people the Scotti (Latin for Irish) and it is said that the Irish gave the Scots their name, their language (Gaelic) and their Christianity.

Gaelic Ireland was socially and politically hierarchical. Provincial kingdoms comprised some 100 to 150 smaller kingdoms (tuatha), each containing a few thousand people. Local wars between them were frequent and brief. The Gaelic kings were rulers of their clan in peacetime, military leaders in war and swore service to superior kings. Ring forts, or raths, on the hill of Tara north of Dublin now mark the home of the Gaels' High Kings, who claimed to be 'rulers of all Ireland'. They had no lawmaking or executive powers but had to defend their position against other kings. The High Kingship could have served as a source of common defence and political identity, but this unity was never effectively achieved.

The organization of Gaelic Ireland was cultural, social and legal rather than political, and operated at the local and family level. The family kin-group

PLATE 3.3 The royal seat of power of the High King of Ireland, on the Hill of Tara, looking on to the north Central Plain, Co. Meath, Ireland. © Design Pics Inc. – RM Content/Alamy

(derbhfhine) owned land and was made up of individuals who descended from one great-grandfather. New kings were elected by the freemen of the tuath. The learned, professional class or Aos Dána included judges, lawyers, medical men, craftsmen, the filí (poets, bards and seers) and the druids or priests of the Celtic religion, Druidism. Despite their tribal groupings and their wars the Gaels shared forms of the common language, customary law (Brehon law), oral poetry, music and a history adapted from ancient legend.

The buildings (and monuments) of the Gaels were hill forts (defensive sites), ring forts (such as the inhabited circular enclosure at Eamhain Mhacha or Navan Fort near Armagh) and the lake dwellings of ordinary people. The residences of the farming classes, whose agricultural technology lasted for centuries, and local lords was the rath, often erected on a hilltop and surrounded by a circular rampart and fence.

It is argued that, despite its diversity and later attacks upon it, Ireland had an individual unity, a form of nationhood and a Gaelic/Celtic culture which lasted until the death of Hugh O'Neill in 1616 after his flight into exile. The Celts embraced Christianity and opposed later Viking, Anglo-Norman and Tudor conquests. They left a history of their presence, such as homes, place names, family names, saints and missionaries, manuscripts, stonework, sculptures and metalwork, a vernacular literature, a majority language until the nineteenth-century famines, a minority language today, native music and a folklore tradition. In the late nineteenth and early twentieth centuries, a literary-based Celtic revival re-created the idea of a common Celtic/Gaelic origin, which was an impetus for the rise of modern Irish nationalism.

Christianity

Although Christianity has had a powerful effect on the history of the island and on Irish identities, its origins in Ireland are uncertain. It is suggested that other missionaries had preceded the Roman-British St Patrick and their missions may have been connected to trading relations with the Romans. The earliest date for a Christian initiative is AD 431, when St Germanus, Bishop of Auxerre in Gaul, proposed to send Palladius to Ireland, who may have worked in Leinster. Religious activity in Ireland in the fifth century was shared by St Patrick and other missionaries. However, the traditional date (AD 432) for the beginning of Patrick's mission is debated and some historians prefer AD 492/3 over AD 461/2 for his death.

Celtic/Gaelic Ireland in early Christian times (fifth and sixth centuries) was a country of warring kings and cattle raids between clans. St Patrick was mainly based in the north or Ulaidh/Ulster with its probable capital at Eamhain Mhacha (Navan Fort) near Armagh, where he established his ecclesiastical centre and which is still the primatial see of both the Roman Catholic Church in Ireland and the Anglican Church of Ireland. Patrick met Ulaidh's rulers, expanded Christianity in the fifth century and introduced Latin and writing.

In the transition stage between Druidism and Christianity, when the latter struggled against the former, many Gaelic rites and deities were abolished and the druids gave way to a Christian priesthood. However, the new religion did not immediately change the social structure. Gaelic Ireland's culture fused with and influenced Christianity on different levels. Bronze Age art and Celtic designs and motifs were incorporated into early Christian art between AD 650 and 800. Designs on stone crosses, manuscripts and metalwork were similar to those on earlier gold and bronze ornaments. Pagan holy places, religious hermits, sacred wells, stones and trees were also incorporated into Christianity. These developments suggest a continued sharing of diverse cultures and practices in the island rather than the sudden destruction of one tradition and its immediate replacement by the new.

Although St Patrick tried to introduce the episcopal system of church government by bishops, monks and monasteries were already established in Ireland. In the sixth and seventh centuries the monastic system developed further, partly through the influence of Celtic monasteries in Scotland and Wales. Irish monasticism contributed to the evangelization of Scotland through a community

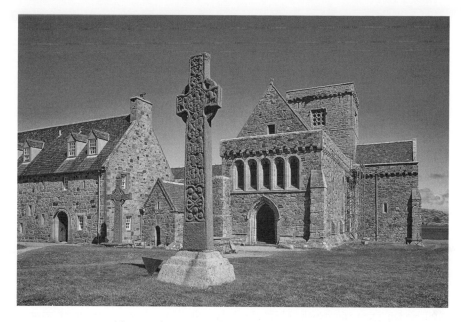

PLATE 3.4 Iona Abbey and Martin's Cross, Inner Hebrides, Argyll, Scotland, where Colm Cille (St Columba/Columb) founded his monastery in 563. © Derek Croucher/Alamy

founded on Iona by St Columba. It is argued that monasteries remained the dominant centres of religious and social life of the Irish people for 500 years. Some, like Bangor and Armagh, were grouped around local families and clan chieftains as prototype ('proto') towns with large populations and represented a different form of church/social organization to the episcopal model practised elsewhere in Europe.

It is argued that the monastic system in Christian Ireland (rather than the Roman Catholic diocesan model) adapted itself to the dispersed settlements of Celtic clans or tribes and served as both a defence and a centre of communal/religious life. Diocesan organization cut across such identities. Traditional history suggests that after Patrick's death, new monasteries were still being created and Ireland's important churches were ruled by abbots.

However, critics suggest that conflict between episcopal and monastic systems does not reflect the reality of the diocese structure. The Church in the seventh century reflected transitional diversity within a single system, in which clerical and monastic functions and administration could be pragmatically combined. But weaknesses in the monastic system eventually led to its replacement by episcopal administration under bishops and clergy.

The conversion of Ireland to Christianity from the fifth century was a gradual but ultimately major event in the lives of the people. Religion became a central, albeit controversial and divisive issue in future centuries as it clashed with politics and as both these forces influenced individual and collective identities. Initially, Christianity opposed paganism on religious, political and social grounds. The later Protestant Reformation and anti-Catholic penal laws in the eighteenth century added religious persecution to political subjection and anti-Reformation views resulted in the Irish having a largely Catholic identification.

Historically, religion in Ireland has also involved strong missionary and evangelical impulses at home and abroad. In the Middle Ages, Irish missionaries travelled to Europe to spread Christianity, culture and education. Irish monks, such as St Columbanus and St Columba, founded monasteries in Britain and Europe as part of their conversion activities. Similarly, in the twentieth and twenty-first centuries, Irish men and women have played a part in Roman Catholic and Protestant missionary enterprises in Africa, Asia and South America.

European scholars saw Ireland as a refuge in the sixth and seventh centuries, and its monasteries became centres of learning in a Celtic/Gaelic golden age, to which manuscripts by Latin and Greek authors were added. Works of art were created in monasteries and accounts of Irish society were also crucially transcribed. These studies and the growth of a Christian faith and literature helped to preserve the Irish language, identity and history, and resulted in a close connection between the people and Christianity.

Viking invasions

Clans or kingdoms of varying size and power were established in Ireland after Celtic/Gaelic immigration. Following conversion to Christianity, the relatively isolated country was raided in the eighth to eleventh centuries by Vikings from Norway and Denmark. The Vikings were not a united force, but operated as individual raiders. Initially, they did not settle but looted the monasteries, stole food and cattle and captured people, who could be sold as slaves. These raids marked the first external attacks since the arrival of the Celts, although there had been violence and plunder in Ireland itself as indigenous groups fought each other and raided monasteries. Irish groups had also colonized parts of western Scotland, Wales and Cornwall between the fourth and sixth centuries.

The first Viking raid was on the island monastery of Lambay off the coast of Co. Dublin in AD 795, although some historians argue for Rathlin Island off the north-east Antrim coast. Celtic/Gaelic Ireland was disunited and lacked a centralized political structure and military resistance to organize its defence. The early assaults were the start of a first Viking Age. The Vikings eventually settled peacefully, assimilated into Celtic/Gaelic society, became traders, arguably built the first Irish towns, such as Arklow and Wexford, and developed urban lifestyles in a mainly rural society. The Viking period lasted for 200 years; their activities varied in extent and intensity; their numbers were relatively small; but they did have influence.

After 837 there was greater inland penetration, although most settlement was still confined to coastal areas at the end of the ninth century. The Vikings began to trade widely in Europe and Ireland, established trading posts at Dublin (841), Wexford and Limerick, and Irish and Viking art styles merged. In the late ninth century the Vikings were not interested in Ireland and Dublin was abandoned in 902. A second Viking Age began in around 915–920. It started with raids, followed by attempts to create permanent bases along the coast. A Viking settlement at Dublin was re-established in 917, with others at Limerick, Waterford and Wexford.

By the mid-tenth century Vikings were settled in Ireland. They had been assimilated into Irish society; converted to Christianity; and were known as Hiberno-Norse. The Norse languages only survived in loan words incorporated into Irish, relating to fishing, shipping and trade. Viking settlements centred on the trading towns of Dublin, Waterford, Cork, Wexford and Limerick. They were not politically powerful and paid tributes or rents to Irish kings. However, their towns expanded trade and developed Ireland's foreign mercantile links.

Although the later history of this period is confused, any potential Viking political and military power was prevented by Brian Boru at the Battle of Clontarf in 1014. However, Clontarf was not solely a conflict between Irish and Vikings. Boru had fought other Irishmen to capture the High Kingship and at Clontarf overcame an army of Dublin Vikings and Leinster Irishmen. Irish history in the Viking period was influenced by royal and church propaganda, shifting alliances and frequent hostilities. Vikings and Irish were divided among themselves, and each group attacked monasteries and towns and killed monks and civilians.

The Vikings made a significant contribution to Ireland as traders and town dwellers, and trading posts, such as Dublin, grew into conventional towns. These urban settlements emphasized the importance of manufacturing, trade and overseas markets, and a mint was established at Dublin in 997. Dublin's harbour and a sharing of trade and business links between Scandinavia, western France and the Mediterranean via the Irish Sea in the tenth and eleventh centuries eventually made it Ireland's principal town and capital. It had specialized craftsmen, a vital import-export trade and Viking styles influenced Irish artwork.

The positive benefits of Viking settlement arguably offset the effects of the early raids. Although debate continues, the traditional common perception of the Vikings as only robbers and plunderers has been modified by historical and archaeological research in recent years, particularly that relating to central Dublin.

Anglo-Norman invasions and settlement

Following 200 years of Viking attacks and settlement, Ireland experienced twelfth-century invasions by Anglo-Normans. They reached the island after their eleventh-century conquests of England and Wales when Normandy had become a strong, feudal state. Military success brought English, Welsh, Norman, Flemish and Breton soldiers into parts of eastern Ireland. The Anglo-Normans illustrated a new expansionist period in European history as populations and economies grew, towns and trade flourished and nations expanded through colonization.

However, the Norman occupation of Ireland was uncoordinated, incomplete and difficult. Many of the new arrivals had no close connections with Normandy. Their interests and power bases were in England and they were initially called 'Anglo-Normans'. Most were later assimilated into Celtic/Gaelic Irish culture by the fifteenth century, but had difficulties in their relationships and identities with both Ireland and England in later centuries.

The first attacks were led by individual Norman barons seeking land or assisting Irish kings in disputes. They invaded in around 1169–1170 from western England and Wales after Dermot MacMurrough, the king of Leinster, invited Richard Fitz Gilbert (alias de Clare or 'Strongbow') to help him in a dynastic conflict. The invasions and settlements were private enterprises and were not controlled or organized centrally by the English king, Henry II.

Henry saw the growing power and Gaelicization of the Anglo-Norman colonists as a threat to his power; he invaded Ireland in around 1171–1172; settled supporters in the island; and asserted his Lordship of Ireland. Popes Adrian IV and Alexander III supported the invasion and Henry's claim, possibly hoping that it might promote Irish church reform. Instead, Norman colonization deprived Celtic/Gaelic Ireland and its people of their independence, even though English kings initially exerted direct authority over only some of Dublin and other parts of the country were largely free from tight royal control.

The Anglo-Norman settlers of the country outside Dublin in 1170 appeared to be English to the Irish and increasingly Irish to England. This unsatisfactory relationship and their identity problem as colonists remained unresolved for centuries as they tried to maintain contact with England. They shared the same civic and legal principles, economic practices, laws, social conventions and political authority as England, but their life in Ireland distanced them gradually from the new English in Dublin and England's power structures.

Settlement in colonial Ireland was conditioned by the fragmented nature of the invasions, and the colonists were concentrated around Dublin and on the south-east coast. They then gradually spread along the valleys and low ground to the south, west and north-east, and controlled transport and communication lines. The colonization process resulted in a base at Dublin (the Pale) and outlying locations among the Irish, protected by Norman castles.

Colonists had to adapt and protect themselves in a partly conquered Ireland. Some in the west integrated by adopting Gaelic customs, speech and family names. Those nearer the Pale mixed Gaelic practices with old English traditions, but remained distant from royal authority. Counties close to Dublin and major towns benefited from the government's legal, military and administrative services; maintained contact with England; and resisted local Irish influences. But most colonists still felt unaccepted as English and saw themselves as 'the middle nation' balancing between the Irish and England.

Despite these problems of alienation, adaptation and partial conquest, Anglo-Norman colonization affected the social, governmental and economic life of Irish society and initiated 750 years of English domination. Nevertheless, the Gaelic language, customs and social organization survived among the Irish.

The Gaelic Irish briefly recovered in the early fourteenth century. They captured the outlying colonial settlements, interrupted communications and isolated the colonies from one another and Dublin. Threats to English kings also came when Scotland briefly challenged English rule in Ireland and tried to assert influence. English rulers in Ireland were concerned, although tensions lessened after the Black Death (plague) in the mid-fourteenth century, which reduced the population and the threat of revolt. But colonial Ireland was still disconnected and identities were fragmented.

Palesmen in Dublin tried to avoid Gaelic influences and the Statutes of Kilkenny in 1366 banned intermarriage with the Irish, prohibited land-leasing with them and restricted trade. But Gaelicization beyond the Pale continued even though the Irish regarded all settlers as foreigners, irrespective of whether they were Gaelicized or born in England. The relationship of Anglicized Palesmen and urban people to outlying settlers was uncomfortable.

English monarchs appointed viceroys or deputies as their representatives in Dublin. They administered the Pale and managed relations with the Irish and colonial lordships. But the king's government in Ireland often had little power and effect. The colony outside the Pale was largely autonomous and control over local areas lay with powerful landed families and chieftains, such as the Earls of Kildare, until the end of the medieval period (1154–1450).

Ireland was politically weak with divided loyalties among people. Palesmen thought that the deputies obstructed their civil rights and connection with the king. They objected to the limited authority of government; wanted to protect their security and prosperity; and proposed that Ireland should become a kingdom rather than a lordship. The Irish should accept the law as the king's subjects and abandon their traditional way of life for an English style. The Palesmen aimed at an English Ireland ruled by themselves as English, but they were ignored and their position became progressively worse.

Colonialism, Protestantism and Catholicism

Between 1485 and 1691, Henry VII (1485–1509) and later English monarchs tried to control a volatile situation by imposing English policies directly upon Ireland through royal deputies, reducing Anglo-Irish influence and centralizing power in the English Crown. They initiated colonization (plantation) policies; supported Protestantism after the English Reformation; and protected Ireland from European threats to its security. The identities of colonists and the indigenous Irish became more firmly fixed by the eighteenth century as they were affected by religious changes, shifts in policy and contested political power. Irish politics and society altered and led to a culturally and religiously diverse population with different allegiances. Tensions increased between the Gaelic Irish, the colonial Anglo-Irish of English or Irish birth who had integrated into Irish culture and new English settlers in the Pale around Dublin.

Domestic and foreign developments in Henry VIII's reign frustrated the Anglo-Irish (or 'Old English') who wanted to maintain the Anglo-Norman conquest, retain their Catholic faith and create an English identity for Ireland and themselves. The king, however, had to protect his throne, guard his new supreme leadership of the Church in England (1534) and assert control over Ireland against threats from popes and European enemies. Henry's introduction of the Protestant Reformation into Ireland from 1537, dissolution of the monasteries and confiscation of rebel property forced the Anglo-Irish ('Old English'), who felt persecuted as Catholics and a 'middle nation', to join the Gaelic Irish in opposition to the Reformation. Internal and external pressures in a Europe divided by Catholicism and Protestantism led Henry to centralize Protestant control of Ireland from England.

Under Edward VI (1547–1553), England became more Protestant. Dublin followed English policies in religion and politics, despite the brief restoration of Roman Catholicism under Queen Mary (1553–1558) and opposition in Ireland against Protestantism. Colonists (such as the Old English) lost their lands and civil rights if they resisted centralized royal control.

Following rebellions in Ulster by Gaelic chieftains, the Protestant Elizabeth I (1558–1603) restored Protestantism and imposed a harsh Irish policy. England was aggressively Protestant and expansionist, and the Elizabethan conquest resulted in Irish Catholic leaders submitting to English forces, which devastated Ulster and Munster.

Under Elizabeth and James I (1603–1625) the English state Church of England had been extended to Ireland from 1560 and the Anglican Church of Ireland was controlled politically by the English rulers in Dublin. But the large majority of the Gaelic population and most Anglo-Irish people inside the Pale were Catholic and the government was concerned about an alliance between the Pale, the Gaelic Irish and Catholic European countries. Many Anglo-Irish had fought with the Elizabethan government and argued that their Catholicism did not limit their allegiance to the Crown. Some settlers outside the Pale fought for the Crown and others were opposed or neutral. The 'Old English' descendants of the Normans struggled for their English rights, but were dismissed by 'New English' settlers.

Identity in Ireland depended upon ancestry and religious affiliation. Since the English conquests were Protestant triumphs, religious discrimination increased. The Old English wanted recognition of their Englishness and Catholicism; were against much government policy; campaigned against Protestant New English settlers; were a strong interest group; owned one-third of Irish land; and controlled Irish trade.

In an attempt to balance various competing interests, James I used a private colonization of Ulster to grant land in Antrim and Down to Lowland Scots. A confused period then ended with the Flight of the Earls (O'Neill and O'Donnell) to Catholic Europe in 1607. They had unsuccessfully resisted English forces and lost status and eventually their estates. Their flight is said to represent the defeat of Gaelic Ireland and its replacement by a mainly Protestant settler class.

In the 1607 Plantation of Ulster the Earls' land was redistributed in mid- and west Ulster (Armagh, Fermanagh, Cavan, Donegal, Tyrone and Coleraine-Londonderry/Derry) among mainly Protestant English, Welsh and Scottish settlers. Many Irish objected to the arrival of the planters and waged intermittent guerrilla attacks against them. The Plantation policy was intended to subdue Ulster through political control, and the migration of New English settlers to all parts of Ireland was encouraged. The Old English survived but they were disadvantaged and could forfeit their land because of their Catholicism.

It seemed that religion rather than ethnicity now separated planter from Gaelic Irish and Old English. But religious identity was complex. Some Scottish settlers were Presbyterians or Catholics; others were Episcopalians who joined the Church of Ireland; some Presbyterians were English puritans; and some Gaelic Irish joined the settlers' Presbyterian congregations.

Religious identities became polarized at one level between Catholicism and the established Anglican Church, but the Presbyterian faith of Scottish immigrants was controlled until the English Civil War. Other Protestant dissenters or non-conformists also experienced discrimination. At a further level, conflicts in England between the Royalist Charles I (1625–1649) and the English Parliament complicated Irish struggles for identity and religion. Charles gained support in Ireland from Catholic groups and in return the Irish and Old English hoped to use Charles and the English Civil War (1642–1648) to regain their status and possessions.

The conflicting identities were apparent when an uprising occurred in 1641 to seize Dublin and expel the New English. The Old English joined the Gaelic Irish as Confederate Catholics against the new settlers and the Protestantism of the English Parliament and its Scottish allies. The uprising was fierce and bloody. It and the English Civil War resulted in the defeat of the Confederate Catholics and victory for the English parliamentary armies.

After the 1641 uprising, the defeat of the Royalists in England and the execution of Charles I (1649), Oliver Cromwell (1653–1658) imposed English rule in Ireland. Catholic and Royalist landowners were banished to Connaught. Most land in Munster, Leinster and Ulster was confiscated and divided among Cromwell's soldiers and supporters. Some land in this Cromwellian land settlement was later returned at the restoration of Charles II (1660–1685), but two-thirds of the land in Ireland remained in Protestant hands.

James II (1685–1688) later gave government positions and militia control to Catholics who supported him in the English Glorious Revolution of 1688. He tried to establish himself in Ireland and arrived in Dublin in 1689. Protestants and Old English settlers were driven out and escaped to Enniskillen and Londonderry/Derry, which James did not capture. His Parliament restored Catholic lands confiscated since 1641 and supporters of the new Protestant English king (William of Orange) William III (1688–1702) lost property and civil rights.

However, William landed at Carrickfergus and, in July 1690 at the Battle of the Boyne, he defeated the Irish forces, but did not capture Limerick. The following year, William's generals defeated the Irish army at Aughrim, and Limerick was forced to capitulate. The Treaty of Limerick (1691) permitted Catholics some religious freedom, and the lands that they had possessed under Charles II were to be restored to them. But the English Parliament forced William to break the Treaty's land concession, and the Old English were socially degraded and their lands lost.

Parliament broke the Limerick terms granting religious toleration by passing the Penal Laws, directed mainly against Catholics, but also Protestant dissenters. Irish commerce and industries (except for linen) were crushed by the English and the Irish export trade to England in many products was stopped. These measures led to gradual economic decline and reactions by some to English attempts to control Ireland. Many Catholics emigrated to Spain and France, and some Protestant dissenters went to America. Seventeenth- and eighteenth-century

PLATE 3.5 Orange parade at Loughgall, Co. Armagh commemorates William III (of Orange) and his victories over the Jacobite forces of James II at the battles of the Boyne and Aughrim, 1690. © AKP Photos/Alamy

colonial Ireland was Protestant Ireland, but it also faced the old difficulties of colonist status and maintaining a satisfactory relationship with England.

By the eighteenth century, settlement, colonization and religion had contributed to the social mixture of modern Ireland and identities and religious polarization between Catholics and Protestants were becoming established. Political events in the nineteenth and twentieth centuries exacerbated the divisions and led to the partition of Ireland and the identities of many Irish people along Catholic (Nationalist) and Protestant (Unionist) lines.

Emigration and immigration

Religious statistics on immigration into Ireland suggest that by the early eighteenth century a quarter of the population were descendants of English and Scottish migrants who had arrived within the previous 200 years. Emigration and immigration have affected Ireland in varying degrees over the centuries and later immigration has led to the establishment of minority groups with specific identities on the island.

Emigration

It is suggested that emigration from Ireland differs from that of other countries because it has involved greater numbers of people than immigration and illustrates tragic episodes in Irish history when people were forced to leave. Debate continues over whether the best or the most deprived left the country; whether emigration damaged Ireland economically as the most gifted left; or benefited the economy because surplus and therefore economically dependent (welfare) labour was reduced. It seems that while many suffering emigrants left because of need, some may have taken advantage of new opportunities and prospered overseas.

There have been various factors impelling Irish emigration over the centuries. Initially monks, missionaries and scholars were motivated to spread knowledge and religious faith in Europe in the Middle Ages. Later emigrants wanted to escape political or religious oppression and colonialization; served as mercenaries in European armies; wanted to avoid the hunger, hardship and deprivation of the famines in the 1840s (particularly in the western Gaeltacht); or generally wished to seek a better life abroad.

Emigration from Ireland increased considerably during the seventeenth and eighteenth centuries and was focused on Europe or British colonies, with Canada as the early main destination. Mass emigration occurred between 1801 and 1921 when it is estimated that some 8 million Irish people permanently left the country. Between the Famine in the mid-nineteenth century and the First World War, the favourite destinations were the United States of America and Great Britain, followed later in the twentieth century by Australia and European countries.

PLATE 3.6 *Famine*, a statue commemorating the Irish famines of the 1840s and 1850s at Custom House Quay, Dublin, Co. Dublin, Ireland. © Imagestate Media Partners Limited – Impact Photos/Alamy

It has been estimated that some 70 million citizens of other countries may be of Irish descent in addition to Irish-born people living abroad temporarily or more permanently due to emigration. This Irish dispersal is centred on English-speaking countries, such as the United States, Great Britain, Canada, Australia, New Zealand, South Africa and the Caribbean. For example, the US Census Bureau in 2004 reported that there were 30.4 million Irish-Americans in the USA or 10.8 per cent of the population. There are also large Irish communities in European countries, such as Great Britain, France and Germany, as well as Japan, Brazil, Argentina and other South American countries (following emigration to Latin America in the eighteenth and nineteenth centuries). An interesting feature of Irish emigration is that equal numbers of women and men have emigrated. This has enabled Irish-born persons to marry within their own ethnic group and prevented a female surplus in Ireland. Relatively high rates of emigration continued following partition in 1921, with more from Ireland than Northern Ireland.

Immigration

Ireland

Historically, Ireland received little immigration because it was remote from Europe, lacked economic appeal and had a forbidding history of emigration. However, immigrants from Eastern Europe in the late nineteenth and early twentieth centuries increased Ireland's small Jewish community, and Italians and Chinese formed distinctive communities and worked in retail and catering. Recent immigrants have been German and Dutch, and some people in the mid-twentieth century immigration from India and Pakistan to Britain were then attracted to Ireland. By the 1980s there were 600 Indians in Ireland, working in retail drapery and later in catering.

Until recently, immigration into modern Ireland was mainly small, controlled refugee movements, but more people have now applied for asylum. Hungarians (1956) and Chileans (1970s) were the first refugee groups to arrive in Ireland under UN sponsorship schemes, but soon left for better opportunities. Some 212 Vietnamese entered in 1979 and have become one of the biggest Asian communities (824). Iranians (26 in 1985) and Bosnians (770 in 1992) gained permission to settle. In the five years up to 1998, about 7,000 refugees arrived in Ireland from Bosnia, other Eastern European countries, Turkey, the Middle East and sub-Saharan Africa. The majority of them sought political asylum. Applications for asylum have risen and the Irish government has now prioritized them according to safe countries of origin.

Ireland has not had a substantial immigration history and there have generally been few racial or ethnic distinctions or overt discrimination. However, the pressure from increased immigration in recent years has focused attention on questions of race and ethnicity. The reaction to immigrant arrivals, such as Romanian gypsies or Roma, has been mixed, occasionally violent and arguably racially motivated.

Ireland experienced economic growth following accession to the EU in 1973 and further improvement through the 1990s. The Celtic Tiger boom led to a decrease in the historical pattern of large-scale emigration by Irish people, but an east to west migration of people resulted in greater economic immigration. In the period 1995 to 2000, approximately a quarter of a million persons migrated to Ireland, of whom about half were returning Irish citizens and the rest were either other Europeans or Americans. Immigrant flows reached a very high peak in 2006 to 2007 at over 100,000 a year.

The Celtic Tiger boom and associated factors had led to significant change as Ireland enjoyed one of the world's highest GDP growth rates, the lowest unemployment ratios in Europe and a booming job market and international profile. But the economy collapsed into recession from 2006–2007, immigration fell sharply and emigration has increased, particularly among young Irish people and returning EU migrants such as Poles, Czechs and Lithuanians.

Immigration implies an increase in newer identities in Ireland. A new question on ethnic or cultural background was included in Ireland's 2006 Census, in which people were invited to choose their ethnic category. Table 3.1 shows that 94.8 per cent of the population was recorded as having a 'White' ethnic or cultural background; 1.1 per cent had a 'Black or Black Irish' background; 1.3 per cent had an 'Asian or Asian Irish' background; 1.1 per cent were classified as 'Other including mixed background'; and 1.7 per cent of the population did not state their

TABLE 3.1 Ethnic/cultural background, Ireland (2006)

Category	Population (thousands)	% of population
White		
Irish	3,645.2	87.4
Irish traveller	22.4	0.5
Any other White background	289.0	6.9
Black or Black Irish		
African	40.5	1.0
Any other Black background	3.8	0.1
Asian or Asian Irish		
Chinese	16.5	0.4
Any other Asian background	35.8	0.9
Other including mixed background	46.4	1.1
Not stated	72.3	1.7
Total	4,172.0	100.0

Source: adapted from Census, 2006, Central Statistics Office, Dublin

ethnicity. These figures indicate that 2.4 per cent of the Republic's population believed that they had a non-White ethnicity (excluding the mixed category). The increase in 'mixed backgrounds' reflects a similar recent rise in population figures for Great Britain.

Allowing for births (245,000) and deaths (114,000), the net immigration of people into Ireland between 2002 and 2006 was 186,000, which at an average annual rate of 37,200 was comparatively high for a country with Ireland's overall population and migration history. The Republic had 96,600 people claiming a non-White ethnicity at the 2006 census and 46,400 who regarded themselves as 'Other including mixed background'.

The breakdown of non-Irish nationals from these general statistics may be seen in Table 3.2. According to these figures, Ireland had 282,572 foreign citizens (6.8 per cent) in its population at the 2006 Census. These figures apparently do not include 1,318 people with no nationality, and 44,279 with no stated nationality. The single largest group of immigrants came from the United Kingdom, followed by (usually seasonal migrants from) Poland, Lithuania and Nigeria. However, many EU migrants have left Ireland due to the 2008 recession.

Nevertheless, Ireland's population increased significantly to 4,172,000 in the 2006 Census and experienced one of the fastest growing populations in Europe. From 2004 to 2006 the growth rate was above 2 per cent. This was due to falling death rates, rising birth rates, relatively high immigration levels and the return of

TABLE 3.2 Non-Irish nationals living in Ireland (2006)

Country of origin	Population (thousands)	% of population
United Kingdom	112,548	2.7
Poland	63,276	1.5
Lithuania	24,628	0.6
Nigeria	16,300	0.4
Latvia	13,319	0.3
United States	12,475	0.3
China	11,161	0.3
Germany	10,289	0.3
Philippines	9,548	0.2
France	9,046	0.2

Source: adapted from the Census 2006, Dublin Central Statistics Office

Irish people (often with foreign-born children) who had emigrated in large numbers in earlier years during periods of high unemployment. Ireland has the youngest population in Europe, with only 11.2 per cent being over age 65. The country is forecast to have the smallest proportion of the 65+ age group in Europe until 2035. Estimated Irish population growths are the second highest in Europe, with a projected 53 per cent growth by 2060 and an increase to 6,057,000 by 2035.

Northern Ireland

Following the partition of Ireland in 1921 rates of migration into and out of Northern Ireland have been similar to those of Ireland. But since 2001, there has been a significant growth in immigration into Northern Ireland from countries outside the UK, such as the Philippines. Following the enlargement of the EU in 2004, considerable numbers of people from the new EU countries, such as Poland, have also arrived. The population at the 2001 Census was 1,685,267, and grew to 1,810,900 by the 2011 Census.

But this increase in immigration from abroad has been accompanied by an increase in people from Northern Ireland moving to other countries on a temporary or permanent basis. In 2005–2006 the highest number of people in recent history (9,100) emigrated from Northern Ireland. This figure did not include those who moved to the rest of the UK or to Ireland. It is suggested that this emigration is part of a general global increase in international migration. The geographical mobility of the Northern Irish population may be seen in the statistic that more than one in four surveyed for the 2006 *NILT Survey* said that they had lived outside Northern Ireland for more than six months. However, in the balance between emigration and immigration, Northern Ireland figures show that 32,000 people entered the province in the year to June 2007 and 22,000 people left so that the population (or net immigration) grew by 10,000 new immigrants. According to the NISRA Agency in 2008, this increase had a greater effect on population figures than the excess of births over deaths.

Northern Ireland has the smallest population of the UK countries. The population is fairly static, as migration roughly balances natural increase. Since partition, emigration from Northern Ireland has tended to outpace immigration, although the net outflow of people from the region has been relatively small, especially when compared with earlier mass Irish emigration before partition. The combination of a relatively high birth rate and small overall emigration has contributed to a gradual rise in the population of Northern Ireland.

During the Troubles, levels of immigration to Northern Ireland were low. However, there has been an increase since the Good Friday (Belfast) Agreement curtailed terrorist activity. Most ethnic minorities live in the Greater Belfast area, although certain groups are attracted to other parts of the province. Minority non-White ethnic groups are apparently only 0.8 per cent of Northern Ireland's population (which includes the 'mixed' category), a lower percentage than that of Ireland at 3.5 per cent.

The first ethnic minority to arrive in significant numbers were the Chinese, who came to Northern Ireland in the 1960s, and there were 4,200 speakers of Chinese languages in 2004. The largest non-native restaurant capacity in Northern Ireland is Chinese, because many of the initial immigrants set up food outlets.

Apart from the Chinese, there are a number of other ethnic minority groups from Asia. Most came from Commonwealth countries such as Pakistan and India (sometimes via Great Britain), with 1,000 Indians arriving by the 1980s to work in retail drapery and later in catering. The influx led to the building of a mosque and a Hindu temple to cater for spiritual needs and an Asian supermarket on the Ormeau Road in Belfast.

Other recent distinctive immigrants arrived in Northern Ireland in the 1990s, such as some 1,000 Portugese. The Portugese community is located primarily in Dungannon, Co. Tyrone but many work in Portadown, Co. Armagh.

There are now about 30,000 Polish people living in Northern Ireland. This large influx has been relatively recent, and has increased since Poland joined the European Union in 2004. Many Poles come on a short-term basis to find work, but numbers can vary according to the prevailing economy and many EU migrants have left since the onset of the 2007–2008 recession. There are a number of other ethnic minorities, primarily from Eastern Europe, such as Hungarians who have moved to smaller towns in the west of the province.

Table 3.3 illustrates ethnic/cultural groups in Northern Ireland. This and Table 3.4 give increased numbers for the 'mixed' category similar to statistics for the Irish and UK populations. Table 3.4 also gives a more detailed breakdown of Northern Irish immigration and ethnic statistics.

TABLE 3.3 Ethnic/cultural groups, Northern Ireland (2001)

Category	Population (thousands)	% of population
White	1,672,698	99.3
Mixed	3,319	0.2
Asian	2,679	0.2
Black	1,136	0.1
Chinese or other ethnic group	5,435	0.3

Source: adapted from Census of the Population, 2001, Northern Ireland Statistics ND Research Agency

TABLE 3.4 Ethnic/cultural background, Northern Ireland (2001)

Category	Population (thousands)	% of population
Irish travellers	1,719	0.1
Mixed	3,317	0.2
Indian	1,579	0.1
Pakistani	683	0.04
Bangladeshi	260	0.02
Other Asian	190	0.01
Black Caribbean	256	0.02
Black African	517	0.03
Other Black	391	0.02
Chinese	4,155	0.25
Other ethnic groups	1,285	0.08
Total	14,352	

Source: adapted from Census of the Population, 2001, Northern Ireland Statistics ND Research Agency

Attitudes to national identity

Northern Ireland

The Good Friday (Belfast) Agreement, 1998 guarantees the 'recognition of the birthright of all the people of Northern Ireland to identify themselves and be accepted as Irish or British, or both, as they may so choose'. Furthermore, Northern Irish citizens are 'all persons born in Northern Ireland and having, at the time of their birth, at least one parent who is a British citizen, an Irish citizen or is otherwise entitled to reside in Northern Ireland without any restriction on their period of residence'. These requirements have posed problems for those who are born in the province but who have no relevant parental or other connection.

Questions of national identity in Northern Ireland are complex. A *Northern Ireland Life and Times Survey (NILT)* ARK in 2010 showed that respondents regarded themselves as British (37 per cent), Northern Irish (28 per cent), Irish (25 per cent), Ulster (4 per cent) and Other (5 per cent). Catholics voted 58 per cent for 'Irish' and 25 per cent for 'Northern Irish'; Protestants rated 'British' at 61 per cent and 'Northern Irish' at 28 per cent; while those of no religion responded with 33 per cent for 'British', 18 per cent for 'Irish' and 37 per cent for 'Northern Irish'. In a *NILT Survey* ARK in 2008, 37 per cent of all categories felt very strongly about being British, but 34 per cent did not and 15 per cent 'not at all'. The identity which scored highest in the 'very strongly' position with 50 per cent was Northern Irish.

Cultural and political identities are problematic in Northern Ireland. They are subject to fundamentally different Nationalist and Unionist perceptions which affect notions of allegiance and group membership. Critics argue that discussion of national identity may also be complicated by the fact that many in Northern Ireland are so conditioned by their own ideologies that they are not willing to accept or tolerate the chosen national identities of others. But survey results indicate that people can hold various combinations of identity and may be more flexible or pragmatic than has been usually granted.

A *NILT Survey* ARK in 2011 reported that 73 per cent of 1,200 Northern Irish respondents were in favour of remaining within the UK. Significantly, 52 per cent of Catholics favoured the union with Britain rather than a united Ireland and only 4 per cent of Protestants want Irish unity.

Ireland

As a result of recent increased immigration, Ireland has had similar problems to Northern Ireland in respect of who may claim Irish citizenship. In the period 2003 to 2005, the country's citizenship laws were changed to 'eliminate an Irish-born child's automatic right to (Irish) citizenship when the parents are not Irish nationals' (MPI).

In terms of attitudes to national identity, a *Eurobarometer 57 – National Standard Report, October, 2002* drew parallels to EU membership and the Nice referendum, 2001. The report found that identity in Irish political culture is related to national pride and a history of nationalism. Just over 70 per cent of Irish respondents said that they were very proud to be Irish, a far higher figure than those recorded by the French, Dutch and Germans. But the Irish have a less well-developed sense of European identity (30 per cent), although pride in being Irish is seen as quite compatible with pride in being European, albeit at a lower level of intensity. A majority are generally positive about and approve of membership of the EU, but admit to fears about the imposition of decisions by the big countries and about loss of national identity and national culture. In the run-up to the first Nice referendum in 2001 (which was rejected by Ireland) indifference to the EU by Irish respondents exceeded enthusiasm by a significant margin.

Exercises

Explain and examine the following terms:

Mesolithic	Connaught	Strongbow
Neolithic	*tuath(a)*	the Pale
River Boyne	High King	Statutes of Kilkenny
Newgrange	Tara	Iona
Beaker Folk	Navan Fort	Plantation of Ulster
Celts	Hugh O'Neill	Munster
St Patrick	monastery	Old English
diocese	Lambay	Church of Ireland
missionary	feudal	New English
Charles I	Oliver Cromwell	immigration
Clontarf	Anglo-Normans	Episcopalians

Write short essays on the following topics:

1   Compare and contrast emigration and immigration patterns in Irish history.

2   Analyse questions of national identity in Northern Ireland or Ireland.

3   Examine the role of the Vikings in Irish history.

Further reading

Balaresque, P. *et al.* (2010) 'A Predominantly Neolithic Origin for European Paternal Lineages', *PLOS Biol.*, 8(1): e1000285

Bramanti, B. *et al.* (2009) 'Genetic Discontinuity between Local Hunter-Gatherers and Central Europe's First Farmers', *Science*, 2 October

Clarke, A. (2006) *The Old English in Ireland* Dublin: Four Courts Press

Connolly, S.J. (ed.) (2007) *Oxford Companion to Irish History* Oxford: Oxford University Press

Kee, R. (1982) *Ireland: A History* London: Abacus

Lalor, B. (ed.) (2003) *The Encyclopaedia of Ireland* Dublin: Gill and Macmillan

Loughrey, P. (1988) *The People of Ireland* Belfast: Appletree Press

Malmström, H. *et al.* (2009) 'Ancient DNA Reveals Lack of Continuity between Neolithic Hunter-Gatherers and Contemporary Scandinavians', *Biology*, 19(20): 1758–1762, 24 September

Oppenheimer, S. (2006) *The Origins of the British: A Genetic Detective Story* London: Constable

Salazar, C. (1998) 'Identities in Ireland: History, Ethnicity and the Nation-state', *European Journal of Cultural Studies*, 1(3): 369–385

Sykes, B. (2006) *Blood of the Isles* London: Bantam Press

Websites

Census, Central Statistics Office, Ireland: http://www.cso.ie/
Northern Ireland census: http://www.nisranew.nisra.gov.uk/census/start.html
Northern Ireland Life and Times, ARK: http://www.ark.ac.uk/nilt

4

Religion

- Religious history
- Religion in Ireland after 1921
- The churches in contemporary Ireland
- Religion in Northern Ireland after 1921
- Religion in Northern Ireland today
- Attitudes to religion
- *Exercises*
- *Further reading*
- *Websites*

The identity of Ireland, for Irish people and for outsiders, has included a strong religious component. That Ireland was 'a land of saints and scholars' implied not only a description of a historical era in which Irish monasteries contributed to the Christianization of Europe but also a description of a distinctively Irish (mainly Catholic) religious practice. Ireland's patron saint, St Patrick, has today become a global symbol of things Irish. St Patrick's Day (17 March) is marked by celebrations across the world. Though these celebrations themselves usually have nothing to do with religious belief, the popular identification of Ireland with its saint continues to associate Irishness with religion. In the twentieth century, the partition of Ireland was the result of the incompatible political goals of mainly Catholic Nationalism and Protestant Unionism. What defined both parts of Ireland, politically as well as culturally, was the influence of organized religion. After the outbreak of the Troubles in 1968/9, the depth of religious division revealed itself again in Northern Ireland and many outsiders assumed that Ireland was still engaged in a 'holy war'. That interpretation does not explain political violence in Northern Ireland, but it is true that religion remains a key marker of political boundaries.

Recently, a different perspective has emerged. It has been argued that Ireland is very rapidly developing the characteristics of a post-Christian society. The authority of church leaders has been weakened and church attendance is falling. Young people especially have become more independent in those areas of sexual morality and family life where religion once had a dominant influence. Society in Ireland and Northern Ireland is becoming both increasingly secular and, with immigration, more multi-faith. While these developments have been observable in the past few decades, it is the case that religion remains important in public and private life in both parts of the island. By international – especially Western European – standards, religious adherence is still strong. Practising membership of church congregations – again, by Western European standards – is notably high in all denominations and most people still associate themselves, if sometimes nominally, with a particular church.

Religious history

The evidence of pre-Christian religion in Ireland remains fragmentary. The likelihood is that it shared much with the paganism of Celtic Europe. It appears that the worship of sacred stones was general and that human sacrifice was

PLATE 4.1 Síle na gCíoch on the church wall of Killnaboy, Co. Clare. Early Christianity incorporated older pagan symbols such as this figure, thought to represent either fertility or the sin of lust. © imagebroker/Alamy

sometimes practised. Fertility both of the land and of women was represented in religious imagery. Possibly the most famous is the Síle na gCíoch, a representation of the Celtic goddess of motherhood. There is mention in later literature of Irish druids who resemble the pagan priesthood common to most of Celtic Europe. Medieval Christian literature celebrated the defeat of the druids and attributed it to the work of St Patrick in the fifth century.

Christian communities in Ireland, probably of captured slaves, actually pre-dated Patrick's arrival in about 432. From Roman Britain, he had been abducted (possibly from what is now Cumbria in north-west England) and enslaved by a raiding Irish warlord. Though Patrick managed to escape from Ireland, he chose to return as a missionary and bishop, beginning a process of evangelization and conversion. Christianization of the island was not immediate but it appears to have been relatively peaceful and very thorough. This was partly a result of the common Christian practice of adopting and transforming older pagan symbolism. For example, Christian holy wells probably had pagan origins and the Síle na gCíoch came to adorn the walls of medieval churches as a means to ward off evil. Patrick's main missionary work had been in the North, a personal cult developed rapidly and the saint's veneration enabled the northern see of Armagh to claim primacy in Ireland in the seventh century. There is little evidence for Patrick's links with Armagh, the claims coming in the centuries after his death, and this claim of primacy was never fully accepted. The so-called primatial controversy was

PLATE 4.2 Representation of St Patrick as a slave and missionary in the window in the Church of Ireland Down Cathedral, Downpatrick. It is believed that the mortal remains of Patrick, the patron saint of Ireland, are buried here. © David Lyons/Alamy

disputed for centuries between Armagh and Dublin. In 1893, the Pope conferred the cardinalship on the Archbishop of Armagh, effectively ending the dispute within the Catholic Church. Armagh had become the primatial see of the reformed (or Protestant) Church of Ireland in the sixteenth century. In both churches, the Archbishop of Armagh has the title Primate of All Ireland and the Archbishop of Dublin has the title Primate of Ireland.

Irish Christianity became respected for the quality of its learning and the beauty of its art (adding scholarship to sainthood). Irish illuminated manuscripts, like the *Book of Kells*, were renowned for the intricacy of style and ornamentation. Irish missionaries, like Colm Cille's (Columba's) mission to Britain and the mission of Columbanus through continental Europe, had a major influence on Christian faith and scholarship. There was a long-standing scholarly consensus that early religious organization in Ireland was dominated by the monastic system and that this made the island unique. It was the authority of abbots rather than the authority of bishops that was decisive and, on matters such as the dating of Easter, the Irish Church was distinctive (though Irish dating was followed in parts of England until the Synod of Whitby in 664).

More recently, scholars have begun to question that traditional consensus and have suggested that the Church in Ireland was probably more akin to the European model than was previously thought. Whatever the judgement, the early Irish Church exerted not only religious authority but also economic and political power. There developed a constant tension between spiritual commitment and worldly corruption, something the Church certainly did share with other parts of Europe. The later condition of the Irish Church led reformers to question its Christian vocation. In the twelfth century, reform was encouraged by the work of St Malachy who acted with the sanction of the Pope. The impact of these reforms reorganized the Church such that bishops now controlled 24 territorial dioceses. Also established were four archbishoprics in Armagh, Cashel, Tuam and Dublin. During this period, Irish monasticism was also transformed by the arrival of the European orders of Cistercian and Benedictine monks and Augustinian canons. These reforms coincided with the Anglo-Norman attempt to control high office in the Irish Church and to make it conform more closely to Roman practice. This was only partially successful and the Irish Church retained its own character. For example, clerical marriage and hereditary bishoprics were commonplace in parts of the country.

The sixteenth-century Protestant Reformation, however, was to have a profound effect on Irish religious history. When Henry VIII broke from Rome in 1533–1534, it was for dynastic, rather than religious, purposes. As king, it was to him, rather than to the Pope, that the Church and its courts should now owe allegiance. This was established in England and Wales by the Act of Supremacy. In 1536, the Irish Parliament passed its own Act of Supremacy and declared Henry to be the 'supreme head of the Church of Ireland'. All church officials had to swear the Oath of Supremacy. This was done with little opposition and no bishop refused, mainly because church doctrine remained undisturbed. Even the dissolution of the monasteries was achieved with relatively little disturbance.

Only as the Reformation gained theological momentum in the course of the sixteenth century did Catholic resistance develop. As a result, the shape of religious history in Ireland was transformed as a more assertive Protestantism was given state sanction. Under Elizabeth I (1558–1603) there was an attempt to impose a thoroughgoing Protestant settlement on the realm. The Act of Uniformity in 1559 required the use by clergy of the Book of Common Prayer and everyone was expected to attend the (Protestant or Reformed) Church of Ireland, now the established church and headed by the monarch. On the one hand, it retained many of the rites and ceremonies as well as much of the liturgy of the Catholic Church, proclaiming the continuous tradition of faith with the early Church of St Patrick. On the other hand, it rejected the authority of the Pope and the alleged innovations in doctrine which were held to be contrary to Scripture. This policy met with stubborn opposition which secured papal approval. Unlike England, the reformed faith failed to become the confession of the majority. The Reformation in Ireland was now understood by that majority to be both religiously and culturally alien. Rather than replacing Catholicism as the religion of the people, the newly established Church of Ireland found itself in opposition to it. This had been unforeseen, and the result was that Ireland became fertile ground for Counter-Reformation ideas and thus a potential threat to the Protestant monarchy in England.

In Ireland, as elsewhere in Europe, religion was bound up with dynastic rivalry and political ambition. However, the government was not strong enough to impose a comprehensive Protestant settlement. As a consequence, it was the vulnerability of the Church of Ireland to Catholic challenge, possibly aided by hostile foreign powers (for example, the Spanish Armada of 1588), that informed policy in succeeding centuries. During this era, compared with other European states, the religious sanctions in Ireland were relatively mild. Catholicism was openly practised. By 1630, there were 17 Catholic bishops and over 1,000 clergy, about one-third of whom had been trained at seminaries in Europe. The Catholic Church felt strong enough to support armed rebellion in the middle years of the seventeenth century, encouraging attacks on the clergy of the Church of Ireland. The statistics are unclear, but during the rebellion of 1641 about 12,000 Protestants, mainly in Ulster, were either killed or died of ill-treatment and this helped set the tone of religious brutality which followed.

Despite severe repression, Catholicism survived the land confiscations and the transportation of priests during the Cromwellian period (1649–1658). Hopes of revival under the reign of James II (1685–1688), who had placed Catholics in positions of authority throughout Ireland, were dashed in 1690 by the victory of William III at the Battle of the Boyne. The Battle of the Boyne and the Battle of Aughrim in 1691 secured the political dominance of Protestantism in Ireland. It also permitted the introduction of the Penal Laws against the Catholic Church.

These laws forbade the entry of foreign priests and banished bishops. They were intended over time to eradicate Catholicism in Ireland and to exclude prominent Catholics from public life. However draconian these laws were in principle, they were only patchily enforced. The Catholic Church continued to operate and a prosperous Catholic gentry and mercantile class emerged in the course of the eighteenth century. The Penal Laws were a sign both of Protestantism's new power and also of its continuing insecurities. The established Church of Ireland did little to evangelize the majority but instead tended to concentrate its attention upon those already converted, many of whom were not native Irish.

The Church of Ireland, then, found itself at odds not only with Catholics but also with Protestant dissenters, mainly Presbyterians resident in Ulster. Presbyterians, who came mainly from Scotland, had settled in Ulster in the sixteenth and seventeenth centuries. Presbyteries, the name given to their organized congregations, prospered under Cromwellian rule. Their loyalty to William III was also rewarded by an increase in financial support from the state, known as the *regium donum*, which was paid to the Presbyterian Synod of Ulster. Their freedom to worship was acknowledged by the 'Ease of Protestant Dissenters', or Toleration Act, of 1719.

The Presbyterians of Ulster resented the dominant role, politically and culturally, of the Church of Ireland. In particular, they resented their requirement to pay a tax, or tithe, for its upkeep, and these grievances and this sense of exclusion encouraged large numbers of Presbyterians to emigrate from Ulster to North America. Their contribution to the cause of the American Revolution and to writing the Constitution of the United States was significant. Radical Ulster Presbyterians also provided the inspiration for the movement of United Irishmen which aimed to overthrow English rule and to institute religious equality in Ireland. In some areas the violent sectarianism of the Rebellion of 1798, in which Catholics took revenge on Protestant landlords and tenants, made Ulster Presbyterians (with also the folk memory of 1641) more inclined in the nineteenth century to make political common cause with the Church of Ireland when Home Rule became the central issue of Irish politics.

One consequence of the 1798 Rebellion was the Irish Act of Union which in 1801 united Ireland with Great Britain. Under the Act of Union, the Church of Ireland and the Church of England were also united 'for ever', an eternity which lasted for only 70 years. In the course of the nineteenth century it became increasingly difficult for the Church of Ireland to defend its privileged position and it came under challenge not only from popular Catholicism in Ireland but also from Parliamentarians at Westminster. In the census of 1861, membership was calculated at 693,300 or 12 per cent of the population of Ireland (in Ulster it was about 25 per cent), and its minority status was dramatically illustrated. In 1869 the Irish Church Act, which came into effect on 1 January 1871, disestablished the Church of Ireland. This meant that it was no longer the state-supported church (disestablishment meant losing at first £16 million, though later £10 million was

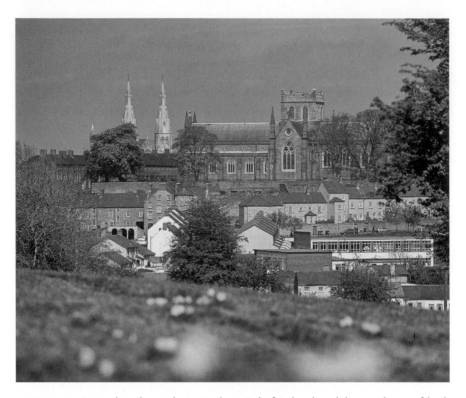

PLATE 4.3 Armagh is the ecclesiastical capital of Ireland and the residence of both Primates of All Ireland (Church of Ireland and Roman Catholic). The Church of Ireland St Patrick's Cathedral is shown in the foreground and the Catholic St Patrick's Cathedral in the background. © scenicireland.com/Christopher Hill Photographic/ Alamy

returned) and the Crown no longer had authority over its appointments. Its affairs were now controlled by a General Synod and the Church of Ireland became a self-governing part of the Anglican Communion.

Because of its democratic basis, Presbyterianism continued to be internally divided with a tendency to split on issues of religious principle. In the early 1800s there were no fewer than six bodies laying claim to legitimacy. One major schism in nineteenth-century Presbyterianism was over the appointment of ministers. Another was over doctrinal orthodoxy. In 1840, the establishment of the General Assembly of the Presbyterian Church resolved most of these issues. Those Presbyterian congregations which remained outside the General Assembly formed the Non-Subscribing Presbyterian Church. A further group of congregations continued as the Reformed Presbyterian Church, a denomination with eighteenth-century origins. The other major Protestant denomination to establish itself in Ireland at this time was Methodism. Originally an evangelical reform movement within Anglicanism in the eighteenth century, it separated from the Church of Ireland to form its own structures in 1878.

The largest denomination in Ireland remained the Catholic Church and the vast majority of Irish people were Catholic. In the nineteenth century the Church was able to turn its numerical strength into a powerful political force to which the government in London increasingly deferred on matters of clerical interest, such as education. Though most of the disabilities of the Penal Laws had been removed by the early years of the century, full Catholic emancipation was only achieved in 1829. The new self-confidence of Catholicism was displayed in the building of churches, schools and hospitals. Its public presence was confirmed by the Synod of Thurles in 1850, the first formal meeting of Catholic bishops since 1642. Under the leadership of Paul Cullen, Archbishop of Armagh (1849–1852) and of Dublin (1852–1878) and the first Irish cardinal, the Church was not only strengthened organizationally, it also underwent a 'devotional revolution'.

This transformed the character of Irish Catholicism and instituted a European-wide trend of doctrinal reform. The importance of familial piety was stressed and Catholic fraternities and associations were promoted amongst the laity. *Ultramontanism*, or accountability to and regulation by Rome, was promoted by Cullen. This was significant since it asserted the autonomy of the Church from the state and attached its allegiance exclusively to the Pope. In principle, therefore, Catholicism and Irish nationalism were not necessary or easy bedfellows. The church hierarchy was suspicious of its radical elements and was instrumental in bringing down the (Protestant) leader of Irish nationalism, Charles Stewart Parnell, when he became involved in a divorce case in 1890 to 1891. The principle of the Church was Cullen's view that the true nationality of Ireland was *Catholic*. Therefore nationalism was acceptable only so long as it did not threaten the true *religion* which was also Catholic.

This was sufficient for the overwhelming majority of Protestants to believe that Irish self-government would mean the dominance of Catholic values in public life. In other words, they believed that Home Rule would be Rome Rule. The *Ne*

PLATE 4.4 A portrait of Cardinal Paul Cullen in St Patrick's College, Drumcondra, Co. Dublin. He was the first Irish cardinal and oversaw changes in Catholic organization and worship which had a profound influence on Irish life in the nineteenth and twentieth centuries. http://multitext.ucc.ie/viewgallery/500

Temere decree, promulgated by the Pope in 1907 and taking effect in 1908, required children of mixed marriages to be raised as Catholics. This was taken as an example of the religious intolerance Protestants would experience in a self-governing, and possibly independent, Ireland. The concentration of Protestants in the northern province of Ulster also bound religion and British Unionism tightly together, even though there were small numbers of Protestant Home Rulers. That concentration gave its argument political weight. The government's solution to this mix of religion and politics was to partition Ireland. The drawing of the political boundary meant that a small Protestant minority remained in the 26 southern counties and a large Catholic minority remained in the six northern counties. For the government in London this appeared a price worth paying to prevent possible civil war in Ireland.

There are problems in examining religion in Ireland exclusively within state boundaries since the structures of the churches are all-Ireland but the religious balance within those boundaries is very different. For example, on an all-Ireland basis the major denominational percentages today would be about 75 per cent Catholic, 7 per cent Church of Ireland, 7 per cent Presbyterian and 1 per cent Methodist. Calculated separately on Ireland and Northern Ireland bases these percentages are very different. In that sense, a state-based approach is still appropriate.

Religion in Ireland after 1921

The separation of Northern Ireland from its jurisdiction made the Irish Free State even more Catholic than Home Rule Ireland would have been. So too did the emigration of large numbers of Protestants either as a consequence of the removal of British troops and administration or sometimes as a result of fear or intimidation. Though numbers in the southern counties had been declining slowly in the nineteenth century, between the census of 1911 and that of 1926 the fall was precipitous. Membership of the Church of Ireland in the territory of the Irish Free State fell from 250,000 to 164,000, a loss of about one-third. By 1961 it had decreased by a further 36 per cent to 104,000 or about 4 per cent of the population. By 1991, Church of Ireland congregations accounted for a mere 2.5 per cent of the population. The other, smaller Protestant Churches witnessed a similar decline. Presbyterian membership fell from 50,000 in 1921 to just over 13,000 in 1991, or 0.4 per cent of the population. The decline in all Protestant denominations was from 10.5 per cent in 1911 to 3.2 per cent in 1991.

This long retreat of the Protestant population, from 1921 to the end of the twentieth century, has been attributed to a number of factors. The *Ne Temere* decree did contribute to reducing Protestant numbers. As a consequence, some Protestant men and women chose not to marry out of their faith and remained single and childless. It was also the case that Protestants were more likely than

Catholics to profess no religion at all. As congregations aged and churches closed, the prospect of extinction became a depressing possibility. That feeling of marginalization found little or no expression in Irish public life and Protestant decline was ignored as a political issue. There was no separate Protestant political party and the majority of southern Protestants accepted the new social order. Unionist politicians in Northern Ireland, on the other hand, pointed to the experience of southern Protestants as proof of the malign effect of the Catholic Church in the affairs of state.

The Catholic Church wielded enormous moral and political authority. This was unsurprising, since Catholics now constituted over 90 per cent of the population. Though it would be misleading to claim that the influence of the Church was always decisive in Irish public life, its influence was pervasive especially in education, health and family matters. Nor was it unpopular. In 1932, for example, over one million people attended the open-air Mass celebrated in Dublin during the international Eucharistic Congress.

The consensus in favour of Catholic values was rarely challenged, and Irish governments faced little opposition in legislatively enforcing those values. On matters such as the censorship of books, films and newspapers and the banning of contraceptives, Catholic influence was manifest. The Free State did not establish any religion but Article 44 of the 1937 Irish Constitution recognized the 'special position of the Holy Catholic Apostolic and Roman Church as the guardian of the Faith professed by the great majority of its citizens'. The Constitution did embrace Catholic teaching in many of its articles. For example, divorce was made unconstitutional. Church–government relations were intimate and political leaders were deferential, but not necessarily subordinate, to Catholic bishops.

One famous example of the overt political influence of the Church was its role in the Mother and Child controversy of 1950–1951. The Minister for Health planned free medical provision for mothers and children under 16. For the Church, the proposed legislation interfered too deeply in family life and appeared to challenge the Church's role in the moral upbringing of children. The government backed down in the face of opposition from the bishops and the Minister resigned. The incident seemed to confirm the power of clerical veto in matters where the Church's interests were most at stake.

This Catholic moral consensus was slow to change not because the Church had power alone but because it had popular support. Surveys showed that weekly attendance at Mass remained remarkably high well into the 1990s. In the mid-1970s it was estimated that attendance was over 90 per cent. In the 1980s it was around 85 per cent. Only in the late 1990s was there evidence of appreciable decline to around 65 per cent. When Pope John Paul II visited Ireland in 1979, he was greeted with enormous public enthusiasm.

Though the 'special position' of the Catholic Church had been removed from the Constitution following a referendum in 1972 (which the bishops had not

PLATE 4.5 The Eucharistic Congress held in Dublin in June 1932 represented a high point of Catholic influence in Ireland. After an open-air Mass in Phoenix Park, Dublin, it is estimated that one million people processed to O'Connell Bridge in the centre of the city where this photograph was taken. http://catalogue.nli.ie/Record/vtls 000241107

opposed), the Church was still able to mobilize popular support on some, though not all, moral issues. Contraception had been legalized for family planning purposes (on doctor's prescription) in 1979 but referenda on abortion in 1983 and on divorce in 1986 confirmed the position of Catholic teaching in these matters. Such victories were short-lived, however. The law relating to homosexuality was liberalized in 1993. Divorce was legalized after another referendum in 1995. Despite referenda on the issue in 1992 and 2002 there is still no right to abortion. However, information about its availability (for example, in English clinics) is now freely available.

The changes in Irish society in recent years have been remarkable and traditional Catholicism has found it hard to adjust. The decline of clerical power can be traced to a number of factors such as changing social expectations and a less deferential public culture. Some commentators have argued that Irish society has become more 'protestant', not in the sense of religious confession but in the sense of the growing importance placed upon individual rights and conscience. Catholics increasingly choose to follow their own conscience on sexual and family issues rather than accepting without question the teachings of the Church.

Interestingly, polls seem to show that the Church is more respected when it speaks on social matters like poverty and inequality than when it speaks on matters like sexual behaviour. This may also be a measure of the secularization, or what others have called the modernization, of Irish society. Certainly the position of the Catholic Church today is very different from what it was only a generation ago. A poll in 2007 found that 82 per cent of parents would let their children make up their own minds about faith compared with only 7 per cent in 1977. Academic research also showed that 75 per cent of Catholic women were in favour of abortion when the woman's health was in danger. They were equally in favour of female priests, something which the Church has long resisted.

The churches in contemporary Ireland

In 2009, according to the *Irish Catholic Directory*, the Catholic population of Ireland stood at just over 3.5 million out of a total of 4,338,587 or about 89 per cent of the population. The biggest diocese (with 200 parishes) is Dublin and the smallest is Achonry in the west of Ireland with 23. The bishops, diocesan and auxiliary, together meet four times per year as the (island-wide) Irish Catholic Bishops Conference (ICBC). The ICBC comprises five Episcopal Commissions which focus on specific aspects of the Church's responsibilities such as education and pastoral care. The purpose is to facilitate cooperation between bishops but not to override their individual pastoral authority. The President of the ICBC is the Primate of the Church, the Archbishop of Armagh, and its day-to-day operations are overseen by a dedicated secretariat. The religious orders in Ireland have their own organization, the Conference of Religious of Ireland (CORI), which was established in 1983 and claims a membership of 136 congregations comprising about 9,000 men and women. These include both male orders such as the Christian Brothers and Cistercians and female orders such the Sisters of Mercy. However, the numbers of clergy and members of orders are falling and there are worrying trends for the future of the Church.

First, of the 2,539 diocesan clergy the majority are over age 60 (average age: 63). The average age of members of religious communities is over 70. Second, there has been a dramatic drop in young people entering the priesthood. In the mid-1960s, there were 1,375 vocations to the priesthood and religious life. In 2003, only 19 priests were ordained. Dioceses are being compelled to 'cluster' parishes to continue the provision of the Mass. Similarly, some parishes have to share priests. In 2008 *The Irish Catholic* newspaper estimated that by 2028 the number in the priesthood would fall to about 1,500. There has also been a decline in attendance at Mass, especially among young people and urban dwellers. In 1999, an IMS survey found that 57 per cent attended Mass and in 2008, according to the International Social Survey Programme, it was down to 43 per cent (and only about 18 per cent of those aged 18 to 24). There are two controversial issues which the Catholic Church may have to address if these trends are to be reversed. The first is clerical celibacy. Ending the prohibition on priests being able to marry, some have argued, could encourage recruitment. The second issue is the ordination of women. The resistance of the Papacy on this issue, argue others, makes the Catholic Church appear out of touch with current attitudes to women's position in society.

This threat of institutional decay has provoked debate within the Church about how it can address the spiritual needs of Irish people as its institutional control has receded. It has been claimed that the Catholic hierarchy has lost the 'moral civil war' and some have argued that a transition is taking place in which clericalism, or power exercised by bishops, is giving way to a church in which the laity should have a greater say. There is an expectation that the Church can become more open, reformers hoping that the modern and the traditional can be accommodated without undermining the Church's spiritual message. Despite the decline in weekly Mass attendance, church-going is still about twice the average for most Western European countries. A socially responsible church, reformers believe, must have something to say to those who do not find spiritual contentment in the material wealth of modern Ireland. This is a mammoth task since clerical authority has been seriously damaged in the past two decades by a series of major scandals. These involved cases of child-sex abuse, the horror of which was compounded by attempts to cover up the evidence or to protect the guilty priests.

Four reports revealed a culture of secrecy. In October 2005, the Ferns Report uncovered child abuse and suppression of evidence in the south-east of Ireland. In May 2009, the Ryan Report revealed the extent of abuse at orphanages and reformatory schools run by religious orders. In November 2009, the Murphy Report detailed clerical child abuse over a 30-year period in the diocese of Dublin. In each case the Church was condemned for its concealment, failure to act and collusion with the police to permit paedophile priests to escape justice. Such was the public outrage that four bishops were compelled to resign. In March 2010 Pope Benedict XVI was obliged to write a pastoral letter to the Irish people in which he conceded that 'grave errors of judgement were made' which challenged the 'credibility and effectiveness' of Catholic leadership. Finally, the Cloyne Report of July 2011 also uncovered falsification of evidence about child abuse. This provoked a diplomatic incident between Rome and the Irish government when the Taoiseach, Enda Kenny, accused the Vatican of putting the reputation of the Church ahead of the children it was supposed to protect.

One of the facts revealed in the Census of 2002 is that the long decline of the Protestant churches in Ireland has been reversed. In the decade since the previous census, Church of Ireland membership had risen by 26,400 to 115,600. In the Census of 2006, this had risen further to 125,585, about 3 per cent of the population. In the same period, Presbyterian membership rose by 7,400 to 23,564 or just over 0.5 per cent of the population. Methodist membership, at 12,160,

TABLE 4.1 Major faith groups in Ireland (2006)

Catholic	3,500,000
Church of Ireland	125,585
Muslim	32,539
Presbyterian	23,564
Orthodox	20,798
Methodist	12,160

Source: Census, 2006, Ireland

had doubled since 1991 though it still constituted only 0.26 per cent of the total population. Together, members of these churches now form 4 per cent of the population.

The overall number of nominal Protestants is likely to be slightly larger, since a proportion of the 6 per cent of 'not stated' or 'no religion' may have a Protestant background. At least one reason for this growth has been immigration which has revived some of the moribund Protestant parishes in Ireland. However, this is only a partial explanation. For instance, many non-Catholic immigrants have established their own so-called migrant-led churches. Recent research by the Irish Inter-Church Meeting has identified 362 such churches and chaplaincies, mainly in the Dublin area but also in most large Irish towns, often sharing premises with established Protestant congregations. There are only about 40 such churches in Northern Ireland, a reflection of its already wide choice of denominational worship and the fact that immigration there has been mainly from Catholic Poland and Lithuania.

However, the fastest-growing church is the Orthodox Church, the membership of which rose from 400 in 1991 to 20,798 in 2006. This may be attributed almost entirely to the influx of immigrants and asylum seekers from Eastern Europe. Immigration is also responsible for the numerical rise in other (so-called) world faiths. The number of Muslims in Ireland increased fivefold between 1991 and 2006 and now stands at 32,539, the third largest religious grouping. In the same period the Hindu community rose from just under 1,000 to 6,082 while the Jewish community has remained stable at about 1,930. These numbers encouraged some to talk of Ireland as a multi-faith society, though the predominance of Christianity, and of the Catholic Church in particular, remains clear (Table 4.1).

Religion in Northern Ireland after 1921

When Northern Ireland was established it had a religious balance of about two-thirds Protestant and one-third Catholic. However, Protestantism in Northern Ireland never had the same homogeneous character as Catholicism in Ireland, being split into a number of denominations both large and small. The variety and energy of these denominations and the vitality of their religious life have made Northern Ireland a distinctive part of the UK as well as a unique part of the island.

The largest Protestant denomination is the Presbyterian Church. Its geographical presence generally matches the extent of Scottish settlement in Ulster during the sixteenth and seventeenth centuries. In the 1926 Census there were 393,000 Presbyterians, just over 31 per cent of Northern Ireland's population. The organization of the Church is not episcopal, or bishop-led, and it reflects the emphasis given to the participant relationship between the congregation and the minister in Presbyterian worship. Though it has an all-Ireland structure, the membership of the Presbyterian Church lies overwhelmingly in Northern Ireland. Indeed, about 30 per cent of its total membership lives in the Belfast area alone. Northern Ireland is organized into 21 Presbyteries with their headquarters in Belfast.

The Church is governed by an annual General Assembly to which every minister and a representative member, or elder, of every congregation on the island is eligible to attend. Its membership, which also includes representatives of women's and youth organizations, is about 1,300. The General Assembly meets for one week each year. The Assembly is responsible for deciding the general policy of the Church and reviews the work of the Assembly's Commissions, Boards and Committees which carry on the day-to-day work of administration. A Moderator, elected for one year, presides over the deliberations of the

PLATE 4.6 The Union Theological College, founded in 1853 in Belfast and initially called the 'Assembly's College' after the General Assembly of the Presbyterian Church in Ireland. It trains students for the ordained ministry as part of the Institute of Theology at the Queen's University, Belfast. © Kirsty McLaren/Alamy

Assembly. The Church permitted women to be elders in 1926 and the Assembly voted for the ordination of women in 1973. Today about 5 per cent of ministers are women. Presbyterian numbers in Northern Ireland remained relatively stable, though from the 1970s onward there began a slow decline. In 1971 there were 406,000 or 26.5 per cent of the population. In 2001 there were 348,742, slightly less than 21 per cent of the population.

The second largest Protestant denomination is the Church of Ireland. In 1926 it had a membership in Northern Ireland of 338,000 or 27 per cent of the population. Though again the Church is all-Ireland in its organization, this figure represented three-quarters of its total membership. The main geographical strength of the Church of Ireland lies in the Belfast area and in the counties of Antrim and Down, though there is also a substantial community in Co. Fermanagh. The Church has two Provinces, Armagh and Dublin. Each has an archbishop and the Primate of All Ireland remains the Archbishop of Armagh. There are 12 dioceses, 7 in the Province of Armagh and 5 in the Province of Dublin, which are subdivided into 466 parishes.

While the Church of Ireland is episcopal, the laity also plays an important role. Members have a say in the election of bishops, except the Archbishop of Armagh who is elected by bishops only, and also in deciding the policy of the Church. Each diocese has its own synod under the presidency of its bishop or archbishop, on which both lay and clerical members serve. The diocesan synod elects clerical and lay members to the General Synod. The General Synod is the supreme authority of the Church and it is divided into two Houses. These are the House of Bishops with 12 members and the House of Representatives with 432 lay members and 216 clergy. The President of the General Synod is the Archbishop of Armagh. A Standing Committee, comprising 71 members and chaired by the Archbishop, is responsible for ensuring that the decisions of the General Synod are carried out. Decisions can be made only if both laity and clergy agree and, though the House of Bishops has a veto, this has never been used. The General Synod legislated for the ordination of female priests in 1990, making the Church of Ireland the first member Church of the Anglican Communion in Europe to take this step. Membership of the Church of Ireland has followed a similar pattern to that of the Presbyterian Church. Numbers in Northern Ireland remained relatively stable until the 1970s when a slow decline became noticeable. In 1971 numbers stood at 334,318 or 22 per cent of the population. In 2001 they stood at 257,788 or 17.6 per cent.

The third largest Protestant denomination is the Methodist Church. Methodist congregations in a local area form a 'circuit'. There are 75 Methodist circuits in Ireland organized into eight geographical districts. The governing body of the Church is the Annual Conference, presided over by the elected President of the Methodist Church in Ireland. Again, the vast majority of Methodists live in Northern Ireland and the Methodist College in Belfast is a respected and high-achieving school. In 1926 there were 49,000 Methodists or 4 per cent of the population. Numbers rose steadily to 72,000 or 5 per cent in the 1960s, falling to just under 60,000 or 3.5 per cent in 2001.

Other Protestant denominations, such as the Baptist Union of Ireland (19,000) and Free Presbyterian Church (12,000), founded by the Reverend Ian Paisley in 1951, also have a majority of their members in Northern Ireland, contributing to its distinctive religious and social character. Together with Pentecostal and other small denominations they constitute about 6 per cent of the population.

The Catholic Church within Northern Ireland finds itself a minority on an island in which it has an overwhelming majority. Its northern Province has six dioceses, some of which overlap the Irish border. Even in Northern Ireland, the Church has the largest membership of all Christian denominations. In 1926 it numbered 420,000 or 33.5 per cent of the population. Despite a higher rate of emigration among Catholics and despite Catholic complaints of religious discrimination by the Unionist government, Church membership has grown steadily. This contrasted with the experience of Protestant communities on the other side of the border. In 1971 there were 562,000 Catholics, constituting nearly 37 per cent of the population. By 1991 this number had risen to 605,639 or 38 per cent. In 2001, this figure was 678,462 or about 41 per cent.

For most of the history of Northern Ireland, there was little dialogue or even contact between Protestant and Catholic clergy. Differences in doctrine were compounded by very different attitudes to politics. If many Catholics believed Protestantism to be heretical, many Protestants believed Catholicism to be in error. There was little popular interest in ecumenism, or the union of Christian churches. Sectarian attitudes and bigotry were common but each community tended to believe that the other side was mainly responsible. For many Catholics, Northern Ireland had been constituted as a Protestant state and sectarianism would only be overcome in a politically united Ireland. Most Protestants believed that a politically united Ireland would mean their decline on the same pattern as co-religionists across the border.

The political violence after 1969 accentuated religious divisions in Northern Ireland. While attacks on churches or church premises did happen, they were not common. When they did happen, such acts prompted condemnation on all sides. However, Republican murders of security force personnel, who were mainly Protestant, and destruction of Protestant businesses meant that it was difficult for Protestant congregations to build understanding with their Catholic counterparts. Loyalist murders of Catholics and their attacks on Catholic property had a similar effect. Protestant and Catholic clergy were often expected to express the anger of their respective communities rather than to promote Christian forgiveness.

The Churches were unable to avoid becoming bound up at times in the controversies of the Troubles. For example, the Catholic Church, despite its opposition to violence, found it difficult to maintain its distance from those members who were involved in the IRA. It faced a particular problem when

TABLE 4.2 Major faith groups in Northern Ireland (2001)	
Catholic	678,462
Presbyterian	348,742
Church of Ireland	257,788
Methodist	60,000
Source: Census, 2001, Northern Ireland	

it came to funerals of IRA members that were accompanied by displays of paramilitary symbolism. The Church of Ireland was also embarrassed by the violent confrontations that took place from the mid-1990s at Drumcree near Portadown. These were caused by the inability of neighbouring Catholic residents and the Orange Order to agree on the route of a traditional Orange parade from the parish church. In both cases, the churches tried to negotiate compromise solutions. The Free Presbyterian Church, of course, was intimately associated with the Democratic Unionist Party led by the Reverend Ian Paisley.

Nevertheless, the past 30 years has witnessed an unparalleled expansion of cross-community, inter-faith and ecumenical organizations. The Corrymeela Community, founded in 1965 to promote good relations between Protestants and Catholics, has now been joined by groups such as the Centre for Contemporary Christianity Ireland and the Faith and Politics Group. The Community Relations Council (CRC), which receives most of its funding from the government, helps to fund faith and community groups in their reconciliation work. The emphasis of the Irish Council of Churches (ICC) has also been peace and reconciliation work, often in cooperation with the Northern Ireland Catholic Council on Social Affairs (NICCOSA). Attention has been focused on producing materials for schools and the Churches' Peace Education Programme has been established in recent years to promote better understanding between young people of different denominations. Leaders of the main churches now meet regularly and there have been inter-church discussions on a range of sensitive religious, political and cultural issues. For example, in 2002 the Church of Ireland and the Methodist Church agreed to work more closely together. Greater under-standing, however, has not brought any nearer the distant prospect of Christian unity (Table 4.2).

Religion in Northern Ireland today

Calculations based on the 2001 Census in Northern Ireland reveal the current religious balance to be about 40.26 per cent Catholic and 45.57 per cent Protestant. Fourteen per cent stated 'no religion'. This statement of religion does not refer to active church membership. Indeed, the evidence in Northern Ireland, as across the border, points to increasing secularization. Some argue that the growing percentage of those who refuse to state a religion suggests the emergence of a 'third community', neither Protestant nor Catholic, but entirely secular in outlook. A *Northern Ireland Life and Times* research paper in 2004 suggested that the 'no religion' category could soon claim equal status with Catholicism and Protestantism. Those most likely to profess no religion at all live in the Belfast area and tend to reside in predominantly Protestant districts. Young people and men are more likely than older people and women to state that they have no religion.

Traditionally, Catholics have had a higher birth rate than Protestants. This continues to be the case, although the evidence suggests that increasing affluence, as elsewhere in Ireland, has encouraged a trend among Catholics for smaller families. There appears now to be a convergence in birth rates for all denominations and a best guess would be a possible equalization of numbers around the mid-twenty-first century. Church attendance continues to be higher among Catholics (two-thirds saying they attend weekly) than Protestants (half of Presbyterians and one-third of Church of Ireland) but both attend more regularly than elsewhere in the UK. In Northern Ireland 45 per cent of the population claim to attend 'regularly' compared with 18 per cent in Scotland and 12 per cent in England.

Though there has been a considerable effort to improve community relations in Northern Ireland, traditional religious attitudes have been slow to change. Opinion on many issues remains conservative. Social gatherings have become more common but shared worship between Protestants and Catholics remains limited. Mixed marriage too remains unusual even though the Catholic Church has significantly moderated its position on *Ne Temere*. It is difficult to gauge figures accurately but marriages between Catholic and Protestant partners today is probably about 10 per cent of all marriages. Surveys suggest that mixed marriage is marginally more acceptable to Catholics than to Protestants. Though it is beginning to diminish, there is still something of a taboo attached to marrying outside one's religious community. Recent research has also shown that this attitude is more likely to be the case (understandably so, perhaps) where sectarian conflict has been at its bitterest over the past 30 years.

A dedicated support group, the Northern Ireland Mixed Marriage Association (NIMMA), exists to help couples deal with the challenges. One institutional attempt to erode the barriers between Catholics and Protestants has been the move to establish integrated schooling. Even here progress has been slow. There are currently 61 integrated schools with about 16,000 pupils. This constitutes only 5 per cent of those of school age, though an Omnibus Survey by Millward Brown Ulster in 2008 showed that 43 per cent of adults were prepared to send their children to an integrated school.

There are only very small numbers of those who profess world faiths in Northern Ireland. Together they constitute about 0.3 per cent of the total population. There has not been the same level of immigration experienced elsewhere in the UK or more recently in Ireland. Though the UK has one of the largest Jewish populations in Europe (283,000), in Northern Ireland there are only about 350 Jews. Muslims, by contrast, have doubled in number from 1,000 in 1991 to 2,000 according to the Census of 2001.

Attitudes to religion

The relationship between religion and public morality is a complex one. Because society in both jurisdictions in Ireland has changed significantly in the past 50 years, it is easy to attribute changes in public morality to the advance of secularism. This term can mean a number of things. It can mean, first, that religious faith is no longer intimately associated with the institutions of the state. It can mean, second, that economic prosperity, private affluence and the professionalization of education, health and welfare provision diminish the role of religion in both public and private life. Both of these meanings apply in both parts of Ireland and help to explain new social realities. Polls show that there is a generational factor at work. Younger people are more likely to have relaxed attitudes about issues such as divorce, abortion and homosexuality than older people and also to be more apathetic about church attendance. However, the more radical meaning of secularization – that people feel no need for religion at all – does not conform to the evidence.

Religion remains a vital element in society on both sides of the border. In comparative European terms, Protestants and Catholics express their beliefs with a distinctive intensity. While attendance at church may be falling, the polls confirm that religious values such as belief in God, heaven and hell, sin and salvation, are still quite deeply held. There is a noticeable trend, however, that is common to most other parts of Europe and North America towards distinguishing institutional observance from personal morality. For example, a *MRBI* survey in 2001 in Ireland found that though 76 per cent thought that religion was an important factor in their lives, on moral issues people were less willing to accept established Catholic teaching. The Catholic Church, in other words, appears to be losing influence in that area where it once concentrated its efforts – the family. Whereas the Catholic Church used to be able to rely on its authority in such matters, its challenge today is to persuade by moral reasoning, made all the more difficult owing to recent scandals.

This is a challenge for all churches, of course, and the difficulty they find is receiving a hearing in a media market crowded with other messages. There exist today organizations which attempt to encourage dialogue and understanding between the churches despite profound doctrinal differences. Most Protestant denominations are members of the Irish Council of Churches (ICC) which exists to promote a common spiritual life and common effort in various social matters.

There is an Irish Inter-Church Meeting (IICM), coordinating contacts between the ICC and the Catholic Church, which meets about every 18 months.

In Northern Ireland, relations between Protestants and Catholics have been the central issue. The popular image of this relationship has been one of conflict. This image of violence is a distortion of reality, since the relationship between Catholics and Protestants is rather one of separation. Individual Catholics and Protestants, of course, meet and engage with one another daily but collectively they tend to live apart. Traditionally, there has been a culture of minimizing social contact, further entrenched as a result of political violence.

In 2003, the *Northern Ireland Young Life and Times Survey* measured religious attitudes among Catholic and Protestant 16-year-olds. Like their counterparts in Ireland, 87 per cent of young people saw themselves as belonging to a particular religion and 59 per cent said that their religious identity was important to them, though this did not necessarily mean that they attended church on a regular basis. Only 10 per cent were willing to admit that they disliked members of the other religion. On the other hand, nearly 50 per cent of respondents said that they felt 'neither favourable nor unfavourable' towards the other side, hardly a positive attitude to reconciliation. The survey also found that social contact was limited. Nearly 90 per cent of young people attended single-religion schools and 65 per cent lived in residential areas that were almost exclusively of one religion. Twenty per cent said that they never socialized at all with members of the other religion. Fifty per cent did so sometimes but not regularly. In a similar survey in 2009, 56 per cent of those aged 18 to 24 said that most or all of their friends were of the same religion as themselves. While there was support for greater contact and better relations between the religious communities, more young people believed that things would stay the same (42 per cent) than that they would improve (36 per cent). Fifteen per cent actually believed they would get worse. The picture this paints is of a society that remains communally divided, even among young people with little or no experience of the violence of the Troubles between 1969 and 1994.

Secularization provides a test for the Churches in both parts of Ireland. It also provides them with continuing opportunities. On the one hand, levels of ignorance among the young were investigated by an Iona Institute/Evangelical Alliance poll in 2007 which showed that basic religious knowledge among those aged 16 to 24 (for example, being able to name the First Commandment) had halved in a generation. There also appears to be little that can be done in the short term to arrest the culture of materialism and individualism which defines contemporary society. On the other hand, one spark of hope may be found in the *Northern Ireland Life and Times Survey* of 2008 where 69 per cent of all respondents say they believe in the existence of God and the figure for those aged 18 to 24 was still 60 per cent. Thus there is no insuperable obstacle to religious faith being made relevant in contemporary conditions, especially since most people in Ireland, wherever they live, continue to say that it is important to them.

Exercises

Explain and examine the following terms:

St Patrick	Penal Laws	Act of Supremacy
Ne Temere Decree	Mother and Child controversy	Christian Brothers
Armagh	primatial	disestablishment
Reformation	ecumenical	congregation
Anglican	episcopal	presbytery
bigotry	secularism	mixed marriage
Irish Council of Churches	integrated schools	General Synod
clerical celibacy	special position of Catholic Church	ordination

Write short essays on the following topics:

1   What were the consequences of the Reformation in Ireland?

2   Discuss the role of the Catholic Church in Irish life.

3   What role does religion play in divisions in Northern Ireland?

4   What are the common problems facing churches today in both parts of the island?

Further reading

Bailey, S. (2008) *Presbyterians in Ireland: Identity in the Twenty-first Century* Basingstoke: Palgrave Macmillan

Crawford, H. (2010) *Outside the Glow: Protestants and Irishness in Independent Ireland* Dublin: University College Dublin Press

Elliott, M. (2002) *The Catholics of Ulster* London: Basic Books

Elliott, M. (2009) *When God Took Sides: Religion and Identity in Ireland – Unfinished History* Oxford: Oxford University Press

Hempton, D. (1996) *Religion and Political Culture in Britain and Ireland: From the Glorious Revolution to the Decline of Empire* Cambridge: Cambridge University Press

McDonagh, E. and Mackey, J. (2002) *Religion and Politics in Ireland* Dublin: Columba Press

Websites

Catholic Church http://www.catholicireland.net/
Church of Ireland http://www.ireland.anglican.org/
Irish Council of Churches http://www.irishchurches.org/
Judaism http://www.jewishireland.org/
Methodist Church http://www.irishmethodist.org/
Muslims http://islamireland.ie/
Presbyterian Church http://www.presbyterianireland.org/

5

Cultural contexts

- ■ Language
- ■ Literature
- ■ The arts
- ■ Sports
- ■ Culture in Ireland
- ■ Culture in Northern Ireland
- ■ *Exercises*
- ■ *Further reading*
- ■ *Websites*

Ireland's cultural history has been conditioned by geography, politics, religion, wealth and poverty, invasions, migration, a conflict-ridden relationship with Britain and partition in 1921. There have been many divisions, such as those between rural and urban areas; Catholics and Protestants; Unionists, Nationalists and Republicans; Irish and English speakers; warring tribes and regions; indigenous populations and immigrants; different social classes; northern and southern parts of the island from 1921; and travellers and settled communities.

Economic improvement, government spending and corporate sponsorship in the twentieth and twenty-first centuries resulted in more cultural opportunities. People now attend or participate in a range of cultural events, hobbies, sports and physical activities. Some are traditional pastimes and others are new, but economic downturns and spending cuts can affect many people's ability to enjoy such opportunities. Different cultural activities contribute to the island's social fabric or civilization, which may be defined representatively as 'a whole way of life' (coined by Raymond Williams), rather than a simple opposition between high (elite) or low (popular) culture.

After periods of neglect, cultural diversity is now more actively promoted in Ireland through government departments, such as the Department of Arts, Heritage and the Gaeltacht and agencies such as Culture Ireland. The counterpart in Northern Ireland is the Department of Culture, Arts and Leisure. Their titles and mission statements suggest a traditional high culture emphasis, such as art, heritage, crafts, dance, design, festivals, film, literature, music, performing arts, photography, theatre, visual arts, museums, galleries, archives, concerts and opera. But these public bodies do debate the meaning of 'culture' at national and international levels and their current programmes include more popular and grass-roots forms.

An ARK *Northern Ireland Life and Times Survey* in 2001 asked respondents what activities they associated with 'culture'. The following proportional results (which could also arguably be applicable to Ireland) were: arts/theatre/museums/ music/dance/books/painting (283); opera/ballet (43); tradition and beliefs (42); Irish dancing/music (39); personal history/ancestors/heritage (35); religion (26); marching/Twelfth (of July) marches (23); sports (16); history (14); livelihood (13); Irish heritage/history (13); Irish culture (12); traditional music/arts/crafts/ dance (12); and different people/backgrounds (11). A majority of respondents (283, 43, 42, 39 and 35) appeared to support traditional ideas of 'culture' but there was also evidence of wider activities, such as livelihoods, different people/ backgrounds and sports.

More personal responses to what constitutes 'culture' (and an ability to discriminate between types) were shown when Northern Irish respondents were asked whether they would regard the following activities as 'cultural': visiting a museum (Yes 77 per cent, No 14 per cent); going to the theatre (66/20); visiting an attraction like the Giant's Causeway (71/24); going to the cinema (21/62/depends what it's about 12); visiting the W5 (mixed) entertainment centre at the Odyssey in Belfast (26/53/depends what it's about 5); going to a play in a local community centre (46/38/depends what it's about 12).

Language

The Irish and English languages have historically been controversial elements in Irish life and influence literature, drama, songs, conversation and political debate. Assuming the continuing central role of English, the questions for Northern Ireland and Ireland (and their politicians) are how widely and fluently Irish is used and whether it will grow or decline.

Article 8 of the 1937 Constitution of Ireland states that Irish is the first official language of Ireland and English is the state's second official language. The latter (Hiberno-English) is an Irish-, plantation- and Cromwellian-influenced dialect of English with distinctive regional characteristics and is the most widely spoken language in the island. About 40.8 per cent of people in Ireland and 10 per cent of people in Northern Ireland claim to speak Irish to varying degrees. Irish evolved from the Gaelic or Goidelic branch of the Celtic languages and is related to Scottish Gaelic, Manx, Welsh, Cornish and Breton. It probably arrived in Ireland during Celtic migrations between 600 and 100 BC. Shelta (a mixture of Irish, Romany and English spoken by travellers), immigrant languages and Ulster Scots in some Northern Irish Unionist communities are also spoken.

The earliest written language form is Primitive Irish Ogham inscriptions scored on stone and wood monuments, which date from the fifth to the seventh centuries AD. This was replaced as the common vernacular language by Old Irish, which is evidenced in written form in the sixth century as glosses in Latin manuscripts after Irish conversion to Christianity. It was the language of Ireland's Golden Age between AD 700 and 850; the simplified language of the late Viking and post-Viking period; and evolved into Middle Irish during the tenth century.

Viking settlements from AD 795 and Anglo-Norman colonization from AD 1169 introduced linguistic diversity (Scandinavian dialects, Norman-French and English), but Middle Irish was used by most of the population. By 1200, Early Modern Irish emerged when Middle Irish, Norse, Norman-French and Old English were assimilated by an Irish-speaking society. It survived from the thirteenth to the sixteenth century as the common language for Ireland, Scotland and the Isle of Man, and later developed into Modern Irish, Scots Gaelic and Manx.

PLATE 5.1 Beginning of Breves Causae of Matthew in the *Book of Kells,* an eighth-century illuminated manuscript held by Trinity College Library, Dublin. © Ancient Art & Architecture Collection Ltd/Alamy

Most of the Irish population was Irish speaking until the nineteenth century, although the large towns used English for administrative and legal purposes. However, political events in the sixteenth and seventeenth centuries, such as the Tudor and Stuart conquests (1534–1610), the Cromwellian settlement (1654), the Williamite war (1689–1691) and the Penal Laws (1695), weakened the positions of Irish, Irish speakers and their cultural institutions. They were replaced by an Anglo-Irish ascendancy and English became the language of government and civic life, although Irish was still spoken by most rural people and some urban workers. English also increased its hold because many Irish-born authors wrote in English; the Penal Laws were gradually relaxed from the 1750s; greater social and economic mobility became available to the Irish; and affluent Irish speakers adopted English and middle-class habits. The Irish language was consequently associated with poverty and social exclusion.

Ironically, rural population growth increased the number of Irish speakers in the early nineteenth century and some four million people spoke Irish in 1835. But poor rural dwellers and Irish were seriously weakened by the famines of the 1840s, deaths and mass emigration. By the 1891 Census, the number of Irish speakers had declined to 680,000; 85 per cent of the population spoke only English; and some 3.5 per cent of children under 10 spoke Irish.

The Irish language also suffered in 1831 when the British government introduced an English-speaking (primary) National School system, in which Irish was prohibited. The English language influenced institutions, education, trade, business and newspapers; and parents discouraged their children from speaking Irish.

However, attitudes had changed as linguistic and political nationalism spread through Europe in the late eighteenth century. Irish Protestants such as William Neilson were interested in Irish and its literature; there was more study in the nineteenth century of Gaelic culture; and Irish language-related activity grew. Further progress was made when the Gaelic League (Conradh na Gaelige) was established in 1893 by the Protestant Douglas Hyde (later the first President of Ireland) and Eoin MacNeill, which arguably started the Gaelic Revival and aimed to promote Irish as the spoken language of the country.

Hyde planned to restore Ireland as an independent nation and to remove the influences of English sport, literature and institutions. Irish was seen as a unifying rather than a divisive force, which could neutralize religion and promote national identity. Interest in Irish culture coincided with other cultural revivals, such as the creation of the Gaelic Athletic Association (GAA), the production of plays about Ireland in English by writers such as W.B. Yeats, J.M. Synge, Sean O'Casey and Lady Gregory, and the founding of the Abbey Theatre in Dublin. Irish also influenced the English of authors such as George Bernard Shaw and Oscar Wilde.

The Gaelic League was successful in connecting the language, Irishness and the separatist political movement. It initially had broad class, political and apolitical support and Irish became important in education. In 1903 1,300 National Schools taught Irish; in 1909 it became a compulsory subject; and by 1915 there were 3,000 qualified teachers of Irish. In spite of its minority position today, the survival of Irish was arguably partly due to the Gaelic League and similar groups, although they failed to create a fully Irish-speaking nation.

PLATE 5.2 Douglas Hyde (1860–1949), linguist, scholar, co-founder of the Gaelic League and first President of Ireland from 1938. © Steppenwolf/Alamy

The Irish language influenced education policy in 1921. The newly independent government argued that the state should become Irish speaking; introduced compulsory Irish at school; and required its knowledge for employment in the civil service. Critics maintained that these measures were counter-productive, lacked popular support, and alienated children and adults who refused to use the language after leaving school. It was alleged that Irish and Gaeltacht areas declined owing to inadequate government policies in the twentieth century.

In a much later effort to address the continuing problem of Irish language usage, the Official Languages Act, 2003 stipulated that Irish government publications be published in both Irish and English. The office of the Official Languages Commissioner was supposed to ensure equal treatment for both languages, but there were weaknesses in the application of the Act, such as a poor general knowledge of Irish. Attempts have been made to support Irish through media, such as Raidió na Gaeltachta (Gaeltacht Radio) and Telefís na Gaeilge (Irish Language Television), now renamed TG4, with limited success. But literature in Irish survived and Irish continued to have an influence on Ireland's cultural identity.

There are still debates about whether (and how) the Irish government should actively encourage the language beyond its status as a school subject at primary and secondary levels. It has initiated a 20-year strategy for the Irish language (2010–2030) which aims to increase the numbers using Irish on a daily basis outside the education system to 250,000. In 2006, it had affirmed its support for the development and preservation of Irish and the Gaeltacht through the Department of Arts, Culture and the Gaeltacht and statutory bodies.

However, censuses and surveys indicate a decline in the use of Irish. According to the 2006 Census, 1.66 million persons (40.8 per cent of the population, compared with 42.8 per cent in a 2002 survey by the Department of Community, Rural and Gaeltacht Affairs) over the age of 3 defined themselves as Irish speakers. (In 2002, an Irish speaker was defined as a person who claimed to speak Irish, but who did not necessarily use it in daily life.) In 2006, more women (45.3 per cent) than men (38.4 per cent) were able to speak Irish. Some 485,000 (29.3 per cent) persons said that they spoke Irish on a daily basis within the education system, while a further 53,500 (3.3 per cent) spoke it on a daily basis outside the education system.

The school-going age groups (5 to 19 years) accounted for 80 per cent of the daily speakers in 2006 compared with 76.8 per cent in 2002. Coincidently, there had been a growth in Irish-medium schools (Gaelscoileanna) at primary and secondary levels in both Ireland and Northern Ireland from 16 in 1972 to some 200 in 2006. However, the 2006 Census pointed out that language ability declines in the immediate post-education age group; recovers for the 45- to 54-year age group; but declines again after age 54.

The Gaeltacht areas cover Co. Waterford, Co. Cork, Co. Galway, Co. Kerry, Co. Donegal, Co. Mayo, Co. Meath and Galway City. Irish speakers represented 70.8 per cent of the population aged 3 years and over within these areas in 2006, reduced from 72.6 per cent in 2002. Fifty-seven per cent of Irish speakers in these areas speak Irish on a daily basis and a further 10.2 per cent on a weekly basis. Some 23 per cent speak Irish less frequently than weekly, while 6.7 per cent had never spoken the language, but critics argue that accurately determining the fluency of Gaeltacht Irish speakers and its extent is problematic.

The language situation in Northern Ireland is reflected in divisions between Unionist and Nationalist communities. Irish has been regarded with suspicion by Unionists who have associated it with a Catholic-dominated Ireland in the south, and lately with Republicanism in Northern Ireland. The language was marginalized; was not taught in Protestant schools; and public signs in Irish were prohibited by the Northern Ireland Parliament until the early 1990s.

In Nationalist communities, an interest in Irish resulted in the establishment of a network of Irish-medium schools, which had been founded in Belfast and Londonderry/Derry by community action. In addition, there was a short-lived Irish-language Belfast newspaper *Lá Nua* (New Day) until 2008; BBC Radio Ulster broadcast a half-hour programme in Irish in the 1980s called *Blas* (Taste); and BBC Northern Ireland showed its first TV programme in the language in the early 1990s.

The 2001 Census reported that 167,487 people (10.4 per cent of the Northern Ireland population) had 'some knowledge of Irish' with the highest concentrations of Irish speakers being in Belfast, Londonderry/Derry, Newry/South Armagh, Central Tyrone (between Dungannon and Omagh) and southern Co. Londonderry (near Maghera): 154,622 were Catholics and 10, 987 were Protestants and 'other Christians'. Most Irish speakers in Northern Ireland speak the Donegal dialect of Ulster Irish. Irish received official recognition in Northern Ireland for the first time in 1998 under the Good Friday (Belfast) Agreement and policy for Irish-medium education is overseen by the Department of Education.

Literature

Ireland has contributed much to literature in English and has particularly influenced English literature. Literature in Irish is the third oldest in Europe (after Greek and Latin) and has substantial written and oral traditions. Both languages are central to Irish cultural history.

Although literacy was probably not widespread in the general population, the arrival of a Latin-based Christianity from the third to the fifth centuries led to a more literate society. The earliest written literature in Old Irish was in manuscript form; dates from the sixth and seventh centuries; and was poetry or prose based on ancient tales and myths. The major early work consisted of four prose sagas or cycles. The Ulster Cycle contains stories about the Ulaid people (and their leader Cú Chulainn) of Ulster and their conflicts with Connaught. The Fenian Cycle covered the regions of Munster and Leinster, and recounts the adventures of Fionn ma Cumhaill (Finn MacCool) and his warriors, the Fianna.

However, Classical Irish poetry became the main literary vehicle in the medieval period rather than prose. Literary form and style were taught in the bardic schools, which produced historians, lawyers and poets who depended on aristocratic patronage. Twelfth-century Anglo-Norman invasions introduced new stories and translations were made from English into Irish. Printing was introduced in Dublin in 1551, but works in Irish were still written in manuscript form.

By the seventeenth century, there was greater English control over Ireland, the Gaelic aristocracy was suppressed and writers lost their patrons. Poetry was still the dominant medium, but its classical forms were replaced in the eighteenth century by more popular styles written for local audiences. Such works were available in print by the nineteenth century, but cheaply produced manuscripts were also copied for an expanding market.

In the nineteenth century, English gradually became the main language. A decline in Irish followed the famines of the 1840s as Irish speakers died or emigrated. Hedge schools (pay schools) provided basic education for children and maintained an Irish native culture, but they were replaced by National Schools in 1831 with obligatory English teaching. Although the English-speaking middle classes became the central cultural force, Ireland's literature and the Irish language have historically benefited from immigration and the Latin, Norman-French, Scottish and English languages. Similarly, during the eighteenth and nineteenth centuries, Irish usage was absorbed into English and influenced literature in English by Irish writers.

In the early twentieth century, some Irish writers felt that the traditional styles of Modern Irish should still be used for literature. But others, such as Patrick Pearse, objected to the old modes. They were influenced by the Gaelic League and successfully argued (implemented in 1945 and 1953) that Irish should incorporate contemporary culture and usage. Irish literature after the Second World War was produced by new poets, novelists and dramatists, and from the 1970s younger writers in Irish attracted an urban readership with edgier themes and styles.

Literature in English by Irish authors has influenced English literature for centuries. Ireland produced writers in English such as satirist Jonathan Swift, Irish-born poet Oliver Goldsmith, Maria Edgeworth (an Ireland-based developer of the realist novel), political theorist Edmund Burke, novelist George Augustus Moore, dramatists Oscar Wilde, Sean O'Casey, J.M. Synge and George Bernard Shaw, poet William Butler Yeats (with Shaw, a Nobel Prize winner), and modern prose writers, such as the influential James Joyce (author of *Ulysses*, 1922), Liam O'Flaherty, Frank O'Connor, Sean O'Faolain and Flann O'Brien.

Many of the earlier writers lived and worked in England and Europe, and had a considerable cross-cultural experience, whether due to a negative reaction to Irish life, career choices or preference. However, the growth of Irish cultural nationalism towards the end of the nineteenth century culminated in the Gaelic Revival and a literary renaissance. Irish nationalists revived traditional Gaelic culture in language, literature, music and dance. W.B. Yeats and John O'Leary used nationalist ideals, literature and legend in the model of a cultural and political nation, which would provide an Irish identity and a quality national literature. Between 1886 and the 1920s, Yeats revived Irish legends and folklore with Synge, Lady Augusta Gregory and Douglas Hyde. Cultural revivalism also included a political dimension, which was linked to the struggle for independence in the early twentieth century.

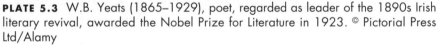

PLATE 5.3 W.B. Yeats (1865–1929), poet, regarded as leader of the 1890s Irish literary revival, awarded the Nobel Prize for Literature in 1923. © Pictorial Press Ltd/Alamy

Later Irish writers in English included Nobel Prize winner (1969), novelist and dramatist Samuel Beckett, who was succeeded by Patrick Kavanagh, Brian Coffey, Paul Durcan and John Montague, and in the 1960s by Eavan Boland and Brendan Kennelly. These writers had universal themes, but some have also examined an Ireland which had developed from rural provincialism to a modern society with greater social inequality, poverty, deprivation, problematic identities, intolerance, increased crime and economic difficulties. Authors such as Edna O'Brien, John McGahern, Roddy Doyle, Dermot Bolger, Colm Tóibín, Éllís Ni Dhuibhne, Dermot Healy and William Trevor gained international reputations and have written about changing values and attitudes in Irish society; the relationship between Ireland and Northern Ireland; and the gap between myth and reality.

In Northern Ireland, poets, playwrights and writers in English have also achieved international recognition, such as Belfast-born C.S. Lewis, with his children's classic *The Chronicles of Narnia*, and the Brontë family, who migrated to England from Co. Down in 1820. The Nobel laureate (1995) Seamus Heaney and poets such as Paul Muldoon, Tom Paulin, Mebdh McGuckian, Derek Mahon and Michael Longley have well-established reputations, as have playwrights Brian Friel and Tom Murphy and novelists Brian Moore, Bernard Mac Laverty and Robert MacLiam Wilson. Some poets have been influenced by Old Irish seventh- and eighth-century epics, and Heaney has translated the twelfth-century Irish poem *Buile Suibhne* ('The Frenzy of Suibhne'/Sweeney) and the Old English *Beowulf*. Northern Irish writers have written about the Troubles since the 1970s and identities in a divided society.

Irish dramatists and plays occupy particular places in literary history and were involved in the literary revival of the late nineteenth century. The early tradition in English consisted of William Congreve in the seventeenth century and Oliver Goldsmith and Richard Brinsley Sheridan in the eighteenth century. They were followed in the nineteenth to twentieth centuries by Oscar Wilde, J.M. Synge, G.B. Shaw, Samuel Beckett, Sean O'Casey, Brian Friel, Sebastian Barry and Billy Roche.

In 1899, Yeats co-founded the Irish Literary Theatre with Lady Gregory and Edward Martyn to present plays of national idealism by Synge and others. The company was renamed the National Theatre Society and moved in 1904 to a

PLATE 5.4 Seamus Heaney (1939–) author, writer, lecturer, poet, awarded the Nobel Prize for Literature in 1995. © jeremy sutton-hibbert/Alamy

music-hall in Abbey Street, Dublin, later known as the Abbey Theatre, which produced Irish national drama. The Abbey Theatre was rebuilt in the mid-1960s and stages classic Irish plays, as well as new works in Irish and English. Dublin's other main theatre, the Gate, was founded in 1928, introduced European plays to Dublin, and now produces Irish and international drama, while the Peacock Theatre, incorporated into the Abbey building, concentrates on experimental plays and works in Irish. There are other small theatres in Dublin, such as the Focus Theatre with its Irish, European and experimental offerings. Theatres and theatre companies are also found outside the capital and provide a range of national and international drama. Galway's Druid Theatre, which performs plays in Irish, is a prominent provincial company and there is an active amateur dramatic movement around the country.

There was no conventional Irish theatre before the twentieth century, but the writing of Irish plays was encouraged by the literary revival and the founding of a theatre (An Taibhdhearc) in 1928, which focused on Irish-language plays. The Abbey Theatre became a bilingual theatre in the 1940s, but Irish-language drama has declined. It lacks funding, big audiences and professional support, although small Irish theatre groups are still working.

The literary revivalists were successful in creating a new, significant national literature. But some critics argue that their high culture and Dublin-based emphasis generally appealed to an educated and intellectual audience and did not

PLATE 5.5 The Grand Opera House (Belfast 1895) has had an eventful history. It has offered variety theatre, music-hall, farce, dance, drama, opera, comedy, musicals, pantomime and family shows. © Tibor Bognar/Alamy

present new European drama. It is suggested that many Irish people were more interested in popular and light-hearted forms of entertainment, such as music-halls, variety theatre and dance clubs. The Abbey Theatre struggled financially until it was subsidized by the Irish Free State in 1924. Nevertheless, the revivalists influenced Nationalists' vision of Ireland as an ancient nation and culture, and they gained global recognition for Irish literature and drama.

Northern Ireland in the early twentieth century did not have a significant literary or artistic reputation. However, the Ulster Literary Theatre (founded in 1902) attracted Catholic and Protestant writers into the literary revival movement and produced folk drama, farce and political satire with lively Ulster themes until it closed in 1934. The Grand Opera House (1895) offered a base for drama and opera production, in addition to popular variety theatre and music-hall. The annual Belfast Festival began in the early 1960s and is a major cultural event, with many varied arts offerings such as literature and drama; and the community West Belfast Festival (1988) offered alternative views to the Troubles. The Waterfront Hall (1997) is a major arts venue in the centre of Belfast. Londonderry/Derry has the influential Field Day Theatre Company, founded in 1980 by international artists such as Seamus Heaney, dramatist Brian Friel, novelist Seamus Deane and actor Stephen Rea.

The arts

The arts have a wide appeal in Ireland and Northern Ireland. Some reflect traditional high culture and others cover aspects of popular culture. They may be self-supporting or receive state grants, lottery funding, corporate sponsorship and public subscriptions.

Music and dance

Ireland has a long musical tradition. The oldest musical instruments are arguably the bodhran (goatskin drum, possibly of Celtic or African origin) and the Irish frame harp, which dates from the tenth century. Irish harpers were known in Europe from the twelfth century and some of their songs have survived. Other instruments appeared later, such as the uilleann pipes (Irish union pipe or bag-pipes), fiddle and four-string Irish banjo (derived from the United States in the nineteenth century).

Ireland's popular music was once seen as culturally distinct from its classical styles and reflected a high and low culture division. In the classical field, Belfast-born John Field was the first Irish composer to develop an international reputation in the early nineteenth century; composer Michael William Balfe wrote operas, such as *The Bohemian Girl* (1843); John McCormack (1884–1945) became a popular and successful operatic and concert tenor; and annual festivals like the Wexford Opera Festival today attract international visitors. The National Symphony Orchestra and the RTÉ Concert Orchestra in Dublin are maintained by the public service broadcaster Radio Telefís Éireann (RTÉ), and are Ireland's main orchestras.

Irish songs had a European audience in the nineteenth to twentieth centuries, and the music which Irish emigrants took to the United States following the 1840s famines contributed to American folk and country music in New York, Boston and Chicago. Traditional Irish music became politically and culturally influential during the linguistic and literary revivals and was connected to notions of national identity and folk history.

Irish society modernized and responded to consumer pressures and international influences in the mid-twentieth century. Music in urban areas became commercially oriented and included British and American jazz, pop and rock and roll. There was a revival in Irish traditional music in the 1960s, inspired by American folk music, civil rights and anti-war campaigns. It was commercially and globally successful and included groups such as the Chieftains, the Dubliners, the Clancy Brothers with Tommy Makem, and Sweeney's Men.

The connection between traditional music and nationalism later grew weaker and commercialization increased. Irish music was developed by musicians, such as Liam O'Flynn, into a form with international appeal which mixed folk and rock, traditional regional variations, different instruments and European cultural influences. Ireland has produced internationally popular rock and pop artists with very varied styles, like U2, Sinéad O'Connor, Hothouse Flowers, the Cranberries and the Corrs.

Northern Ireland's music is often associated stereotypically with either Nationalist or Unionist traditions. Internationally popular Irish folk music has largely Nationalist/Catholic origins, but may also be enjoyed by Unionists/Protestants. It is centred on the traditional styles of the céili (ceilidh) or informal musical gatherings which originate from Scottish, French, English and Austrian sources. Unionist musical culture is often based on local marching bands, with small drums (now replacing the larger Lambeg drum) and fife or flute, but other music mixes local traditions with cosmopolitan influences.

Northern Irish music has had internationally recognized classical artists, such as composer and conductor Hamilton Harty; flautist James Galway; pianist Barry Douglas; and composer Elaine Agnew. Van Morrison is a major rock musician and Stiff Little Fingers were involved in British 1970s punk rock. Traditional Irish folk-singing by artists like the McPeake Family later blended pop and folk and became very popular. Northern Ireland and Belfast in particular have a lively musical culture covering many different styles and fashions.

Ireland has a long tradition of folk dancing. Solo dancing consists of fast footwork and high kicks, with a straight upper body and arm position. The appeal and transformation of Irish dancing grew with the Gaelic revival of traditional music and later led to the creation of internationally successful stage productions, such as *Riverdance* and *Lord of the Dance* in the 1990s, in which large numbers of solo artists performed collectively.

Visual and fine arts

The earliest evidence of Irish visual art is the stone carvings at Neolithic sites such as Newgrange; Bronze Age gold objects and artwork; Celtic brooches, gold ornaments and metalwork; and illuminated manuscripts produced by monks in Irish and Scottish monasteries during the fifth to ninth centuries. The *Book of Kells* is an important Middle Ages example of art and calligraphy and the creation of manuscripts continued into the age of printing around 1551.

Later Irish painters gained international recognition after the seventeenth century, such as the eighteenth-century landscape artists James Barry, George Barret and Nathaniel Hone, Sr. Barret, Hone and the English painter, Sir Joshua Reynolds, founded the Royal Academy of Arts in 1768. Representative nineteenth-century painters were the impressionist Nathaniel Hone, Jr., the portraitist Walter F. Osborne, landscapist James Arthur O'Connor and the history painter Daniel Maclise.

An Irish painting tradition developed during the nineteenth and twentieth centuries and artists gained international reputations, such as the portraitists Sir John Lavery and Roderic O'Connor, the figurative painters John ('Jack') Yeats, landscape artist Paul Henry, cubist painter Mainie Jellett, stained-glass artist Evie Hone and portraitist William Orpen. Modern artists appeared in the mid-twentieth century, such as Louis de Brocquy, the Belfast-born Daniel O'Neill and Norah McGuinness. Today, Ireland's fine arts scene is growing, is internationally recognized, and major annual exhibitions, such as the Exhibition of the Royal Hibernian Academy, the Oireachtas Exhibition and the Exhibition of Living Art, present the work of painters, sculptors and artists working in stained glass.

Northern Irish visual artists in the twentieth century reacted to the Troubles and prevailing conservative landscape traditions. Some artists moved to Dublin or London and others in the 1980s examined problems of identity, conflict and place. The visual arts world expanded, as new artists used installation, video and digital technology art forms. But the art market was undeveloped and artists still moved to Ireland, where they received better state support.

Architecture

Ireland's prehistoric peoples erected many menhirs (large upright stones), megalithic tombs often covered with stone slabs, such as dolmens and cromlechs, and stone forts, which date from 2000 to 1000 BC. An important construction is the Neolithic Newgrange passage tomb in eastern Ireland with spiral wall art. Its site has a circle of standing stones, similar to Stonehenge in England, and probably dates from about 3000 BC.

Ireland's later architectural heritage is influenced by English and European fashions and adaptations to local conditions. The medieval Romanesque style is reflected in religious architecture, such as the twelfth-century Cormac's Chapel on the Rock of Cashel in Co. Tipperary. The Anglo-Normans brought Norman stone castles to Ireland in the twelfth century and used the European Gothic style in the Dublin cathedrals of St Patrick's and Christ Church. The need for defensible structures in the fifteenth to seventeenth centuries resulted in many fortified houses with heights from three to six storeys. The architecture of the rural Irish cottage was influenced by available local raw materials, finance and a harsh climate, and consequently produced characteristic one-storey structures with small windows and thatched roofs.

During the eighteenth and early nineteenth centuries the Anglo-Irish aristocracy built substantial homes, and civic planning schemes transformed villages and urban architecture in towns and cities, such as Dublin's public buildings and squares. But much traditional architecture was destroyed in twentieth-century slum clearance and replaced by homogeneous, functional, low-rise housing. The Georgian Society and An Taisce (the National Trust of Ireland) try to protect Ireland's architectural heritage and control speculative property development of old buildings, such as Dublin's eighteenth-century properties. However, some Georgian houses north of the Liffey are in a poor state and need either state or private support.

In Northern Ireland there are a few impressive eighteenth-century country mansions, large farmhouses, urban terraced houses and remnants of the past, such as the Norman Carrickfergus Castle of 1177 and parts of the historic city of Londonderry/Derry. But it is felt that the buildings of Northern Ireland are generally undistinguished owing to industrial growth in the nineteenth century and lack of organized town planning, although there is some interesting industrial architecture. In Belfast, a fine City Hall was erected in 1906, slums were cleared and recent projects in Laganside and the Titanic Quarter may improve the cityscape.

Film

Irish film has achieved recent success under directors like Neil Jordan and Jim Sheridan and with works such as *My Left Foot* (1989), *The Crying Game* (1992), *Michael Collins* (1996) and *The General* (1998). Contemporary Irish film examines national identity, terrorism, politics, a violent past and a changing society. It is argued that these themes enable writers to challenge stereotypes and myths about Ireland and the Irish (both internal and external).

The film industry is growing at a local level in Northern Ireland and actors and directors such as Liam Neeson, Stephen Rea and Kenneth Branagh are internationally recognized. Many films have depicted Northern Irish society and locations, such as Carol Reed's *Odd Man Out* (1947) and *Cal* (1984), directed by Pat O'Connor, and Belfast initiated an annual film festival in 2000. A fledgling film studio has started in the Paint Hall of theTitanic Quarter in central Belfast.

Sports

The Gaelic Athletic Association (GAA) echoed the nationalist aims of the 1891 to 1922 cultural revivals. It was founded by Michael Cusack and Maurice Davin in 1884 and opposed English influence and games such as cricket and rugby union. It tried to build a genuine Irish identity by promoting Gaelic football, hurling/camogie and other Irish team sports, based on Croke Park in Dublin. The GAA was supported by the Catholic Church and nationalist politicians such as Michael Davitt and Charles Stewart Parnell. Its members were prohibited from playing foreign sports until the ban was lifted in 1971. The GAA divided the island on club-county-province levels. Based on the provinces of Connaught, Munster, Leinster and Ulster, the 32 counties of the island (including Northern Ireland) compete in provincial knockout rounds of All Ireland Championships, from which two surviving teams contest the finals.

Ater restricting Fenian influence in the association and the fall of Parnell, the GAA became a non-violent and non-revolutionary nationalist organization. As popular culture developed, amateur hurling and Gaelic football became big spectator sports. The Anglo-Irish War and the civil war hindered participation in sports, but the GAA recovered and has played a central part in Irish life. In April 2005, Croke Park was opened to soccer and rugby union. This gesture was significant because Croke Park was the location where British paramilitaries had fired on a Gaelic football match in 1920, killing 13 people.

There is both mixing and separation at representative levels. Sports such as Gaelic football, hurling and rugby union are organized on an all-island basis, with one team representing Ireland in international competitions. In addition, the British Lions and Irish Lions rugby union team consists of players from England, Ireland, Scotland and Wales, who tour Australia, New Zealand and South Africa. Sports such as soccer have separate organizing bodies in Northern Ireland and Ireland, and field national teams in international and World Cup football. At the Olympic Games, a person from Northern Ireland can choose to represent either the Great Britain and Northern Ireland team or the Ireland national team.

Ireland

Gaelic football is the most popular sport in Ireland and has 34 per cent of sports attendances, followed by hurling at 23 per cent, soccer at 16 per cent and rugby union at 8 per cent, with the All-Ireland Football Final being the most watched sporting event in Ireland. Swimming, golf, aerobics, soccer, cycling, Gaelic football and billiards/snooker have the highest levels of personal participation.

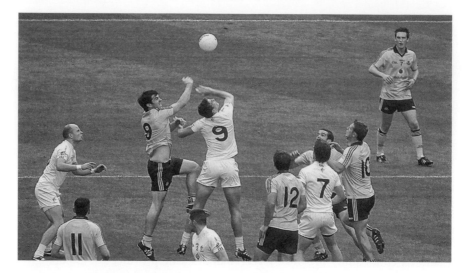

PLATE 5.6 This Gaelic football match was between Dublin (winners) and Kildare in the Leinster Championship semi-final at Croke Park, Dublin, 26 June 2011. © Mark Moloney/Demotix/Demotix/Corbis

Gaelic football resembles soccer and rugby. Players run holding the leather ball for no more than four paces, after which they must bounce, kick or punch it. One point is scored for putting the ball over the crossbar between the posts and three points are awarded for putting it in the net. The game is played by both men and women in teams of 15 for two 30-minute periods. The final of the inter-county competition (All-Ireland Final) is held at Croke Park.

Hurling, originating in the thirteenth century, is similar to field hockey and is named after the stick (the caman or 'hurley') with which the sport is played. Players use the hurley (similar to a hockey stick but with a shorter and wider blade) to hit the ball along the ground or into the air. They can also kick the ball or hit it with the flat of their hands. The leather-covered sliothar (ball) can be either caught preparatory to hitting it or carried on the stick. Teams of 15 players each try to score a point by hitting the ball over the eight-foot-high goal crossbar. Players can score a goal (cúl) worth three points by hitting the ball under the crossbar past the goalkeeper. The female version of hurling is camogie. Teams compete in the All-Ireland Senior Hurling Championship and the final is held at Croke Park.

Soccer has become more popular, partly due to television coverage of matches in the UK, and the relative success of Ireland in European and World Cup competitions. Rugby union is followed at club and national levels. Horse-racing, such as the Galway Races festival in July, is a very popular spectator sport and Irish breeders have produced some of the world's finest thoroughbreds in, for example, Co. Kildare. Professional cycling attracts a wide following; cricket is played at local and national levels and Ireland beat England in 2011 at a World Cup Group series; and water surfing, sailing and golf are popular hobbies.

TABLE 5.1 Top exercise and sporting activities by active persons in Ireland (2007)

Event	%
Walking	39.3
Aerobics/keep fit	13.0
Swimming	8.0
Golf	7.6
Soccer	7.1
Other	25.1

Source: adapted from *Quarterly National Household Survey*, Central Statistics Office, Ireland, December 2007

According to the *Quarterly National Household Survey, 2007*, 62.8 per cent of persons overage 15 in Ireland said that they had participated in physical activities for exercise, recreation or sport (Table 5.1). Activity was highest among people in work and students, and lowest among the unemployed, those with home duties and the retired. Female participation at 64.4 per cent was higher than males at 61.3 per cent.

The motivation to exercise and participation was mainly related to improving health (58.6 per cent), with a social element being the second most common reason (20.7 per cent). Some 22.6 per cent of active persons had participated in physical exercise or sports activities five or more times per week and 35.3 per cent participated once or twice per week.

Northern Ireland

Sports are popular in Northern Ireland among observers and participants. In the Catholic community, Gaelic football and hurling among men and camogie among women are favourites. Among Protestants, the most popular games are rugby union, cricket and field hockey. Soccer and golf are followed in both Catholic and Protestant communities, with support for English football clubs. Gaelic football, hurling and handball are increasingly played by Protestants. Fishing is popular; the province has fine coarse fishing with bream and roach; and salmon and trout fishing attract international visitors. Hill-walking courses and beaches are again attracting overseas visitors following the end of the Troubles.

In Northern Ireland, the 2009/10 *Continuous Household Survey* (Table 5.2) reported that 46 per cent of respondents participated in sport and physical activity; more males (54 per cent) than females (41 per cent) took part; 37 per cent of respondents participated at least one day a week; and 63 per cent of respondents spend no time participating in any type of sport or physical activity during the

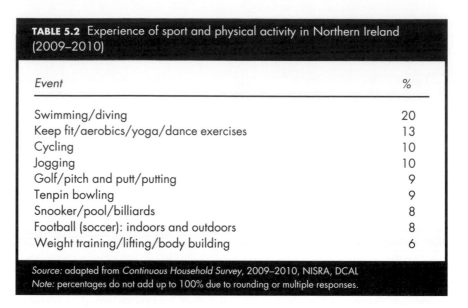

TABLE 5.2 Experience of sport and physical activity in Northern Ireland (2009–2010)

Event	%
Swimming/diving	20
Keep fit/aerobics/yoga/dance exercises	13
Cycling	10
Jogging	10
Golf/pitch and putt/putting	9
Tenpin bowling	9
Snooker/pool/billiards	8
Football (soccer): indoors and outdoors	8
Weight training/lifting/body building	6

Source: adapted from *Continuous Household Survey*, 2009–2010, NISRA, DCAL
Note: percentages do not add up to 100% due to rounding or multiple responses.

week. Some 32 per cent of respondents attended a sporting event as a spectator in Northern Ireland and 16 per cent attended a sporting event outside Northern Ireland. Fifty per cent of respondents were 'very' or 'fairly satisfied' with the sports provision in Northern Ireland, a drop from 53 per cent in 2008/2009.

Other polls, such as the 2009 *Northern Ireland Life and Times Survey*, have similar results. They show the decreasing amount of time that people spend in sport and physical activity (compared with Ireland); disparities between male and female participation and age groups; and agreement that Northern Ireland's Executive should spend more money on sport. Sport, exercise and physical activity are viewed positively but government spending cuts may further affect people's ability to participate in and watch sports.

Culture in Ireland

Following independence in 1921 Irish politicians concentrated on state building rather than cultural policy and the arts. Fianna Fáil gained power in the 1930s and held office for many years. It supported non-governmental cultural initiatives which had party approval and reflected Irish traditions. The fine arts, orchestras, concerts, operas and dance were associated with aristocratic and English control and did not receive state funding. Critics opposed such views, but cultural policies did not develop for some 20 years.

Artists and commentators in the early twentieth century argued that Ireland was rooted in the past, driven by economic and financial considerations, and had a mediocre cultural life. James Joyce escaped what he saw as Ireland's suffocating closed-mindedness. While many writers stayed and campaigned for freedom of expression, a lack of state support for the arts led to public cynicism about politicians. Film and literature suffered as censorship laws in 1923 (film) and 1929 (books) were introduced. Disillusioned artists, such as George Bernard Shaw, left Ireland.

The theatre initially avoided censorship and financial problems when a state subsidy was granted to the Abbey Theatre in 1925. The Gate Theatre was established in 1928 and brought international drama and new production styles to Dublin. However, general artistic alienation and censorship continued, with no firm cultural policy and uncertain developments of the visual arts, museums and the National Library.

But significant change did occur in 1951 when the Arts Council (An Chomhairle Ealaíon) was created. It was responsible for painting, sculpture, architecture, music, drama, literature, industrial design, the fine arts and applied arts. Despite economic and social stagnation in the 1950s, the Council gradually increased its influence and funding and began to place the arts more centrally in Irish life. The Arts Council now receives an annual grant from the state and distributes finance, scholarships and awards to the arts and artists. Cultural policy is debated and formulated by the Department of Arts, Heritage and the Gaeltacht. Individual writers, artists, architects and composers are aided with financial support from the Aosdána organization, created in 1981 by the Arts Council. The establishment of a national lottery in 1986 substantially increased funding for the arts, culture and sports by having some lottery income awarded to 'good causes'.

Cultural institutions were gradually created, such as the Kilkenny Design Workshops in 1965, a new Abbey Theatre in 1966, also known as the National Theatre of Ireland (including the experimental Peacock Theatre), an extension to the National Gallery and the new Cork Opera House in 1963 (renovated in 1993). A National Concert Hall was founded in 1981, and now offers classical, popular, operatic, choral, jazz and ballet. An Irish television station was established in 1961; television brought many social and cultural changes; opened up Irish society; and helped liberalize the censorship of books, film and newspapers, although censor classification and legal restrictions continue.

Changes also came in 1969 when creative writers, sculptors, composers and painters living and working in Ireland no longer paid income tax on earnings. Artists gained greater public acceptance. New art galleries and reorganized art colleges revitalized cultural life. But there was still no unified state policy for the arts, although a Fine Gael/Labour government in 1973 showed increased interest in cultural planning. The Arts Council was restructured; given increased powers under the Taoiseach's Department; and became more accountable to the public and accessible to the media.

It was further strengthened in 1975 when the Abbey Theatre, the Gate Theatre, the Irish Theatre Company, the Irish Ballet Company and the Dublin Theatre Festival were placed under the Council's control. An extension to the

Chester Beatty Library and Museum near Dublin Castle (with collections from Asia, the Middle East, North Africa and Europe) was built and local authorities increased financing of the arts.

However, substantial regional provision for galleries, theatres, museums and film centres outside Dublin was still lacking in the 1990s and there was no government-funded film board. Attitudes changed somewhat in 1993 when the Minister for Arts, Culture and the Gaeltacht was given a full Cabinet post and cultural initiatives developed. Earlier negative views about culture and the arts had decreased by the end of the twentieth century and were replaced by a new vitality. However, although government-supported culture and greater artistic freedom are now more established features of Irish life than in 1921, debate and controversy still occur over funding and responsibility for national arts policy.

There is a variety of artistic and cultural work in Ireland, such as street theatre and poetry, rock musicians, painters and sculptors, traditional music, dancing and opera. Irish artists analyse the realities of their society in films, books and plays as the old insularity and suspicion decrease. More people are now exposed to the arts, but Ireland still faces competition from Anglo-American media, the decline of the Irish language, globalization and a lack of cultural provision in some areas of the country, such as the midlands.

Other institutions also deliver and fund arts and cultural policies. Most of Ireland's major museums, galleries, libraries and learned societies are located in Dublin, such as the National Museum of Ireland, the National Gallery of Ireland and the National Library of Ireland, which has over 500,000 volumes and is the largest public library. Trinity College Library, founded in 1601, has some 2.8 million volumes. Many cities and towns have public libraries, museums and a variety of heritage centres, which document local history.

The National Museum has impressive exhibits in the fields of art, industry and natural history, and maintains collections of Irish silver, glass, textiles and lace. It has a collection of Viking artefacts, medieval relics and fine metalwork examples of the early Christian period such as the Tara Brooch, the Ardagh Chalice and the Moylough Bell Shrine (all dating from the eighth century), as well as the Lismore Crozier and the Cross of Cong (both twelfth century). Dublin's National Gallery has a large collection of paintings covering many schools of Irish and European art. Under British rule a number of Anglo-Irish cultural institutions were established that successfully adapted to changing conditions. These include the Royal Irish Academy (1785) with science and the humanities, the Royal Dublin Society (1731) with agriculture, art and science, the Royal Hibernian Academy of Arts (1823) with the fine arts and the Royal Irish Academy of Music (1848).

According to an Arts Council survey in 2006 to 2007, expenditure on the arts by local authorities in Ireland doubled to €55 million in 2005 and there had been more varied programmes and partnerships with other bodies. There was increased funding and provision for festivals and traditional arts; more arts offerings for young people; more arts programmes on radio and television; a more lively film sector; and new arts technology.

The survey found that Irish people generally have positive views about the arts. Respondents thought that arts education in schools was as important as science education (82 per cent); arts activity helped tourism in Ireland (91 per cent); the arts have become more available in the past 10 years (85 per cent); it was as important to provide arts amenities as sports amenities (75 per cent); and there should be increased arts spending by government (56 per cent) and local authorities (55 per cent). These views were reflected in attendance at arts activities in 2006, as shown in Table 5.3.

The survey revealed large increases since 1994 in the popularity of mainstream film and rock/pop events; smaller increases for literature/poetry reading and contemporary dance; and decreases for variety shows/pantomime, art exhibitions, country and western music and plays. Respondents had moved increasingly

TABLE 5.3 Attendance at arts activities in Ireland (2006–2007)

Event	Proportion of respondents
Mainstream film	57
A play	30
Rock or popular music	28
Open-air street theatre/spectacle	19
Traditional Irish or folk music	19
Stand-up comedy	18
Musical	17
Variety show/pantomime	16
Art exhibitions	15
Circus	13
Country and western music	10
Traditional/folk dance	8
Jazz/blues music	7
Classical music concert or recital	7
Art-house film	5
World music	5
Readings (e.g. literature/poetry)	5
Opera	4
Contemporary dance	3
Ballet	2
Other live music performance	17
Other dance performance	7

Source: adapted from Arts Council, Hibernia Consulting, *The Public and the Arts*, Ireland 2006–2007 (proportional figures based on 1,210 responses)

from conventional or subsidized art forms to genres like open-air street theatre, stand-up comedy and circus. The leading music genres (by purchase) were rock or popular music (50 per cent); traditional Irish or folk music (22 per cent); country and western music (16 per cent); classical music concert or recital (11 per cent); and jazz/blues music (10 per cent).The number of respondents attending at least one arts event (85 per cent) in 2006 was also higher than the number in six other countries (Northern Ireland, Scotland, Wales, England, France and the USA), where the figures varied between 73 and 84 per cent.

However, participation in the arts was less than attendance, with only 19 per cent of respondents saying that they had taken part in at least one type of arts activity. The top participatory events were playing a musical instrument for one's own pleasure (8 per cent out of 1,210 responses); helping with running an arts event (7 per cent); painting/drawing/sculpture (6 per cent); choir singing (5 per cent); set dancing (5 per cent); playing a musical instrument to an audience (4 per cent); performing a play/drama (4 per cent); photography as artistic activity (3 per cent); writing (3 per cent); and writing any music (2 per cent).

A new question was asked in 2006 about reading for pleasure. Sixty-four per cent of people said that they had read a book from at least one of the following categories, with 36 per cent saying that they had not read any. The most popular type of reading was a novel, story or play (51 per cent). The other categories included biography or autobiography and non-fictional or factual work. In terms of gender, 73 per cent of women and 54 per cent of men had read a book from at least one of the categories.

Culture in Northern Ireland

The relationship between native and foreign influences has historically conditioned cultural life in the north-east of the island. Prehistoric sites, archaeological artefacts, Viking remains, Norman castles, regional images in ancient manuscripts, legends and myths illustrate earlier cultures in Ulster before the sixteenth-century Tudor invasions or the English/Scottish plantations of the seventeenth century. These identifiable roots and influences have fashioned a complex contemporary culture in Northern Ireland and are apparent in practices, ceremonies and festivals, which have been overlaid by global influences. Northern Ireland has comprised two main sectarian communities in recent centuries, which have been joined by later immigrant groups. Differences of opinion and behaviour mark daily life and relations between these people. Linguistic terms, artistic expression and historical events can mean different things to Unionists, Nationalists and others.

Generally, Irish music and dance, Gaelic football, hurling and community festivals form a cultural focus among Nationalists. Some identify with Ireland, want to preserve the Irish language and support a network of Irish-medium schools. Among Unionists, cultural life, although differentiated from that of mainland Britain, is influenced by trends in the UK. Loyalties in Protestant working-class neighbourhoods often centre on Orange Order activities and the tradition of marching bands, particularly in the marching season between Easter and 12 July, which commemorates the Battle of the Boyne and William III's victory in 1690 over the Catholic King James II. The marches may pass through majority-Catholic communities and provoke hostility from the Nationalist community.

Public and cultural spaces are traditionally defined as Nationalist, Unionist or mixed. It may be possible to interact in some middle-class, student and other areas, but most neighbourhoods are religiously or politically homogeneous and may be bordered by 49 'peace walls', which separate the two main communities, are covered with murals and graffiti, and are the reality of division or separation. Most people have tended to interact only with fellow community members in both urban and rural areas. Sectarian conflict often exists where the boundaries are contested. Rural areas may experience little overt confrontation, but bitterness does remain and some atrocities in the Troubles occurred in the countryside.

There is limited contact between Catholic and Protestant children and school education is mainly denominational. In 2009, Catholic children faced threats as they went to and from school across sectarian boundaries in North Belfast. Such divisions still affect daily life in Northern Ireland, despite some improvement in relations following the Good Friday (Belfast) Agreement, 1998.

Northern Ireland's communities traditionally tend to be conservative in their social and religious outlooks. Church attendance is high (but declining), family life is central (although increasingly subject to breakdown), divorce levels (while growing) are relatively low in European terms and community ties are strong (but arguably weakening). Catholic and Protestant attitudes to sexual morality and abortion are similar, although some views on contraception and divorce are not shared. The number of mixed Catholic–Protestant marriages has risen, but is a small percentage of all marriages. Protestant family sizes decreased during the twentieth century, but Catholic families remained larger. Social attitudes in rural and small-town areas are arguably more conservative than those in the cities.

Sectarian conflict is reflected in film, drama, poetry, fiction and the visual arts, although the north-east and Belfast lacked major artistic reputations in the nineteenth and early twentieth centuries. However, Nationalist and Unionist communities have since produced internationally known writers, poets, actors and musicians, many of whom have protested against political and sectarian violence. Government agencies also attempt to reconcile divisions and create a cultural identity in the province.

Northern Ireland today has an Arts Council, which encourages the arts, and a Department of Culture, Arts and Leisure is responsible for arts policy. These institutions have given some governmental impetus for artistic development. The reopening of the Grand Opera House in 1980 was important for Belfast's position in the performing arts, but Northern Ireland has other theatres and a touring company based at the University of Ulster at Coleraine. The Council also sponsors art exhibitions, some of which tour the province. There was little development in the visual arts in the nineteenth century, but painting and poetry now have strong reputations as the north-east has moved into a more expressive and expansive arts scene.

More funding has been given to the arts by local councils and the Heritage Lottery Fund distributes a share of UK National Lottery finance, which has been used to build new theatres and arts centres in, for example, Londonderry/Derry and Armagh. The multi-purpose conference, arts and entertainment Waterfront Hall in Belfast was completed in 1997, and a cultural quarter near the city centre has been developed. Classical music is mainly imported, but Belfast has a symphony orchestra and a youth orchestra, and has developed one of the largest festivals (ranging from classical to pop music) in the UK.

Among cultural institutions, the Ulster Museum (1892) in Belfast is the national museum and art gallery and has a large collection of local and international art and antiquities, with Londonderry/Derry and Armagh also having permanent art galleries. Belfast has the Belfast Central Library (1888), the Queen's University Library (1849) and the Linen Hall Library (1788), a private institution with central collections of Irish literature, political materials and newspapers. The Ulster Folk and Transport Museum (1958), at Cultra near Belfast, is one of the oldest cultural heritage sites in the UK and illustrates peasant origins in Northern Ireland. The Ulster-American Folk Park (1976) at Omagh is also a heritage centre, which details the experience of Irish emigrants to the United States. The Armagh Observatory was founded by Archbishop Richard Robinson in 1790, and is now independent, supported by state aid. It has links with observatories abroad and cooperates with the Armagh Planetarium. There is also a major maritime museum, the Harbour Museum, in Londonderry/Derry.

Nevertheless, there are mixed (and sometimes contradictory) public responses to the cultural scene in Northern Ireland. An ARK *Northern Ireland Life and Times Survey* in 2001 reported that 51 per cent of respondents thought that the province now offers more cultural events and attractions than in the past; 95 per cent thought that this was a good thing; and that those responsible for this increase were district councils/local government (50 per cent), government departments at Stormont (23 per cent), private business (26 per cent) or community groups (28 per cent). However, in responding to a question about the relevance of the arts in Northern Ireland, 56 per cent of respondents did not think that it was very (or not at all) important to go to or take part in cultural events. When asked whether they did anything regularly in their leisure time that they identified with culture, 74 per cent said No, 21 per cent said Yes and 5 per cent did not know.

In identifying 'cultural' events in their regular leisure time activities, the majority (48 per cent) mentioned museums, art galleries, theatre or concerts. Others identified amateur dramatics (6 per cent), dancing (6 per cent), painting

(5 per cent) and listening to music (5 per cent). They considered that increases in cultural events were a good thing because they brought people from different religions together (56 per cent) and brought people together socially (54 per cent). However, 38 per cent were not interested in cultural events and 30 per cent didn't have time to attend. Others blamed expense (20 per cent), lack of information (17 per cent), inability to drive (10 per cent), health problems (7 per cent), too old (7 per cent) and that cultural events were not really for people like them (15 per cent).

Respondents did not appear to be enthusiastic when asked whether going to or taking part in cultural events was important for their leisure activities: 6 per cent said very important; quite important (23 per cent); neither important nor unimportant (14 per cent); not very important (23 per cent); not at all important (33 per cent); and 3 per cent did not know.

However, 10 years on from the above report, a 2009/2010 *Continuous Household Survey* from the Northern Ireland Department of Culture, Arts and Leisure reported that 73 per cent said that they had attended *at least one* arts event in 2009/2010 (higher than the 67 per cent in 2008/2009), with males at 69 per cent and females at 75 per cent. The most popular event attended by respondents was film at a cinema or other venue (52 per cent), followed by play or drama (24 per cent), rock or pop music (21 per cent), other theatre (16 per cent), a museum (11 per cent), other live music event (12 per cent), community festival (12 per cent), exhibition or collection of art or photography (11 per cent), a craft exhibition (9 per cent), and folk, traditional or world music (9 per cent). There was an increase in the proportion of respondents who *participated* in arts activities and/or attended arts events in 2009/2010 (76 per cent) than in 2008/2009 (71 per cent), and the range of items indicated a widening in what was recognized as 'culture' and 'the arts'.

Seventy-one per cent of respondents were satisfied with arts provision in 2009/2010 (65 per cent in 2008/2009); and 32 per cent of respondents said that they had participated in (rather than observed) at least one arts activity (29 per cent men and 34 per cent women), which was higher than the 25 per cent in 2008/2009. Most popular participatory arts activities were textile crafts (9 per cent), playing a musical instrument for one's own pleasure (8 per cent), other dance (7 per cent), painting/drawing/printmaking/sculpture (7 per cent) and photography as art (4 per cent).

However, the economic downturn and government cuts in 2007/2008 had an impact on culture and leisure activities in Northern Ireland. A survey of 1,180 respondents by the Department of Culture in 2009 found that 16 per cent of people attended fewer cultural and leisure activities. Nearly a quarter said that they had spent less money; about one-fifth said that they had visited the cinema less and 16 per cent had gone to fewer music concerts; 10 per cent went to fewer sports events as a paying spectator; but more people were using public libraries.

Exercises

Explain and examine the following terms:

culture	the Ardagh Chalice	the Ulster Cycle
peace walls	Ogham	Jonathan Swift
Lambeg drum	Anglo-Irish ascendancy	Samuel Beckett
thatched roofs	Gaelic League	Heritage Lottery Fund
Waterfront Hall	Celtic Revival	the Gate Theatre
Douglas Hyde	Gaeltacht	Ulster Literary Theatre
the marching season	Ulster Scots	Waterfront Hall
hurling	W.B. Yeats	bodhran
Sean O'Casey	James Joyce	John McCormack
Seamus Heaney	Abbey Theatre	céilí
RTE	Chester Beatty Library	*Riverdance*
the *Book of Kells*	Georgian Society	Cormac's Chapel
National Museum of Ireland	Arts Council	Gaelic Athletic Association
Grand Opera House	sectarian	Linen Hall Library
Gaelic football	Harbour Museum	camogie

Write short essays on the following topics:

1   Compare and contrast the survey results on culture/arts in Ireland and Northern Ireland.

2   Discuss the state and relevance of the Irish language in Ireland and Northern Ireland.

3   Briefly examine the historical development of literature in Ireland and Northern Ireland and discuss the relevance of the Gaelic literary revival.

Further reading

Bairner, A. (ed.) (2005) *Sport and the Irish: Histories, Identities, Issues* Dublin: UCD Press

Brown, T. (1982) *Ireland: A Social and Cultural History 1922–79* London: Fontana

Burke, P. (2006) *What is Cultural History?* Cambridge: Polity Press

Carlson, J. (ed.) (1990) *Banned in Ireland: Censorship and the Irish Writer* London: Routledge

Coohill, J. (2000) *Ireland:A Short History* Oxford: Oneworld Publications

Cronin, M. (1999) *Sport and Nationalism in Ireland: Gaelic Games, Soccer and Irish Identity since 1884* Dublin: Four Courts Press

De Burca, M. (1999) *The GAA: A History* Dublin: Gill and Macmillan

Hindley, R. (1990) *The Death of the Irish Language* London: Routledge

Hussey, G. (1994) *Ireland Today: Anatomy of a Changing State* London: Viking

Jeffares, A.N. (1997) *A Pocket History of Irish Literature* Dublin: O'Brien Press

Lee, J.J. (1989) *Ireland 1912–1985: Politics and Society* Cambridge: Cambridge University Press

Sugden, J. and Harvie, S. (1995) *Sport and Community Relations in Northern Ireland* Coleraine: Centre for the Study of Conflict: University of Ulster

Welsh, R. and Stewart, B. (eds) (1996) *The Oxford Companion to Irish Literature* Oxford: Clarendon Press

Williams, R. (1981) *Culture* London: Fontana

Websites

ARK (Access Research Knowledge, Northern Ireland): www.ark.ac.uk

Arts Council, Ireland: www.artscouncil.ie

CAIN website (Northern Ireland): cain.ulst.ac

CELT online cultural history resource: www.ucc.ie/celt/

Central Statistics Office (Ireland): cso.ie

Culture Ireland: http://www.cultureireland.gov.ie/

Department for Arts, Heritage and the Gaeltacht: http://www.pobail.ie/

Department of Culture, Arts and Leisure, Northern Ireland: www.dcalni.gov.uk

Gaelic Athletic Association (GAA): www.gaa.ie

National Library of Ireland: www.nli.ie

Northern Ireland Life and Times Survey: www.ark.ac.uk/nilt

6

Politics and government

Medieval Ireland was divided into small Gaelic 'kingdoms', some of whose rulers, like the O'Neills in Ulster, were able to assert their authority over local rival chieftains. Some of these chieftains aspired to overlordship or high kingship of Ireland, like Rory O'Connor, the last High King, who died in 1198. Though the idea of island-wide kingship dates from the seventh century, there was no centralized administrative machinery. The precarious status of Irish rule was revealed when Dermot MacMurrough, deposed King of Leinster, sought Anglo-Norman assistance to recover his lands. The arrival in Ireland between 1169 and 1170 of Anglo-Norman troops, under the ambitious Richard Fitz Gilbert (also known as Strongbow), shifted the balance of military and political power. King Henry II of England was wary of permitting commanders like Strongbow an independent base in Ireland and in 1171/1172 he asserted his lordship over Ireland, which had been granted in 1156 by Pope Adrian IV (the only English Pope). This asserted the authority of the English Crown, and thereafter, until the sixteenth century, kingship of England brought with it lordship of Ireland.

Anglo-Norman and Tudor Ireland

The control exerted by the Anglo-Norman system of government was variable. It was most developed along the eastern seaboard from Dublin to Cork where Anglo-Norman settlement was most securely defended. It was mainly absent in the west and in the north. Royal authority was exercised through a chief justiciar (or Lord Deputy, later Lord Lieutenant) who governed on the king's behalf. While in theory the writ of lordship ran throughout the whole island, in practice Anglo-Norman – or English – governance co-existed uneasily with Gaelic traditions and its future seemed precarious. As the Statutes of Kilkenny (1366) confirmed, there was concern about the subversion of its social order by native ways. Measures, such as laws on language and customs, were put in place to protect it. By the fifteenth century royal governance was still on the defensive and effectively confined to the eastern counties of Dublin, Louth, Meath and Kildare, known as the 'English Pale'. It was in the Pale that administrative structures most closely replicated those in England while those areas 'beyond the Pale' retained their distinct Gaelic character. Moreover, the concern of the English Crown with the loyalty of royal servants in Ireland was shown in Poynings' Law (1494) which required the approval of the king and the English Privy Council (the Crown's close advisers) for summoning an Irish Parliament and for all draft laws.

In the course of the sixteenth century, the Tudor monarchy attempted an ambitious policy of extending royal sovereignty throughout the island. In 1541, Ireland was created a kingdom and Henry VIII of England also took the title of King of Ireland. This was done for a number of reasons. The first was an attempt to integrate the Gaelic lords into a modern political structure and to change them from 'enemies', potential or actual, to loyal 'subjects'. The second was finally to implant English law and custom throughout Ireland in return for confirming the land tenure of Irish lords. The third was to secure the Crown in Ireland against challenge from Catholic monarchs of Europe following Henry's break with Rome. These objectives were only partially successful and when Queen Elizabeth I was excommunicated by the Pope in 1570, the nightmare of European Catholic powers conspiring with disloyal Irish subjects became all too real. The Elizabethan era involved continuous military campaigning, for example, the so-called Nine Years War (1594–1603), in order to affirm the authority of the Crown over Gaelic tradition.

It was not until 1603, with the accession to the throne of James I, that the power of the Crown was finally established throughout the island. Ulster was the last province to be subdued and the 'Flight of the Earls' – O'Neill, O'Donnell and Maguire – from Ulster in 1607 symbolized the end of Gaelic resistance, paving the way for Ulster's further 'plantation' by settlers from Great Britain. However, royal authority continued to be threatened throughout the seventeenth century by Catholic disaffection and by the intrigue of European powers. About 12,000, mostly Protestant, settlers were either killed or died of ill-treatment in the rebellion of 1641. In this brutal century, political and religious authority was imposed by equally brutal methods such as those associated with Oliver Cromwell's campaign of 1649 to 1650. Probably 4,000 died in Cromwell's sieges of Drogheda and Wexford in 1649. Thereafter, the Catholic 'Old English' lords suffered political marginalization at the hands of the Protestant 'New English' settlers. Their hopes of recovering power in alliance with the equally marginalized 'native Irish' were dashed by the victory of William III over James II at the Battle of the Boyne in 1690 and the Battle of Aughrim in 1691. As a consequence, the eighteenth century became one of Protestant ascendancy. Plantation and forfeiture meant that Catholic lords now held only 14 per cent of the land.

However, the late seventeenth and early eighteenth centuries witnessed a change in that ascendancy's self-understanding from English to Irish patriotism. The example of the American Revolution provided an opportunity for the assertion of Irish parliamentary autonomy in 1782. Another serious threat was posed by Republicanism, a mix of Ulster Presbyterianism and revolutionary ideas from America and France, which led to the 1798 Rebellion. This period also saw the beginnings of the Orange Order (1795) to defend the Williamite Settlement. By 1798 it had 470 lodges throughout the island. The 1798 Rebellion provoked a review of Anglo-Irish relations and the consequence was the Act of Union (1800). On 1 January 1801 the United Kingdom of Great Britain and Ireland

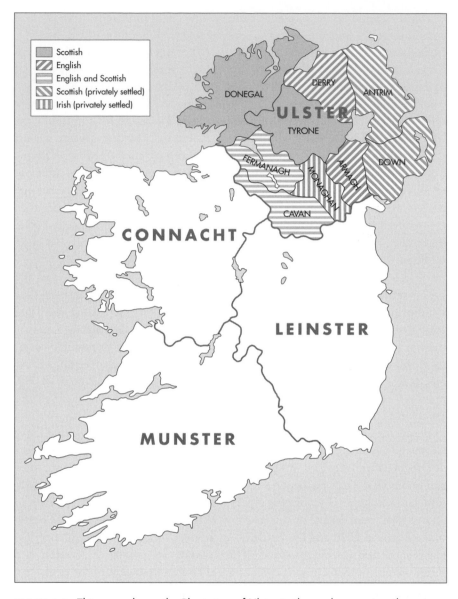

PLATE 6.1 This map shows the Plantation of Ulster in the early seventeenth century. It covered the counties of Londonderry, Tyrone, Fermanagh, Armagh, Cavan and Donegal, but not Down and Antrim, which were already 'planted'. (Source: James G. Leyisum, *The Scottish Irish: A Social History*, University of North Carolina Press, Chapel Hill, NC, 1962, p. 93.)

came into existence. The Irish Parliament was dissolved and Ireland was now represented in London by 100 MPs in the House of Commons, and 28 lords and one Anglican archbishop plus three bishops in the House of Lords. The legislative union of the two islands did not remove the necessity for a separate executive in Dublin. A Lord Lieutenant represented the Crown and a Chief Secretary was responsible for the conduct of government policy.

Home Rule and partition

Those members of the old Irish Parliament who opposed the Union did so in part because they identified the Irish nation as exclusively Protestant. Catholics tended to favour the Union because they thought it would be followed rapidly by measures of emancipation, removing the last vestiges of public exclusion. Similarly, Irish Presbyterians saw the Union as a way to remove the remaining civil and religious restrictions maintained by the established Church of Ireland. The refusal of Kings George III and IV to grant emancipation rapidly soured Catholic opinion and later encouraged a popular movement under the leadership of Daniel O'Connell (1775–1847) to promote emancipation. The Catholic Association, formed in 1825, achieved that goal in 1829. From December 1832 O'Connell refocused Catholic agitation on repeal of the Act of Union itself. By now most Irish Protestants had accommodated themselves to the Union and for them the association of Catholicism with repeal was threatening. When Gladstone, the Liberal Prime Minister, responding to the growth of Irish nationalist pressure, committed the government in 1885/1886 to a policy of Home Rule for Ireland, the political divisions between Catholic and Protestant became firmly drawn.

Home Rule was not without its Protestant supporters and it was the Protestant Isaac Butt (1813–1879) who founded the Home Rule movement in 1870. Home Rule envisaged a separate parliament for Ireland for exclusively domestic matters with the UK Parliament remaining responsible for all other matters. Charles Stewart Parnell (1846–1891), also a Protestant, promoted Home Rule through leadership of a disciplined Irish Parliamentary Party in the House of Commons and it was the discipline of Nationalist MPs that compelled a corresponding organization on the part of Irish Unionists. Unionism combined the mainly Anglican southern landed gentry and professional class with the mainly Presbyterian northern business elites, behind whom stood popular Protestantism in Ulster (which contained 75 per cent of Protestants in Ireland). It too espoused an Irish identity but one firmly within the UK, arguing that the prosperity and progress of Ireland was bound up with the maintenance of the Union. They also feared that Home Rule could be the first step towards Irish independence.

Home Rule bills failed to pass in 1886 and in 1893, owing to opposition in the House of Lords (which had a veto). When the Liberal government, with Irish Party support, introduced a third bill in 1912, this provoked organized resistance

PLATE 6.2 The death toll of the Easter Rebellion in Dublin 1916 was 450. Of these, 132 were soldiers (pictured) or police, 254 civilians and 64 rebels. The Rebellion was deeply unpopular at the time but it proved to be a key moment in the history of Irish republicanism. © Bettmann/Corbis

from Ulster Unionists. They threatened to establish their own government if Home Rule was enacted and prepared for military resistance in the form of the Ulster Volunteer Force (UVF), with arms smuggled from Germany in April 1914. In July 1914 the Nationalist Irish Volunteers brought in arms, also from Germany. This created the potential for civil war. Though the leader of the Irish Party, John Redmond (1856–1918), was to see the Home Rule bill enacted in 1914, events in Ireland were overtaken by the outbreak of the First World War. The Home Rule Act, without any firm commitment on the future position of Ulster, was suspended for the duration of the war. To begin with, Nationalists and Unionists were equally committed to the war effort and some hoped that a common sacrifice might heal old political divisions. Of the 200,000 Irish recruits to the British forces, it is estimated that some 35,000 were to die in action between 1914 and 1918.

At Easter 1916 an armed group of Irish Volunteers, under the direction of the secret Irish Republican Brotherhood (IRB), declared Ireland an independent republic and fought the British Army on the streets of Dublin. Though this rebellion had little popular support at the time, the execution of its leaders and subsequent coercive measures swayed public opinion. A more radical, republican, form of Irish Nationalism took root, also provoked by the threat of military conscription. The political party of Sinn Féin was reconstituted with openly republican principles in 1917 by one of the 1916 rebels, Éamon de Valera. In the General Election of 1918 Sinn Féin won a majority of Irish parliamentary seats (73 out of 105) except in Ulster which returned a majority of Unionists (23 out of 37). Sinn Féin took this result as a mandate for an Irish Republic and Unionists took it as a mandate for a separate jurisdiction in Ulster.

Here was the ground for the subsequent partition of Ireland – not as a result of British policy alone but as a result of competing democratic mandates. The Government of Ireland Act (1920) formally acknowledged the partition of Ireland into 26 southern counties and 6 northern counties, the former called Southern Ireland and the latter, Northern Ireland. However, in that Act both remained part of the UK and partition was assumed to be temporary. Though the Irish Republican Army (IRA) fought a campaign in the Anglo-Irish War (1919–1921) against any formal connection with the British Crown, the Irish Republic proclaimed in 1916 was traded in the Anglo-Irish Treaty of 1921 for substantial political independence. This Treaty conceded to the 26 southern counties dominion status within the British Empire. This went further than the 1920 Act (which only became operative in Northern Ireland) and the new entity in the south became known as the Irish Free State.

Ireland after 1921: the political framework

In January 1922 the Treaty was only narrowly accepted by Irish Republican deputies (64 votes to 57). Though the Treaty was generally popular and supported by the Catholic Church, the anti-Treaty faction led by de Valera refused to accept the oath of allegiance to the British Crown. It was this symbolic betrayal of the 1916 Rebellion – not the partition of Ireland – which split Sinn Féin. The split led to a civil war (1922–1923) between the Free State government and the anti-Treaty IRA, resulting in the deaths of about 1,000 people. Despite victory for the government, there was no formal acceptance of the Free State by its opponents and the legacy of civil war divisions continued to influence Irish politics for generations.

The Constitution of the Irish Free State was enacted in 1922 and it was a compromise between popular republicanism and constitutional monarchy. On the one hand, it proclaimed that all powers and authority of government 'derived from the people of Ireland'. On the other hand, it recognized the Crown, acknowledged the Crown's representative in Ireland, the Governor-General, and permitted legal appeal to the judicial committee of the Privy Council in London. Moreover, the traditions of British parliamentary democracy were evident in the institutions of government. The Parliament, or Oireachtas, was bicameral, consisting of the Dáil (chamber of deputies) and the Seanad (senate). The Dáil, the main legislative chamber, was elected for a maximum of seven years with deputies (Teachtaí Dála, or TDs) representing between 20,000 and 30,000 constituents. The Seanad was composed of 60 members and had powers to delay bills sent by the Dáil. Its purpose was to provide representation of 'important aspects of the Nation's life' (Article 30 of the Constitution) and this originally involved a special place for Protestants. An Executive Council, modelled on the British Cabinet, chaired by the President of the Executive Council, was responsible for the conduct of government. The Constitution actually provided limited restraint on the powers of the Executive Council since it could (following British precedent) amend constitutional provisions by ordinary law. The Free State government took over the old civil service and administrative departments in Dublin. However, only 180 former members of the Royal Irish Constabulary (RIC) continued in the new police force, An Garda Síochána (Guards of the Peace), which was formed in August 1923. Nearly 1,000 members of the RIC joined the newly formed Royal Ulster Constabulary (RUC) in Northern Ireland.

The solidity of Irish parliamentary democracy was confirmed when, following the General Election of 1932, there was a fairly smooth transfer of authority from the pro-Treaty party Cumann na nGaedhal to its old civil war rivals, now led by de Valera under the banner of Fianna Fáil. Fianna Fáil had no allegiance to the Treaty. In the course of the next five years it proceeded to dismantle the main elements of the British connection. It abolished the royal oath, the right of appeal to the Privy Council, and in 1936 removed the Seanad and the Governor-General. Since Fianna Fáil also held the 1922 Constitution to be illegitimate, de Valera began a new draft in 1935 which was passed in the Dáil in June 1937 by 62 votes to 48.

The 1937 Constitution and the Republic of Ireland Act, 1948

The new Constitution (Bunreacht na hÉireann) reaffirmed that the powers of political institutions derived from the people but emphasized Ireland's status as an independent state. Article 2 expressed a controversial assertion of *de jure* sovereignty over the six counties of Northern Ireland by proclaiming the national territory to be 'the whole island of Ireland'. Article 3 accepted *de facto* that Northern Ireland was outside the Constitution's jurisdiction and provided that 'pending the re-integration of the national territory' Irish law would apply only in the 26 counties.

The Constitution left intact the institutions of parliamentary democracy bequeathed by its predecessor, even re-establishing the Seanad. The one major change was the office of a directly elected President to replace the Governor-General. Until Easter 1949, however, the formal Irish Head of State continued to be King George VI. The 1937 Constitution was a fundamental document in the way that the 1922 Constitution was not. Amendment required a popular referendum and the validity of laws under the Constitution could be referred to the Supreme Court for review. Though Catholic social teaching had influenced legislation after 1921, the 1937 Constitution went further by formally recognizing in Article 44 'the special position of the Holy Catholic Apostolic and Roman Church as the guardian of the Faith professed by the great majority' of Irish citizens. This 'special position' was removed by referendum in 1972. If a Protestant Parliament and a Protestant state was the image of Unionist Northern Ireland, then de Valera's Constitution consolidated his vision of southern Ireland as a Catholic state for a Catholic nation. The Republic of Ireland Act, 1948 'declared that the description of the State shall be the Republic of Ireland'. This Act cut the remaining connections to the Crown and to the British Commonwealth. Symbolically, it came into effect on Easter Day 1949.

Political institutions

The 1937 Constitution has been amended over the years by referenda to take account of European Union membership, social changes and the peace process in Northern Ireland, but these amendments have not altered significantly the relationships between domestic institutions.

The President

The President is directly elected, holds office for seven years and can be re-elected for one further term. Candidates for the office must be nominated by at least 20 members of the Oireachtas or by four local councils. In practice, presidential candidates are usually chosen by the major political parties and on two occasions there was an agreed candidate. The President became Head of State after Easter 1949 (replacing the British monarch). The office is expected to be above party politics and normally the President will act only on the advice and with the consent of the government. The functions of the office are mainly ceremonial but the President does have the power to refer a bill to the Supreme Court to test its constitutionality (apart from money bills and bills to amend the Constitution). Political controversy over one such referral, the Emergency Powers bill, led to the resignation of President Ó Dálaigh in 1976. The office also provides an opportunity to promote a distinctive image of the state. De Valera's two-term presidency (1959–1973) embodied continuity and tradition. Mary Robinson's presidency (1990–1997) – she was the first woman to hold the office – embodied change and innovation as Ireland self-consciously modernized and liberalized. Mary McAleese (1997–2011) was the first President to come from Northern Ireland and symbolized a new relationship between Ireland and the UK. The presidential election of 2011 was unusually controversial. Martin McGuinness of

PLATE 6.3 Mary Robinson was, in 1990, the first woman to become President of Ireland. Her presidency was symbolic of a changing Ireland, more liberal, secular and inclusive. © Allstar Picture Library/Alamy

Sinn Féin, allegedly a former chief of staff on the IRA's Army Council, sought election on the platform of being a peacemaker in Northern Ireland but many thought his election would symbolize a return to the past. The current President, Michael D. Higgins, has made social inclusion the theme of his seven-year term.

It has been suggested that both the so-called Irish 'diaspora' – Irish citizens living abroad – and citizens of Northern Ireland should be allowed to vote in presidential elections. The one reform which the Fine Gael–Labour Coalition elected in 2011 has proposed is to reduce the presidential term to five years from 2018.

The Dáil

The Dáil is the main legislative, or lawmaking, chamber of the Irish Parliament. It comprises 166 members representing 43 constituencies, elected by proportional representation (PR) for a maximum term of five years. Constituency boundaries

TABLE 6.1 Irish presidents since 1938

Douglas Hyde	1938–1945
Seán O'Ceallaigh	1945–1959
Éamon de Valera	1959–1973
Erskine Childers	1973–1974 (died in office)
Cearbhall Ó Dálaigh	1974–1976 (resigned)
Patrick Hillery	1976–1990
Mary Robinson	1990–1997 (resigned a few months before end of term)
Mary McAleese	1997–2011
Michael D. Higgins	2011–

are regularly revised by an independent commission. The Dáil is presided over by the Ceann Comhairle or Speaker. Normally it sits for three sessions per year (about 95 days in total) and usually meets for three days (about 30 hours) each week, Tuesday through Thursday. The Fine Gael–Labour Coalition, elected in 2011, intends to use Friday sittings as well to discuss committee reports and Private Members' business. The main formal work of the Dáil is the passage of legislation and its procedures show the influence of British parliamentary practice. Legislation passes through a number of readings or stages as set out in Figure 6.1.

If there are no amendments by the Seanad, or if the Dáil accepts Seanad amendments, the bill is sent to the President for signing into law. If the Dáil disagrees with Seanad amendments the bill is sent back to the Seanad for further

First reading: formal notification of the bill.

↓

Second reading: general debate on the principles of the bill. No amendments are accepted and the bill is voted for or against in its entirety.

↓

Committee stage: the bill is debated in detail in one of the specialist committees of the Dáil and detailed amendments are either accepted or rejected.

↓

Report stage: at this stage the Dáil has an opportunity to insert further amendments.

↓

Third reading: final reading of the bill before it passes to the second chamber, the Seanad. The Seanad cannot amend money bills (legislation dealing with finance).

FIGURE 6.1 Passage of legislation through the Dáil

reflection. The Seanad can either accept the will of the Dáil or delay – but not reject – the final passage of the bill.

As in most parliamentary democracies the government, or executive branch, controls the business of the Dáil because it normally has a majority of TDs. Amendments to bills are usually government amendments or those that the government is willing to accept.

Since executives play such an extensive role in modern societies, one of the other key functions of a legislature is the task of scrutiny. The Dáil adopted the British model of parliamentary questions and latterly of parliamentary select committees. TDs have the opportunity to put oral and written questions to government ministers on policy matters within their departmental responsibilities. The system of parliamentary questioning is extensive and well developed. In 2009, for example, about 54,000 questions were answered. It is used by TDs to raise issues of national importance, party advantage or, most frequently, of specific interest to their constituents. Since 1997, a system of parliamentary committees has been established. There are three main types of committee. First, select committees of the Dáil and Seanad which are responsible for dealing with the committee stages of parliamentary bills. Second, there are joint committees comprising the select committees of the Dáil and Seanad sitting together to monitor and scrutinize issues relevant to specific government departments. For example, the respective Dáil and Seanad select committees on Foreign Affairs and Trade sit together as the Joint Committee on Foreign Affairs and Trade. Third, there are standing committees, such as the (Dáil-only) Committee of Public Accounts which scrutinizes reports of government expenditure.

The Seanad

The Seanad comprises 60 members. The vision of the Seanad in the 1937 Constitution was one of vocational or interest representation, a reflection of Catholic social philosophy at the time. However, since the electorate for the Seanad is mainly composed of party politicians its membership reflects their priorities. Forty-three Senators are elected from five panels (Figure 6.2). About 1,000 persons are eligible to vote in these panels, comprising county and city councillors, members of the Dáil and outgoing Senators.

Agriculture	11 seats
Culture and education	5 seats
Industry and commerce	9 seats
Labour	11 seats
Public administration	7 seats

FIGURE 6.2 Senate panels

A further six Senators are elected by university graduates: three by the National University of Ireland and three by Trinity College Dublin. The remaining 11 are appointed by the Taoiseach, usually ensuring a government majority in the chamber. Though it plays a useful role in taking some of the burden of legislative and committee work, the powers of the Seanad are limited. It is now common for the government to use the Seanad to introduce legislation and it normally meets only on Wednesdays and Thursdays. The Fine Gael–Labour Coalition elected in 2011 is committed to abolishing the Seanad and has promised a referendum on its future.

Criticisms of Irish parliamentary democracy

One of the traditional criticisms of TDs is that they focus too much on their constituents' interests and too little on influencing legislation or scrutinizing ministers and public officials. The localism of TDs and the ineffectiveness of the legislature, it is suggested, have been the reasons for many corruption scandals in recent years.

The Oireachtas committee system has also been criticized for being ineffective, weak and limited in powers. In particular, it has been criticized for failing to oversee financial policy properly and, along with the whole political system, was brought into disrepute by the banking crisis of 2008. The Fine Gael–Labour Coalition intends to give committees greater power and responsibility. They will be permitted to introduce legislation; government will enable committees to consider the general scheme of bills before publication; and parliamentary time will be made available to debate committee reports. The proposal in the Thirtieth Amendment to the Constitution to grant committees full powers to investigate matters of public interest was rejected in a referendum held at the same time as the presidential election of October 2011.

Others argue that the conduct of business in the Oireachtas requires greater professionalism and expertise. The perceived ineffectiveness of Parliament may be due neither to the facilities for debate nor to the opportunities for scrutiny but to the tight discipline of party organization. The large 'payroll' vote of government ministers in the Dáil and the aspiration of backbench TDs to achieve government office provide incentives for partisan politics rather than for a common parliamentary viewpoint. However, this is a common problem for parliaments and not exclusively an Irish issue.

Government

The exercise of executive authority in Ireland follows the UK model. The Taoiseach, or Prime Minister, is elected by the Dáil and heads a Cabinet of

Ministers. These ministers are responsible to the Dáil for their respective departments of state. The Cabinet operates on the principle of collective responsibility
and ministers are required to defend the policy of government as a whole, even
if that government is a coalition of different parties. While there is no constitutional limit on the number of departments, the Constitution specifies that the
government should contain a minimum of 7 and a maximum of 15 members.
No more than two may be members of the Seanad. As in the British system, there
is no separation of the executive and legislature and the political effectiveness of
the government rests upon support in the Dáil. Government is the source
of nearly all legislation. The Cabinet, normally chaired by the Taioseach or his
deputy, the Tánaiste, is the central decision-making body of government. The
Taoiseach has the power to call a general election and can recommend dissolution
of Parliament to the President at any time, though he or she must resign on losing
a vote of confidence in the Dáil. Like the British Prime Minister, the Taoiseach
also exerts considerable political authority over Cabinet colleagues whom he or
she may dismiss. Unlike the British Prime Minister, the Taoiseach heads a separate
Department of the Taoiseach that coordinates responsibilities in domestic and
international affairs. Recently, Northern Ireland has featured prominently among
that department's concerns. Other responsibilities include public service reform,
Ireland's relations with the European Union and coordination of relations with
business and the trade unions. Government business in the Dáil is managed by
the Chief Whip who attends Cabinet meetings but does not have a vote. The
Chief Whip is responsible to the Taoiseach with the task of ensuring that party
discipline is maintained and that legislative objectives are secured.

The Irish Civil Service too has traditionally operated on the British model of
neutrality: loyalty to ministers, giving impartial advice and administering policy,
irrespective of the political complexion of government. This, of course, is an ideal
but it still informs the ethos of public service. The Public Service Management
Act, 1997 set out for the first time in law the functions and responsibilities of
departmental secretaries general and heads of offices. Ireland is a unitary state
and its government is highly centralized in Dublin; recently the intention has
been to decentralize administration in order to spread regionally the employment
benefits of modern public service. In 2003/2004, the government announced
proposals to relocate about 11,000 civil servants and the headquarters of some
departments outside the capital. By 2010 only about 3,000 Civil Service jobs had
been relocated. The financial crisis in 2008 meant that it was unlikely that
expenditure on the programme of decentralization would go ahead.

Local government

Modern local government in Ireland can be traced to the Local Government Act
(1898) that restructured and democratized the nineteenth-century administrative

patchwork. In 1999 the Constitution was amended to recognize formally local government and it specified that elections be held every five years. The Department of Environment, Community and Local Government oversees the local government system. There are 75 Town Councils, 29 County Councils, 5 Borough Councils and 5 City Councils. There are also eight Regional Authorities, established in 1994, which coordinate some of the functions of the councils and are responsible for the implementation of EU funding. Furthermore, two Regional Assemblies – Midland and Western, and Southern and Eastern – were set up in 1999 to promote coordination of public services. The Irish local government system is distinguished by the division between its political and managerial aspects. Executive decisions are taken mainly by the City or County Manager and are presented to the elected councillors for ratification. This managerial procedure was designed to address public complaints about corruption and discrimination. Managers are selected by an independent Local Appointments Commission and appointed for seven-year terms.

As in the British system, local authority powers are conferred by government and most of its finance, about 75 per cent, is centrally allocated as well. The rest is mainly raised through a local rating system on property. Local government is relatively weak and the power of councillors is limited, but they do have an important influence over local planning applications. Like TDs, councillors tend to act as mediators between constituents and the local bureaucracy.

Parties and elections

The electoral system in Ireland is conducted according to the single transferable vote (STV) system of proportional representation (PR). For Dáil elections there are 43 multi-member constituencies which, depending on population, return between three and five TDs. Voters rank candidates by putting '1' against their first choice (known as the first preference vote) and 2, 3, 4, etc. lower preferences as they wish. This permits the voter to choose not only between parties but between candidates representing the same party. To be elected, a candidate must achieve a 'quota' which is calculated by dividing the number of votes cast in a constituency by the number of seats plus one and then adding one to the number. The formula is:

$$\text{Quota} = \frac{\text{Total number of valid votes}}{\text{Number of seats} + 1} + 1$$

The election count involves redistribution of the votes of those already over the quota and the elimination and redistribution of the votes of the lowest-placed candidate. This process continues until all the seats are filled.

The two major parties in Ireland can trace their origins to the split in Sinn Féin over the Anglo-Irish Treaty of 1921. Historically the most successful of these parties, Fianna Fáil (FF), was founded in 1926. By 1932 it had become the largest party and secured an overall majority in the Dáil with the support of the Irish Labour Party. The party was responsible for framing the Constitution of 1937. In the 1938 election FF won a majority of the votes and seats and did so again in 1977. It enjoyed two periods in office of 16 years' duration – 1932 to 1948 and 1957 to 1973. FF became one of the most successful political parties in Europe and came to think of itself (like the Conservative Party in the UK) as the natural party of government. Although it has been unable to govern alone since 1989, FF continued to be the dominant partner when in coalition. Indeed, its main partner in recent coalitions – the Progressive Democrats (PDs) – was a party formed in 1985 by FF dissidents critical of the party's then leader Charles Haughey. The PDs were dissolved in 2009. Of the nine Irish Presidents, six have been FF nominations.

The traditional electoral success of FF was its cross-class appeal. It presented itself as the party of republican patriotism, the Irish language and international neutrality. Not only did it appeal to Ireland's large rural constituency, it also had a base among the urban working class. Nor did the populist inheritance of FF's policy diminish its support among the business community. The party is organized in local branches which provide delegates to constituency-level bodies known as Comhairle Dáilcheantair (Constituency Councils) which select candidates for national and European elections. The Ard-Fheis (Annual Conference) is officially the supreme governing body, electing the President of the party. However, the President is always the parliamentary party leader and policy-making is mainly the responsibility of ministers (when in government) or spokespersons (when in opposition).

Though it achieved an average of over 40 per cent of the vote between 1945 and 2007, FF performed disastrously in the General Election of 2011. As the major governing party, the electorate blamed FF for the banking crisis and associated it with corruption and incompetence. The collapse of popular support was dramatic. In the election of 2007, FF took just under 42 per cent of the vote and had 77 TDs. In 2011, it took just 17.4 per cent of the vote and was reduced to 20 TDs. A further sign of its electoral weakness was the decision not to nominate a candidate for the 2011 presidential election, though one of the candidates, Seán Gallagher, who polled nearly 30 per cent of the vote, had been closely associated with FF. The party must now struggle to make itself a credible party of government again and this may take a generation.

The second major party, Fine Gael (FG), developed out of the pro-Treaty Cumann na nGaedheal which had governed until 1932. Established in 1933, it became the main opposition party in the state. Traditionally, the party's appeal has been to a conservative constituency of large farmers and the urban middle class. Because of its more moderate nationalism, FG attracted the support of the Protestant minority even though FG was part of the government coalition which established the Irish Republic in 1949. In the 1960s the party developed a European-style identity promoted by its later leader Garrett Fitzgerald, trying to

PLATE 6.4 Fine Gael leader Enda Kenny in front of an election poster during the general election campaign of 2011. In a dramatic result, Fine Gael became the largest party in the Dáil for the first time in its history and Kenny became Taoiseach in a new governing coalition with Labour. © Stephen Power/Alamy

position itself alongside European Christian Democratic parties. This centrist appeal enabled the party to form coalition governments with Labour in the 1970s and 1980s and with Labour and the Democratic Left in the 1990s. In the post-war period, FG had about one-third of the vote and in 1982 it recorded its best performance with 39 per cent. Over the next 20 years the party's vote slipped, and in the General Election of 2002 it returned its worst result since 1948 with only 22.5 per cent. In 2007, however, its vote recovered to 27.3 per cent and by 2011, profiting from FF's collapse, it became the largest party with 36 per cent of the vote, winning 76 seats in the Dáil.

Like FF, the party organization is based on local branches which, in delegate bodies, select candidates for local councils and the Dáil. Again, like FF, the Ard-Fheis is the supreme governing body, though the major decisions on policy are taken by the leader and senior members of the party.

A number of smaller populist or socialist parties have periodically challenged the two-party dominance of FF and FG. The importance of nationalism, the significance of old civil war divisions in party politics and the size of the rural electorate have made it difficult for socialist or left-of-centre parties to achieve electoral success. The most enduring has been the Labour Party, though it too has strong nationalist sympathies and is marked by the history of the civil war. One of its major successes was the election of Mary Robinson, a Labour member, as President in 1990. In 1992 Labour achieved a surprising 19 per cent of the vote but the party's role as 'king-maker' in governing coalitions – first FF and then FG – did not secure its appeal and its vote halved at the election in 1997. In 1998 it agreed to merge with the smaller left-wing party, the Democratic Left. This merger did not deliver an immediate electoral breakthrough. However, as the economic crisis undermined support for FF, Labour also profited electorally. In 2011 it emerged as the second largest party with 19.4 per cent of the vote and 37 Dáil seats. Its candidate, Michael D. Higgins, became the ninth Irish President in 2011.

In recent years Sinn Féin, formerly the political wing of the Provisional IRA, has benefited from the peace process in Northern Ireland and political disaffection in working-class areas to make an impact in Irish party politics. In 1986 the party dropped its policy of abstention from the Dáil. In 1997 it won its first Dáil seat and took five seats in 2002. In 2007 it achieved just under 7 per cent of the vote, losing one Dáil seat. However, in 2011 SF emerged as the fourth party in the state with just under 10 per cent of the vote and 14 Dáil seats. As an all-Ireland party, it is discussed further in the following section. The Green Party won nearly 5 per cent of the vote in 2007 and, with six seats in the Dáil, formed part of the governing coalition with FF. However, in the election of 2011 its vote fell to below 2 per cent and the party lost all of its seats.

Northern Ireland after 1921: the political framework

The Government of Ireland Act of 1920 established institutions that were to govern Northern Ireland from 1921 to 1972, though Northern Ireland continued to have representation in the Westminster Parliament. In the 1918 General Election, 30 Westminster MPs represented the six counties which were to form Northern Ireland. The 1920 Act reduced these to 13. In 1982 the number of seats was increased to 18, though representation will fall to 16 when, according to legislation passed in 2011, the House of Commons is reduced to 600 MPs. The Crown in Northern Ireland was represented by a Governor who conducted the ceremonial duties of the monarch. It was the convention at Westminster that matters devolved to Northern Ireland would not be subject to scrutiny. As a consequence, the Parliament of Northern Ireland was accorded substantial autonomy.

The Northern Ireland Parliament was bicameral and became known from 1932 as Stormont after its new building in East Belfast. The House of Commons consisted of a fixed number of 52 seats and elections were to be held every five years. The original system of election was by PR (STV) in multi-member con-stituencies. To secure its majority, in 1929 the Unionist government abolished PR and introduced simple majority voting in single-member constituencies. This made little difference to Unionist Party dominance of the House of Commons, since it never held fewer than 32 seats. The second chamber, the Senate, consisted of 26 seats held for a term of two Parliaments. Twenty-four members of the Senate were elected by the House of Commons and the remaining two were the Lord Mayor of Belfast and the Mayor of Londonderry/Derry. It was not politically significant and had little power. Government was fashioned on the Westminster model. It consisted of a Prime Minister who led a Cabinet of departmental ministers. It managed devolved matters such as education, agriculture, local government, policing and the courts. The principle of collective responsibility consolidated the control of the Unionist Party over Parliament, since up to one half of Unionist MPs could hold some sort of government post. The administration of policy was managed by a separate Northern Ireland Civil Service (NICS), again modelled on British practice.

For most of the Northern Ireland Parliament's existence, Catholic disaffection with Unionist political control and their exclusion from political influence was poorly organized and ineffective. This changed after 1967 with the emergence of the Northern Ireland Civil Rights Association (NICRA). NICRA demanded an end to discriminatory practices in local government elections, fairer allocation of public housing and reform of security policy. Through protest marches and demonstrations, it focused world attention on policing and administration in Northern Ireland. By 1970 civil rights protest compelled the Unionist government, under pressure from London, to concede most of NICRA's demands.

The Troubles

Confrontation over civil rights claims between Unionists and Nationalists became violent throughout 1968 and 1969, with widespread rioting and destruction of property. British troops were deployed in August 1969 to 'aid the civil power' in the preservation of law and order. At first British soldiers were welcomed by Catholics as protection against what Nationalists saw as a Unionist police force, but this soon changed as the newly formed Provisional IRA (or Provos) went on the offensive against what it saw as British 'occupation forces'. The Provisional IRA had split from the old (Official) IRA in 1969. Whereas the OIRA tended to advocate a socialist solution to communal division, the PIRA represented a return to militant nationalism and began a systematic campaign of bombing and shootings to achieve Irish unity. It grew in support after a failed attempt to intern IRA activists in August 1971 and after the army's shooting dead of 13 people when rioting broke out at a civil rights protest in Londonderry/Derry on 30 January 1972, an event known as 'Bloody Sunday'. David Cameron as Prime Minister of the UK apologized on behalf of the British government for this event following the publication of the Saville Inquiry Report in 2010.

On 21 July 1972 the IRA exploded over 20 bombs in Belfast, killing 9 people and seriously injuring 130. This became known as Bloody Friday. Though the annual death-toll fell steadily throughout the 1970s, Nationalist sympathy for Republican prisoners who died in the Hunger Strike of 1981 helped sustain the IRA's campaign for another decade. In the 1980s it had been supplied with automatic weapons and explosives by Libya's Colonel Gaddafi. By this time the IRA had developed into an efficient terrorist organization capable not only of attacks in Northern Ireland but also of bombing cities in England and British Army bases in Germany. It almost succeeded in killing the British Prime Minister Mrs Thatcher and senior members of her Cabinet in 1984. A number of Protestant and Loyalist terror groups also emerged during this period, the largest being the Ulster Defence Association (UDA) and the Ulster Volunteer Force (UVF). Both of these organizations were mainly responsible for murdering innocent Catholics. The campaigns of both Republican and Loyalist paramilitaries were arguably strategically ineffective but they did frustrate attempts at agreement in Northern Ireland.

According to the most systematic survey, by the end of 1998 (the year of the Good Friday (Belfast) Agreement) 3,636 people had died in the Troubles (Table 6.2). About 58 per cent of these deaths can be attributed to Republicans, more than half to the IRA alone, and about 33 per cent to Loyalist paramilitaries. The police and army were together responsible for 10 per cent of all deaths. Civilians suffered most casualties, the highest incidence being in North and West Belfast.

PLATE 6.5 A member of the Royal Ulster Constabulary (RUC) and soldiers of the British Army in action in Belfast, 1981. In the course of the Troubles 300 RUC officers and 503 soldiers lost their lives. © Homer Sykes/Alamy

TABLE 6.2 Deaths in the Troubles (1966–1998)	
Catholic civilians	1,232
Protestant civilians	698
Police and local security forces	509
Army	503
Republicans	392
Loyalists	144
Other	158 (mainly deaths outside Northern Ireland)
Total	3,636

Source: D. McKittrick *et al.*, *Lost Lives* (1999)

The years with the largest number of fatalities were 1972 (496) and 1976 (308). Improvements in security techniques and intelligence gathering were largely successful in containing terrorist violence such that by the early 1990s the futility of the IRA's campaign was clear. Republicans and Loyalists both called ceasefires in 1994 in order to engage in political talks about the future of Northern Ireland. However, the Real IRA (Republicans who reject the Belfast Agreement) planted a car bomb in Omagh on 15 August 1998, killing 29 people. This so-called 'dissident republican' activity continues as a threat to public safety. In recent years four security personnel – two soldiers and two Catholic policemen – have died as a result of Real IRA attacks.

Direct rule

When the Northern Ireland Parliament was prorogued in 1972, direct rule was introduced. Direct rule meant that Westminster took responsibility for matters previously transferred to Stormont. This was given effect by the Northern Ireland (Temporary Provisions) Act, 1972. Political direction was provided by the Secretary of State for Northern Ireland who sat in the Cabinet in London. The Secretary of State was responsible for the conduct of policy in Northern Ireland and for representing its interests on the international stage. The Secretary of State had a team of junior ministers to whom were delegated the responsibilities of distinct Northern Ireland departments. The Northern Ireland Office (NIO), a Department of State created in 1972, dealt with political and terrorist issues. A Cabinet Committee on Northern Ireland, chaired by the Prime Minister, oversaw the security and strategic aspects of Northern Ireland policy. This policy involved a series of 'political initiatives'.

Between 1972 and 1974 the object was the construction of devolved government based on power-sharing between Unionists and Nationalists and a new relationship between Northern Ireland and the Republic. The first was legislated for in the Northern Ireland Constitution Act, 1973 which provided for an Assembly and an Executive. The second was agreed at Sunningdale in December 1973 and provided for a Council of Ireland as a linking institution between the two parts of Ireland. This initiative failed in 1974 as a result of the Loyalist (Ulster Workers' Council) general strike and Unionist rejection of the Council of Ireland. After 1979 the Conservative government of Margaret Thatcher tried a further initiative. An elected Assembly (1982–1986) was established to which powers could be devolved so long as there was cross-party consensus. This was known as 'rolling devolution' but it failed owing to a Nationalist boycott of the Assembly.

The Anglo-Irish Agreement (AIA) of 1985, signed by Margaret Thatcher and Garrett Fitzgerald, was an inter-governmental approach committing the British and Irish governments to work cooperatively to seek a solution in Northern Ireland. It put the 'Irish dimension' first. The institutions of the Agreement – the Anglo-Irish Conference and Secretariat – gave the Government of Ireland a consultative role in the affairs of Northern Ireland. However, the AIA itself became part of the problem and the need to accommodate Unionist rejection of the Agreement led to renewed talks between the British and Irish governments and the Northern Ireland parties in 1991 and 1992.

In 1993, the strategy changed again. It involved the British and Irish governments seeking to promote inclusive political talks. This meant bringing the extremes (Republicans and Loyalists) into political talks about Northern Ireland's future. This became known as 'the peace process'. In the Downing Street Declaration of December 1993, the British and Irish Prime Ministers (John Major and Albert Reynolds) set out the democratic principles for any future settlement in Northern Ireland. After 1996, multi-party talks chaired by former US Senator George Mitchell commenced, but because of a temporary breach in the IRA's ceasefire, Sinn Féin was not admitted until September 1997. Talks were conducted in a three-strand format as set out in Figure 6.3.

Strand one – negotiations about the devolved institutions involving the Northern Ireland parties and the British government.

Strand two – negotiations about north–south relationships involving the Northern Ireland parties and the British and Irish governments.

Strand three – negotiations about British–Irish inter-governmental relationships involving the two governments alone.

FIGURE 6.3 Three-strand format in multi-party talks, 1997

The outcome was the Good Friday (Belfast) Agreement of April 1998 and it incorporated the democratic and constitutional principles set out in the previous decade. The main institutions of the Agreement were:

- A legislative Assembly responsible for devolved matters, taking decisions on the basis of parallel Unionist/Nationalist consent.
- An Executive, chaired by a First Minister and Deputy First Minister, responsible for a programme of government. The Executive is a 'compulsory coalition' with seats allocated between the parties according to a mathematical formula (the d'Hondt system).
- A North/South Ministerial Council (NSMC) to consult on cross-border cooperation between the Northern Ireland Executive and the Government of the Republic of Ireland. The NSMC oversees the operation of six north/south bodies, such as Waterways Ireland, operating on an all-island basis and assists, where appropriate, cooperation between Belfast and Dublin in six further areas such as agriculture, health and tourism.
- A British–Irish Council comprising representatives of the British and Irish governments, representatives of the newly devolved institutions in Northern Ireland, Scotland and Wales, and representatives from the Isle of Man and the Channel Islands, to consult on matters of mutual interest.
- Cooperation between London and Dublin in a new British–Irish Inter-governmental Conference, replacing the Anglo-Irish Agreement of 1985.

On 22 May 1998, the Agreement was approved in referenda in Northern Ireland and the Republic of Ireland. The vote in favour in Northern Ireland was 71.1 per cent, though this vote concealed the fact that only a small majority of Unionists (about 51 per cent) was in favour. In the Republic of Ireland 94.4 per cent voted in favour. One consequence of that vote was the requirement to modify Articles 2 and 3 of the Irish Constitution to accept the principle of consent in Northern Ireland. This was supported by 94 per cent of the Irish electorate in a further referendum held in June 1998.

The institutions did not become operative until December 1999 owing to a fundamental difference of interpretation between Unionists and Sinn Féin about when the IRA was required to hand over its weapons ('decommissioning'). Subsequently there were four suspensions of devolution, the most protracted between October 2002 and May 2007 following allegations of an IRA spy network in the Assembly. In September 2005 the final decommissioning of IRA weapons took place. The St Andrews Agreement of October 2006 set out an arrangement, brokered by the two governments, for power-sharing between the (now) two largest parties, SF and the Democratic Unionist Party (DUP). This Agreement did not change the basic structure of the 1998 Good Friday (Belfast) Agreement, but did contain some new provisions. These included a statutory ministerial code, which required decisions to have the full consent of the Executive and not just that of the individual minister; and changes to the procedure for appointing the First and Deputy First Minister. Both strengthened the position of the DUP and SF. There was also a requirement, demanded by the DUP, that all parties demonstrate acceptance of the new Police Service of Northern Ireland (PSNI). This permitted devolution to be restored on 8 May 2007.

Assembly and Executive

The Northern Ireland Assembly, presided over by a Speaker, is the legislative body for devolved matters like education and health. There are 108 Members of the Legislative Assembly (MLAs), or one MLA per 16,565 of the population. The Assembly meets in plenary session on Mondays and Tuesdays for formal debates and ministerial questions. MLAs are required to designate themselves according to communal identity – Unionist, Nationalist or Other – in order to test cross-community support on certain Assembly votes.

Most of the day-to-day work of the Assembly is conducted in committees, the membership of which reflects the composition of the Assembly as a whole. There are three types of committee: Statutory, Standing and Ad Hoc. By far the most important are the 12 Statutory Committees which shadow the Executive Departments. They are part of the legislative process, discussing the detailed aspects of primary legislation. They also review and advise on departmental budgets, can hold enquires and make reports. Statutory committees can also initiate legislation. Each committee normally has 11 members but such is the

PLATE 6.6 The Chamber of the Northern Ireland Assembly, Parliament Buildings, Stormont, Belfast. The photograph shows a plenary session of the Assembly presided over by the Speaker. © Design Pics Inc. – RM Content/Alamy

scope and burden of work that most MLAs sit on more than one committee. The legislative stages in the Assembly are:

- First stage: Introduction of a bill.
- Second stage: Debate and vote on the general principles of a bill.
- Committee stage: Detailed investigation by a committee and the publication of a report for consideration by the Assembly.
- Consideration stage: Consideration of and vote by the Assembly on the details of a bill, including proposed amendments.
- Further consideration stage: Consideration by the Assembly of further proposed amendments to a bill.
- Final stage: Passing or rejecting of a bill by the Assembly, without further amendment.
- Royal assent.

The Office of First and Deputy First Minister (OFMDFM) coordinates the Executive and aims to ensure the effective delivery of public administration. The Northern Ireland Executive (or Executive Committee) is not a voluntary but a compulsory coalition. The Executive represents an inclusive form of power-sharing and parties with sufficient seats in the Assembly take up posts on the Executive by right. Currently there are five parties in the Executive: two Unionist, one Republican, one Nationalist and one cross-community, the Alliance Party. The exception to the rule is the Alliance which, though smaller than the other parties, has two ministers. It was necessary to appoint a 'neutral' or non-communal minister to take initial responsibility for policing and justice in 2010 and the Alliance Party leader, David Ford, took up that position. Though the Executive is required to agree a collective programme for government and a budget, ministers often act on party rather than collective principles. In the Executive of 1999 to 2002, the two DUP ministers even refused to take part in formal meetings and saw themselves as an 'internal opposition'. This changed after May 2007 and the DUP now plays a leading part in the Executive under a newly amended Ministerial Code which stresses collective responsibility.

Criticisms of the institutions

Critics have argued that the new institutions make good government in Northern Ireland difficult to achieve. First, it is claimed that there is no commitment to an agreed political community and that power is not so much shared as divided up. Second, it is believed that the formation of the Executive on strict proportionality has fragmented public administration and prevented 'joined-up' government. It took the Executive more than six months from the Assembly election in May 2011 to propose a draft Programme for Government, 2011–2015. Third, another major complaint is that there is no effective political opposition in the Assembly. If all the major parties have positions in government, it is argued, there is little incentive for MLAs to hold the Executive to account. Though most people prefer administrative difficulties and political delay to political violence, the tendency of political institutions to postpone decisions rather than to make them may possibly alienate the electorate in the future.

Local government

The Local Government (NI) Act of 1972 entailed a drastic reduction in the powers of local government. Seventy-three elected local authorities were replaced by 26 councils based on district towns and the cities of Belfast and Londonderry/Derry. The introduction of PR (STV) reversed the simple majority procedure enacted by the Unionist government in 1922. Control of public housing and education was removed from councils. Now that devolved government has been restored, reform of local government has come on to the political agenda again. A Review of Public Administration, which reported in 2005, suggested reducing the 26 councils to 7 – Belfast and 6 others – with a maximum membership of 50 councillors. It also suggested returning planning powers to local level. This caused political controversy between the political parties. The draft Programme for Government announced in November 2011 proposes to establish an 11-council model for local government by 2015.

Political parties

Division between parties in Northern Ireland has been on the constitutional question: should Northern Ireland remain part of the United Kingdom or should Northern Ireland become part of a united Ireland? Support for Unionist parties is overwhelmingly Protestant and support for Nationalist and Republican parties is overwhelmingly Catholic. A small number of parties have competed for a cross-community vote. Only the Alliance Party, formed in April 1970, has played a sustained role. Its electoral support is about 8 per cent.

Unionist political parties

The Ulster Unionist Party (UUP) can trace its origins to the Ulster Unionist Council (UUC), a collection of organizations established in 1905 to resist Home Rule. It was associated with the Protestant Orange Order which continued to have direct representation in the UUC until 2005. Between 1921 and 1972 the UUP was the party of government and the dominant force both in Unionism and in Northern Ireland. In elections to the Northern Ireland Parliament the party usually won three-quarters of the seats with about 50 per cent of the vote. It split in 1973/1974 when its leader, Brian Faulkner, took part in the power-sharing Executive with Nationalists. A reunited UUP again became the largest Unionist party and its leadership resisted power-sharing devolution. When David Trimble was made leader in 1995 he committed the UUP to a negotiated settlement, calculating that an inclusive agreement with Nationalists was the best way to secure the Union. However, the party's electoral support has declined steadily, from 27 per cent in the Assembly election of 2003 to just over 13 per cent in 2011; it is now only the third largest party in terms of seats (16). Until 1974 the UUP maintained a direct organizational link with the British Conservative (and Unionist) Party. In 2009, the Ulster Unionists again formed an alliance with the local Conservative Party to form the Ulster Conservatives and Unionist – New Force (UCUNF). Under this label in the 2010 Westminster General Election, it lost its only seat in the House of Commons.

The Democratic Unionist Party (DUP) was founded by the Reverend Ian Paisley in 1971. For most of its history the DUP was the 'junior' party to the UUP but has since overtaken it. Historically, the DUP favoured a comprehensive devolved arrangement within the UK but, like the UUP, opposed executive power-sharing and an institutionalized Irish dimension. It refused to participate in the multi-party talks when Republicans were admitted in 1997 and opposed the Good Friday (Belfast) Agreement of 1998. The DUP modified its opposition after 2003 and argued for a 'renegotiation' of the Agreement to secure a 'fair deal' for Protestants. It claimed that the St Andrews Agreement of 2006 satisfied that agenda. In May 2007 the DUP took the First Minister's post. By this time the DUP was the largest party in Northern Ireland, securing over 30 per cent of the vote in the Assembly election of 2007. In the Assembly elections of 2011 it maintained that percentage and has 38 seats, while in the Westminster election of 2010 the DUP polled 25 per cent of the Northern Ireland vote and won eight seats.

Nationalist and Republican political parties

The Social Democratic and Labour Party (SDLP) was formed in August 1970. It was a coalition of political interests, bringing together elements of the Catholic Nationalist Party, civil rights activists and the Catholic labour tradition. Though its constitution stressed socialist objectives, the main purpose of the party was to promote the cause of Irish unity by agreement. The SDLP became the dominant party among Catholic voters owing to its rejection of IRA violence. Under the leadership of Gerry Fitt, it seemed to have achieved most of its immediate policy objectives in the power-sharing Executive/Council of Ireland in 1973/1974. The collapse of that body encouraged the SDLP to take a different strategy under the leadership of John Hume after 1979.

The SDLP was instrumental in promoting the Anglo–Irish Agreement of 1985. In the late 1980s and early 1990s, Hume tried to develop an agreed position with Sinn Féin (SF) and the Irish government on the future of Northern Ireland. Some have argued that this association with SF, while important for ending violence, helped undermine the SDLP's position of leadership within Catholic politics. In the Northern Ireland Assembly election of 1998 it was still the largest Nationalist party with 22 per cent of the vote. In the Assembly election of 2003 it was overtaken by SF (24 per cent to the SDLP's 18 per cent). In the Assembly elections of 2011 its vote fell to just over 14 per cent and 14 seats, while in the Westminster election of 2010 the party retained its three seats.

Sinn Féin (SF) was traditionally an abstentionist party both north and south of the Irish border. Under the leadership of Gerry Adams, SF has been able to transform itself from an adjunct to the IRA into a serious political party on the island of Ireland. In the past 30 years the party went through two distinct phases. The first was to advocate a parallel strategy of violence and politics, known as the 'ballot box and Armalite' strategy. In the Westminster General Election of 1983 SF won just over 13 per cent of the vote but IRA violence acted as an electoral disincentive. The second phase led to IRA ceasefires in 1994 and 1996. By 2000, SF had become a party of government in the country it had pledged to destroy. It is now the second party in the Assembly with 27 per cent of the vote and 29 seats. In the 2010 Westminster General Election, SF actually emerged as the largest single party in Northern Ireland with 25.5 per cent of the vote. It has five MPs at Westminster (though they still do not take their seats).

Attitudes to politics and government

In a poll in 2001 conducted by MRBI, citizens of Ireland revealed that government and politicians had a very limited influence on how they thought about the world. Only 2 per cent thought that they were an important factor compared with 71 per cent who thought that family and home were most important. However, levels of interest in Irish politics appear to be high. Another MRBI poll in the same year showed that 72 per cent were either fairly or very interested in political affairs. However, a Eurobarometer national survey in 2007 suggested that 'interest' did not mean 'active' interest. It found that only 10 per cent discussed political matters frequently, 58 per cent discussed them occasionally and 17 per cent never discussed them at all. In that same survey, 43 per cent trusted the Dáil and 41 per cent trusted the government. This was a comparatively low level of trust in European terms, especially in 2007 when the Irish economy was doing so well. It confirms the rather low expectation of politicians found in an IMS poll of May 2002. People were asked if they thought politicians, if elected, would deliver on promises made during an election campaign. Sixty-nine per cent believed they would not and only 21 per cent believed they would. Trust in Irish politics hit a low in 2010 when another Eurobarometer poll found that only 15 per cent of voters had confidence in their government and even fewer – 13 per cent – had confidence in their political parties. A *Red C* poll in May 2010 found that only 36 per cent of respondents thought that Ireland was 'heading in the right direction' politically.

On Northern Ireland, the overwhelming majority of citizens in Ireland continue to support the Good Friday (Belfast) Agreement. In 2001, an MRBI poll showed that 40 per cent did not think there would ever be a united Ireland and only 27 per cent believed they would see Irish unity within their own lifetime. A poll in the *Sunday Independent* in 2005 found that 45 per cent of those questioned would not vote for a united Ireland. While most would like to see a united Ireland, few believe it is of immediate importance and even fewer are willing to pay for it.

In 2001 the *Northern Ireland Life and Times Survey* (NILT) asked whether people thought that within the next 20 years there would be a United Ireland. Twenty-nine per cent of respondents thought it either likely or very likely and 52 per cent thought it either unlikely or very unlikely. A NILT survey published in 2011 showed that only 16 per cent of the total population and 33 per cent of Catholics favoured a united Ireland. There is probably some symmetry between Catholic opinion in Northern Ireland and views in the rest of Ireland. There is an aspiration for a united Ireland but it is not seen as an immediate priority or possibility. Protestants remain strongly opposed.

Figures show that approval of the current institutions in Northern Ireland remains mixed. Few express unqualified satisfaction with the *practice* if not the *idea* of them. Perhaps the most telling response is what is known as the 'zero-sum' or 'win/lose' question. The 2007 NILT survey asked: Does a political gain for one religious tradition usually result in a loss of ground for the other? Only 31 per cent disagreed. Trust in politicians remains low. The 2009 NILT survey showed that only 15 per cent trusted politicians 'a fair amount' while 36 per cent said they didn't trust them at all. Most reserved their judgement. An IPSIS/MORI survey commissioned by the Assembly in 2010 found that 61 per cent had little interest in its work and 75 per cent thought that the present system of government was not working properly. Only 29 per cent could name one MLA. It seems that, for the moment at least, people want politicians to deal with 'bread-and-butter' issues and not to continue the dispute over Northern Ireland's constitutional position.

Exercises

Explain and examine the following terms:

the Pale	plantation	ascendancy
Orange Order	Home Rule	UVF
IRA	Éamon de Valera	Articles 2 and 3

decommissioning   TD   MLA
Dáil   Taoiseach   STV
OFMDFM   Stormont   Troubles
Bloody Sunday 1972   Bloody Friday 1972   peace process
direct rule   Assembly   power-sharing
partition   zero-sum   Good Friday (Belfast)
                                                    Agreement

Write short essays on the following topics:

1   Discuss the ways in which TDs make government accountable. How effective are
    they?

2   Explain the divisions between the major parties in Ireland. Are these changing?

3   What do you understand by the term *devolution* in Northern Ireland?

4   How do the political institutions in Northern Ireland today accommodate the
    interests of all parties?

Further reading

Adshead, M. and Tonge, J. (2009) *Politics in Ireland: Convergence and Divergence in a Two-Polity Island* Basingstoke: Macmillan.

Bew, P. (2009) *Ireland: The Politics of Enmity 1789–2006* Oxford: Oxford University Press

Coakley, J. and Gallagher, M. (2009) *Politics in the Republic of Ireland* (5th edition) London: Routledge.

Edwards, A. (2011) *The Northern Ireland Troubles* London: Osprey

Knox, C. (2010) *Devolution and the Governance of Northern Ireland* Manchester: Manchester University Press

McKittrick, D., Kelters, S., Feeney B. and Thornton, C. (1999) *Lost Lives: The Stories of the Men, Women and Children who Died as a Result of the Northern Ireland Troubles* Edinburgh: Mainstream Books

Patterson, H. (2007) *Ireland since 1939: The Persistence of Conflict* London: Penguin Books

Websites

CAIN Web Service – Conflict and Politics in Northern Ireland http://cain.ulst.ac.uk/

Government of Ireland information service http://www.gov.ie/

Irish Parliament (Oireachtas) http://www.oireachtas.ie/parliament/

Northern Ireland Assembly http://www.niassembly.gov.uk/

Northern Ireland Executive http://www.northernireland.gov.uk/

7

International relations

The subject of international relations presents some difficulties in the Irish case. Today Ireland is a sovereign state and has an international presence like that of any other small nation. For example, it has diplomatic relations with 107 countries and has over 40 embassies throughout the world, comprising around 340 officials and 300 locally recruited staff. It also has a seat in the United Nations and is a member state of the European Union. Northern Ireland, on the other hand, is a region of the UK and foreign policy remains the responsibility of Her Majesty's Government in London. Recently, international relations came to mean something different in Northern Ireland. There the 'internationalization' of the Troubles was either the extent to which paramilitary campaigns drew upon external sources for arms, such as Libyan support for the IRA, or the extent to which external support was sought for a political settlement, such as American involvement in the peace process of the 1990s. After 1921 the Irish state sought to confirm its separate identity from the United Kingdom (UK). By contrast, the Unionist government in Northern Ireland sought to confirm its place in the UK. The partition or border issue dominated relationships between Belfast and Dublin and between Dublin and London. On the one hand, the Irish state has never accepted that Northern Ireland is entirely foreign, even though it has been the External or Foreign Affairs Minister who has normally dealt with the issue. On the other hand, the Irish state's *foreign* policy has been significantly influenced by the Northern Ireland question.

Empire and Commonwealth

Following the Act of Union which came into effect on 1 January 1801, Ireland became an integral part of the United Kingdom of Great Britain and Ireland and participated in building the British Empire. The Irish contribution, Catholic and Protestant, to the imperial enterprise was significant. Ireland's soldiers helped to garrison it, its civil servants helped to administer it and its emigrants helped to settle it. However, the relationship with the Empire, like in the rest of the UK, was complex. It is easy to assume that Irish Nationalists were universally opposed to the Empire but this was far from being the case. Irish political leaders in the nineteenth century often shared with British politicians a common imperial outlook. In the main they sought proper acknowledgement of the Irish contribution to the Empire by acceptance of Irish self-government within it. One of the arguments made by Nationalists in favour of Home Rule was that by settling

Ireland's remaining grievance with England, the Empire would be more securely founded and Ireland could remain a loyal member of it. Indeed, the Irish Parliamentary Party looked to other members of the Empire for support in this policy. For example, the Canadian House of Commons passed resolutions in favour of Irish Home Rule, as did the Australian Parliament. Moreover, other members of the Empire looked to Irish self-government as an opportunity to establish a more equal association of nations. Even the English imperialist Cecil Rhodes made donations to the Irish Parliamentary Party.

By contrast, Unionist opposition to Home Rule was based on the argument that Irish self-government was a first step towards the dissolution not only of the UK but also of the Empire. In 1886 this issue had split Gladstone's Liberal Party and strengthened the Conservative and Unionist influence in British politics. A second Home Rule bill was defeated in the House of Lords in 1893. The Unionist position by then continued to stress the threat that Home Rule would pose to the integrity of the Empire. As the possibility of a European war became more likely, Unionists also argued that Home Rule would weaken the UK's security and pose a threat to the idea of collective imperial defence. Ulster Unionists in particular defended the proposition that their position within the UK should not be

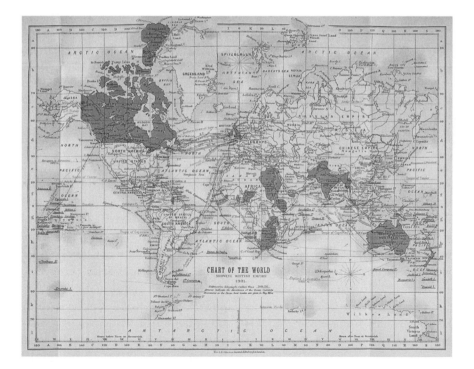

PLATE 7.1 A map showing (shaded) the extent of the British Empire in 1901. The Irish contribution to the Empire, its administration, settlement and defence was significant.
© Classic Image/Alamy

measured by mere numbers. Rather, it should be tested by their sympathy with 'the world mission of the British Empire', which was defined as the cause of civil and religious freedom. Such imperial sentiment was not confined to Unionists. Arthur Griffith, who helped to found Sinn Féin in 1905, looked to the Dual Monarchy of the Austro-Hungarian Empire as the model for a new Anglo-Hibernian – rather than British – Empire. However, it was questionable whether Griffith was serious about an enduring Irish role in the Empire.

Nationalist and Unionist leaders built their very different cases within an imperial set of references. However, a more radical though less popular tendency within Nationalism combined republicanism and militarism into a fundamental rejection of the British connection and, with it, of the Empire. Republicans had inherited a hatred of England from the time of the United Irishmen Rebellion of 1798. Their action also had an imperial scope. For example, the Fenian Brotherhood in the United States, made up of Irish emigrants who had fought in the American Civil War, carried out armed attacks on British Canada in 1866, 1870 and 1871. The Fenians also carried out sporadic bombing campaigns in England in the 1860s, 1870s and 1880s. The Irish Republican Brotherhood (IRB), a small revolutionary group that grew out of the Fenians, exploited public concern about the Boer War in South Africa (1899–1902) to promote the separatist cause in Ireland. Socialists like the Marxist James Connolly also used the Boer War to oppose Irish recruitment for armed service in the Empire and to denounce the oppression inherent in imperialism. However, this was not the view of the majority of Irish people.

When the first World War broke out in 1914, John Redmond, leader of the Irish Parliamentary Party, called on Irishmen to enlist in the army. His hope was that service against a common enemy would help unite Catholic and Protestant and assist the implementation of Home Rule (passed by Parliament in 1914 but suspended until after the war). The Easter Rebellion of 1916 and its aftermath, involving armed Irish Volunteers under IRB leadership and Connolly's Citizen Army, destroyed Redmond's hopes. It not only transformed Irish politics but transformed republicans from a minority into a mass movement. Rebels such as Patrick Pearse proclaimed a republic, expressed sympathy for the German war effort and the surviving leaders later exploited opposition to military conscription in Ireland. The effect of mass support for republicanism created new demands for Irish sovereignty that were to be addressed in negotiations with the British government for an Anglo-Irish Treaty in 1921.

Under the terms of that Treaty the Irish Free State became a self-governing Dominion – like Canada and Australia – within the British Empire or, as it later became known, the British Commonwealth of Nations. This conceded substantial autonomy on domestic matters to the government in Dublin but limited independence in international relations. Opponents of the Treaty were not immediately concerned about partition (they thought that Northern Ireland could not survive) but about sovereignty. They argued that the Free State was denied the ability to make decisions about war and peace because the British retained defence facilities in what were known as the 'Treaty ports'. Their use in war would automatically involve the Free State in British conflicts. Furthermore, the Commonwealth connection meant that international treaties would be determined by British rather than Irish priorities. Supporters of the Treaty like Michael Collins, the principal leader of the Irish Republican Army (IRA) in the War of Independence 1919 to 1921, later argued that it provided the Irish government with the freedom to achieve freedom. The Commonwealth association was justified on the basis that the other Dominions could help the Free State enlarge its autonomy. This set the policy for the first decade of the Irish state.

Under the leadership of the pro-Treaty party Cumann na nGaedheal, founded in 1923, international relations until 1932 were based on membership of not only the Commonwealth but also the League of Nations, which had been founded after the First World War to secure international peace. Along with the other Dominions, the Irish Free State promoted the idea of an equal association of independent nations within the Commonwealth. This objective was substantially achieved in the Statute of Westminster in 1931 which gave legislative autonomy to the Dominions.

Nevertheless, when the anti-Treaty Fianna Fáil party came to power in 1932 a policy of disengagement from the Commonwealth was instituted. The External Relations Act of 1936 diminished significantly Irish involvement in the Commonwealth, and Éire/Ireland (as the Free State was to be renamed in the 1937 Constitution) became a sovereign, independent state in all but name. In that sense, the proclamation of the Republic of Ireland Act on Easter Sunday 1949, which ended the Irish state's membership of the Commonwealth, was not a revolutionary act. In the 1930s, the Irish Prime Minister Éamon de Valera used the League of Nations in Geneva to proclaim the virtues of collective security and the rights of small nations. He also used the opportunity of an international forum to condemn the partition of Ireland. On all counts, the League failed to satisfy Irish ambitions.

The Unionist government of Northern Ireland, established under the Government of Ireland Act, 1920, exercised its option under the 1921 Treaty to remain within the UK and so bound by its international obligations. While governments in Dublin pursued a policy of loosening the British connection, the government in Belfast proclaimed Northern Ireland's solidarity with, and its contribution to, British foreign policy. Northern Ireland's attitude was of vital importance with the outbreak of the Second World War in 1939. Its participation in the Allied war effort complemented Unionist arguments about their loyalty in the First World War of 1914 to 1918, loyalty which, they believed, should – and did – sustain Northern Ireland's position within the UK.

First and Second World Wars

In 1914 both the Irish Nationalist leader John Redmond and the Unionist leader Sir Edward Carson committed their followers to the war effort. For the former the war was about the rights of small nations against German aggression and thus a claim on the British government to fulfil the right of Ireland to self-determination. For the latter the war was about the fidelity of Ulster Unionists to the British imperial mission. Redmond's National Volunteers joined the 10th and 16th Irish Divisions while Carson's Ulster Volunteers contributed 13 battalions to the 36th Ulster Division. Together over 210,000 Irishmen volunteered for military service between 1914 and 1918 (compared with 2,000 who took part in the Easter Rebellion of 1916) and of those about 35,000 died. The most dramatic loss of life occurred on 1 July 1916 when the 36th Ulster Division suffered heavy casualties on the first two days of the Battle of the Somme, about one-third being killed, wounded or missing in action. The 16th Irish Division later saw action at the Somme and both divisions took part in the Battle of Messines in Flanders.

PLATE 7.2 The remains of a former British trench at the Battle of the Somme, 1916. In July, the 36th Ulster Division suffered 5,000 casualties with over 2,000 killed. The 16th Irish Division was to suffer similar casualties at the Somme in September 1916. © Photos 12/Alamy

While the sacrifice at the Somme became one of the founding myths of Northern Ireland Unionism, the sacrifice of Irish soldiers was later played down by the Free State which naturally looked instead to the Easter Rebellion of 1916. Only very recently has the Irish state begun to acknowledge officially its dead not only in the First but also in the Second World War. For example, the Irish Round Tower in Flanders, honouring the 36th Ulster and 16th Irish Divisions who fought together there, was jointly opened on 11 November 1998 by Queen Elizabeth II, President Mary McAleese and the King of Belgium.

In the Second World War of 1939 to 1945, Northern Ireland played a significant role in the struggle against the Axis powers. Its strategic importance increased once the Treaty ports had been returned to the Irish government in 1938. Northern Ireland then provided a base from which to defend the Atlantic sea routes. Londonderry/Derry in the north-west was a key port for the Allied navies and Northern Ireland airfields provided facilities for the Allied air forces in the task of convoy protection and submarine detection. In 1941, seaplanes flying from Lough Erne in County Fermanagh helped spot the German battleship *Bismarck*. Between 1942 and 1945 over 120,000 United States troops were stationed in Northern Ireland in transit to England and, after June 1944, to Northern Europe. About 40,000 men and women from Northern Ireland volunteered to serve in the British armed forces (unlike the rest of the UK, there was no military conscription in Northern Ireland). The shipyards and aircraft factories of Belfast were also important for the war effort and they were the intended targets of two German air raids in April and May 1941. Over 1,000 people were killed and about half the housing stock of the city was damaged. Some historians have questioned the extent of Northern Ireland's contribution, pointing to the higher incidence of strikes and lower productivity in the war industries compared with the rest of the UK. Nevertheless, the Unionist government's commitment to the war was ultimately the crucial factor.

In 1939 the Irish government confirmed its independence of the UK by asserting its neutrality in the war. It was able to do this because the return of the Treaty ports meant that no part of its territory could be used for offensive operations against the Axis powers. The government in Dublin successfully lobbied the British Cabinet against military conscription in Northern Ireland and de Valera refused to trade neutrality for Irish unity when it was offered (in very vague terms) by Winston Churchill in June 1940 and again after the Japanese attack on Pearl Harbor in 1941. In the early stages of the war, the Irish government expected a German victory and there were those who believed that Irish neutrality would be looked upon benevolently by Berlin.

So detached was Ireland from events that the Second World War was known only as 'The Emergency' and most evidence of the conflict was suppressed by heavy government censorship. Though the tide of war changed in the next few years, Ireland continued to maintain neutrality. In practice, Irish neutrality tacitly favoured the Allies. There was, for example, intelligence cooperation and the

Emergency Powers Act, 1939 was used to suppress the pro-Nazi elements in the IRA. Some Irish citizens volunteered to fight and many of them went to Great Britain to work. About 45,000 men and women from the Free State joined the British forces and around 200,000, some already resident in Great Britain, found work in British armament factories. Sympathetic historians claim that this sort of benign neutrality was the best that the Irish government could do given the country's deep political divisions. Those who are less sympathetic believe it was a shameful period, symbolized by de Valera's message of condolence to the German Legation on the death of Hitler in 1945.

The consequences of the Second World War were important in the politics of the island. The inward-looking culture of Irish politics had been strengthened. More importantly, relationships with the UK and the United States were soured by the Irish state's role during the conflict. Even Ireland's desire to participate in the United Nations was frustrated by a Soviet Union veto until December 1955. By contrast, the international reputation of the Northern Ireland government

PLATE 7.3 General Eisenhower inspecting troops near City Hall, Belfast in August 1945 when he received the freedom of the city. Northern Ireland played a crucial role in the Second World War. 120,000 US servicemen were stationed there and Londonderry/Derry was an important base for the US navy. Courtesy of the Public Record Office of Northern Ireland

substantially improved. Significantly, its relationship with Westminster prospered. In response to the declaration by Ireland of the Republic, the British government passed the Ireland Act, 1949. This confirmed Northern Ireland's position within the UK conditional only on the consent of the Northern Ireland Parliament. The Irish government's neutrality in the war, in other words, had helped entrench partition of the island.

UK–Irish relations

From the beginning, the Northern Ireland Question loomed large in Anglo-Irish relations. Supporters of the Anglo-Irish Treaty had mistakenly expected that the Boundary Commission (1924–1925) would remove sufficient territory from Northern Ireland to make it unviable as a political unit. When the anti-Treaty Fianna Fáil took office in 1932, the case against partition was the constant theme of the Irish government's relations with British ministers. A six-year dispute between the governments, known as the Economic War, was resolved in 1938 with Anglo-Irish agreements that restored normal trade between the two countries. In the 1937 Constitution of Ireland, Articles 2 and 3 laid claim to jurisdiction over the whole territory of the island. After the Second World War, the language of Irish policy was strongly anti-partitionist which encouraged the hostility of the Unionist government in Belfast and did little to promote good relations with London. During this same period Northern Ireland benefited from the expansion of the British Welfare State and the Unionist government became more secure. The differential in material well-being of the two parts of Ireland was increasingly pronounced, making a serious policy of Irish unity a distant prospect. It was only in the 1960s that traditional anti-partitionism began to moderate and moves towards cross-border understanding hesitantly got underway.

Under Seán Lemass, who became Taoiseach in 1959, there were new approaches to both the British government and Northern Ireland. The Anglo-Irish Free Trade Agreement was concluded in 1965 and represented a change from the protectionist mentality of the previous era. Lemass began a new openness to Unionists and in 1965 he met the Northern Ireland Prime Minister, Terence O'Neill. Irish unity was still the objective but there was no longer the expectation that it could be imposed on Northern Ireland. Lemass believed that unity would be a product of the modernization of Irish economy and society. On the other hand, O'Neill believed that modernization would create a more stable Northern Ireland as Catholics and Protestants prospered, helping to ease political relationships on the island.

However, the outbreak of the Troubles in 1969 and the engagement of British troops in Northern Ireland rekindled old animosities. In 1970 two members of the Irish government, Charles Haughey and Neil Blaney, were charged but subsequently acquitted with illegally importing arms to equip the Provisional

IRA. Though violence was repudiated by the government, this was a very dangerous period in Anglo-Irish relations. On 2 February 1972, the British Embassy in Dublin was destroyed by a mob following the funerals of those shot by British troops in Londonderry/Derry on Bloody Sunday. A more cooperative attitude was evident in the Sunningdale Agreement of 1973 that was to complement power-sharing devolution within Northern Ireland. The proposed Council of Ireland would have linked the administrations of both parts of the island. However, the failure of the Irish government to acknowledge unambiguously Northern Ireland's constitutional status within the UK (there was no offer to change Articles 2 and 3 of the Constitution which laid territorial claim to Northern Ireland) contributed to Sunningdale's collapse. This failure led Fianna Fáil governments after 1977 to return to hardline nationalism. In 1980 the Taoiseach, Charles Haughey, even demanded British withdrawal from Northern Ireland.

The removal of the Unionist-controlled Northern Ireland Parliament in 1972 made possible direct intergovernmental negotiations between London and Dublin about Northern Ireland's future. This is what happened in the course of the 1980s. After 1982, Fine Gael-led governments of Garrett Fitzgerald negotiated with Margaret Thatcher's Conservative government and the result was the Anglo-Irish Agreement of 1985. That Agreement, through its Inter-governmental Conference, gave the Irish government a formal input into British policy in Northern Ireland. This represented a significant victory for Irish diplomacy and a significant defeat for Ulster Unionism.

After 1985, Anglo-Irish cooperation on Northern Ireland became the norm. In the 1990s, the two governments co-sponsored talks about Northern Ireland's future and jointly managed the peace process. The Good Friday (Belfast) Agreement of 1998 confirmed the close relationship and instituted two Irish dimensions in Northern Ireland. The first is the North–South Ministerial Council which brings together ministers from the Northern Ireland Executive and the Irish government to develop cooperation within the island on matters of mutual interest. It oversees cross-border policies, programmes and bodies on the island. The second is the British–Irish Inter-governmental Conference which continues coordination of policy between London and Dublin. However, the territorial claim contained in Articles 2 and 3 of the Irish Constitution was amended to accept the principle of consent for Irish unity.

Since 1969, then, Anglo-Irish relations have changed substantially. The Irish government is accepted by the British government as a partner in securing political stability in Northern Ireland. The international strategy of the Irish government is no longer determined by the need to talk about Irish unity. It is now accepted that Northern Ireland remains within the UK because that is the wish of the majority but also that Irish governments have a role to play in protecting the rights of the Catholic minority. In June 2010, the then Taoiseach, Brian Cowen, announced after a meeting with Prime Minister David Cameron at 10 Downing

TABLE 7.1 North–South implementation bodies (1998)
Inland Waterways
Food Safety
Trade and Business Development
Special EU Programmes
Language
Aquaculture and Marine Matters
Source: the Good Friday (Belfast) Agreement, 1998

PLATE 7.4 L–R: President Mary McAleese, Queen Elizabeth II, Prince Philip and Martin McAleese attending a State Dinner in Dublin, May 2011. The visit by the Queen was the first by a British monarch since 1911 and an important statement of reconciliation between the two states. (Photo by Samir Hussein/WireImage)

Street that Queen Elizabeth II would visit Ireland in 2011. He said there was no longer any reason to deny 'those normal courtesies of friendly neighbouring states exchanging visits through heads of state'.

The Queen's visit in May 2011 was the first visit to Ireland by a reigning monarch since George V in 1911 and the first-ever visit by a UK Head of State to independent Ireland. It was judged to be an outstanding success, including a formal welcome by President Mary McAleese at her official residence of Áras an Uachtaráin (formerly the residence of the Lord Lieutenant of Ireland). The Queen took part in ceremonies at the Garden of Remembrance (for Irish rebels against British rule) and the National War Memorial Gardens (for the Irish dead of the two world wars). The symbolism of reconciliation was very clear.

European Union

When the UK applied to join the (then) European Economic Community (EEC) in 1961, Ireland also applied. For the Irish government membership of the EEC was an important element of the policy of modernization which was thought necessary to overcome the economic stagnation and political isolation of the post-war period. It was also part of a strategy to provide a new framework for Irish foreign policy. Within the institutions of the EEC, it was believed, the interests of a small state like Ireland could be protected and its voice more respectfully heard. The French veto in 1963 on the UK's application was also a blow to Ireland's hopes. In 1973 it was finally admitted along with the UK and Denmark following a referendum in which 83 per cent voted in favour of membership. Northern Ireland, as part of the UK, also entered the EEC at the same time. After 1974 the Labour government in the UK renegotiated terms of entry and held a referendum on membership in 1975. The result in Northern Ireland showed that on a very low turn-out of 47 per cent only 52 per cent had voted in favour of staying in the EEC. However, many had expected a negative result because the major Unionist parties had campaigned for a 'No' vote.

Membership of the European Community – after 1992, the European Union (EU) – helped transform Ireland's status in international affairs. In the first 50 years of Irish independence, isolation and protection were assumed to be the guarantees of national sovereignty. It was generally accepted that this approach had failed to deliver either economic prosperity or diplomatic influence. It was the qualification – or 'pooling' – of national sovereignty involved in the process of European integration that helped deliver these objectives. The first two decades of EU membership did not show rapid improvements in comparative living standards, though farmers in both parts of Ireland benefited immediately from the Common Agricultural Policy (CAP). The CAP provided a guaranteed price for produce fixed at a level much higher than the world market price. Between 1973 and 2010 Irish farmers received over €45 billion from the CAP. Since the agricultural budget is guaranteed up to 2013 and constitutes about 33 per cent of EU expenditure, Ireland will continue to benefit disproportionately from CAP funding.

European structural funds – designed to promote economic and social cohesion across the European Union – also benefited Ireland by helping to finance its transport and communications infrastructure. By the end of 2010 Ireland had received nearly €20 billion in structural funds. It is only after 2013 that economists calculate that Ireland could possibly become a net contributor to the EU budget. In the early 1990s, per capita incomes in Ireland were still 75 per cent of the EU average. By the beginning of the new millennium per capita incomes had reached the EU average. Not all of this material improvement can be attributed to the EU but membership was crucial for the strategy of attracting foreign investment which fed the so-called Irish Celtic Tiger economy.

The major Irish political parties have been keenly supportive of European integration and the public has responded to their lead. There have been votes in favour of changing the Constitution of Ireland to accord with European treaties in 1972, 1987, 1992 and 1998. This political rule was first broken with the rejection of the Nice Treaty in a referendum in June 2001. This caused substantial embarrassment to the Irish government because it threatened to block the enlargement of the EU eastwards and to damage Ireland's reputation. Though all the major parties and the Catholic Church had recommended a 'Yes' vote, the result on a very low turn-out of 34 per cent was 54 per cent against and 46 per cent in favour. The major concerns were that Ireland could lose EU funding as (former communist) Central European states were admitted and that Ireland's traditional neutrality could be compromised by the development of an EU military Rapid Reaction Force. The Treaty was put to a second referendum in October 2002 with an article excluding Irish participation in common European defence. On a poll of 49 per cent, 63 per cent voted in favour.

The political rule was broken a second time when in June 2008 voters rejected the Lisbon Treaty by 53 per cent to 47 per cent. Ireland was the only EU member state required to hold a referendum. This Treaty was designed to make decision-making in the EU more efficient to reflect its new size of 27 members. Polls found that the main reasons for voting against the Treaty were neutrality, military pacts and the issue of abortion. Once again, the Irish government was compelled to hold another referendum in June 2009. This time 67 per cent of Irish voters voted 'Yes'. In the period between the two referenda the Irish government had negotiated guarantees on its sovereignty. However, one important reason for the shift in public opinion was the banking crisis and the fear that a negative vote would mean Ireland losing European financial assistance.

Over the years, membership of the EU has enabled the Irish state to develop a new self-confidence in its relations with the UK. The politics of the currency provides one example of this. Before 1978 the Irish pound had been linked to parity with the British pound and both currencies were used freely throughout the island. After 1979, Ireland – but not the UK – joined the European Monetary System, leading to a break in parity. This also had the effect of creating two exchange rates on the island, so creating a new currency border with Northern Ireland. On 1 January 1999 Ireland, but not the UK, joined the single European currency or euro zone. Traditionally, Ireland has defended the European

PLATE 7.5 A meeting of the European Union (EU) Heads of State and Government in Brussels, June 2010. Membership of the EU has been a central part of Ireland's foreign policy since 1973. Northern Ireland's interests in the EU are represented by the government of the UK. Georges Gobet/AFP/Getty Images

Commission's role as policy initiator in the EU. This is why concerns were expressed about the Lisbon Treaty which proposed to remove the right of each state to an automatic post in the Commission. The Irish government has supported the Commission as the institution best suited to protect the interests of small states. It has been suspicious of attempts to shift power towards an inter-governmental arrangement where the larger states, like the UK, would have the decisive say. Currently, the Irish Commissioner is Máire Geoghegan-Quinn who holds the portfolio for Research and Innovation. Of the European Commission's five Secretaries-General – or chief administrator – two have been Irish, including the current holder, Catherine Day. Until 2010, the Head of the Commission Delegation to the United States – the EU's most important ambassadorial position – was a former Taoiseach, John Bruton.

Confusingly, though the Lisbon Treaty created a new post of President of the European Council (currently Herman van Rompuy), it remains the case that the Presidency of the EU rotates every six months between member states. Holding the Presidency has permitted Ireland a prominence in world affairs incommensurate with its size. Ireland has held the Presidency six times: in 1975, 1979, 1984, 1990, 1996 and 2004. The Presidency requires intensive administrative effort by Irish civil servants in Dublin and Brussels. Ministers chair EU Council meetings and supervise working groups of officials. The diplomatic style of a country helps determine the effectiveness of any Presidency and Irish governments have prided themselves on their efficient conduct of EU business. In 2004 the Irish

Presidency helped secure agreement on a draft European Constitution (though this was later replaced by the Lisbon Treaty).

Furthermore, the day-to-day business of the EU has eroded the old boundaries between domestic and international policy. Irish ministers attend regular EU Council (inter-governmental) meetings, for example, on finance and agriculture, and Irish civil servants are frequently engaged in the committees of both the Council and Commission. The Europeanization of Irish policy-making is one of the most conspicuous changes of the past 30 years. This is also apparent, although to a lesser degree, in party politics. Ireland has 12 Members of the European Parliament (MEPs) out of 736 who sit not as national delegations but in separate party groups. The EP has legislative, budgetary and supervisory powers and has grown in political influence in the past two decades.

The growing scope and domestic effect of the EU has required both an administrative and political response. A Minister of State, responsible to the Minister for Foreign Affairs, has a special brief for European matters. The Department of Foreign Affairs takes the lead administrative role in EU matters, along with the Department of the Taoiseach, in the coordination of Irish EU policy. The Department of Finance has oversight of EU funding and the Department of Agriculture's business is almost entirely decided at EU level through the CAP. Ireland's Permanent Representative in Brussels acts as a sort of ambassador to the EU and monitors Irish interests at the highest official level in the Committee of Permanent Representatives (COREPER). Parliamentary scrutiny of EU and international relations is the job of the Oireachtas Joint Committees on Foreign Affairs and on European Affairs. Though foreign policy remains a matter of sovereign decision-making, Ireland's international relations are increasingly advanced within the framework of the EU's Common Foreign and Security Policy (CFSP). Indeed, as Ireland plans to cut back the number of its embassies – for example, to the Vatican – some have proposed that Ireland should rely more heavily on the newly established EU diplomatic service, the European External Action Service (EEAS).

Nevertheless, criticism of the EU has become much more vocal in Ireland in recent years. There is a widespread feeling that the role played by the European Central Bank (ECB) and by some EU governments, especially Germany and France, during the recent financial crisis means that Ireland has 'lost' rather than 'pooled' its sovereignty. Ireland shares this feeling with other, similarly affected states like Portugal, Greece and even Italy, but anti-EU sentiment is qualified by the recognition that there is little alternative but to work within the main lines of EU policy. An *Irish Times*/Ipsos MRBI poll published in October 2011 showed that while voters were dissatisfied with the way in which the EU was run, there was continued strong support for membership of the EU. Sixty-seven per cent said it was better to be inside the EU than to be outside.

Unlike the Irish state, Northern Ireland's input into the EU policy process is channelled through the UK government. Devolution, following the Belfast

Agreement of 1998, did not affect that relationship since control of EU matters is a power reserved to London. There have been complaints at times that the UK's negotiating position on certain agricultural and fishing matters has not adequately recognized Northern Ireland's distinctive needs.

However, the relevant ministers in the Northern Ireland Executive are generally consulted on UK negotiating positions in the EU. Today there is a European Policy and Coordination Unit (EPCU) in the Office of the First and Deputy First Minister (OFMDFM) which coordinates the views of the Northern Ireland Executive in relation to the EU and liaises with the government in London. In 2001 the Office of the Northern Ireland Executive was established in Brussels as the main administrative hub of Northern Ireland's relations with EU institutions. It monitors EU developments affecting local interests and is concerned to make sure that Northern Ireland's voice is heard. Like the European offices of the Scottish government and the Welsh Assembly government, the Office of the Northern Ireland Executive comes under the general scope of the UK Permanent Representation. Invest Northern Ireland, Northern Ireland's economic development agency, is based in the Office to attract inward investment from European countries. Northern Ireland has also become a member of the Conference of Peripheral Maritime Regions (CPMR) which articulates the concerns of those areas outside the central core of Europe. Northern Ireland also has three MEPs out of the UK's national quota of 72.

The nationalist Social Democratic and Labour Party (SDLP) has consistently argued that in the EU Northern Ireland would be better represented by a common, all-Ireland approach. Others, again mainly in the SDLP, have looked to the EU as a model for resolving the political conflict in Northern Ireland. Unionists on the other hand have been generally critical of the process of European integration and have expressed concerns about the erosion of British sovereignty. Sinn Féin has made a similar case about Irish sovereignty. The EU helps fund regional development, sponsors programmes for cross-border cooperation and provides limited funding to underpin the peace process in Northern Ireland. Unlike Ireland, the UK has always been a net contributor to the EU budget. It is difficult to make a regional assessment for Northern Ireland alone but, given its large agricultural sector, it is likely that Northern Ireland is marginally a net beneficiary of EU membership. However, in 2011 Northern Ireland's Finance Minister, Sammy Wilson, claimed that Northern Ireland (within the UK) would be financially better off outside the EU.

United Nations and security

After the Second World War Ireland did not join the North Atlantic Treaty Organization (NATO) set up in 1949 by North American and West European states for mutual security against the Soviet Union. The Irish Minister of External

Affairs at the time, Seán McBride, privately told the American envoy that Ireland would join if partition was ended, but this was never considered practical. Ireland sought membership of the United Nations (UN) but its application was vetoed by the Soviet Union until 1955. After 1955, Ireland used the UN to assert its neutrality. This meant that in theory it did not take sides in the Cold War but in practice, owing to the Catholic Church's anti-communism, it supported the West politically.

Ireland has promoted the authority of the UN as the appropriate body to resolve international conflicts. As participants in UN peacekeeping missions, the Irish military has been able to make a practical, if small, contribution to the principle of collective security. The total strength of the Irish Defence Forces today is just under 10,000 with a reserve of about 12,000. Since 1958, Irish forces have been involved in tours of duty in over 50 separate missions. The criteria to be met for any deployment are threefold: the operation must be mandated by the UN; it must be approved by the government; and if there is to be a deployment of more than 12 personnel, it must be approved by a resolution of Dáil Éireann. Currently, Irish forces serve on UN missions in Kosovo, Congo, Western Sahara and the Middle East. In 2000, Ireland was elected for a two-year term as a non-permanent member of the UN Security Council and it saw its role as providing a voice for smaller nations. On international aid, the Irish government has expressed its commitment to the UN target for overseas development of 0.7 per cent of GNP. Its spending in 2010 – 0.5 per cent or about €671 million – continues to fall short of that figure. It is mainly focused on programmes in sub-Saharan Africa.

Though the principle of neutrality is one that is popular and one to which all the major parties subscribe, its operation by the Irish government has often been determined by pragmatism. In 1990 United States planes were permitted to refuel at Shannon Airport en route to the First Gulf War against Iraq. The justification was that the war had been sanctioned by the UN. In 2003 during the Second Gulf War against Iraq, US planes also used Shannon Airport although this time there was no UN mandate. The reason in both cases was the need to maintain good relations with the United States. One of the reasons for the rejection of the EU Nice Treaty in 2000 and the Lisbon Treaty in 2008 was the question of military neutrality. Though the Seville European Council in 2002 accepted Ireland's National Declaration on neutrality and the Irish government has made any future participation in a common European defence arrangement conditional upon a national referendum, concern still persists about the drift of policy.

Ireland committed a battalion-strength force to the new EU Rapid Reaction Force but only for humanitarian and peacekeeping duties within the European area. Since 1999 Ireland has also been a member of the NATO-sponsored Partnership for Peace (PfP) which is designed to encourage cooperation between European states in peacekeeping and humanitarian operations. It now has a delegation at NATO Headquarters in Brussels and observer status at Western European Union (WEU). Since 2002 Ireland has provided non-combatant staff for the International Security Assistance Force (ISAF) in Afghanistan.

PLATE 7.6 On 21 May 2011 Secretary of State Owen Patterson, First Minister Peter Robinson and Jeffrey Donaldson MP took the General Salute as part of the Conferment of the Freedom of the City of Lisburn on the Royal Irish Regiment (RIR) on its return from a tour of duty in Afghanistan. © Ken Mack

Northern Ireland's place within the UK integrates it into Britain's defence commitments. Its strategic significance within Western defence has diminished since 1945, especially with the ending of the Cold War after 1989. Army regiments that have recruited in Northern Ireland have been involved in most post-Second World War conflicts involving the UK, from Korea in 1951 to Afghanistan today. The modern, locally recruited Royal Irish Regiment (RIR) is unique in the British Army in that it consists of one air assault battalion, liable for worldwide service, and one reserve battalion of part-time soldiers exclusively based in Northern Ireland. The regiment, according to its mission statement, 'seeks to recruit soldiers of Irish origin or background to serve anywhere in the world where UK forces are deployed'. Recently, the RIR has served tours of combat duty in Iraq and Afghanistan.

United States of America

In the United States those of an Ulster Protestant background (known later in the nineteenth century as Scotch-Irish) were a major political influence in the War of Independence of 1775 to 1782. After the Great Famine in Ireland in the mid-1840s there was large Irish Catholic migration to the US. Between 1845 and 1855 about 1.5 million emigrated there. It has been estimated that about 3 million had moved to the US by 1900. One consequence of Catholic immigration was Irish-American support for political nationalism. Large Irish communities in cities like New York and Boston provided an important resource of money and political influence for the cause of Irish independence. The Fenian movement that influenced the revolutionary tradition in Ireland also had its origins in the US. Irish-American influence, directly through the Democratic Party and indirectly through newspapers and lobbying, exerted pressure on the British government during the negotiation of the Anglo-Irish Treaty in 1921. Democratic Party administrations, as a rule, have been more sympathetic to Irish Nationalist claims than have those of the Republican Party.

However, US influence upon Ireland should not be exaggerated; nor should Irish influence upon US policy. The US government was alienated by Irish neutrality in the Second World War, had cool relations with the Irish government over its refusal to join NATO and gave only limited support to Ireland's application for membership of the UN before 1955. The strategic relationship with the UK – what is known in the UK as the 'special relationship' – has been more important than either the Irish or Northern Ireland Question and American diplomats still regard the UK as the closest ally of the US, especially during the recent wars in Iraq and Afghanistan.

It would also be wrong to assume that Irish-American influence is homogeneous. After 1969, the so-called Irish-American lobby was sympathetic to the nationalist cause in Northern Ireland but was divided between majority support for constitutional politics and minority, but vocal, support for the IRA. The diplomatic resources of the Irish government were employed in favour of promoting support for constitutionalism. The object was to use American influence to persuade the British government that there should be a common Anglo-Irish approach to Northern Ireland. The Anglo-Irish Agreement of 1985 may be attributed in part to this persuasion.

However, it was only under the Clinton Presidency (1992–2000) that there was sustained and direct US involvement in Northern Ireland. That Administration actively supported the peace process and encouraged the use of the St Patrick's Day celebrations in Washington as a venue for discussion between politicians from both parts of Ireland. Clinton visited Ireland three times during his Presidency and this showed an unprecedented expression of American interest in Irish affairs. Former Democratic Party Senator George Mitchell became Chairman of the talks that led to the Good Friday (Belfast) Agreement of 1998 and he continued to play a crucial role in the review of that Agreement in 1999. After 2001, the Bush Presidency was much less engaged though it did keep a Special Envoy with responsibility to monitor the peace process in Northern Ireland. President Obama (who discovered that a maternal ancestor had migrated to America from Ireland in 1850) has continued that restrained approach and shows little policy interest in Irish affairs.

Internationalization and Irish global communities

In the twenty-first century, the politics of both parts of Ireland are now set within a European framework and their respective economies are integrated into the global system. The island has experienced an internationalization common to other parts of the world. In the Irish context, however, internationalization also has a specific historical meaning. There was a traditional concern in nationalism to 'internationalize' the Irish Question and this involved the attempt to find a diplomatic counterweight to British authority in the island. At the beginning of the twentieth century, the Dominions were looked to in support of Home Rule. After 1916, Sinn Féin leaders called on American support in the cause of independence. The Free State used Commonwealth membership after 1921 to expand its constitutional autonomy and, when he came to office in 1932, de Valera used the League of Nations to prepare for Irish neutrality in the Second World War. In the early post-war period the Irish government tried to internationalize its campaign against Northern Ireland though to little effect. The echo of that failed policy was heard again in the UN when in 1969, following the outbreak of the Troubles, the Irish government – ignoring the UK's permanent membership of the Security Council – requested support for an international peacekeeping force in Northern Ireland.

Internationalization has been a tactic of nationalism and republicanism within Northern Ireland. The former leader of the SDLP, John Hume, used his contacts in the US, such as the late Senator Edward Kennedy, to encourage Congressional interest in an all-Ireland settlement. His membership of the European Parliament from 1979 to 2004 was also employed to press for EC/EU involvement. For Hume, European institutions provided a model for the peaceful resolution of conflict and in 1992 the SDLP even proposed that the EC appoint a member of any future Northern Ireland Executive.

Republicans have tried to bring international pressure to bear in a number of ways. In the 1980s, the IRA secured arms from Colonel Gaddafi's Libya (which had also sent money in the 1970s to Loyalist paramilitaries), raised funds in the US and, even after the Belfast Agreement, engaged with guerrillas in Colombia. Sinn Féin has been keen to identify Republican claims with liberation struggles elsewhere such as those of the African National Council (ANC) in South Africa, the Palestinians in the Middle East and with Fidel Castro's Cuba. None of these examples has any real relevance to Northern Ireland and in the 1990s this revolutionary image was played down when the Sinn Féin leadership shifted its attention to securing the US administration's support for the peace process.

These political efforts at internationalization have an appeal owing to the extent of Irish global communities. What today has become known as the Irish 'diaspora' is a matter of dispute. In 1990, the then President of Ireland, Mary Robinson, claimed that 70 million people worldwide were partially descended from Irish emigrants. According to the US Census Bureau (2004), there were 30.4 million Irish-Americans in the US, of whom some 50 per cent would be Protestant. Canada, Australia and New Zealand also have large Irish communities of both religious denominations. Migration to Great Britain, mainly to England and Scotland, has been a common experience for families in both parts of Ireland and the history of cities like Liverpool and Glasgow owes much to the Irish connection. Most Irish settlers integrated into British society and only the surname of succeeding generations would indicate their Irish origin. At the time of the Queen's visit to Ireland in 2011, the British Foreign and Commonwealth Office estimated that around 6 million people in the UK have an Irish parent or grandparent and that more than 100,000 Irish residents were born in the UK. Abroad, Irish Catholics have often retained a distinctive ethnic identity, in part because they were differentiated from the Protestant cultures of the US, UK and Commonwealth Dominions in a way that the Protestant Irish were not; and in part because the balanced emigration of men and women permitted marriage within the group.

Emigration was a common European experience in the nineteenth and twentieth centuries but it has had peculiarly negative associations in Irish Nationalist history. The expectation placed in Irish independence was that economic prosperity would see the population grow to 20 million. The failure after 1921 to reverse what was known as the 'evil' of emigration became a mark of national shame. The policy of political isolation and economic protection worsened rather than improved matters. After independence, the population declined from 3 million in 1921 to slightly under that figure 40 years later. In the same period, the population of Northern Ireland rose by one-sixth to 1.5 million. Only after the 1960s did the population in independent Ireland begin to rise slowly. Rapid economic growth in the late 1990s encouraged inward migration to both parts of the island such that the population in Ireland is now about 4.5 million and in Northern Ireland about 1.8 million.

In addition, in the 1990s the meaning of diaspora changed from a symbol of former oppression (famine) and political failure (isolation) to a symbol of global opportunity. The Irish abroad, especially in the US, have been redefined as a resource to encourage inward investment and to promote Irish interests. The global 'rebranding' of Ireland as a dynamic place for new business and as a land of innovative citizens now complements an older image of Ireland as a relaxing place for vacations. Together these two brand images have been used to market Irish goods abroad, the best-known example of which has been the globalized 'Irish' pub. The other side of that coin has been the importation to Ireland of diasporic forms of Irishness, most notably in the recent Americanization of St Patrick's Day celebrations.

Attitudes to internationalization

Irish government foreign policy has consisted of three pillars: neutrality, support for UN collective security and membership of the EU. Opinion polls consistently reveal that these policies are popular with the general public. An MRBI poll in 2001 showed that 72 per cent wanted Ireland to continue its policy of neutrality. However, the link between neutrality and UN collective security is a complex one and the public's attitude is equally complex. In 2002, respondents were asked in an MRBI poll about Ireland's role on the UN Security Council and whether, if Iraq failed to comply with UN resolutions on arms inspection, Ireland should vote in favour of military action. Fifty-nine per cent replied that it should not. This answer showed that most respondents suspected that the US determination to go to war in Iraq threatened to compromise Irish neutrality as well as to weaken the principle of UN collective security.

When the Irish electorate failed to ratify the Nice Treaty in 2000 it appeared that they were voting against any participation in EU security and were having doubts about enlargement of the EU to incorporate Eastern and Central European states. A series of MRBI polls in 2001 actually showed that 59 per cent favoured enlargement. About half of the people believed that Ireland should participate in the EU's Rapid Reaction Force providing its tasks were peacekeeping ones. The Irish government's policy of maintaining a seat in the EU Commission also met with popular approval. On the question of whether Ireland should integrate fully within the EU or whether it should do all it can to protect its independence, opinion is evenly divided. However, that is not the choice that most people feel has to be made. The history of EU membership has encouraged Irish people to believe that integration has helped to sustain their independence, especially against the UK.

A 2008 Millward Brown/IMS poll for the Department of Foreign Affairs showed that 60 per cent of Irish citizens believed that Ireland's interests were best secured by full involvement in the EU. A Eurobarometer report in 2008 also confirmed that 73 per cent of Irish voters believed that the EU was 'a good thing'. In 2010, another Eurobarometer poll showed that 81 per cent thought that Ireland had benefited from EU membership. These findings contradict the opinion sometimes expressed in the media that the public has been alienated from the EU by the austerity measures required in exchange for financially assisting Irish banks.

A British Council survey in 2003 found that in economic, social and cultural terms 73 per cent of Irish respondents felt themselves to be 'closer to Boston than Berlin'. In other words, 30 years of European integration seemed to have had little impact on the long-standing connections between the US and Ireland. In sum, one can say that although a large majority of Irish people think that membership of the EU is beneficial, they still have (like most people in the UK as well) strong transatlantic cultural and political sympathies. Indeed, the same British Council survey also revealed that attitudes to UK–Irish relations have become very positive. Eighty-one per cent thought that the relationship between the British and Irish governments ranged from good to excellent and 75 per cent believed they had improved in the past 10 years. These findings challenge the view of popular hostility between the British and the Irish. The vast majority were happy to welcome the Queen on her visit to Ireland in 2011 and, according to a report in the *Catholic Herald*, over 80 per cent approved.

In Northern Ireland, opinion poll findings tend to show that there is little difference between Protestant and Catholic attitudes on key international issues. For example, in the *Northern Ireland Life and Times Survey* of 2002 both religious communities tended towards a common view on the EU. Catholics were only marginally more likely than Protestants to think of themselves as 'European'. Just over 30 per cent of all respondents thought of themselves in this way while 67 per cent never thought of themselves as European. On the best long-term European policy for the UK, only 6 per cent advocated leaving the EU. Opinion was equally divided between those who preferred the status quo and those who wanted the EU to integrate further. Thirty per cent preferred the powers of the EU to stay the same and 30 per cent wanted those powers to increase. Forty-six per cent agreed that EU membership was a 'good thing' for Northern Ireland.

The survey suggested that most people had little active interest in or knowledge of the EU. Half of all respondents had no opinion about the impact of EU membership on Northern Ireland. However, a 2006 survey carried out by Gallup on behalf of the European Commission seemed to show that people in Northern Ireland were the most aware of all UK regions of the benefits of EU membership. In particular, Northern Ireland was most positive in its attitude towards the economic and social benefits of EU membership. Seventy-six per cent agreed that the EU had benefited exporters and 60 per cent that it had improved working conditions. On the larger question of the UK's influence in the world the *Northern Ireland Life and Times Survey* of 2003 again demonstrated that there was little difference in attitude between Protestants and Catholics. Thirty-eight per cent of all respondents believed that the UK continued to have either a great deal or quite a lot of influence in international affairs.

As one might expect, there is a large difference between the communities in Northern Ireland when it comes to relations with the Republic of Ireland. The *Northern Ireland Life and Times Survey* of 2003 showed that 34 per cent of Catholics wanted the Irish government to have a lot of involvement in Northern Ireland while 63 per cent of Protestants wanted it to have no involvement at all. However, there was a middle ground of 30 per cent of Protestants and 49 per cent of Catholics who agreed that the Irish government should have a little involvement. This particular response represents an acknowledgement of the political realities of Anglo-Irish cooperation since the 1980s.

Exercises

Explain and examine the following terms:

sovereignty	Dominion status	Fenian movement
British Empire	Boundary Commission	Commonwealth
Irish neutrality	League of Nations	internationalization
United Nations	MEP	Dominions
the Irish Constitution	Lisbon Treaty	European Commission
euro zone	Irish diaspora	Irish America
Emergency Powers Act 1939	NATO	Royal Irish Regiment
Department of Foreign Affairs	the Somme	American special envoy

Write short essays on the following topics:

1   Describe the difference in international status between Ireland and Northern Ireland.

2   What role has Northern Ireland played in relations between the British and Irish governments?

3   How important is the European Union in the foreign policy of Ireland?

4   Describe the different roles played today by the military forces of the UK and Ireland.

Further reading

Barton, B. (1995) *Northern Ireland in the Second World War* Belfast: Ulster Historical Foundation

Farrington, C. (ed.) (2008) *Global Change, Civil Society and the Northern Ireland Peace Process: Implementing the Political Settlement* Basingstoke: Palgrave Macmillan

Howe, S. (2000) *Ireland and Empire: Colonial Legacies in Irish History and Culture* Oxford: Oxford University Press

Kenny, K. (2005) *Ireland and the British Empire* Oxford: Oxford University Press

Keogh, D. (2005) *Twentieth-century Ireland: Revolution and State Building* Dublin: Gill and Macmillan

Laffan, B. and O'Mahony, J. (2008) *Ireland and the European Union* Basingstoke: Palgrave Macmillan

Websites

Defence Forces of Ireland: http://www.military.ie/

European Commission Representation in Ireland:

http://ec.europa.eu/ireland/press_office/index_en.htm
European Commission Office Northern Ireland:
http://ec.europa.eu/unitedkingdom/about_us/office_in_northern_ireland/index_en.htm
Irish Department of Foreign Affairs: http://www.dfa.ie/home/index.aspx
Royal Irish Regiment: http://www.army.mod.uk/infantry/regiments/3409.aspx
UK Foreign and Commonwealth Office: http://www.fco.gov.uk/en/

8

Irish legal systems

This chapter examines significant periods of Irish legal history; sources of Irish law; and legal systems in the north and south of the island as they have developed from 1921 to the present.

Early forms of Irish law were initially shared with and then gradually overtaken by English law from the twelfth century as Anglo-Normans colonized Ireland and used the law to politically control the country. Ireland was part of the United Kingdom (UK) from 1801 until partition in 1921. Contemporary law, legal professions and courts in Northern Ireland and Ireland have consequently been influenced by English legal models.

However, these systems now differ from each other. Ireland adopted written constitutions, referendums and Supreme and High Courts with judicial review powers (scrutiny over legislation and executive action) following independence from Great Britain. Northern Irish legal structures share similarities with those of England/Wales, but further devolved powers to the Assembly and Executive may in future increase differences.

Legal history

Key periods in Irish history illustrate the development of legal practices and structures in the island and the changing relationship between Ireland and Great Britain.

Early Irish law

Brehon law was an early form of Irish law. It was introduced by European immigrants from about 1000 BC and was initially in oral form. The first written law covered the later Gaelic period and is evidenced in Old Irish law manuscripts from between the seventh and ninth centuries AD. These were written and studied at monasteries and law schools, and were later expanded by twelfth- to sixteenth-century glosses and commentaries.

The legal system did not apparently distinguish between civil and criminal offences and applied restorative justice. The injured party brought an action against the offender and claimed appropriate compensation. The parties accepted negotiated judgments and there was no official implementation of decisions. The Brehons were a scholar class, presided over hearings and were mediators who followed established traditions. But Brehon law could be developed in the light of changing circumstances.

PLATE 8.1 Redwood Castle (Co. Tipperary) is still occupied. It was built by the Normans in 1200 and leased to the MacEgan family from about 1350. They were Brehons who practised Brehon law and established a school of history and law in the castle. © Angela Commins

Ireland initially comprised scattered warring tribes with no centralized political or legal authority. As their wealth and power increased, some later became kingdoms. They had complex social patterns and rules based on status, property and kinship hierarchies. Brehon law and early Irish society were influenced by ancient sagas, myths and the arrival of Christianity in the fifth century with its canon (ecclesiastical) law and retributive justice.

Medieval law: 1169 to 1600

Medieval law lasted from the first Norman invasion of Ireland in 1169 until 1600. The Anglo-Normans initially settled the area around Dublin (later known as the Pale), where they introduced English common (judge-made) law, land law, criminal law, legal remedies and evidential proof. Conflicts between settlers were decided by English law and Brehon law was used by the Irish. Irish and English legal systems coexisted for 400 years, sometimes in conflict, but also influencing each other. In the twelfth century, attempts were made to allow the Irish access to the common law and equal rights with Anglo-Normans. The common law was gradually extended to the Irish in the Pale (although many used Brehon law) and was slowly applied outside the Pale from the seventeenth century on.

There was some mixing between the two societies and their legal systems. But concern at the Gaelicization (adoption of Gaelic customs) of the Anglo-

Normans resulted in the Statutes of Kilkenny, 1366, which attempted to preserve English control over the Pale and to prevent social interaction, such as marriage between Irish and Anglo-Irish and use of the Irish language. The statutes arguably failed in their defensive aims.

English influence over Ireland fluctuated in the medieval period. It was felt that stronger control of the Pale, a more powerful English Parliament and greater uniformity between England and Ireland were needed. Although the Irish Parliament had passed its own legislation since the thirteenth century, Poynings' Law in 1494/1495 ruled that English law should be used in Ireland and the Irish Parliament operated only after royal permission was granted. The law (repealed in 1782) neutralized Irish parliamentary opposition to the king, increased uniformity between the two countries and promoted English control over Ireland.

Nevertheless, two main legal systems (English and Brehon) still operated together and other structures also functioned in Ireland from the Norman Conquest until the seventeenth century. Local areas were given by English monarchs to earls who created courts (palatinates or liberties). Royal administrative authority was delegated to the earls, who ran their own legal systems and probably used both common and Brehon law.

English rule and law: 1600 to 1801

The period from 1600 to 1801 illustrated the growing strength of English common and statute law and the eventual integration of Ireland into the United Kingdom (UK) by the Act of Union, 1801. But political changes and Irish insurrections affected legal matters. English law in the early fifteenth century had been restricted to the Pale, and Ulster in the north-east became a powerful Gaelic area of Ireland. However, Ulster's independence ended with the defeat by the English of Hugh O'Neill, Earl of Tyrone, in 1603, and the subsequent Flight of the Earls in 1607. It is argued that this event marked the decline of Irish legal, political and social authority, extended English law and led to England's domination of Ireland. Irish lords accepted the king's courts and plantation policies were implemented.

Although the extent of English law and political power in this period is debated, Brehon law was banned in 1603 under James I and English law was applied by local magistrates and royal representatives by 1617. By 1691, English courts had jurisdiction over all of Ireland and canon law courts were also controlled by the state. But struggles for political, religious, social and legal power continued between the Irish Parliament, the English Parliament and the Crown.

English law governed relations between the Irish and English. Penal laws against Catholics were imposed between the sixteenth and eighteenth centuries. Catholics were prohibited from owning land, practising law, building schools, voting in elections and serving in Parliament. Many of these laws were repealed at the end of the eighteenth century and most restrictions were removed in 1829, although there is doubt about how strictly the laws were enforced.

Ireland and England continued to contest legal supremacy. The Irish Parliament maintained that it had the right to legislate for Ireland and that the Irish House of Lords headed a separate Irish court system. The British Parliament rejected these claims and insisted that it could legislate for Ireland. Legal conflict reflected instability in the island, which led to the Catholic insurrection of 1798 with massacres and violence. English politicians recognized the need for more direct control and the Act of Union, 1801 was passed, which created the United Kingdom of Great Britain and Ireland (UK). Irish MPs sat in the Westminster Parliament, which legislated for Ireland and Great Britain. Legal disputes in Ireland were resolved by resident magistrates, with appeals to the English courts, and the UK House of Lords was the final court of appeal for most Irish and English/Welsh cases.

The nineteenth century

The period from 1801 until 1916 saw the uneven implementation of the Act of Union as Ireland in the nineteenth century was affected by political and legal developments. Most Westminster law was binding on the whole of the UK and resulted in greater uniformity between the jurisdictions. But some Westminster legislation was specific to Ireland and attempted to solve its particular social and political issues.

There was a major nineteenth-century reorganization of courts in the UK. A Judicature Act in 1877 reorganized the Irish court system, and laws on landlord and tenant, land and rights of tenants were reformed. These areas became increasingly important and politically contentious as the nineteenth century progressed and were connected to a campaign for Irish Home Rule.

1916 to 1924

The years 1916 to 1924 witnessed crucial events in Irish history, political and legal changes and increasing conflict. Although the 1916 Easter Rising against British rule was crushed, electoral success for Sinn Féin in 1918 led to the Dáil Éireannn of 1919, the announcement of a Republic of Ireland and discussions on an outline constitution. The Dáil rejected English law and reintroduced Brehon law. Two legal systems (official and revolutionary) temporarily operated together. Conflict continued with the 1919 to 1921 Anglo-Irish War of Independence.

This conflict was resolved by the signing of the Anglo-Irish Treaty in 1921, which effectively partitioned Ireland into two jurisdictions with the south as a Free State within the British Empire swearing allegiance to the Crown (rather than an independent republic). The north became Northern Ireland under the earlier Government of Ireland Act, 1920. This Act was delayed by the First World War and came into force in 1921. It devolved legislative authority to make laws for six counties in Northern Ireland to a Northern Ireland Parliament, but also guarded against abuse of the Parliament's powers. It was subject to the sovereignty of the UK Parliament at Westminster, which could impose direct rule over the province. The Act created an independent court system based on the English model, with appeal to the UK Court of Appeal and the House of Lords in London.

However, a civil war broke out in 1922/1923 between the new Irish Army and anti-Treaty forces who wanted an Irish Republic, which would unite north and south. The Irish Provisional government won and the Dàil had ratified the 1922 Constitution of the Irish Free State. Government and authority would be derived from the people through referendums. The Oireachtas (Parliament) comprised the king (represented by the Governor-General), the Dáil and the Senate, and was an independent legislature for the 26 counties of the Free State. An English model court system was created by the Courts of Justice Act, 1924.

The formation of the Irish Free State illustrated the complex history of Ireland. Article 73 of the Constitution transferred pre-1922 English, Irish and UK parliamentary law into Irish law, except for that of the first Dáil and statutes incompatible with the Constitution. There was also a continuation of pre-1922 common law judicial precedents of Ireland and Britain.

The 1922 Constitution was accepted by the British government and a majority of Treaty-supporting Irish Free State voters. It incorporated a parliamentary and common law system of law (British and Irish) into a constitutional model. The Constitution contained an oath of allegiance to the monarch, the office of Governor-General and legal appeal to the Privy Council. It was a compromise between past and present models and a work in progress.

Post-1924

The twentieth century saw the development of constitutional and parliamentary systems. Although English and Irish parliamentarism ('unwritten/uncodified' constitutionalism) had existed since the thirteenth century, written/codified constitutions in Ireland appeared with the creation of the Irish Free State in 1922 and Ireland in 1937 in addition to parliamentary features. Northern Ireland has a parliamentary-based system and an 'unwritten/uncodified' Constitution.

An example of parliamentary authority occurred in 1972 when the UK Parliament, faced with disorder in Northern Ireland, used legislative sovereignty to suspend the Northern Ireland Parliament and substitute lawmaking by Orders in Council from Westminster (direct rule). Attempts were made from 1974 to 1986 to return devolved legislative powers back to Northern Ireland, but all failed and direct rule continued. Eventually, a devolved Assembly was formed following the Good Friday (Belfast) Agreement, 1998, but there were breaks in the continuity of the Assembly and a return to direct rule until 2007. Much Westminster parliamentary authority (devolved matters) has now been transferred to the Assembly, save for *excepted matters* like defence, the armed forces, immigration and taxation, which are still handled by the Westminster Parliament. Some *reserved matters* in policing and justice powers (such as the prerogative of mercy in terrorism cases, drug classification, security of explosives and the Serious Organized Crime Agency (SOCA)) are still organized from London. But the transfer of most other justice and policing powers from Westminster to the Northern Ireland Assembly/Executive was achieved in 2010.

Constitutionalism operates alongside parliamentarianism in Ireland. The 1937 Constitution (like the 1922 Constitution) upheld existing legislation and common law in Ireland (Article 50) and pre-1922 UK statutes are still in force. The Oireachtas, government and courts from 1922 were also retained. Articles 12 to 14 provided for an elected president as head of state (replacing the monarch) with discretionary powers, the Senate was reformed and the Taoiseach gained prime-ministerial powers. Article 34 gave the Supreme Court power to review the constitutionality of new legislation and executive action. Articles 40 to 45 allegedly reflected Catholic social thinking on family, education, property and religious rights. Articles 46 to 47 provided for the amendment of the Constitution by popular referendum. By 1937, 41 of the original articles of the 1922 Constitution were amended or abolished. These changes illustrated a more independent constitutionalism and a focus on Irish national identity.

Despite criticism of the powers of the President, the position of the Catholic Church and Article 3 which arguably recognized partition, the Constitution was approved by referendum in 1937. Since the 1960s, Irish courts have recognized additional rights, such as a right to marital privacy and a right to withdraw one's labour. The 1922 right of appeal from the Irish courts to the Judicial Committee of the British Privy Council was abolished by constitutional amendment in 1933, thus eroding more of the historical British connection.

Ireland's growing international status in the twentieth century has also resulted in legal and constitutional changes. For example, admission to the European Economic Community (EEC, now EU) in 1973 meant that European law takes precedence over Irish domestic law and appeal on questions of European law goes to the European Court of Justice (ECJ). Northern Ireland has EU status owing to the accession of the UK to the EEC in 1973.

Criminal and civil law

Most legal cases in Northern Ireland and Ireland are divided into either criminal or civil law and are resolved in criminal or civil courts.

Criminal law protects society by punishing those (the accused or defendants) who commit crimes, such as theft, assault or murder, which, together with the punishments, may be defined in statute or common law. In criminal law a person is innocent until proven guilty and the evidence must show guilt 'beyond a reasonable doubt'. In Northern Ireland, the state through the Director of Public Prosecutions (DPP) prosecutes an individual or group generally at a public (but sometimes closed) trial in order to establish guilt or innocence. In Ireland, Article 30.3 of the 1937 Constitution stipulates that 'All crimes and offences . . . shall be prosecuted in the name of the People and at the suit of the Attorney-General or some other person authorized in accordance with law to act for that purpose.'

The result of a prosecution may be a fine, imprisonment or community service if found guilty or an acquittal if found innocent. The punishment is supposed to act as a deterrent to potential offenders and indicates society's attitudes on a range of activities. The defining features of criminal law are the social control role of the state/people as prosecutor and the element of punishment for a guilty party. Minor crimes are called misdemeanors or summary offences, which can be mainly tried in the lower courts. Serious crimes are known as indictable offences (also as headline crimes in Ireland) and are tried in the higher courts.

Civil law settles disputes between individuals, companies or organizations based on statutes or case law built up over centuries. It deals with claims for compensation (usually financial) brought by a person or group (plaintiff, claimant or complainant) who has suffered loss or damage (for example, from a breach of contract, negligence or discrimination) at the hands of another individual or group (defendant). In civil law, cases must be proved on a 'balance of probabilities' (over a 50 per cent probability that the defendant is responsible). Civil cases may be decided by negotiation and settlement before trial to avoid cost and uncertainty of the result or by a judge (and sometimes a jury) after trial. The civil law attempts to mediate between opposing forces and to restore social and personal balance.

Trials or negotiations in Northern Ireland and Ireland are adversarial contests between opposed parties. They present evidence, supported by witnesses, which can be challenged by lawyers (barristers or solicitors) from the other side. Decisions or findings of fact are made by juries or (sometimes) judges and the latter usually decide the sentence or punishment.

The jury system

Common to the trial systems in both Ireland and Northern Ireland is the important role of the jury, mainly in criminal cases. A jury is a sworn body of 12 people chosen at random to give a common-sense, impartial verdict of guilt or innocence on the basis of the evidence presented to them in a court of law. They generally do not decide the sentence or judgment, although they may perform this function in some civil matters. Non-jury trials may still be heard only before one judge in exceptional cases in Northern Ireland or before three judges in Ireland.

Sources of Irish law

Ireland and Northern Ireland have similar primary sources of law, although Ireland has a written Constitution and Northern Ireland's Constitution is unwritten/

uncodified. There are also obligations imposed upon both legal systems by inter-national conventions.

Northern Ireland

Since the UK is divided into three legal jurisdictions, there are differences in law and procedure between England/Wales, Scotland and Northern Ireland. Most law in Northern Ireland today derives from UK Parliament and Northern Ireland Assembly statutes, common (or judge-made case) law and European Union law.

Northern Ireland's legal history has created a complex law system, which still contains ancient sources. It includes Acts of Irish and English Parliaments until the 1801 Act of Union; Acts passed by UK Parliaments from 1801 to 1921; Acts of the Northern Ireland Parliament between 1921 and 1972; Orders in Council enacted under the Northern Ireland Acts of 1971 and 1974; Acts passed by the Northern Ireland Assembly from 2000 on devolved matters; Delegated Legislation/Statutory Instruments by Departments of the Northern Ireland Executive and the British government; and Acts of the UK Parliament on excepted or reserved matters which apply to Northern Ireland.

Common law (case or judge-made law) consists of precedents or decisions in court cases usually made by judges in the higher courts, which must be followed by lower courts in similar cases. New precedents usually stem from judges in the higher courts and lower courts are bound to apply them (binding precedent). Precedent can accommodate changed circumstances and new decisions are applied to future, similar cases. Northern Ireland court cases are collected in the Northern Ireland Law Reports.

European Union (EU) law has become progressively more important since the entry of the United Kingdom (UK) into the EEC in 1973. It is directly applicable throughout the UK; is superior to UK domestic law when there are conflicts with EU law; and accounts for some 75 per cent of all legislation in the UK (including that which is relevant for Northern Ireland).

Ireland

Law in Ireland reflects the complexities of Irish history. It has sources in common law, statute law, delegated legislation, constitutional law, legal treatises, European law and international conventions.

The 1922 Constitution of the Irish Free State introduced a constitutionalism which contrasted with the uncodified system of Britain and was the basic law of the state's legal order. Irish and English legislation from the past 800 years that had been applied to the 26 counties, which had not been revoked and which was compatible with the Constitution, was also incorporated into the system. Article 50 of the Constitution of Ireland, 1937 carried out the same function. The

Constitution can only be amended by a referendum of the people and contains fundamental rights of citizens, such as freedom of speech and expression.

The Constitution is the source of legitimate power held by the legislative, judicial and executive branches of government. The Supreme Court and High Court exercise judicial review over legislation and executive action, with the former having the final say on the validity of law. These courts may annul acts of the executive and legislature that are incompatible with or breach the Constitution and the decisions may be significant for society.

Parliamentary and common law traditions are still central, as in Northern Ireland. Since 1922, statute law of the Irish Free State and Ireland has been created by Acts of the Oireachtas (Parliament). A bill now passes through three stages in both Dáil and Seanad (committee, report and final formal stages). It is then sent to the President for signature and becomes the law of the land. Delegated or secondary legislation consists of orders or regulations made by an appropriate minister and civil servants, which are authorized in the original Act.

Ireland has a common law legal system. Precedents made in higher courts before independence, like the House of Lords, are valid. Judges also apply the principles of English equity (or fairness in cases where the common law is considered too harsh and inflexible).

European law is an important source of Irish law and stems from the decision in 1973 by constitutional referendum to join the then EEC, now the European Union (EU). Today, EU law is the largest source of law in Ireland. Previously, the Irish Constitution was superior to any other form of law, but it is now subservient to the Treaty of Rome and EU law. EU membership means that Ireland is obliged to accept EU law in the form of regulations, directives and decisions which have effect in Ireland depending on the different types of legislation. Irish citizens have access to the European Court of Justice (ECJ) as a Court of First Instance, and Irish laws and cases may be appealed to the ECJ if principles and/or aspects of EU law are infringed, such as equality and equal pay cases.

Ireland's signature to international conventions provides further legal sources and obligations. For example, the European Convention on Human Rights enables Irish citizens to claim rights through the European Court of Human Rights (ECHR) in Strasbourg, or, following the incorporation of the European Convention on Human Rights Act, 2003 into Irish law, interpretatively through the courts in Ireland. Under international law, treaties become part of Ireland's domestic law if they are incorporated by the Oireachtas, subject to the Supreme Court's review of their constitutionality.

Accepted legal treatises by legal writers and experts may also contribute to the sources of Irish law. Other influences include membership of the United Nations, the Council of Europe and the World Trade Organization, Roman Catholic teaching and natural law.

Ireland: legal system after 1921

Ireland's legal system in the early twentieth century underwent major changes and a gradual separation from British structures. The Irish Free State and its Constitution were enacted in 1921 and 1922 respectively and an English model court system was created in 1924. A second Irish Constitution was enacted in 1937, together with the renaming of Ireland. In 1948 the Republic of Ireland Act was passed, but the 1937 Constitution and the courts remained.

The courts system and judges

The present courts structure of Ireland was laid down in the 1937 Constitution and became operative with the Courts (Establishment and Constitution) Act, 1961. Between 1937 and 1961, courts were controlled by the 1922 Constitution, the Courts of Justice Act, 1924 and the 1937 Constitution's transition provisions in Articles 34 to 37 (Figure 8.1).

The current Courts Service of Ireland has a managerial function and was established in 1998. It organizes the courts and provides assistance and information. It is not responsible for the administration of justice, which is a judicial function. Judges in their court roles are independent of the Courts Service and are paid by the state.

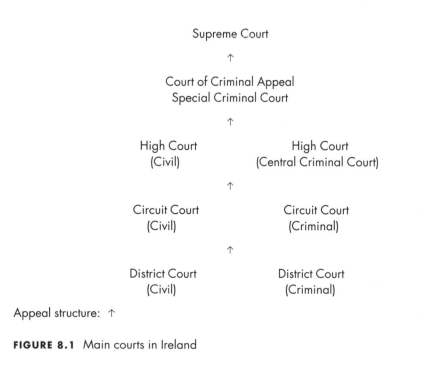

Appeal structure: ↑

FIGURE 8.1 Main courts in Ireland

PLATE 8.2 The Four Courts on the northern bank of the River Liffey in central Dublin contain the Supreme Court and the High Court and other offices such as the Bar Council. © B1 Images Ltd/Alamy

Court hearings must usually be held in public (except for specific cases which are closed) and criminal trials for indictable (non-summary) offences must generally take place before a jury. However, two types of serious crimes may be tried without a jury: trials before military tribunals and special courts. Article 38 of the Constitution empowers the Dáil to establish special courts when conventional courts are considered unable to deliver justice. For example, the Special Criminal Court tries those accused of being members of proscribed paramilitary organizations (like the Real IRA) and organized crime gangs.

The courts system comprises the superior courts of the Supreme Court, the High Court (which also functions as the Central Criminal Court), the Special Criminal Court and the Court of Criminal Appeal. The lower courts are the district courts and the circuit courts.

The superior courts

The Supreme Court and the High Court are the only courts which are established by the Constitution. Other superior courts are established by law; that is, by the Oireachtas or its component parts such as the Dáil.

The *Supreme Court* is the highest judicial authority or 'Court of Final Appeal' in Ireland for all civil and criminal matters. It usually only hears appeals on points of law, but it also decides the constitutionality of bills of the Oireachtas submitted to it by the President of Ireland (Article 26) and the compatibility of activities by government bodies with the Constitution. Its interpretations of the Constitution and the law (judicial review) are final, unless contrary to EU law, which takes precedence. The Supreme Court comprises a Chief Justice, the President of the High Court as an ex-officio member and a minimum of seven Justices. They are appointed by the President of Ireland on the advice of the government, which is advised by a judicial advisory board. The Court sits in divisions of three, five or seven justices and more important cases must be heard by at least five.

The *High Court* also has judicial review authority to interpret the Constitution and to determine the compatibility of executive and legislative actions with the Constitution and the law, but does not have the final word (held by the Supreme Court and the ECJ). It can determine matters of law or fact, civil or criminal, tries serious criminal and civil cases as a trial court and hears some appeals from lower courts. It is headed by a President and has 17 Justices, most of whom are male and Catholic, although there have been Protestant, Jewish and female judges.

Sitting as a criminal court, the High Court is called the *Central Criminal Court*; its trials are held before a judge and jury; and it has unlimited criminal jurisdiction. Appeal from its decisions is to the *Court of Criminal Appeal*, which comprises a Supreme Court judge and two High Court judges chosen by the Chief Justice. It also hears appeals of indictable criminal offences tried in the Circuit Court (see below) and the High Court (criminal cases).

A *Special Criminal Court* was established in 1972 with jurisdiction to try terrorism and organized crime cases without a jury. Three judges from the District, Circuit and High Courts sit on each case, and appeal from this court is to the Court of Criminal Appeal.

The lower courts

Beneath the superior courts are the Circuit Court and the District Court. They are established by law and handle a considerable amount of work at more accessible court levels.

The *Circuit Court* has a President, 37 judges, and the President of the District Court acts as an additional judge. Ireland is divided into eight circuits and at least one judge is assigned to each circuit. Dublin may have 10 judges and Cork 3, and sittings are held throughout the legal year and may vary in length. There are 26 Circuit Court offices in the country with a County Registrar in charge of the work of each office.

The Circuit Court has a limited and local jurisdiction and is divided into four main legal areas: civil law, criminal law, family law and jury service. Civil jurisdiction is usually limited to claims which do not exceed €38,092 (2011), but may be unlimited if all parties agree. The Court has a shared jurisdiction in family law with the High Court and may deal with judicial separation, divorce, nullity and appeals from the District Court. It may make custody and access orders, maintenance, protection and barring orders. The court has the same criminal jurisdiction as the Central Criminal Court in indictable offences except murder, rape, aggravated sexual assault, treason and piracy, and a case is heard before a judge and jury. Local trials may be transferred to the Dublin Circuit Criminal Court if appropriate. Responsibility for jury selection for the Circuit Criminal Court lies with the County Registrar in each of the 26 counties. Appeals from District Courts are made to the Circuit Court.

The *District Court* is the main (and busiest) arena for summary jurisdiction in Ireland (similar to Magistrates' Courts in Northern Ireland and England/Wales) and consists of a President and 63 judges. The country is divided into 40 districts and one judge is assigned to each district, with more in the Dublin Metropolitan District. They deal summarily with minor criminal offences, small civil claims, liquor licensing and some family law applications.

The civil jurisdiction of the Court is limited to damages up to €6,348 (2011) and can renew liquor licences and grant lottery licences. In family law matters, it can award guardianship, protection and barring orders and maintenance up to €150 a week. Its criminal jurisdiction is limited to summary offences heard without a jury (excluding murder, treason, rape and aggravated sexual assault) with a maximum punishment of 12 months' imprisonment. But indictable offences may also be tried if the accused, the judge and the Director of Public Prosecutions agree and the punishment does not exceed 12 months' imprisonment. Bail hearings for offences triable by both the District and Circuit Courts are heard at the District Court, which is also responsible for indicting accused persons and sending them for trial at the Circuit Court and the Central Criminal Court.

The legal profession

The legal profession in Ireland is closely connected to the courts system and is divided (as in the United Kingdom and Northern Ireland) into the two branches of barristers and solicitors. Solicitors are mainly involved in pre-trial work, although they may (since 1971) appear in both higher and lower courts, and from 2002 can be appointed as High Court judges without first becoming a Senior Counsel (SC). However, relatively few solicitors appear in the higher courts. Barristers are usually briefed by solicitors and work both in the preparation of trial documents and as advocates in all courts. Generally, a person seeking legal help must consult a solicitor and is not allowed to approach a barrister directly. Barristers wear a traditional black gown but, since 1995, may choose whether or not to wear the horsehair wig.

In order to qualify as solicitors, students generally obtain a university degree (or other preliminary courses) and continue to the incorporated Law Society's legal courses at Blackhall Place in Dublin, which are combined with periods of paid practical apprenticeship in a law firm. At present there are about 3,700 qualified solicitors in Ireland. The Law Society is their representative body and is responsible for the education, admission, enrolment, discipline and regulation of the profession. It administers a compensation fund, to which claims may be made from individuals and institutions suffering alleged legal malpractice from the profession.

PLATE 8.3 The Bar Council is the professional body for barristers in Ireland. It is a self-appointed, self-regulated private voluntary association created in Dublin in 1897 and reorganized in 1907. Today, it has a number of sites, such as here, the Distillery Building, Church Street, Dublin. © George Carter/Alamy

Student barristers (averaging 60 per cent men and 40 per cent women annually) usually obtain a degree in law and then attend vocational courses at the barristers' college, King's Inns in Dublin, prior to taking examinations and obtaining a Barrister-at-Law degree. The Bar Council is responsible for discipline within the Bar (body of barristers), and controls entry to the profession, although in 2007 the Irish government ruled that the Council had no statutory right to set professional standards for Irish barristers. Training is expensive; students must 'eat dinners' (dine regularly in college) and become a 'devil' or apprentice to a senior barrister for a year. Young barristers then embark upon a precarious career as sole practitioners with many obstacles and expenses. There are some 1,500 barristers in Ireland divided into junior and senior ranks and successful practitioners can achieve high incomes. Appointment to Senior Counsel (the inner bar) by the Supreme Court and the government is known as 'taking silk' because a silk gown is then worn in court. The state is represented at solicitor level by the Chief State Solicitor and at barrister level by the Attorney-General.

There have been campaigns in Ireland, as there have been in England/Wales, to reform and modernize the legal profession; to fuse (merge) the two branches into one type of lawyer; to avoid duplication of services and expense; to allow direct access to barristers by clients; to simplify the legal process; and to make the profession more representative of society. The Law Society and the Bar Council have tried to rectify some of the criticisms, and the profession is responding to consumer criticisms of its monopolies, privileges and restrictive practices.

The judiciary

Judicial authority is vested in legally qualified judges, including district justices. But there is no equivalent in Ireland to the lay magistrates (justices of the peace) in England/Wales and Northern Ireland. Technically, the President of Ireland appoints the judges, but acts on the advice of the government and guidance from the Attorney-General.

Judges serve for life or until retirement (at age 70) but may be removed from office for 'stated misbehaviour or incapacity'. The procedure for removing a judge of the Supreme Court or High Court from office is specified in the Constitution, but by law (statute) this also applies to judges of the lower courts. In effect, judges can only be removed 'upon joint resolutions passed by the Dáil Éireann and by Seanad Éireann calling for. . .removal' (Article 35.4). After a resolution is approved the judge is dismissed by the President, but the dismissal procedure can be problematic and no judge has been removed from office since 1921.

The Constitution gives the higher courts the right to decide on the validity of any laws passed by the legislature, and states that 'all judges shall be independent in the exercise of their judicial functions and subject only to the Constitution and the law' (Article 35.2). The judges are chosen from barristers of high standing and it is generally agreed that after appointment judges do not show any political bias or favouritism in their judgments.

While it is suggested that independent commissions or public hearings should examine judicial appointments, Irish judges have a reputation for incorruptibility and neutrality, and the distinction between legislature and judiciary has been maintained. But senior judges increasingly give their personal views on national matters, such as the abortion debate in 1992.

Judges are mainly male, middle-aged and with long experience as barristers in the courts. They are usually Catholics, mostly middle class, from moneyed families; have had a Catholic single-sex education; and arguably reflect establishment values. Nevertheless, the Supreme Court is a strong force in law reform, and its independent authority allows it to resolve issues that politicians have often failed to address. Its frequently liberal views have sometimes conflicted with those of Catholic conservatives, such as on contraception, abortion, women serving on juries and discrimination against married women under taxation laws.

The police force, security and prisons

The An Garda Síochána (Guardians of the Peace), established in 1922, are a national police force headed by a Commissioner who is responsible to the Minister for Justice and are under the operational command of a senior local officer. The country is divided into 23 police divisions, with 5 of them in Dublin. The Gardaí control subversive and criminal activity in the country by paramilitary and criminal groups and cooperate with the Police Service of Northern Ireland (PSNI – formerly the Royal Ulster Constabulary (RUC)).

The Gardaí were formed after the creation of the Irish Free State and won acceptance, against initial sectarian and political opposition. The force consists of uniformed and unarmed men and women, who may be armed in certain circumstances. Some members have detective duties, are usually plainclothes officers and may be armed. The number of full-time regular police officers and civilian employees in 2011 was 14,500. Generally, the military defence units do not support the police force and remain separate from political institutions, although they may share duties with the police in security situations.

The police force is generally well regarded as a responsible body with high standards of behaviour and good relations exist between the Gardaí and the population. However, there is some minority distrust and accusations of police violence. There is an Independent Complaints Board and a Complaints Appeal Board to deal with complaints from the public about improper police conduct. The Boards include barristers, solicitors, laypeople and senior Gardaí. Irish police are legally prohibited from taking strike action, but are represented by associations in claims for better pay and conditions. They are operating in a contemporary era of security concerns, terrorism, drug pushers, financial fraud, violence and youth crime, and have to deal with associated problems of urban living and unemployment.

The average daily number of prisoners in custody in Ireland in 2011 according to the Irish Prison Service was 4,257. This figure included sentenced prisoners and those on trial and remand. The number of prisoners increased between 1997 and 2004, fell slightly in 2005 and increased again in 2011. The conditions of the prisons have improved slightly, but many are still overcrowded, and lack education, recreation, therapy and rehabilitation programmes. It is argued that the selection criteria for prison staff, their training, supervision and discipline need improvement, and that brutality, discrimination and neglect are endemic in the system.

Legal aid

The legal system is expensive and not easily available for those without the personal means to pay for it. Citizens who need financial and professional help to fight a legal case may have to apply for legal aid in order to access justice and the courts. Although free legal aid in criminal cases has been obtainable since 1962 under certain conditions, free civil legal aid was not. In 1969 students and lawyers organized Free Legal Advice Centres (FLAC) to fill the gap in aid and some lawyers give their services free (pro bono) to needy clients in public interest and some private cases. But campaigns for a more comprehensive free state service have not succeeded because governments (as in other countries) have been unwilling to fund the expense.

The European Court of Human Rights in Strasbourg provided a partial civil breakthrough. It obliged Ireland to provide free legal aid in civil cases when the government was in breach of the European Convention on Human Rights. In 1979 a Legal Aid Board was established to provide civil legal aid on the basis of a means test of claimants' resources. It administers the scheme for civil aid and advice, obtains the services of solicitors and barristers for persons of limited means, and provides legal services in cases of civil debt, matrimonial cases and negligence. However, it has suffered from lack of funds and adequate government support, and does not cover areas such as unfair dismissal or social welfare. Additionally, the costs of going to law are rising and it is argued that the country cannot afford legal aid without increased personal contributions.

Northern Ireland: legal system after 1921

The Government of Ireland Act (1920) established Northern Ireland as a semi-autonomous separate entity, but still a part of the UK. It provided for a devolved Parliament in Belfast with legislative powers, an independent court system and an appeal structure to the English Court of Appeal and House of Lords. However, the Westminster Parliament retained the power to exercise direct rule in the province. The Northern Ireland Parliament was suspended in 1972 owing to the emergency situation in the province and direct rule was imposed from London. The British Army was drafted into Northern Ireland to assist the police force, the (then) Royal Ulster Constabulary (RUC), in maintaining law and order.

Unsuccessful attempts were made in the 1970s and 1980s to create devolved political structures and power-sharing between Nationalist and Unionist communities. However, since the Good Friday (Belfast) Agreement in 1998, a multi-party Northern Ireland Assembly and Executive have been established. Following a period of conflict and suspension of the institutions, devolution was restored to Northern Ireland in 2007 and legislative and executive powers over most matters were transferred to the Assembly and Executive. The UK Secretary of State and Ministry of Justice were previously responsible for Northern Ireland's constitutional and security issues, and oversaw law and order, policing, criminal justice and the prison service, but policing, prison and justice powers were eventually devolved to the Assembly in 2010.

The justice system

The UK does not have a unified court and justice system, and England/Wales, Scotland and Northern Ireland organize many of their own legal affairs. Northern Ireland is a common law and parliamentary jurisdiction. Its laws are created by the Northern Ireland Assembly in devolved matters and the UK Parliament in excepted and reserved matters.

In criminal matters, a new Public Prosecution Service for Northern Ireland (PPS) was established in 2005 headed by a Director of Public Prosecutions (DPP). The PPS is the principal prosecuting authority and takes decisions to prosecute (or not) in criminal cases which are investigated by the police.

Following the devolution of justice responsibilities to Northern Ireland, a new independent post of Attorney-General for Northern Ireland was created. The Attorney-General is the chief legal adviser to the Northern Ireland Executive for both civil and criminal cases in devolved matters and is the Executive's representative in the courts. The DPP is now appointed by the Attorney-General for Northern Ireland.

The courts system

Civil and criminal courts are responsible for the administration of justice in the province. They consist of superior and inferior courts, which are administered by the Northern Ireland Court Service and reflect a similar courts structure to England/Wales (Figure 8.2).

The *Supreme Court* in London is the highest civil and criminal court of appeal in the UK (including some Scottish civil cases). The Constitutional Reform Act, 2005 transferred (in 2009) the judicial functions of the UK House of Lords to the new Supreme Court, which is independent of and separate from the Westminster

The Supreme Court of the UK

↑

The Court of Judicature
High Court

The Court of Appeal   Crown Court

↑

County Court
Magistrates' Court

Appeal structure: ↑

FIGURE 8.2 Main courts in Northern Ireland

PLATE 8.4 The UK Supreme Court was established (2009) in Parliament Square, London. It took over the role of the House of Lords as the supreme court of appeal for many purposes in the UK. © Justin Kase z02z/Alamy

Parliament. There are 12 Justices of the Supreme Court, headed by a President, who hear appeals mainly on points of law in cases of public importance arising from lower courts and an appeal case may be heard by up to five Justices. However, since EU law is superior to UK law in areas of conflict between the two systems, issues which arise in the Northern Ireland domestic courts and political system may also be subject to EU law.

Following the Constitutional Reform Act, 2005, the former Northern Ireland Supreme Court of Judicature became the *Court of Judicature* in 2009. It comprises the Court of Appeal, High Court and Crown Court. Its personnel are headed by the Lord Chief Justice of Northern Ireland (established in 1922), who is the head of the judiciary in the province.

The *Court of Appeal* is the highest court located in Northern Ireland and sits at the Royal Courts of Justice in Belfast. It has three Lords Justices of Appeal and the Lord Chief Justice, who is the President of the Court, and a case will usually be heard by three judges. It hears appeals on points of law in criminal matters from the Crown Court and in civil matters from the High Court. It also hears appeals on points of law from county courts, magistrates' courts and tribunals. Appeal from the Court of Appeal is to the Supreme Court of the UK.

The *High Court* is divided into three divisions (Queen's Bench, Family Division and Chancery Division) after the English model and is located in the Royal Courts of Justice, Belfast. It hears complex or expensive civil cases, such as

PLATE 8.5 The Royal Courts of Justice is the location of the Court of Judicature which comprises the Court of Appeal, the High Court and the Crown Court. The building in Chichester Street, Belfast was opened in 1933. © JFox images/Alamy

those in contract, taxation and matrimonial matters, which are assigned to the divisions according to the nature of the case, and handles appeals from county courts. The High Court hears bail applications in terrorist cases and other bail cases on appeal. Its judges consist of the Lord Chief Justice and 10 High Court judges.

The *Crown Court* hears serious (indictable/'either-way') criminal cases before a jury of 12 men/women randomly chosen from members of the public, which determines guilt on the basis of facts presented in court, and a judge who pronounces sentence or punishment on a guilty person. In some circumstances of law and evidence, the defendant may appeal the decision to the Court of Appeal. The Crown Court also hears appeals from the Magistrates' Court in criminal cases. The Lord Chief Justice is President of the Court and Lords Justices of Appeal, High Court judges and County Court judges may serve in the Crown Court.

While jury trial has historically been a right at criminal and some civil levels in the UK, this was suspended in Northern Ireland in 1972 in the case of 'Diplock courts'. People charged with politically motivated paramilitary offences were tried in non-jury courts with a single judge who decided the guilt of the defendant and the punishment. The practice was ended in 2007, apart from exceptional cases, but remains in Ireland.

The lower *County Court* adjudicates on lesser civil matters and cases are heard before a judge, who decides the outcome. The County Court has 17 County Court judges (with 31 deputies) serving seven divisions or geographical areas and four District judges (with five deputies). They hear a range of civil disputes which are less expensive (up to £15,000) than those in the High Court, such as recovery of debts, trespass or negligence. The County Court (including family care centres) deals with most domestic cases, but more complex matters may be heard in the High Court. The County Court also deals with licence applications and appeals from civil and family decisions of magistrates' courts.

The Small Claims Court is an important, informal, cost-effective and speedy part of the County Court. It hears consumer claims, complaints and minor civil cases (up to £2,000), thus avoiding a large, expensive trial. The cases are usually decided by arbitration without a solicitor or barrister to represent the applicant and a district judge decides the claims.

Lay (non-legally trained) magistrates in the lower *Magistrates' Courts* deal summarily with minor matters (and the large majority of all criminal cases). Magistrates' courts consist of 21 Petty Sessions Districts, with 15 resident magistrates. Although there are no Magistrates' Courts in Ireland, this ancient English structure continues in Northern Ireland.

All criminal cases start in the Magistrates' Court ideally in the local district in which the offence occurred. Magistrates conduct preliminary hearings to see whether a case is serious enough to be sent for trial to a Crown Court, which hears indictable cases. Less serious ('summary') criminal cases can be dealt with entirely by a Magistrates' Court. Summary offences are those where the maximum

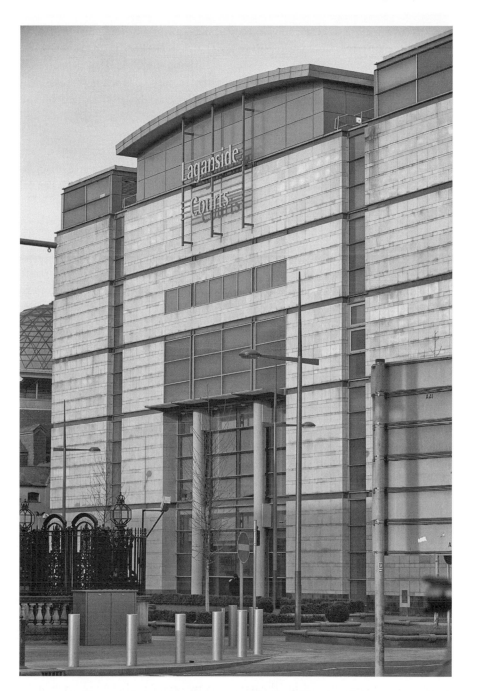

PLATE 8.6 The new Laganside Courts complex in Belfast is a large, purpose-built contemporary building opened in 2002. It houses six Crown, five County and five Magistrates' Courts as well as legal offices. © JoeFoxDublin/Alamy

penalty is a fine of £2,000 and/or six months' imprisonment. They include most traffic offences and some public order offences. In some ('either-way') cases, defendants can decide whether their case should be heard by a magistrate or in a Crown Court. Cases involving juveniles (Youth Courts) and some civil and domestic cases (Family Proceedings Courts) can also be handled by the Magistrates' Court system. The latter deals with adoption, maintenance and domestic violence.

Magistrates sit without a jury. In court they listen to the evidence and decide whether the person accused of the offence (the defendant) is guilty and, if so, fix the sentence. If a magistrate hears a case involving a child or children between 10 and 17 years of age, two members of a lay panel will sit with him or her on the bench.

Other courts

There are additional lower courts, such as Coroners' Courts with three full-time coroners covering Northern Ireland, who investigate sudden, violent or unexplained deaths and may hold inquests or order post-mortem examinations; an Enforcement of Judgment Office dealing with money orders or judgments concerning the possession of land and property; and Tribunals under a Tribunals Administration Service which resolve matters relating to social benefits, employment rights and mental health.

The legal profession

The self-regulating legal profession in Northern Ireland (as in Ireland) is divided into barristers and solicitors. Solicitors are generally involved with non-advocacy work, although they now have rights of audience in the Crown Court, County Court, Magistrates' Courts and Tribunals. Barristers prepare legal pleadings and may appear as advocates in all courts. Barristers are organized by the General Council of the Bar/the Inn of Court of Northern Ireland and solicitors by the Northern Ireland Law Society in Belfast. Both receive vocational training at the Institute of Professional Legal Studies at Queen's University and their training includes practical work with experienced lawyers. Graduate professional legal education is also provided at the Magee campus of the University of Ulster, which leads to a solicitor qualification. Solicitors and barristers may practise in Northern Ireland and Ireland. A few barristers may be hired directly by clients, but historically have been instructed by solicitors.

The Bar Executive Council and its Professional Conduct Committee is responsible for discipline within the Bar (collective name for barristers), while the Law Society performs the same function for solicitors. Any complaint about the handling of a case by the Law Society may be sent to the Lay Observer for investigation. The Lay Observer may recommend that a case be taken to the Solicitors' Disciplinary Tribunal, which is independent of the Law Society and hearings are usually in private. The Legal Services Review Group found in its 2006 report that relatively few complaints were made about lawyers in Northern Ireland.

Qualified Bar students are 'called to the bar' by the Lord Chief Justice of Northern Ireland and are divided into junior and senior counsel. Applications to 'take silk' are submitted to a panel, with successful applicants (who now include solicitors) being appointed to senior status as Queen's Counsel (QC) by the monarch on the advice of the Minister of Justice and an appointments panel. The QC wears a silk gown in court, appears in specialist cases, can claim larger fees and may have ambitions of advancement to a judgeship.

The armed forces, the police and security

Following partition, policing was the responsibility of the Royal Ulster Constabulary (RUC), established in 1922. It mostly recruited from the Unionist (Protestant) community and was distrusted by many in the Nationalist (Catholic) community. The RUC initially had a Catholic membership of 21 per cent, but by 1970 this had dropped to 10 per cent, and continued to fall.

Although armed forces have normally not been used in policing, following civil unrest in August 1969, British troops were sent at the request of the Northern Ireland government to patrol Londonderry/Derry and Belfast. The army played a controversial role in controlling the violence of the 1970s and 1980s and supporting police structures.

Since devolution in 1998, the army, border outposts and bases have been much reduced. The number of British troops in the province reached a maximum of 20,000 but dropped to 11,000 in 2005. It was intended to reduce the military presence, depending on the IRA keeping to its 2005 commitment to end the armed campaign and resume weapons decommissioning.

The 1998 Good Friday (Belfast) Agreement recommended a reformed and smaller police force, and encouraged recruitment from Nationalists. The Patten Commission report, 2000 advocated changes in police practices and structures. Most of its recommendations, such as changing the RUC's name to the Police Service of Northern Ireland (PSNI), have been implemented. In 2011 full-time regular police officers numbered 7,500 with 2,700 staff and 30 per cent of the officers were Catholics.

The PSNI investigates criminal offences and is responsible for civil order and traffic control under the direction of a chief constable. It is organized into District Command Units (DCUs) based on local council areas. The PSNI is subject to the Freedom of Information Act, 2000 and details may be accessed, under the strict provisions of the Act. The Police Ombudsman is independent and investigates complaints about the conduct of the police. Unlike other police forces in the United Kingdom and generally in Ireland, the PSNI is armed.

The Northern Ireland Policing Board was established in 2001 and reconstituted in 2007. It is a non-departmental public body comprising members of the

Assembly and independent members of the public, who, from 2010, are appointed by the Minister of Justice. It supervises the activities of the PSNI; sets targets for police performance; monitors a police Code of Ethics; and appoints independent community observers to supervise police selection. District policing partnerships were set up by the Board to cooperate with local councils and members of the public to produce guidelines for policing and community identity.

Security forces and the police have powers to combat terrorism and to arrest and interrogate individuals suspected of terrorist offences. The number of people charged with terrorist or other serious public order offences reached a height of 1,400 in the early 1970s but declined by some four-fifths by the early twenty-first century, as Loyalist and IRA prisoners were released early from prison under the Belfast Agreement, 1998.

Prisons

The high-security Maze prison, in Maze, Co. Down, contained prisoners who had committed serious offences in the Troubles and who represented the struggle between Unionists and Nationalists. Its 1,700 prisoners were divided along paramilitary and ideological lines. The prison was subject to protests, violence, hunger strikes and attempts at mass escape. Most prisoners were released under the Belfast Agreement and the prison was closed in 2000.

Following devolution, the Northern Ireland Prison Service as an agency of the Department of Justice is responsible for running the prisons, which are overseen by Independent Monitoring Boards. According to the Prison Service website, the number of prisoners in custody (sentenced prisoners and those on trial and remand) in 2011 in the province's three prisons was 1,600. While there was a fall in the average daily number of prisoners in custody between 1997 and 2001, there have been annual increases from 2001.

Public Prosecution Service

The Public Prosecution Service for Northern Ireland (PPS) has had responsibility for the prosecution of criminal cases since 2005 and is headed by the Director of Public Prosecutions for Northern Ireland. Generally, offences committed in Northern Ireland and Ireland are prosecuted there. However, it is possible to be prosecuted in Northern Ireland for an offence committed in Ireland and vice versa, such as murder, manslaughter, kidnapping, road traffic offences, criminal damage and offences against the person.

Criminal Cases Review Commission

Concern in the UK over unsafe criminal convictions led to the creation of an independent Criminal Cases Review Commission in 1995 to examine in England/

Wales and Northern Ireland convictions and sentences which might involve miscarriages of justice. The Commission reviews these cases on appeal from the Crown Court and Magistrates' Court.

The Commission cannot overturn a conviction or change a sentence. It examines cases where the conviction may be unsafe in the light of new evidence, police malpractice, wrong application of the law, inadequate courtroom procedure or omissions. Cases are referred to the Court of Appeal or Crown Court. According to the Supreme Court, 2011, the court may decide that 'on the basis of the facts as they are now known, the defendant should not have been convicted or that conviction could not possibly be based on those facts'.

Youth Justice Agency

The Youth Justice Agency of Northern Ireland replaced the Juvenile Justice Board in 2003. It aims to prevent offending by children and to reduce youth crime. It operates community and youth conference services for children at risk and offenders, as well as the Juvenile Justice Centre which provides custodial facilities for children referred by the courts system.

Legal aid

The Northern Ireland Legal Services Commission was appointed in 2003 and is sponsored by the Northern Ireland Court Service. It is responsible for providing publicly funded legal services in Northern Ireland and includes both civil and criminal legal aid. Individuals may go to a solicitor who is registered to provide services and who establishes whether or not a person is entitled to legal aid. In order to obtain legal advice, assistance or representation, income and capital must be below certain limits. Criminal legal aid is more readily available than civil legal aid, where some services are excluded, such as conveyancing, welfare, wills, defamation, business matters or personal injury. Legal aid may not cover all the costs of a case and winners may have to repay their legal aid.

The UK legal aid scheme has been reduced in recent years, although Northern Ireland receives more public legal aid funding than England/Wales. It is argued that only the poorest people obtain state help; cuts have been made in the service while costs are rising; and lawyers threaten to withdraw from the scheme because it is unprofitable. Yet the number of claimants is increasing, suggesting that larger numbers of people need but may not qualify for legal help and representation. Arguably, this creates a two-tier system of justice for those who can afford legal services and those receiving public funds, while a further group falls between the two extremes and cannot access justice. Nevertheless, in a reorganization of the legal system, ministers aim to cut the annual legal aid bill of £100 million.

Crime and punishment

In Ireland and Northern Ireland, a person may be found guilty or not guilty of a criminal charge. A not-guilty verdict results in acquittal and possible award of costs. A guilty verdict results in a fine, imprisonment, community service, probation or a suspended prison sentence. Capital punishment by hanging for murder was abolished in 1973 in Northern Ireland and in Ireland by law in 1990, although it has been prohibited by the Constitution only since 2002.

Crime statistics in both parts of the island are not as prolific as in Great Britain and other European countries, but reporting of crime to the police can be inaccurate, filed inadequately or ignored. The calculation and interpretation of overall crime may therefore be problematic since statistics vary and are derived from different sources such as the police, individual-based public surveys and official reports. A complicating factor in assessing the incidence of crime is whether fear of crime is greater than its reality.

The top seven crime categories recorded by Ireland's Central Statistics Office based on Garda statistics in 2010 (with 2009 figures in brackets) were theft and related offences including vehicle theft, 76,852 (77,031); public order and other social code offences, 54,926 (57,351); burglary and related offences, 25,380 (26,911); dangerous or negligent acts, 12,086 (15,532); attempts/threats to murder, assaults, harassments and related offences, 17,550 (18,353); controlled drug offences, 20,057 (21,983); and robbery, extortion and hijacking offences, 3,195 (2,491). In addition, there were homicide offences, 83 (84) consisting of murder and manslaughter 53 (56) and dangerous driving leading to death 30 (28).

These figures suggest that the overall crime rate in Ireland continued to fall in 2010 compared with 2009, although the picture is complicated and the general category of theft remained high. There were increases in individual types of crime, such as robbery, hijacking-related offences, extortion, drug cultivation (for example, cannabis), drug sales and supply, and sexual offences. Other offences registered declines, like homicide, burglaries, overall drug offences, drug- and drink-driving, gun crime and public order crime. Some crimes, such as robbery, could be related to the economic recession, unemployment and redundancies in Garda membership (resulting in reduced police coverage).

The main crime categories recorded by the Police Service of Northern Ireland in 2010 to 2011 (contrasted with 2009 to 2010 in brackets) were offences against the person, 29,437 (29,880); theft, 25,437(26,605); criminal damage, 25,003 (26,450); burglary, 11,942 (12,584); other notifiable offences, such as blackmail, kidnapping, drug offences and dangerous driving, 5,520 (5,560); fraud and forgery, 3,032 (3,352); sexual offences, 2,120 (1,944); robbery, 1,306 (1,276); and offences against the state, 1,243 (1,488).

In total, 105,040 crimes were reported by the PSNI in 2010 to 2011 which was a decrease of 4,099 from 2009 to 2010 and the lowest crime figure reported for 13 years. The overall clear-up or detection rate had improved by 1.5 per cent to 27.3 per cent (which is still relatively low); urban regions accounted for 57,114 reported crimes and rural regions for 47,926.

There were overall decreases in offences against the person, burglary, theft, fraud and forgery, criminal damage, offences against the state and other notifiable offences, although, unlike Ireland, offences against the person ranked higher than theft in general categories. There were decreases in other specific areas such as road deaths, domestic abuse, sectarian, racist, disability and faith/religion incidents, but an increase in homophobic offences. There were increases in sexual offences, robberies, drug seizures and drug arrests. The largest proportional increase (36 per cent) was in the number of recorded drug-trafficking offences.

In terms of the security situation in the province, arrests under terrorism legislation increased, as did the number of people charged after arrest. There were 99 bombing incidents in 2010 to 2011 (twice the number in 2009 to 2010), but fewer shooting incidents. Paramilitary shootings and casualties also decreased. The PSNI acknowledges on its crime websites that it has to operate in a difficult security environment, but claims that policing is working, crime is decreasing and it is slowly gaining the support of local communities.

Within both jurisdictions cannabis resin accounted for both the largest number of drug seizures and the largest quantity of drugs seized. The other types of drugs most frequently seized during 2006 in Ireland were cocaine powder and heroin, while in Northern Ireland between 2007 and 2008 they were cannabis herbal and ecstasy tablets.

Historically, Ireland has had a low crime rate compared with Northern Ireland, Great Britain and other EU nations, with the lowest murder rate, fewer assaults per head of population and falling rates of serious violent crime. However, reported violence in individual areas against women (rapes and indecent assaults), common minor assaults, attacks on police officers and arrests for aggravated drunkenness have grown. Although violent gangs and casual murder are relatively few, Ireland does have drug-related problems, criminal activities and urbanized crime, mostly committed by young men from difficult backgrounds. In the housing estates of parts of Dublin, unemployment is above the national average, and a major component of rising crime and antisocial behaviour. Similar patterns of criminal activity are also found in Northern Ireland, especially in the deprived urban ghetto areas of Belfast, and dissident Republican and Loyalist sectarian violence continues.

Attitudes to the Irish legal systems

An investigation by *The Times* (London, 21 April 2011) found that the Northern Ireland justice system faced difficulties following the delayed devolution of law and order powers from Westminster to Stormont in 2010. It reported that Northern Irish politicians were trying to address fundamental issues, modernize unreformed structures and cut the costs, waste and trial delays of criminal justice, which had seen a rise in the legal aid budget, a duplication of lawyers' work and an increase in their fees. Prisons were inadequate and costly with too many prison officers and not enough rehabilitation programmes. The Justice Minister of Northern Ireland accepted that the justice system was unsustainable and needed to be overhauled and replaced by a new culture of justice and prisons. *The Times* report argued that many problems were due to entrenched practices after years of sectarian conflict and a preoccupation with security. It was felt that Northern Ireland needed to develop its own legal system. A later report in *The Times* (26 May 2011) suggested that government ministers and judges are conscious of the need for change and optimistic that it can be achieved.

Criminologists (see Further reading) are also critical of legal structures and attitudes to crime in Ireland. They argue that the criminal justice system has deficiencies and slow rates of progress. Attempts to deal with these problems have arguably been ineffective in crime prevention or in the rehabilitation of offenders, and reflect an inability to address the social concerns related to crime and delinquency. However, despite alarmist media reporting and the fact that crime increased as Ireland industrialized and urbanized in the twentieth century, the incidence of crime today is low compared with North European countries, and very low when compared with the US. By global standards, there are very few murders, manslaughters, rapes, incest cases, aggravated assaults and armed robberies, but drug cases are increasing and the clear-up rates for crimes are low.

However, it is maintained that suggestions for improvements in Ireland's legal system are not always followed up quickly enough. Reform bodies argue for computerization of crime-related information; better coordination of policies and practices; research into the socio-economic factors behind crime and delinquency; examinations of the problem of recidivism (reoffending); consistent sentencing; more alternatives to prison; reduction in the number of remands for persons awaiting trial; building of new and purpose-built prisons and penal facilities; reduction of overcrowding; provision of progressive correctional practices; and the need to approach matters of crime and punishment objectively and humanely.

Views about Irish legal systems may be compared with opinion poll results. International polls suggest that there is a widespread fear of crime in many countries, which may not equate with its actuality. The Central Statistics Office, Cork (CSO) compiled a statistical profile of Ireland north and south in 2008 which first asked about perceptions of safety when walking alone in a neighbourhood or specific area after dark. The *Quality Household Survey* in Ireland and the Northern Ireland *Crime Survey* found the following results:

	Ireland (%)	Northern Ireland (%)
Very safe	25	26
Safe/fairly safe	49	41
A bit unsafe/unsafe	21	22
Very unsafe	5	11

Note: The base for Ireland was 29,388 respondents in the 18+ age group and 3,774 in the 16+ age group for Northern Ireland, which was acceptable in terms of the respective populations.

Overall, 74 per cent of respondents from Ireland reported that they felt 'very safe' or 'safe' walking alone in their neighbourhood after dark and 67 per cent of respondents from Northern Ireland reported feeling 'very safe' or 'fairly safe' when walking alone in their area after dark, indicating a statistically small 7 per cent difference in the two countries.

The same surveys also asked people about their perception of safety when alone in their homes after dark or at night with the following results:

	Ireland (%)	Northern Ireland (%)
Very safe	41	47
Safe/fairly safe	52	41
Unsafe/a bit unsafe	6	9
Very unsafe	1	2

Note: The base for Ireland was 29,450 in the 18+ age group and for Northern Ireland was 3,789 respondents in the 16+ age group.

Overall, 93 per cent of Ireland respondents reported that they felt 'very safe' or 'safe' alone in their home after dark. Among Northern Ireland respondents, 88 per cent reported that they felt 'very safe' or 'fairly safe' when alone in their own home at night. Statistically, there were small differences between the two countries in the main categories and fewer in the 'very unsafe'/'unsafe/a bit unsafe' categories. These results indicate that levels of fear are not appreciably greater in the north than in the south and may imply that respondents *feel* that Northern Ireland does not have much higher crime levels than Ireland.

Exercises

Explain and examine the following terms:

Supreme Court(s)	the Pale	referendum
the Statutes of Kilkenny	constitutionalism	judicial review
Gaelicization	Brehon law	Poynings' Law
Act of Union	palatinates	legal aid
Penal Laws	common law	Dáil
canon law	Judicature Acts	parliamentarianism
statute law	Anglo-Irish Treaty	Oireachtas
civil law	Assembly	President
amendment	rehabilitation	rights
EU law	jury	criminal law
compensation	barrister	Act of Parliament
delegated legislation	equity	High Court
misdemeanours	uncodified	ombudsman
European Law	conventions	Attorney-General

Write short essays on the following topics:

1   Discuss the relationship of Irish and English law in Irish history.

2   Compare and contrast the legal professions in Northern Ireland and the Republic.

3   Compare the types and incidence of crimes in Northern Ireland and the Republic.

Further reading

Byrne, R. and McCutcheon, P. (2001) *The Irish Legal System* Dublin: Butterworths

Dickson, B. (1997) *Concordance of English, Northern Irish and Irish Legislation* Belfast: Irish Association of Law Teachers

Dickson, B. (2005) *The Legal System of Northern Ireland* Belfast: SLS Legal Publications

Doolan, B. (2007) *Principles of Irish Law* Dublin: Gill and Macmillan

Faulkner, M., Kelly, G. and Turley, P. (1993) *Your Guide to Irish Law* Dublin: Gill and Macmillan

Hanly, C. (2006) *Introduction to Irish Criminal Law* Dublin: Gill and Macmillan

Hussey, G. (1994) *Ireland Today: An Anatomy of a Changing State* London: Viking

Kelly, F. (1988) *A Guide to Early Irish Law* Dublin: Dublin Institute for Advanced Studies

Kelly, K. (2004) *ECHR and Irish Law* Dublin: Jordan Publishing

Kilcommins, S., O'Donnell, I., O'Sullivan, E. and Vaughan, B. (2005) *Crime, Punishment and the Search for Order in Ireland* Dublin: Institute of Public Administration

McCullagh, C. (1996) *Crime in Ireland: A Sociological Introduction* Cork: Cork University Press

Murdoch, H. (2000) *A Dictionary of Irish Law* Dublin: Topaz Publications

O'Donnell, I. and O'Sullivan, E. (2001) *Crime Control in Ireland: The Politics of Intolerance* Cork: Cork University Press

O'Mahony, P. (2000) *Prison Policy in Ireland: Criminal Justice versus Social Justice* Cork: Cork University Press

O'Mahony, P. (ed.) (2008) *Criminal Justice in Ireland* Dublin: Institute of Public Administration

Parnell, H. (2003) *A History of the Penal Laws against the Irish Catholics, from the Treaty of Limerick to the Union* Dublin: Lawbook Exchange

Riagain, D.O. (2003) *Language and Law in Northern Ireland* Belfast: Studies in Language, Culture and Politics, Queen's University Belfast

Sinder, J. (2001) 'Irish Legal History: An Overview and Guide to the Sources' *Law Library Journal* 231, American Association of Law Libraries Volume 93, Number 2, spring, pp. 232–60

Statistical Yearbook of Ireland (2008) Dublin: Edition Central Statistics Office (CSO)

Walker, C. and Starmer, K. (eds) (1999) *Miscarriages of Justice: A Review of Justice in Error* Oxford: Oxford University Press. (Includes 'Miscarriage of Justice in Northern Ireland', Dickson, B. p. 287 and 'Miscarriage of Justice in Ireland', Walsh, D., p. 304)

Walsh, D. (2000) *Bloody Sunday and the Rule of Law in Northern Ireland* London: Palgrave Macmillan

Whyte, G., Hogan, G. and Kelly, J.M. (2003) *The Irish Constitution* London: Butterworths

Websites

British and Irish Legal Information Institute: www.bailii.org

Coroners Service for Northern Ireland: www.coronersni.gov.uk

Courts Service of Ireland: http://www.courts.ie

Department of Justice and Equality, Ireland: www.justice.ie

Irish Law site at University College Cork: www.irishlaw.org

Irish Legal Information Institute: www.ucc.ie/law/irlii/index.php

King's Inns, Dublin: www.kingsinns.ie

Law Society of Northern Ireland: www.lawsoc-ni.org

Ministry of Justice, UK: www.justice.gov.uk

Northern Ireland Courts: www.courtsni.gov.uk

Northern Ireland Policing Board: www.nipolicingboard.org.uk

Northern Ireland Prisons Service: www.niprisonservice.gov.uk

Office of the Attorney-General of Ireland: www.attorneygeneral.ie

Police Ombudsman for Northern Ireland: www.policeombudsman.org

Police Service of Northern Ireland: www.psni.police.uk

Public Prosecution Service, Northern Ireland: www.ppsni.gov.uk

Supreme Court Decisions: http://www.bailii.org/ie/cases/IESC

Supreme Court of Ireland: http://www.supremecourt.ie/

Youth Justice Agency, Northern Ireland: www.youthjusticeagencyni.gov.uk

9

Economic systems

- Economic history
- Ireland: economic system after 1921: strategies, structures and performance
- Economic strategies
- Economic performance
- Economic structures
- Northern Ireland: economic system after 1921: strategies, structures and performance
- Economic strategies
- Economic performance
- Economic structures
- Attitudes to economic systems
- *Exercises*
- *Further reading*
- *Websites*

The economic systems on the island of Ireland have changed greatly in the past century. For most of the twentieth century the standard of living in independent Ireland was below the Western European average. The general impression was of economic backwardness and industrial stagnation. By the beginning of the twenty-first century it had the fastest rate of economic growth and was looked upon as a model for new member states of the European Union. Then the banking crisis of 2008 severely weakened the Irish financial system, brought economic crisis and forced the government to seek international support. At the start of the twentieth century Northern Ireland, especially the Belfast region, had a modern industrial economy and its manufacturing strength made it very different from the agricultural-based economy of the rest of the island. By the middle of the century, the long-term decline of Northern Ireland's key industries such as linen, engineering and shipbuilding threatened the region's economic prosperity. It now relies on a large public sector and, following the financial crisis of 2008, faces difficulties in trying to develop a flourishing private sector. Today, both parts of the island are integrated into the global market and both face the same competitive challenges.

Economic history

Until relatively recently, the dominant sector of the economy in Ireland was agriculture. The climate and the soil of the island disposed agricultural activity towards pasture and livestock. Ownership of cattle was a traditional measure of wealth and status. As production for the market became increasingly important from the seventeenth century onwards, the value of livestock products – beef, butter and pork – increased. Between 1750 and 1830 Ireland also became an exporter of grain as war and instability in Europe drove up prices. The main market for these exports was Great Britain.

However, the flourishing export market in agricultural goods did not mean that Irish people were themselves deprived of sustenance. For most of their history, the Irish had sufficient stocks to feed themselves as long as they avoided the common catastrophe of rural economies – harvest failure. The most important addition to the diet of the Irish population from the mid-eighteenth century onwards was the potato. Cultivated sparingly in Ulster in the seventeenth century, it later became a staple food throughout the island. One acre of land could produce at least 6 tons of potatoes and this was enough to feed an average family and whatever livestock (mainly pigs) it possessed. The availability of the potato meant that the agricultural economy could divert resources towards serving the rapidly expanding export market in Great Britain. It also meant that over the next 100 years the Irish population was the fastest growing in Europe. At the beginning of the eighteenth century the Irish population was about 2 million. By the end of the century it had risen to 4.5 million and, by the 1840s, to just over 8 million. The danger was *over*-reliance on the potato and the threat of serious famine if the harvest failed.

Famine was not unknown. There had been harvest failure in 1740 to 1741 that resulted in around 500,000 deaths or nearly one-sixth of the total population. About 80,000 also died owing to bad harvests in 1816 to 1817. However, the Great Famine of 1845 to 1849 represented a human catastrophe for most of the island. Three harvests out of four failed due to potato blight and it is estimated that about 1 million people or just over 12 per cent of the population perished from either disease or starvation, or both. The response of the government in London was hesitant and, by today's standards, unconscionably limited. The west of Ireland, in particular, was severely affected and the famine also affected

PLATE 9.1 Irish peat diggers watched by the landowner. Peat was an important part of the agricultural economy, providing fuel and employment. © Pictorial Press Ltd/ Alamy

disproportionately the poor, that 60 per cent of the population with plots of land under 5 acres. The social demoralization and economic distress of this event encouraged large-scale emigration throughout the rest of the century.

As a consequence, the Irish population declined by about one-third between 1850 and 1921. Those who remained began to experience greater prosperity and living standards in general improved. The size of farms increased and a series of Land Acts between 1870 and 1909 brought about a social transformation as British governments helped tenants to buy their land. The old landlord system, dominated by a few, was replaced by a system of owner-occupation, extended to the many. Incomes also rose steadily from about 40 per cent of the British level at the time of the Famine to about 60 per cent by 1914. Prosperity was greatest in the north-east of Ireland because, uniquely on the island, the Belfast region had undergone an industrial revolution in the middle decades of the nineteenth century. Whereas industry in southern cities was mainly concerned with brewing, distilling or food processing (for example, the Guinness brewery in Dublin) the north-east witnessed the emergence of factory production and a modern industrial economy.

By the beginning of the twentieth century Belfast's mills dominated the world's market in linen manufacture, employing over 50,000 workers, the majority of whom were women. Belfast's shipbuilders produced about 8 per cent of world, and 25 per cent of UK, tonnage. The Harland and Wolff shipyard, builders of the *Titanic* which was launched in 1911, alone employed over 9,000 workers. The development of these two major industries created the conditions for wider growth in related production such as heavy engineering. The population of the city, which had been 70,000 in 1841, rose to 400,000 in 1901, temporarily outstripping Dublin. What is remarkable about the industrialization of the Belfast region is that the north-east, like the rest of Ireland, lacked the raw materials for a manufacturing economy. It had no natural reserves of coal and iron but depended entirely on access to sources in Great Britain. It also depended for its markets on Great Britain and the British Empire. The distinction between the industrial north-east and the agricultural south and west of Ireland was the economic basis for political divisions over Home Rule.

For Unionists in Ulster, the Union after 1801 provided the framework for economic growth and prosperity. They believed that the interests of the north-east were similar to the interests of the other manufacturing regions of the UK and that British free trade was essential to prosperity. Ulster Unionists also suspected that a Home Rule Parliament could impose tariff barriers between Ireland and Great Britain. Irish Nationalists took a different view and believed that Irish self-government was required to promote and protect domestic industry. It was thought that protection would promote local industry, end emigration and improve Irish living standards. Nationalists could not provide Ulster Unionists with any compelling economic arguments for Home Rule; nor were Unionist counter-arguments persuasive to Nationalists.

Ireland: economic system after 1921: strategies, structures and performance

With 55 per cent of the population directly engaged in farming and its produce contributing one-third of gross domestic product (GDP), agriculture and its needs dominated the thinking of Free State governments after 1922. Moreover, most of the country's exports, such as food processing and brewing, were agricultural-related. Manufacturing accounted for only 8 per cent of employment. Though Ireland was now largely politically autonomous from the UK, economically it remained tightly bound up with it. The Irish currency was fixed at parity with the British pound; the British market was the destination for 97 per cent of Ireland's exports and Britain supplied 80 per cent of all Ireland's imports. The pro-Treaty governments between 1921 and 1932 were reluctant to interfere with trading relationships between Ireland and Britain and especially wary of imposing tariffs on British imports. It was feared that tariffs would raise costs for Irish agriculture and invite retaliation from the British government, in turn damaging Irish exports. The large farmers who provided the core support for the pro-Treaty governing party Cumann na nGaedheal (formed in 1923) wanted to maintain unrestricted access to the British market for their livestock. Equally, big business wanted to secure the existing trade in food products and drink. These exports increased satisfactorily, if not dramatically, in the decade after 1922. Domestically, this period was one of economic conservatism. The government was keen to balance the budget; for example, it cut expenditure on old-age pensions and was reluctant to interfere in the working of the market, though it did set up the Electricity Supply Board (ESB) in 1927 to meet the country's energy needs. It was the election in 1932 of a Fianna Fáil government, led by Éamon de Valera, which brought about a far-reaching change of policy. Protection became the new strategy.

Economic strategies

In part protection was a response to the worldwide economic depression that followed the Wall Street Crash of 1929. In part it was also the implementation of a key element of a more radical nationalist ideology that espoused self-sufficiency, was suspicious of external influences and sought to represent the interests of small farmers and local business. The ideal was Ireland as a small, closed economy and the policy of protection was to encourage domestic sub-stitutes, both agricultural and manufactured, for foreign produce. A larger political objective was to reduce the dependence of the country upon the British market. The range of trade controls rose steeply after 1932 and the Irish government imposed some of the highest tariffs in Europe. The state became more actively involved in industrial regulation not only by promoting local enterprise through preferential loans but also, in the Control of Manufactures Act (1932), by requiring Irish ownership of businesses registered in the country. Between 1932 and 1938, the so-called 'Economic War' with Britain disrupted the exchange trade of Irish cattle for British coal. The effects of protection were mixed. Irish industrial output did rise but the scope for growth was limited since the market for its products was mainly domestic and not international. The state subsidy of crop production did reduce grain imports but there was a decline in traditional livestock exports because animal feed was more expensive. The population did show a marginal increase but unemployment also rose significantly throughout the 1930s.

There was deeper economic stagnation between 1939 and 1945 as the Second World War isolated the Irish economy even more. Industrial and agricultural production were depressed, unemployment rose (despite many workers leaving to find employment in the British war industries) and living standards fell. While there was growth in the 1950s of about 1 per cent of GDP per annum, Ireland's performance was miserable compared with other states in Western Europe. By 1961 the population had fallen to 2.8 million as lower living standards encouraged emigration, mainly to the UK.

A change of strategy was initiated in the 1960s which helped transform Ireland from a small, *closed* to a small, *open* economy. This change was signalled in 1958 by the publication of a report by T.K. Whitaker, a key official at the Department of Finance. Whitaker's report, *Economic Development*, argued that it was essential to shift policy from protecting the domestic market to free trade and export-led growth. This meant attracting high levels of foreign investment. At the same time, the government adopted the fashionable rhetoric of economic planning and, also in 1958, announced a Programme for Economic Expansion. The Programme anticipated growth of 2 per cent per annum but the rate of growth over the next five years was actually double that. The lesson was learnt. Economic expansion and better living standards required openness to world trade and attractiveness to foreign investment as well as public investment in welfare services and education.

The Anglo-Irish Free Trade Agreement was negotiated in 1965, Ireland acceded to the General Agreement on Tariffs and Trade (GATT) in 1967 and the country joined (along with the UK) what was then called the European Economic Community in 1973. This strategy was not without its critics and not without its problems. It was argued that Ireland's reliance on foreign direct investment (FDI) left it vulnerable to downturns in world market conditions. Overseas firms taking advantage of Irish tax incentives might just as easily move their investments elsewhere. Moreover, competition within Europe would hit the most vulnerable industries and these were likely to be the Irish-owned firms that had survived behind national tariff barriers.

Despite the evidence of the relative success of this new strategy and despite general prosperity after 1973, especially as farmers profited from the European Common Agricultural Policy (CAP), Irish economic performance was far from spectacular. Though the population was rising along with living standards,

PLATE 9.2 A Ryanair jet arrives at Dublin Airport. Ryanair is famous for developing the so-called 'no frills' or 'low budget' style of air travel and came to symbolize the new entrepreneurial spirit of modern Ireland. It flies about 72 million passengers annually. © Lightworks Media/Alamy

emigration remained a concern throughout the 1980s and the first half of the 1990s. There was widespread satisfaction that access to European markets was progressively reducing Ireland's import/export reliance on the UK. If analysts were generally agreed that Europe had benefited Ireland politically, the overall balance of economic advantage in Europe was less clear-cut.

Very few expected the dramatic boom that was to occur after 1993 when Ireland took advantage of the Single European Market. This unprecedented boom, known as the Celtic Tiger, was due in part to a change in state management of the economy. Unlike the high-spending governments of the late 1970s and early 1980s, economic policy in the 1990s was designed to maintain tight control of public finances, sustain a pro-business culture and keep down wage inflation. The transformation of the economy in such a short period was remarkable. The culture of Ireland also appeared to undergo a similar transformation. The new world of budget airline *Ryanair* rather than the old world of the film *Ryan's Daughter* expressed the spirit of modern Irish enterprise.

Economic performance

In 1950, 93 per cent of Irish exports went to the UK. In 1960 the figure was 75 per cent. By the end of the century less than 25 per cent of Irish exports went to the UK market. UK imports now constitute less than 40 per cent of Irish trade.

This change reveals both the growth of the Irish economy and its diversification. A significant factor in the new export pattern has been membership of the European Union and Irish access to an integrated continental market. However, this pattern was developing before entry to the EU in 1973 and has continued since 1973 as a consequence of globalization. A symbol of the relationship between the two economies had been parity between the Irish and British currencies. The government had sufficient confidence in the long-term prospects of the domestic and European economy to break the connection with the British pound and join the European Monetary System (EMS) in 1979. This effectively linked the Irish currency to the German mark but the change did not deliver the financial stability expected of it. Nevertheless, Ireland, unlike the UK, committed itself to Economic and Monetary Union (EMU) and on 1 January 2002 replaced its own independent banknotes and coinage with the Euro. Arguments that accession to the euro threatened the ability of Irish governments to manage the economy were discounted, though this was an argument that returned in 2008 in the wake of the financial crisis.

European membership was important in other respects. The country received substantial monetary transfers not only from the CAP but also from the European regional fund. It is popularly believed that European money was the main source of recent Irish prosperity even though economists tend to reject this claim. The consensus is that EU subsidies contributed about 0.5 per cent additional annual growth to the economy throughout the 1990s but this must be put into the perspective of average annual growth rates of about 7 per cent. European money did help to improve Ireland's infrastructure, especially the development of new telecommunications networks and the beginning of a modern road network. During the 1990s, European aid contributed to the €2.5 billion spent on road improvements and it continues to support ambitious motorway projects over the next 15 years, estimated at €12 billion. Equally, investment in telecommunications of about €3 billion transformed the Irish network and deregulation of the market has made it more competitive. Some commentators believe that just as important as European funding is the adoption of a more professional attitude in the public sector and a more entrepreneurial culture in the private sector. Importantly, the country's ability to attract FDI is mainly due to Irish access to EU markets. The importance of this sector to the health of the Irish economy has become vital. In the 2008 to 2012 Business Environment Ranking of the Economist Intelligence Unit, Ireland was placed eleventh out of 82 countries in terms of its attractiveness for foreign business.

At the high point of the Celtic Tiger in 2006 to 2007 there were over 1,100 foreign-owned companies in Ireland, providing employment for about 150,000 out of a total employed workforce of 1,795,000. These companies generated about 70 per cent of all manufacturing output and about 85 per cent of all manufacturing exports. Nearly half of these companies were American subsidiaries (the US supplied two-thirds of all inward investment in 2010) and Ireland receives about 25 per cent of all US FDI in Europe. FDI has been concentrated in important growth sectors such as information and communications technology, life and health sciences (such as pharmaceuticals), financial services, but also in less skilled international customer services (telephone call centres). In recent years, Ireland has become an important microchip producer and the world's largest exporter of computer software. One-third of all personal computers sold in Europe are manufactured in Ireland. Most of the large drug companies have established facilities in the country. The attractiveness of Ireland for overseas investment was attributed to its comparatively highly educated workforce, low corporation tax (12.5 per cent) and (for Americans) its English-speaking culture. Ireland's young population also gave it an advantage.

Traditionally, the high Irish birth rate was understood as part of the economic problem since its consequences were either high unemployment or enforced emigration. In the 1990s it became part of the solution. Ireland has the youngest population in Europe: 40 per cent are under the age of 25 and 70 per cent are under the age of 45. Increased participation of women in the workforce also contributed to boosting economic growth. Women now comprise 42 per cent of the workforce compared with less than 10 per cent a generation earlier. Importantly for a nation so deeply affected by the Great Famine, the population has grown to over 4 million. This is the highest figure recorded for the 26 counties of Ireland since 1871. Though the Irish birth rate is falling, the new experience of immigration has sustained modest population growth. From 2000 to 2008, about 200,000 immigrants from Central and Eastern European states came to work in Ireland and an Economic and Social Research Institute (ESRI) study estimated that 6 per cent of economic growth in this period could be attributed to foreign labour. Irish people also returned from abroad, an indication that emigration is no longer considered a permanent step.

In a short space of time, Ireland has become a highly industrialized economy with agriculture now contributing just 5 per cent of GDP. Sixty-five per cent of Irish employment is now in services of all kinds, public and commercial. A sign of this change was Dublin's high-tech International Financial Services Centre which opened in 1987, host to half of the world's top 50 banks and to half of the top 20 insurance companies. Individual prosperity rose sharply. House prices more than doubled between 1987 and 2004. Irish families also benefited from higher welfare expenditure, especially in health and education, which redressed government cutbacks of the 1980s. Welfare spending tripled from around €9 billion in 1997 to €26 billion in 2004. In this era of the Celtic Tiger most people had never been so prosperous and the country celebrated a new economic self-confidence.

Unfortunately there was another side to this prosperity. When Ireland joined the euro, interest rates fell from 7 per cent to 3 per cent and this helped fuel a property investment boom. The buoyant economy encouraged a record-breaking construction of new housing and 20 per cent of economic growth in Ireland between 2000 and 2008 may be attributed to house building alone. Tax relief on

PLATE 9.3 The Irish Financial Services Centre in Dublin was established in 1987. It houses financial institutions along with legal, accountancy and taxation firms and remains a very visible sign of Ireland's economic development. © Steppenwolf/Alamy

mortgages also encouraged property speculation at home and abroad. Irish banks became dangerously over-extended in funding what proved to be an inflated 'property bubble'. They had borrowed heavily to finance loans to property developers both at home and abroad. This was allowed to occur because government regulation was too lax. When that bubble burst in 2008, the construction industry contracted by 51 per cent (leaving in its wake so-called 'ghost estates' or housing developments with no tenants), house prices fell (by over 40 per cent from the high point of the boom), household indebtedness rose dramatically (by 2010 over 150,000 households were in 'negative equity', i.e. the amount of their property mortgage was greater than the value of their home) and the Irish banking system almost collapsed. This was part of a global crisis, of course, but two official reports into the banking crisis published in 2010 argued that a substantial part of the blame can be laid at the door of poor financial regulation, poor lending standards and poor credit judgement. The then President of Ireland, Mary McAleese, famously called it 'blinkered hubris'.

Ireland became the first euro zone country to enter recession, in September 2008. To reassure investors and the financial markets, the government responded by guaranteeing the debts of six Irish-owned banks, in effect a guarantee of €440 billion or twice Ireland's annual GDP. In 2009 and 2010 the Anglo-Irish Bank and the Irish Nationwide Building Society were nationalized but a more comprehensive solution to the banking crisis was the setting up of the National Asset Management Agency (NAMA) in the autumn of 2009. Essentially, this removed

PLATE 9.4 A so-called 'ghost estate' in Enniscrone, Co. Sligo. Ghost estates comprise a development of ten or more houses in which more than 50 per cent are unoccupied or uncompleted. They are the legacy of Ireland's property boom. © JoeFox/Alamy

to government (and Irish taxpayers) the 'toxic' or bad assets from the Irish banks (estimated at €81 billion). The Fianna Fáil government also reacted with stringent measures to restore public finances. In a series of budgets after 2008, a deflationary policy of public expenditure cuts, tax increases and reductions in public sector wages was pursued in order to restore international confidence. In November 2010 the government was compelled to negotiate a 'bail-out' package of €85 billion from the so-called 'troika' of the European Central Bank, International Monetary Fund and European Commission. Since 2008 GDP has fallen by 12 per cent while unemployment has risen to over 14 per cent, and economic emigration has once more become a feature of Irish life. Some commentators argue that Ireland has gone through 15 years of unprecedented growth only to waste its advantages. Others believe that once the lessons of the property disaster have been digested, Ireland can look forward again to rising living standards because the non-banking, export-led sectors of the economy remain sound.

Economic structures

State control of economic structures has been used for strategic purposes such as economic development and the provision of public transport. Today there are 100 so-called state-sponsored bodies employing 57,500 people in the commercial sector. They are responsible for a wide range of functions including tourism, postal services and transport. In the 1990s, the Irish government privatized some of the 'commercial semi-states' like steel and telecommunications, and liberalized other sectors such as air transport and electricity supply. In 2006, the national airline Aer Lingus was privatized, its rival Ryanair taking a 30 per cent stake in the company. In all cases, the purpose has been to increase efficiency through the application of market disciplines. This was a common development throughout the world and the government was adapting to the changing demands of the global market.

In this regard, one of Ireland's success stories has been the Industrial Development Agency (IDA), established originally in 1949 as the Industrial Development Authority. After 1958, the IDA was charged with securing FDI and the promotion of Irish exports. In 1969 it became an autonomous, state-sponsored body responsible for all aspects of industrial development. From 1994 IDA Ireland has been charged exclusively with attracting foreign investment and promoting international competitiveness (while domestic industry became the responsibility of Enterprise Ireland). It selectively targeted international companies in pharmaceuticals, e-commerce and telecommunications. Today, the IDA supports about 1,000 companies employing over 139,000 people and these jobs are mainly export-oriented. Enterprise Ireland has helped domestic manufacturers and service providers enter global markets. Its main objective is to assist Irish business in the use of modern technology, in the development of business plans and in the promotion of innovation.

About one-third of the Irish labour force is organized into trade unions. The Irish Congress of Trade Unions (ICTU) is the main coordinating body in both jurisdictions on the island. Forty-eight of its 55 affiliated unions are mainly based in Ireland. This constitutes a membership of 602,000, now mainly in the public sector, of which 46 per cent are women. The Irish Business Confederation (IBEC) represents the interests of employers. The structure of industrial relations underwent an important change in 1987 with the arrangement of 'social partnership'. Corporate agreement between government, employers and trade unions about employment, welfare and growth was not new in Irish politics but had fallen out of favour. However, in the mid-1980s it appeared essential to prevent economic chaos. Large pay increases, rising inflation, high taxation and heavy government debt of 120 per cent of GDP (much higher than the crisis of 2008) were threatening to erode business competitiveness and international confidence. The Fianna Fáil government, with the support of the opposition Fine Gael, set about reducing public borrowing and expenditure. To secure public support for these measures it negotiated a deal on wage restraint with the trade unions and employers. In return, trade unions were given some influence over employment decisions and welfare policy. This Programme for National Recovery helped stabilize the economy and social partnership was identified as one of the key elements making Ireland attractive for FDI. In 2009 relationships between the government and public sector unions broke down over the imposition of pay cuts to deal with the financial crisis. In the private sector it has become increasingly common for individual deals to be struck between unions and employers. However, government and unions have shown interest in a revised form of partnership or 'social dialogue', though its policy scope is unclear.

The organization representing Irish farmers, the Irish Farmers Association (IFA), was founded in 1955 and reorganized in 2006 with a membership today of 85,000. Of the total land area of 7 million hectares, 5 million are utilized for agriculture and forestry. Cattle and dairy products remain the dominant sectors. However, agriculture has declined in economic significance. In 1989 it employed 15 per cent of the workforce. Today it employs about 7 per cent (130,000), contributes about 3 per cent of GDP or 8 per cent if food processing is included, and 8.5 per cent of Irish exports. It is expected that the number of farms will decline by about one-third in the next decade and of these only about 20 per cent will be full-time commercial enterprises. Agricultural policy is almost entirely decided in Brussels.

Ireland's monetary policy is now also decided within the EU. Since 1 June 1998, Ireland has been a member of the European System of Central Banks (ESCB), consisting of the European Central Bank (ECB) and the central banks of the EU member states. From 1 January 1999, the Governing Council of the ECB has made the decisions on monetary policy and interest rates for those states like Ireland participating in European Monetary Union (EMU). The Governor of the Central Bank of Ireland is a member of the ECB's Governing Council. Indeed, it was Ireland's commitment to the EMU project which helped secure substantial EU funds to improve roads and telecommunications. Unfortunately, membership of the euro zone, especially its low interest rates, helped inflate the property bubble in Ireland between 2000 and 2008 and contributed to the failure of the Irish banking system. Addressing the so-called 'sovereign debt' crisis within the euro zone is likely to mean that in the future Ireland's financial independence will be even more constrained.

Northern Ireland: economic system after 1921: strategies, structures and performance

On the eve of the First World War, the Belfast region was producing one-third of Irish industrial output and two-thirds of all industrial exports. The city's manufacturing wealth was based upon shipbuilding and linen. Londonderry/Derry, the second city in Ulster, had developed an important shirt-making industry. The First World War stimulated industrial production and brought new affluence to Ulster because of the demand for ships, textiles and food. The brief economic boom that followed the war in 1919 to 1920 provided another boost to Ulster's traditional industries. Therefore, the economic basis of Ulster Unionist opposition to breaking the Union with Great Britain was probably stronger in 1921 than it had been for a generation. Improved trade with the rest of Ireland would never have compensated for the disruption of trade with the rest of the UK. Nor was it clear that Ulster agriculture would have benefited outside the Union. However, the staple industries of Northern Ireland were to experience two serious challenges: new international competitors and the world economic crises of the 1920s and 1930s.

Economic strategies

The key economic strategy of the Northern Ireland government had been the same as its key political strategy – to stay within the UK. Economic policy was decided in London on the basis of UK, rather than regional, needs. Northern Ireland's particular condition reflected the general state of the British economy and on most statistical measurements its performance was below the UK average. Like the rest of the country in the inter-war years Northern Ireland suffered high and persistent unemployment, often four times the national average (though other regions, like South Wales, experienced deeper economic problems). In the 1920s the rate of unemployment fluctuated between 13 and 24 per cent and averaged around 19 per cent of the workforce. In the 1930s it averaged around 27 per cent. A number of reasons may be given for the depressed state of the Northern Ireland economy in this period. The first was that, as a free-trading country, the UK was open to the shifts in the world economy and the experience of the 1920s was a classic transition from boom to bust. Linen and shipbuilding had expanded their capacity to meet both wartime and peacetime demand. Suddenly they were confronted with large overcapacity while facing competition from newly industrializing countries like Japan and Sweden.

Though Belfast yards managed to retain their proportion of UK shipping launches throughout the 1920s they were severely hit by the world slump after 1929. The main yard of Harland and Wolff struggled to recover in the 1930s. Because it had never specialized in military vessels it was deprived of government contracts that helped shipyards elsewhere in the UK. Linen suffered due to a decline in demand, a fashion change as much as an economic one. It was more expensive and needed more care than other fabrics. Employment in the industry fell from 75,000 in 1924 to 56,000 in 1930 and output slumped by 25 per cent. Agriculture, which employed a quarter of the workforce, also suffered from international trends and experienced prolonged depression during this period. However, the farming sector was not as badly hit as other parts of the UK.

Northern Ireland also had difficulty in compensating for its declining industries by attracting new ones like cars, chemicals and electrical products, though in 1937 the aircraft manufacturers Short Brothers established a factory in Belfast. A smaller proportion of the region's workforce was in these expanding sectors despite the efforts of the Northern Ireland government to encourage their development under the New Industries (Development) Acts of 1932 and 1937. The existence of the devolved Parliament was probably to Northern Ireland's economic disadvantage. Northern Ireland was expected to look after its own domestic problems and only by the late 1930s did the UK government accept the need for equal funding.

PLATE 9.5 The gantry cranes 'Samson' and 'Goliath' at Harland and Wolff shipyard in Belfast. Shipbuilding, once one of Northern Ireland's major industries, declined throughout the twentieth century. Today most of Harland and Wolff's business is making turbines for offshore wind farms. © Eirepix/Alamy

The Second World War provided an important boost to Northern Ireland's economy. Shipbuilding and aircraft production received important wartime contracts and this work also benefited engineering firms supplying necessary components. The linen mills profited from the demands for military uniforms and tents. Agriculture also took advantage of the demand for foodstuffs. The problem was no longer how to market surplus production but how to maximize production. Unemployment fell sharply and the differentials in living standards between Northern Ireland and the Free State became more pronounced. Northern Ireland not only experienced wartime economic prosperity but also benefited from the UK's post-war Welfare State. For a Unionist government the political merit of the Welfare State was that it underscored the difference between a modern Northern Ireland and a less developed independent Ireland.

The advantages of the Welfare State were not only the entitlements it conferred in healthcare and social security but also the funds it made available to equalize economic opportunities throughout the UK. For a relatively disadvantaged region like Northern Ireland this was obviously significant. In the 20 years after 1945 there was a sevenfold increase in government expenditure which both improved the quality of life and created new jobs in the public sector. For the first time, the Northern Ireland government could draw upon UK financial resources to encourage the development of industry. It was acknowledged that there would be a long-term decline in shipbuilding and linen and that it was important to encourage alternative forms of employment. Despite rising prosperity, unemployment remained a problem and averaged 7.5 per cent throughout the 1950s. The shipbuilding workforce declined further, from 20,000 in 1950 (about 10 per cent of all manufacturing jobs) to 9,000 by the mid-1960s. Linen continued to face increased competition from artificial fibres. Agricultural labour declined by one-third.

A new strategy was required, and it involved encouraging industrial diversification and securing foreign investment. Here Northern Ireland anticipated the successful policy of the Irish government. Investment grants, tax incentives, low rents and prebuilt factories were used to attract FDI. Fifty thousand new jobs were created between 1945 and 1965, mainly in the petrochemical and manmade fibres industries. Personal incomes more than doubled after 1945. Indeed, the 1960s began with optimism as the Northern Ireland government unveiled a number of strategic plans for the future development of regional employment, higher education, transport infrastructure and even a new city – Craigavon – in mid-Ulster.

Such optimism was to fade as Northern Ireland experienced the impact of political violence in the late 1960s and the world oil crisis of 1973. In the 1970s and 1980s Northern Ireland underwent a process of deindustrialization that matched the experience of other regions of the UK. Employment in manufacturing fell by 50 per cent and the numbers engaged in farming fell by a similar proportion. Many of the multinational branch factories established in the 1960s closed as their parent companies relocated activity. The manmade fibre industry collapsed completely. One problem was the lack of emerging local industry to compensate for the loss of jobs in foreign-owned business. Unemployment rose to 20 per cent in the early 1980s and attracting FDI was made more difficult by the bombing campaign of the IRA. Though much of the analysis is speculative, one estimate is that the Troubles cost about 22,000 jobs.

Following the suspension of the Northern Ireland Parliament in 1972, public expenditure rose incrementally under direct rule from London. The figures are quite revealing. In the course of the next 20 years, public expenditure accounted for 65 per cent of GDP. Forty per cent of the workforce was employed in the public sector and the jobs of many in the private sector depended upon government contracts. This became known as the 'subvention' or the difference between what Northern Ireland could finance from its own resources and what is actually spent. In the 1960s this averaged about 7 per cent of public expenditure. By 1994 it was 33 per cent or £3.5 billion. In 2011 it was £9 billion or about £5,000 per person. Critics coined the term 'dependence economy' to describe this condition. Others argued that such expenditure was justified owing to Northern Ireland's special needs. In one way it indicated the significance of being part of the UK, since the equivalent cost to the Irish government would have been about one-tenth of Ireland's GDP. Nevertheless, the economy did show signs of improvement in the 1990s, coinciding with the winding down of political violence.

Northern Ireland remains one of the least prosperous regions of the UK, though it was the most prosperous region on the island of Ireland until the mid-1980s. The four reasons traditionally given for its economic disadvantage are relatively high unemployment, low economic activity rate, a high birth rate and low productivity. Between 1990 and 2006 all of these indicators of disadvantage showed substantial improvement. The unemployment rate fell below the EU average and there was an improvement in the economic activity rate (though at 70 per cent of those eligible for work, it is still low by UK standards). The relatively high birth rate, formerly believed to be a problem, was now thought to be one of the region's economic advantages. Sixty per cent of the population is under 40 years old and 23 per cent under 16 years. This comparatively youthful population is a resource for new industry and a market for consumer goods. Between 1997 and 2002, the Northern Ireland economy experienced real growth of over 13 per cent. There was also a diversification of Northern Ireland's exports. Partly this diversification may be attributed to the renewed success in attracting FDI. One-third of investment comes from the rest of the UK, 26 per cent from America, 19 per cent from Ireland and 13 per cent from other EU countries. About 80 per cent of FDI goes into the knowledge-based sector such as computer software, telecommunications and financial services.

At the same time government measures to address claims of economic discrimination have been successful. There was a substantial improvement in the employment profile of Catholics. Fifty-five per cent of all employees are Protestant and 45 per cent are Catholic compared with a potential working population of 57 per cent Protestant and 43 per cent Catholic. In the course of the past 25 years Catholics have become well represented (and in some cases, over-represented) in managerial, administrative and professional positions, especially in the public sector. Though there are still complaints about discrimination today these are as likely to come from Unionist as from Nationalist politicians.

Economic performance

Manufacturing now accounts for only 11 per cent of jobs in Northern Ireland. In 2011 unemployment stood at just under 7 per cent, slightly lower than the UK average and the EU average of 10 per cent. However, figures for youth unemployment and long-term unemployment were higher than the UK average. The accountancy firm Price Waterhouse Coopers estimated that about 124,000 new jobs were created between 1998 and 2008, but that one-third of these were lost in the economic recession of the next two years. Like the rest of Ireland, there had been a speculative property boom between 1998 and 2008 (about €3.5 billion of the property assets acquired by NAMA are in Northern Ireland). From a peak in 2007, house prices in Northern Ireland have dropped by about 37 per cent. This severely affected employment in construction which fell by a quarter between 2008 and 2011. Unlike Ireland, which has a strong exporting sector, growth in Northern Ireland is limited by the lack of export-led industry. In 2010, a report by First Trust Bank argued that if Northern Ireland were an independent country the gap between public expenditure and taxes raised would leave it with a budget deficit of 26 per cent of GDP (compared with Ireland's 12 per cent). This remains academic since it is *not* independent but an economic region of the UK. However, the reliance of the Northern Ireland economy on the public sector has become a political issue.

In a BBC television interview before the General Election of May 2010, the leader of the Conservative Party and later Prime Minister, David Cameron, singled out Northern Ireland as an example of a region in which the 'state accounts for a bigger share of the economy than it did in the communist countries in the old eastern bloc'. This, he claimed, was unsustainable. The problem had been recognized already by Northern Ireland's First Minister Peter Robinson who said in 2006 that the 'over-large' public sector acted as a disincentive to private enterprise. It has been argued that one way of stimulating growth would be to cut corporation tax in Northern Ireland to the Irish level of 12.5 per cent. Some economists predict that this could, over 10 to 15 years, generate an extra 60,000 new jobs and improve income per head by about 14 per cent. However, this would require a corresponding cut of about £300 million in the grant which the Northern Ireland Executive receives from London and some argue that this would be a bad trade-off.

Northern Ireland will share the public expenditure cuts which the Conservative–Liberal Democrat Coalition outlined in the emergency budget of June 2010. UK borrowing is to be cut over five years from £149 billion (11 per cent of GDP) to £20 billion (1 per cent) and public expenditure in some areas could be cut by as much as 25 per cent. Public expenditure in Northern Ireland is 22 per cent higher than the UK average and the consensus of economists is that there is no longer a convincing 'special case' argument now that the Troubles have ended. Under current budgetary plans agreed by the Northern Ireland Executive in March 2011, there will be reductions of 7 per cent in current and 37 per cent in capital spending over the period to 2015. The best that has been predicted for Northern Ireland is that recovery will be flat, what some economists have called 'jobless growth'.

Economic structures

Major economic decisions affecting Northern Ireland continue to be made by the UK government. Since the UK does not participate in the European single currency, interest rates for Northern Ireland are set by the Bank of England. Local banks in Northern Ireland can issue their own banknotes within the overall regulatory framework set by the Bank of England. As a provincial capital, Belfast never developed a large market in financial services. Between 1921 and 1972, the Northern Ireland government had few autonomous economic powers. The Ministry of Commerce was charged with encouraging industrial development and it did have some limited scope for providing business incentives. For 10 years between 1955 and 1965, the Northern Ireland Development Council (NIDC) promoted and lobbied for investment. The NIDC was the forerunner of a number of agencies in the 1970s and 1980s whose task was to support job creation. These included the Local Enterprise Development Unit (LEDU), established in 1971, which concentrated on assisting indigenous firms; and the Industrial Development Board (IDB), established in 1982, which concentrated on securing external investment. The latest such agency is Invest Northern Ireland, established in 2002, which amalgamated all other development structures. It aims to promote research and development, to help businesses achieve higher levels of growth and to encourage an enterprise culture in cooperation with universities and the public sector. Like the IDA in Ireland, its main purpose is to attract high-quality, knowledge-based FDI.

Most of the economic organizations in Northern Ireland are linked with those in the rest of the UK. The Confederation of British Industry (CBI), for example, represents the interests of local business and is affiliated to the national organization. The recognized trade union organization for Northern Ireland is the Northern Ireland Committee of the Irish Congress of Trade Unions. Although part of an island-wide organization, (NIC) ICTU is responsible for dealing with matters relating exclusively to Northern Ireland. It also represents Northern Ireland

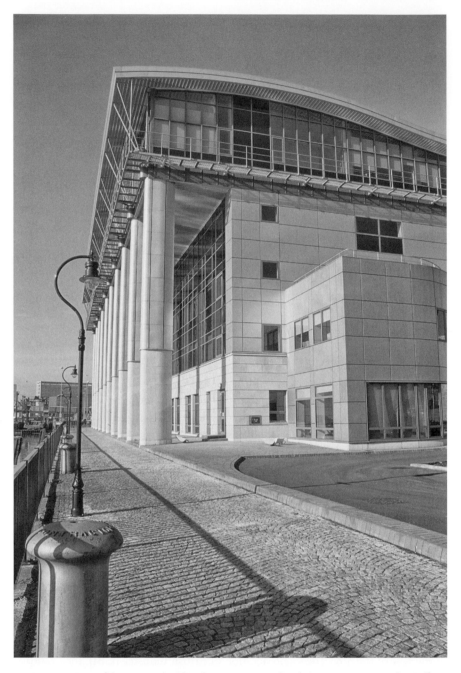

PLATE 9.6 Part of the major dockland regeneration development at Laganside, Belfast. It represents a new, post-industrial city combining offices, retail and leisure space as well as private housing. © Design Pics Inc./Alamy

members at the UK Trades Union Congress (TUC). This arrangement is a curious product of Irish history. Until the mid-1960s, the Northern Ireland government refused to recognize ICTU because of its Dublin base and its Ireland-wide affiliation. For reasons of political goodwill and to assist the project of economic planning, the Unionist government changed its position in 1964. Of the trade unions affiliated to ICTU, 36 are based mainly within Northern Ireland and have a collective membership of 216,000. Business leaders and trade union officials serve on a range of government agencies and play a major part in public life. Together with the Economic Development Forum (EDF), established in 1999, representatives of the CBI, of (NIC) ICTU and from the voluntary and education sectors advise on issues relating to the competitiveness of the Northern Ireland economy.

The provisions of the Good Friday (Belfast) Agreement in 1998 have potential implications for economic relations on the island. One of the north/south bodies, the Trade and Business Development Body, operates as InterTrade Ireland. Under the direction of the inter-governmental North/South Ministerial Council it collaborates with the Department of Enterprise, Trade and Development in Northern Ireland and the Department of Jobs, Enterprise and Innovation in Ireland. Its main concern is promoting north/south trade and business cooperation. Since its establishment in 1999, cross-border trade has doubled but this has more to do with general economic trends than with political action. One-third of cross-border trade is still in agricultural produce and livestock. In the case of tourism, a publicly owned limited company has been established by the Irish Tourist Board (Bord Fáilte) and the Northern Ireland Tourist Board to jointly market the island of Ireland. Tourism contributes 4 per cent of GDP in Northern Ireland.

There are those who argue that a single-island economy is developing and that a new axis of growth now exists in what has been called the Belfast–Dublin Corridor. They also point to the cross-investment in businesses operating north and south of the border, like Ulster Television (UTV). However, cross-border trade remains a small component of island economic activity and significant structural obstacles remain, such as different tax, interest rates and currencies. More importantly, the two parts of the island have been competitors for FDI.

Attitudes to economic systems

Opinion polls a decade ago revealed a rather pessimistic view of economic prospects. In the early 1990s one of the major issues in Ireland remained the high level of emigration. The public mood reflected that traditional concern, despite the fact that the Irish economy had been growing steadily since the late 1980s. This mood was to change as the extraordinary boom of the Celtic Tiger economy brought with it unprecedented prosperity. Popular perception of individual and familial improvement was pronounced throughout the 1990s but became more anxious when the exceptionally high rates of growth slowed after 2001.

Most people in Ireland are agreed on two things. First, they think that partnership agreements between employers, trade unions and government are important for national well-being. Second, they believe that the introduction of the euro meant that Irish people were paying more for goods and services. An IMS poll of May 2002 discovered that nearly 89 per cent agreed that prices had gone up as a result of the new currency. No one thought they were paying less. This reflected a widespread feeling that economic success also meant increased pressure on families with average incomes owing to the rise in the cost of living. The press ran stories on 'rip-off Ireland' similar to stories in the British press about 'rip-off Britain'. Some critics have gone further and argued that one effect of the Celtic Tiger about which too little was heard was the increase in social inequality. However, research by ESRI has shown that prosperity was more equally shared than these critics claimed. A series of TNS-MRBI polls in 2009 revealed the public mood in the depth of the financial crisis. A poll in February 2009 showed that only 35 per cent thought that taxes should be increased to meet the financial crisis and opinion was evenly divided over whether Irish banks should be nationalized – 36 per cent supported nationalization while 38 per cent opposed it. The vast majority (70 per cent) favoured cuts in public expenditure. In September 2009 the public was clear that salary cuts (58 per cent) were preferable to redundancies (26 per cent) as a way to reduce the public sector pay bill. Despite government reassurances, another TNS-MRBI poll in September 2009 showed that 75 per cent were opposed to any cuts in welfare benefits. Most people did not believe things would get better soon. An Ipsos-MRBI poll in September 2010 found that 70 per cent thought the worst of the crisis was yet to come.

Strikingly, a poll by the *Irish Independent*/Millward Brown Lansdowne published in February 2011 revealed that just over one-third thought that their savings were secure in Irish banks while almost half believed they were unsafe. Sixty-one per cent said that they had had a pay cut since 2008 and nearly 40 per cent had experienced reductions in hours of work. There seemed to be an age factor at work. Those who admitted they had been affected least by the recession were likely to be older or retired. That finding emphasizes how the recent economic crisis has affected prospects for youth employment and has disproportionately hit middle-income earners.

Equally, the public mood about Northern Ireland's economy was often bleak in the 1970s and 1980s and it was common for commentators to speak of it as the 'basket case' of Europe. There was a feeling of irreversible industrial decline made worse by terrorist violence. However, the mood began to change with the economic upturn in the 1990s. The benefits of the so-called 'peace dividend' after 1998 were visible when Belfast became a thriving entertainment city once again and prosperity and house prices rose. Many of the traditional attitudes, though, still prevail. There is a feeling that wealth is unequally divided and that the gap between rich and poor is widening. Despite claims that an entrepreneurial culture has put down new roots, survey evidence suggests otherwise (as do the economic data). In 2000, for example, *The Northern Life and Times Survey* found that only a quarter of respondents would work more to earn more. Sixty-three per cent only wanted to go on working the same hours for the same money (the survey did not ask whether people wanted to work less and earn more). Despite the widespread belief that large public sector employment made working in the private sector less attractive, *The Life and Times Survey* found the opposite. Though 92 per cent thought that job security was either important or very important, a majority of respondents, 53 per cent, said they would prefer to have a job in the private sector. Job satisfaction also proved to be high. Taking a generational perspective, most people thought that they had better prospects in life than their parents. In 2009, *The Life and Times Survey* asked: 'If you were to consider your life in general these days, how happy or unhappy would you say you are on the whole?' Despite the bad economic news, 35 per cent pronounced themselves very happy and another 56 per cent, fairly happy.

On the other hand, there is not much faith in the ability of local politicians to manage the economy. In a survey of the 100 top companies in March 2011, a *Belfast Telegraph* poll found that only 8 per cent had any confidence in the Northern Ireland Executive's capacity to address the issues facing the local economy. Over half were either not very confident or not confident at all. The rest were simply not sure.

Exercises

Explain and examine the following terms:

the Great Famine	Harland and Wolff	tariffs
free trade	Economic War	T.K. Whitaker
FDI	Common Agricultural Policy	Celtic Tiger
property bubble	ghost estates	negative equity
bail-out fund	National Asset Management Agency	toxic loans
troika	export-led growth	privatization
IDA	social partnership	linen
Craigavon	subvention	recession

Write short essays on the following topics:

1 What economic issues contributed to political differences over Home Rule between Unionists and Nationalists?

2 Explain the rise of the 'Celtic Tiger' economy.

3 What were the causes of the banking crisis in Ireland in 2008?

4 Discuss the reasons for Northern Ireland's heavy reliance upon the public sector.

Further reading

Barry, F. (ed.) (1999) *Understanding Ireland's Economic Growth* London: Macmillan

Foster, R. (2007) *Luck and the Irish: A Brief History of Change c. 1970–2000* London: Allen Lane

Hogan, J., Donnelly, P.F. and O'Rourke, B.F. (eds) (2010) *Irish Business & Society: Governing, Participating & Transforming in the 21st Century* Dublin: Gill and Macmillan

Johnson, D. and Kennedy, L. (2003) 'The Two Economies in Ireland in the Twentieth Century', in J. Hill (ed.) *A New History of Ireland* Oxford: Oxford University Press

Smith, N. (2005) *Showcasing Globalisation? The Political Economy of the Irish Republic* Manchester: Manchester University Press

Websites

Central Statistics Office Ireland: http://www.cso.ie/

Confederation of British Industry: http://www.cbi.org.uk/

Department of Enterprise Trade and Development (Northern Ireland): http://www.detini.gov.uk/index.htm

Department of Finance (Ireland): http://www.finance.gov.ie/ViewDoc.asp?fn=/home.asp&m=0

Economic and Social Research Institute (Ireland): http://www.esri.ie/

IDA Ireland: http://www.idaireland.com/

Invest Northern Ireland: http://www.detini.gov.uk/index.htm

Irish Business and Employers Federation: http://www.ictuni.org/

Irish Congress of Trade Unions: http://www.ictu.ie/

Irish Congress of Trade Unions (Northern Ireland Committee): http://www.ictuni.org/

Northern Ireland Statistics and Research Agency: http://www.nisra.gov.uk/

10

Social systems

- Social services history
- Social services in Ireland after 1921
- Social security and poverty
- Health provision in Ireland
- Housing
- Social services in Northern Ireland after 1921
- Social security and poverty
- Healthcare
- Housing
- Attitudes to social services
- *Exercises*
- *Further reading*
- *Websites*

In the twentieth century the most far-reaching change in the lives of ordinary people in both parts of Ireland was the development of universal public welfare. The availability of social benefits in times of unemployment, of healthcare in times of sickness and of adequate housing in times of need, transformed the lives of the great majority of people. It also transformed the public's expectations of the state. It is now taken for granted that it is the duty of government to ensure that everyone has a decent standard of living. In the past, a moral case to look after the poor and distressed was recognized but welfare relied on individual or collective charity. There was no acknowledgement that welfare was a *right* of the individual rather than a *duty* of the wealthy. The modern idea of public welfare is based on entitlement and not on charity. It is mainly funded by taxation (compulsion) and not by charitable giving (choice). The most effective way of achieving basic welfare for everyone has been through forms of general taxation and social insurance in state-sponsored schemes. The term that emerged to describe this modern idea was 'the Welfare State'.

Though the state today does play the major role in social service provision in both parts of the island, the voluntary or charitable sector continues to function. Voluntary organizations and religious bodies provide services either from their own resources or in partnership with the state. There is also a private sector which is based upon insurance contributions paid by individuals and families over and above state taxation. One of the central arguments for comprehensive state welfare benefits is that it aids economic efficiency. A healthy, well-educated, materially secure workforce is good for business. One of the central arguments against universal welfare benefits is that it may encourage dependency on state 'hand-outs'. Around those two arguments certain questions are asked of the social services. What level of welfare encourages efficiency and avoids dependency? What structures best meet social needs but deliver value for money? What level of taxation should people be required to pay? These common questions continue to be addressed by the different social service structures in both parts of Ireland.

Social services history

Ancient Irish tradition had assumed that the care of the old and the sick was the responsibility of the family or kin group. As in other European societies, the idea of organized efforts to deal with destitution and illness only emerged late in Irish history. Unlike the English Poor Law, which can be traced to the sixteenth century and required church parishes to pay for the relief of poverty, no such model existed in Ireland. The distinction between 'correcting' or punishing the poor and helping them was a fine one since the distinction between criminality and poverty was thought to be marginal. For instance, the 'houses of industry' established in eighteenth-century Ireland as refuges for the poor were also designed as prisons for beggars and the unemployed. Most of the inmates of these houses of industry were there against their will. Children fared worse than adults. The foundling hospitals for homeless children in Dublin and Cork had death rates of over 60 per cent.

Towards the end of the eighteenth century, policy began to differentiate between categories of 'eligibility' or between those who were deserving of assistance and those who were not. This represented the emergence of an important distinction between poverty and correction which helped transform attitudes in the course of the nineteenth century. The late eighteenth century also witnessed the construction of 'voluntary' hospitals in Irish towns financed mainly by wealthy Protestants. In the early nineteenth century, Catholic hospitals were also built, run by female religious orders such as the Sisters of Charity and the Sisters of Mercy.

After the Act of Union in 1801, Irish social conditions became an issue of parliamentary concern in London. A number of Acts were passed providing for the establishment of medical dispensaries (1805) and fever hospitals (1807 and 1818) in every county. However, the most significant change in Ireland followed the general review of the operation of the English Poor Law. The outcome of this review was the Poor Law Amendment Act of 1834 which was applied in England and Wales and later in Scotland. This Act became the model for the Irish Poor Law of 1838. For the first time Ireland had a national system funded by local rates and this represented a significant improvement on the old charitable arrangements. The country was divided into 130 'unions' (163 in 1850) and in each union poor relief was the responsibility of a Board of Guardians elected by those, mainly landowners, paying the poor rate.

In 1847 a separate Irish Poor Law Commission was established. Each union had a workhouse which provided 'indoor relief' to those deemed worthy of assistance. Only families could seek admission but once admitted they were separated. The workhouse also provided schooling and medical facilities. In many Irish towns, the workhouse infirmary later became the local hospital. The principle of the workhouse was that of 'less eligibility' which meant that those applying for assistance had to be in a condition of poverty *worse* than that of the very poorest in work. The lingering notion that a penalty should attach to poverty remained under the Poor Law. In 1905 over 45,000 vulnerable people inhabited Irish workhouses. Of these, two-thirds were either sick or aged and infirm. Children and unmarried mothers made up one-sixth of the total.

In the 1830s it was estimated that there were nearly 2.5 million 'desperately poor' in Ireland out of a population of about 8 million. Officials feared that the

PLATE 10.1 Carrickmacross Workhouse, Co. Monaghan. This workhouse was opened in 1842 and designed to accommodate 500 inmates. During the Famine in 1847 a separate fever hospital was erected on the site. © Ros Drinkwater/Alamy

extent of Irish rural poverty and a high birth rate would make the Poor Law unmanageable. Not enough was – or thought *should* be – done to avert widespread starvation and disease. The Great Famine of 1845 to 1849 simply overwhelmed the system. Workhouses had been designed to cope with 80,000 paupers but by 1851 they were dealing with more than three times that total. The government resorted to a number of additional measures in response to the disaster. It suspended one of the principles of the Poor Law and provided 'outdoor relief', especially in the form of soup kitchens. After the Famine, large-scale emigration became one way of exporting the problem of Irish poverty. Emigration meant that the numbers of those relying on the Poor Law fell after the middle of the century. They were to rise again by the end of the century. By 1885 nearly 55,000 people were in receipt of outdoor relief. In 1905 the figure was over 58,000 but by this time outdoor relief involved a range of benefits.

Ireland, however, was not without innovations in welfare provision. The Congested Districts Board of 1891 used public money to raise living conditions, develop new rural infrastructure and provide work opportunities for agricultural labour. A series of Labourers Acts in the late nineteenth and early twentieth centuries significantly improved housing conditions in the countryside. Public health improved as a consequence. By contrast, the living conditions of some urban dwellers, especially those in the tenements of Dublin, were generally acknowledged to be a disgrace. Immediately before the First World War overcrowding in Dublin was widespread, with 23 per cent of families living in one-room accommodation. Sixty-six per cent of working-class housing was classified as substandard. By contrast, the terraced houses of industrial Belfast, built on the same pattern as those in urban England, provided a better standard of

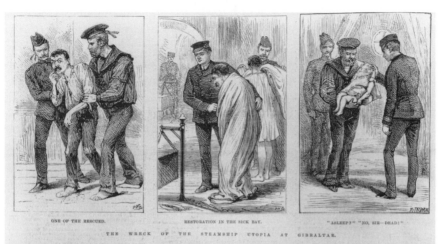

ONE OF THE RESCUED.   RESTORATION IN THE SICK BAY.   "ASLEEP?" "NO, SIR—DEAD!"

THE   WRECK   OF   THE   STEAMSHIP   UTOPIA   AT   GIBRALTAR.

WRECK OF THE UTOPIA AT GIBRALTAR.
The terrible disaster in the harbour of Gibraltar, when the great steam-ship, carrying over eight hundred Italian emigrants on their voyage to New York, drifted foul of H.M.S. Anson at the anchorage, tore a hole in her bottom with the pointed ram of the ironclad battle-ship, and sank in ten minutes amid a violent gale and high sea, preventing the relief of those on board the Utopia, will long be remembered. Great praise is due to the efforts of the seamen of her Majesty's ships, and of the Swedish frigate Freya, to rescue the men, women, and children struggling in the water. The Freya picked up forty-three persons; thirty-nine were picked up by the Rodney, thirty-three by the Anson, two by the Immortalité,

twenty-two by the Curlew, forty-six by the Camperdown, and six by the Amber. Some of those rescued from the water presently died of exhaustion. A correspondent, Mr. C. W. Cole, furnishes sketches of the scene when they were taken on board the Anson. The total loss of life was 576, while about three hundred were saved, including half the crew.

RELIEF OF IRISH DISTRESS.
The measures for the relief of local distress in some districts of Ireland, undertaken by Mr. A. J. Balfour, the Chief Secretary, after his tour of personal inspection early in the winter, and partly aided by a large public subscription fund, as well as by the Government, have been steadily in opera-

tion. The duty of selecting, procuring, and distributing the seed potatoes is imposed on the guardians of each poor-law union, and they are empowered to contract for the supply, and secure the best possible article for seed. Inspectors are chosen by the Local Government Board, who act with the Committee of the Board of Guardians, supply them with forms of tender, and inspect the potatoes as they are delivered to the people. When the seed supplied does not come up to the sample, or is insufficient in quantity, the inspectors communicate with the contractors, who in all cases make good the loss without any extra expense to the Union. Our Illustration shows the scene at the Board-room of the Clonakilty Union, in the western part of the county of Cork, when applicants for seed potatoes were in attendance.

PLATE 10.2 'Relief of Irish Distress', from *The Illustrated London News* 1891. Such images helped to sustain pressure on the government to improve social conditions in Ireland, especially in rural areas. Private Collection/The Bridgeman Art Library

accommodation. Poor housing conditions were also responsible for some major diseases. At the beginning of the century, tuberculosis (TB) accounted for 16 per cent of all deaths and it was to remain a serious problem in both parts of the island until the middle decades of the twentieth century. Indeed, such was the scale of the disease that a Northern Ireland Tuberculosis Authority was established after partition. High child mortality in Irish towns was a product of limited hygiene, poor sanitation and the absence of proper postnatal medical care.

In the two decades before 1921, the reforms that established the basis for the modern Welfare State in Great Britain were also applied in Ireland. Compensation for injury or death at work was introduced in 1897. Old-age pensions were legislated for by the Liberal government in 1908 and this increased public expenditure in Ireland by about one-third. Just over 4 per cent of the Irish population were drawing pensions by 1909, about four times more than in England. Almost a quarter of all old-age pension expenditure went to Ireland. Because the cost of living was lower than in Great Britain, Irish pensioners benefited disproportionately. The introduction of old-age pensions also reduced reliance on the Poor Law. The National Insurance Act of 1911 provided for unemployment, sickness and maternity benefits. This was overseen by the Irish Insurance Commission. By 1914, 700,000 workers were insured under the terms of the Act. However, the system of medical insurance was not applied in Ireland owing to resistance by the Irish Parliamentary Party, the Catholic Church and many doctors.

Social services in Ireland after 1921

During the debate on the National Insurance Act of 1911, Irish Nationalists argued that British legislation was not always suited to Irish conditions. What Nationalists sought was a native scheme that better served the interests of Irish people. After 1921, the Irish government had the opportunity to fashion a system appropriate to Irish conditions. One of the first things it did was actually to reduce old-age pensions. Until recently the substantial difference between Ireland and the UK lay in the financial resources available for spending on social services. This meant that Irish governments were unable to provide services as comprehensive, universal or as generous as those in place in Great Britain and Northern Ireland. From the mid-1990s, however, economic growth allowed Ireland to catch up with, and in some cases to overtake, the UK in welfare provision.

Self-government did not encourage a radically new approach to social services. A number of factors – economic, social and political – operated against it. A relatively low national income, a powerful Catholic Church and conservative political elite limited the extension of welfare. In the first two decades of the Irish Free State, health and social services were the responsibilities of the Minister for Local Government. Delivery of services was often left up to local initiative, the churches (Catholic and Protestant) and the voluntary sector. The family continued to play a key role as a provider of first and last resort. In 1947 the Department of Social Welfare took control of most publicly funded schemes and the Social Welfare Act of 1952 improved and extended access to benefits.

However, reform in Ireland was rather piecemeal and was much less ambitious than the welfare system of the UK. In this situation emigration, especially to England, remained the option that many Irish citizens took. Even in the more optimistic 1960s the figures tell an important story. Between 1961 and 1966, 33 per cent of young men and 30 per cent of young women aged between 20 and 24 left the country.

Growing prosperity from the 1960s onward helped to change matters. Public services were improved, new allowances introduced, the scope of existing schemes extended and payments increased. There was an active programme of public housing and slum clearance such that nearly half of the country's housing stock in 1990 had been built after 1970. The age for drawing an old-age pension was reduced from 70 to 65 and a wide range of supplementary benefits were provided for disadvantaged groups like single parents and deserted wives. More generous pay-related allowances were introduced for the unemployed. Unfortunately, this growth in the provision and cost of social services coincided with the economic downturn of the mid-1970s to mid-1980s. The rapid expansion of public expenditure combined with poor political management created a financial crisis for the Irish state. In the mid-1980s about one-third of adults were in receipt of welfare payments. Government debt had become unsustainable, high taxation was deterring economic activity and a radical cutback in welfare spending became necessary.

Austerity measures were imposed after 1987 although they were accompanied by agreements with trade unions and employers to maintain essential welfare payments. This national consensus underpinned a programme of tax and expenditure reform that established the platform for Ireland's astonishing economic prosperity from the mid-1990s. As the economy boomed, social services benefited from the increased revenues. Remarkably, Irish governments for a while were able to increase social spending while reducing the level of public expenditure as a percentage of GDP. Between 1989 and 2009 expenditure on social welfare (excluding healthcare) grew from just under €3.5 billion to €21 billion, from 27 per cent of public expenditure in 1989 to 35 per cent in 2009. This was about 12 per cent of GDP – €10 billion coming from direct taxes and €11 billion from the Social Insurance Fund (employer and employee contributions). Ninety years after independence, Ireland had achieved economic development on a par with its European neighbours. It now possessed a system of social services as good as any in Europe, but it also had the same difficulty in paying for those services, a difficulty made more acute by the economic crisis of 2008.

Social security and poverty

The concept of social security used to be narrow and meant providing a sub-sistence standard of living. Today the concept is much wider, involving the notion of 'social inclusion'. This was formally acknowledged in the government's National Action Plan against Poverty and Social Exclusion (2003–2005). Inclusion means that welfare policies should also help people to participate fully in society and the object is equal opportunity for all citizens. The challenge for government is to balance rising expectations and costs with taxation.

There are three types of social welfare payments in Ireland – social insurance, means tested and universal. By the early 1960s social insurance for those in work provided a comprehensive range of payments. However, over one-third of the population – including farmers and the self-employed – was not included in the scheme. For those not covered by social insurance, the state provided from general taxation social assistance on a means-tested basis. Social assistance provided less generous benefits than those available under social insurance. Other payments, such as child benefit, are universal. The history of social security in Ireland has been one of both the progressive extension of social insurance to all employees and the progressive expansion of means-tested benefits. From the mid-1960s to the mid-1980s, social security benefits tended to increase more than the rate of inflation. This had the effect of narrowing the differential between welfare and low-paid employment. In particular, old people received relatively generous treatment. One further development was convergence in the value of insurance-based and means-tested benefits. Between 1999 and 2009 the real value of social security payments more than doubled.

Social insurance payments fund a range of contributory pension schemes as well as disability, maternity and unemployment benefits. They are available to those who satisfy what are called Pay-Related Social Insurance (PRSI) conditions. Individuals pay into a Social Insurance Fund and entitlement varies according to benefit claimed and contributions paid. Unemployment benefit – called Jobseeker's Benefit in Ireland – is earnings-related and lasts between 9 and 12 months. Thereafter, one is entitled to Jobseeker's Assistance which is means tested but unlimited in duration. Social assistance also covers a range of means-tested, non-contributory pensions and other supplementary allowances. The Department of Social Protection administers all programmes of social insurance and social assistance. Individual circumstances are dealt with by deciding officers acting according to social welfare legislation. Those who feel they have been treated unfairly can take their case to the Social Welfare Appeals Office which is an independent body. The cost of administering social welfare in Ireland is among the highest in the EU. In 2010 about 1.8 million persons (including dependants) out of a population of 4.5 million were drawing some sort of welfare benefit.

In recent years high annual rates of economic growth and near to full employment meant that the government could deliver more for less. What was distinctive about the Irish system in this era of affluence, as some observers noted, was a decline in 'welfare effort'. As prosperity increased, the ratio of welfare expenditure to national wealth declined and the level of welfare benefits lagged behind the growth in incomes. One consequence was a widening gap in society between the best and the least well-off. This was not unique to Ireland, of course, but some critics argue that this has entrenched poverty and created new problems of disadvantage and exclusion. Nevertheless, important advances in addressing the problems of poverty were made.

In developed countries like Ireland, poverty is normally defined in the range of 40 to 70 per cent of average household income. In 2001 about 25 per cent of families fell below the 50 per cent line (consistent poverty). Over the past 20 years social expenditure has been used very successfully to alleviate this degree of poverty. The objective of the Irish government, according to the National Anti-Poverty Strategy of 1997, was to reduce by 2007 the total number of those who were consistently poor to less than 10 per cent. In that year the national figure was just over 5 per cent. Recently, the goal has been to end consistent poverty completely by 2016. The progress made in Ireland can be measured by the condition of child poverty. In 1987 25 per cent of children were estimated to live in households that were defined as having high levels of deprivation. By 2007, according to the End Child Poverty Coalition, 7.4 per cent of children (76,000) were living in consistent poverty. Since disadvantaged children are more likely to do poorly at school, to become single parents, to be unemployed or to go to prison, spending on child poverty is a good investment for the state. The government can claim some success in working towards this goal. In terms of comparative poverty levels, Ireland is now on a par with the UK.

One of the most important causes of poverty, and a significant welfare cost, is long-term unemployment. By 2011 the unemployment rate had risen to 14 per cent, higher than the EU average. Of these, 113,000 were designated as long-term unemployed – that is, without work for more than a year. This was very different from only a few years previously when sustained economic growth had been the key to reducing poverty in Ireland, mainly by reducing unemployment. Unemployment payments in Ireland are less generous than many EU states but today are higher than in Northern Ireland. However, the UK's comprehensive system of benefits and its free healthcare compensates for that differential.

The economic crisis in Ireland after 2008 has compelled the government to reduce public expenditure. Budgets for 2010 and 2011 have seen social welfare payments, including public service pensions above €12,000 a year, cut by 4 per cent. There have been cuts across the board in allowances along with increases in employees' PRSI contributions. In sustaining social welfare over the next 20 years, however, Ireland has one advantage that many developed European states do not have. It has a relatively young population and relatively few old-age pensioners. It has actually fewer dependants per worker today than a generation ago. The tax base for current welfare spending is thus potentially solid. In Ireland welfare challenges will be the same as those in the rest of Europe. These include funding pensions, dealing with the healthcare problems of increased longevity and managing the consequences of social change.

Health provision in Ireland

According to the 1989 *Report of the Commission on Health Funding*, healthcare is high on people's priority list and this continues to be the case. Ireland, like other European countries, now has a very different set of health issues to address. At the beginning of the twentieth century the problem was disease resulting from poverty. At the beginning of the twenty-first century the problem is disease resulting from affluence, like obesity. The long-term issue will be providing care for a population that is living longer and expecting more from its health service.

Unlike the UK, Ireland never developed a structure of health provision universally free at the point of use and no government has proposed implementing one. The public health system has two categories of entitlement. Category 1 permits free healthcare. It is determined by a means test and those eligible are granted a medical card. This entitles holders and their children to free general practitioner (GP) services, dental treatment, medicines and hospital care. Since 2010 they have had to pay a prescription charge set at a monthly ceiling of €10 per family. In 2010 there were 1,502,807 persons with a medical card. Category 2 patients, the rest of the population, are entitled to hospital care subject to a basic daily charge of €75 up to a maximum of €750 in a year. Charges do not apply to maternity services or to certain childhood illnesses. Category 2 patients have also to pay for the services of a GP for which there are no set charges. Some may be eligible, depending on personal circumstances, for a GP visit card. The GP visit card was introduced in 2005 to extend free GP treatment to individuals and families on moderate incomes. Just over 100,000 can access this provision. Category 2 patients pay for most prescription medicines. Those suffering from long-term conditions, however, can get exemptions and there is also a partial rebate scheme for costly drug treatment. Ninety per cent of public healthcare expenditure is paid for out of general taxation and the rest from social insurance contributions. Health expenditure has risen consistently to about 8 per cent of GDP, slightly below the EU average.

Because healthcare is not universally free at point of use as it is in the UK, about half of the population – 2,246,000 – is now covered by some form of private health insurance. Until the changes introduced by the 1994 Health Insurance Act there was one monopoly provider of insurance, the semi-state Voluntary Health Insurance Board (VHI). The VHI was established in 1957 to cover those not eligible for means-tested public hospital treatment. However, insurance proved popular among more people than just those in its target group because the premiums provided better quality care and more immediate treatment. Though

VHI remains the largest provider (62 per cent of the market), there are today two other major health insurance companies: Quinn Healthcare (23 per cent) and Hibernia Aviva (11 per cent). They both deliver a similar range of plans and benefits to VHI and it is possible to switch between providers.

The Health Insurance Authority (HIA), established in 2001, is an independent statutory regulator, responsible for applying the government's rules on private insurance under the Health Insurance Acts. It monitors the health insurance market and advises the Minister for Health. The regulatory system is based on the principles of community rating, open enrolment, lifetime cover and minimum benefit, and it aims to equalize health insurance costs across age and need. In the definition of the HIA, open enrolment and lifetime cover mean that insurers must accept all applicants and guarantee their right to renew policies regardless of age or health status. Community rating means that everyone is charged the same premium for a particular plan, irrespective of age, gender and the state of their health. These principles constitute what is known as 'risk equalization'. The government has proposed the development of a new risk equalization scheme which will start in 2013 and is currently planning for its implementation. The intention is also to privatize VHI and to increase competition and choice in the market. The financial crisis of 2008 has had an effect on the health insurance market. The HIA estimates that younger people are less likely to take out health insurance and more likely to allow their policies to lapse. In 2009, for example, 120,000 members left VHI and it reported a loss of €42 million.

The general practitioner (GP) or local doctor system provides a mix of free, insured or private services. There are about 2,500 GPs in Ireland with a similar ratio per head of population as in the UK (52: 100,000). As in the UK, GPs provide immediate diagnosis or treatment and serve as the referral agency for hospital consultancy and outpatient treatment. A doctor may set up in general practice with the approval of the Medical Council, the profession's regulatory body. Patients can choose their doctor, though medical card holders are limited to a panel of doctors who are part of the General Medical Services (GMS) scheme. However, a survey commissioned by the health insurer Quinn found that about half of Irish adults avoid going to the GP because of cost.

There are three different types of hospital in Ireland: Health Service Executive (HSE) hospitals, voluntary public hospitals and private hospitals. The first are state owned as well as funded. The second are run largely by religious orders but funded almost entirely by the state. Because of the decline in numbers in these orders, some voluntary public hospitals have been either closed or transferred to the state. Private hospitals do not receive direct public funding, though the state may contract with them to perform certain operations. Most public hospitals also provide some limited private healthcare. There is also a distinction between specialist hospitals (for example, cancer hospitals) and general hospitals.

Health policy is made by the Department of Health in consultation with professional agencies and the voluntary sector. The Chief Medical Officer advises the Department on clinical matters. In 2003 the government announced a thoroughgoing Health Service Reform Programme which involved the abolition of the old Health Board structure, the reorganization of the Department of Health and the establishment of the Health Service Executive (HSE) to manage health as a national entity. The HSE was established by the Health Act, 2004 and became operative on 1 January 2005. The Health Information and Quality Authority (HIQA) was established in 2007 to promote best medical practice throughout the country. These reforms represented a significant change in Ireland's approach to healthcare. With a budget of about €15 billion per annum, the HSE manages healthcare in four administrative areas comprising 32 local health offices. It is responsible for delivering healthcare (hospitals and GP services), community care (such as nursing care, physiotherapy and occupational therapy) and personal social services (specialist social workers, home-help and daycare). It is the responsibility of the HSE to implement the health strategies determined by the Department, for example, on obesity (2005), mental health (2006) and cancer (2006). It is also charged with carrying out efficiency savings such as reduced inpatient care imposed upon hospitals in 2010. As in the UK, one of the pressing policy issues in recent years has been to bring down hospital waiting lists. Of the complaints made by patients to the HSE, most concerned waiting times. Nevertheless, a report by the National Treatment Purchase Fund in 2010 estimated that the average wait for hospital treatment (public patients) was about 2.5 months, the lowest it had ever been.

Housing

There are three main categories of housing in Ireland. The first is owner occupation or private housing. The second is state-subsidized local authority or publicly rented housing. The third is privately rented housing. Over the course of the past century there has been a shift towards very high levels of owner occupation. In 1922, less than 10 per cent of the population lived in private housing. Today the figure is over 80 per cent. There has been a corresponding decline in those renting privately or living in public housing. About 9 per cent of the population today live in local authority housing and 9 per cent in privately rented accommodation. There are a number of reasons for this. Economic growth has increased the disposable income available for house purchase and, more recently, low mortgage rates made house buying more attractive. One other factor was the introduction of purchase schemes which permitted local authority tenants to buy their rented properties.

The Tenant Purchase Scheme (TPS) allowed local authority tenants to buy their house after one year at its estimated market value minus discounts calculated

PLATE 10.3 Advertising for detached family homes in a new estate in the village of Abbeydorn, Co. Kerry. Today, over 80 per cent of the population live in private housing. © David Lyons/Alamy

on years of occupancy. The transformation was dramatic. From the 1980s when the scheme was introduced, two-thirds of the local authority stock of 300,000 houses passed into private ownership. In 2010 the government announced that the TPS would be wound down and replaced by the Incremental Purchase Scheme (IPS). The objective of this scheme is to make it possible for low-income households to purchase new local authority housing. The argument in favour of selling public housing is that it improves the condition of the housing stock as people take responsibility for their own properties. It also increases the wealth of ordinary people who now possess a valuable capital asset. It has certainly been a popular policy. The argument against it is that it makes it more difficult to provide housing for those in need as investment in the sector declines and as private house prices increase. There are now about 45,000 households on local authority waiting lists. Of these, one-third are single persons, one-third single parents and the rest poor families who cannot afford either to rent or buy in the private sector. The *National Development Plan 2007–2013: Transforming Ireland* set out new targets for public housing. The Plan expects that 63,000 houses and flats will be built or acquired over the period. One other policy response has been the Affordable Housing Scheme which assists lower income families to buy their own home. Housing associations and housing cooperatives (responsible for about 1 per cent of homes) also assist those who are unable to rent or buy privately.

Homelessness remains a problem, though the figures for homelessness in Ireland are unreliable (unlike those in Northern Ireland). Ninety per cent of the

PLATE 10.4 A homeless person begging on the streets of Dublin. Though the majority of people benefited from the sustained growth of the Celtic Tiger economy in the 1990s and 2000s, problems of homelessness remained for a few. © Adrian Muttitt/Alamy

homeless recognized by the Department of Environment, Community and Local Government are housed in emergency 'bed and breakfast' accommodation. Others are helped by voluntary organizations which run hostels and temporary shelters. To address this problem the government produced a new strategy *The Way Home 2008–2013*. According to its vision, long-term homelessness (the occupation of emergency accommodation for longer than six months) will be progressively eliminated throughout Ireland.

The other side of the Irish housing experience has been the astonishing building boom in the owner-occupied sector from the early 1990s. For example, 80,000 new houses were built in 2004 while the UK, with a population 15 times larger than Ireland's, built only 160,000. The economic and social impact of this building boom is covered in Chapter 9.

Social services in Northern Ireland after 1921

The 1920 Government of Ireland Act reserved most taxation powers to the UK Parliament. It was expected that Northern Ireland would pay for its own services and also make a contribution to common UK services like defence. The Northern Ireland government argued for parity of provision with other parts of the UK. It was a straightforward principle. If people in Northern Ireland paid the same rates of tax as everyone else in the UK then they were entitled to the same standard of social services. On most measures of social deprivation, Northern Ireland required higher levels of social expenditure (what was known as 'leeway'). In the hardest years of the economic depression between the First and Second World Wars, nearly 25 per cent of the workforce was unemployed. Housing conditions were comparatively poor and it was estimated that during the inter-war years only half of the new houses that were required were actually built.

The workhouse system of the old Poor Law still applied in Northern Ireland. The workhouse population averaged about 5,000 each year between 1921 and 1939. Most of the hospitals were workhouse infirmaries and facilities for mothers and children were poor. However, two new maternity hospitals and a hospital for sick children were built in Belfast during this period. The 1930 National Health Insurance Act (Northern Ireland) introduced free GP treatment but only for those covered by insurance. The local character of social service provision also remained in place. Low rates of assistance for the unemployed and destitute led to serious riots in Belfast in 1932.

The argument for parity of services was finally conceded by the Treasury in the Simon Agreement of 1938. After the Second World War Northern Ireland was included in the framework of the British Welfare State and this was under-written in 1946 by social service agreements between the government in Belfast and the Treasury in London. British National Insurance and National Assistance schemes for the unemployed were extended to Northern Ireland. Subsequently, changes in unemployment benefit, pension rates and other welfare payments have been applied on the same basis as in the rest of the UK.

During the period between 1945 and 1951, the Northern Ireland government followed the legislative programme of the Labour government in the UK. For example, the National Health Service (NHS) was established by the 1948 Health Services Act (Northern Ireland). The Act provided for a comprehensive range of medical services paid out of general taxation. One measure of the success of the new health programmes was the decline in deaths from tuberculosis (TB). In 1946 the death rate was 83 per 100,000. A decade later it had fallen to 12.5 and thereafter TB was progressively eradicated. In 1970, the Northern Ireland government decided to integrate the delivery of health and social services, mainly as a result of the reorganization of local government, and this organizational structure has remained. In short, the objective of policy was that Northern Ireland should move 'step-by-step' with the UK. The consequence was that for most of recent history public spending has been higher, benefits have been more extensive and healthcare more universal in Northern Ireland than in independent Ireland. Today public expenditure per head of the population is also 29 per cent higher in Northern Ireland than in the rest of the UK.

In 1944, it was estimated that Northern Ireland needed about 200,000 new houses, many as a result of German aerial bombing in 1941. After the Second World War, the government subsidized provision of what were known as 'council houses' – houses rented from local authorities. The Northern Ireland Housing Trust (NIHT) was also established in 1945 to add to the public housing stock. A programme of slum clearance was implemented, though many houses, in both rural and urban areas, remained substandard. One of the major grievances of the Catholic community was that housing was allocated by Unionist-controlled councils on a discriminatory basis. This has been disputed by some economists who argue that the share of Catholic public housing was proportionate to the number of Catholic households. However, the Cameron Report of 1969 into the riots of that year had identified the provision of housing as one of the major causes. In order to end charges of discrimination and to provide a transparent system of public housing allocation, the Northern Ireland Housing Executive (NIHE) was set up in 1971. This centralized the management of public housing. More importantly, its procedures were accepted as being fair. With additional funding after 1972, the NIHE was able to address the legacy of poor housing and made Northern Ireland a model of public sector provision.

The active terrorist campaigns from 1970 to 1996 did surprisingly little to disrupt the effective delivery of social services. Indeed, they strengthened the case of those who argued for higher state investment in Northern Ireland's public services in order to counteract the effects of political violence. The immediate impact of direct rule from London was to increase public expenditure by one-third between 1972 and 1975. Between 1970 and 1990 public expenditure in Northern Ireland doubled and Northern Ireland continued to be generously treated in relation to other UK regions. Though some of this growth was accounted for by spending on security, most of it was absorbed by spending on health and social services. However, terrorism did have significant effects on housing. By forcing or encouraging population movement, it led to increased communal segregation.

Social security and poverty

The unemployment and social security system in Northern Ireland operates on the same principles as elsewhere in the UK. There are two forms of entitlement. The first, under the National Insurance Scheme of 1948, provides unemployment benefit, sickness benefit and retirement pensions. Employed persons, their employers and the state pay contributions to the National Insurance Fund. Under the Social Security Administration (Northern Ireland) Act 1992, benefits are payable out of the Northern Ireland National Insurance Fund (NINIF). The Social Security Administration (Northern Ireland) Act 1992 put the NINIF under the management of Her Majesty's Revenue & Customs (HMRC). Control of National Insurance contributions is an 'excepted matter' because benefit rates are applied uniformly across the whole of the UK. This means that matters relating to National Insurance are the responsibility of UK Treasury ministers and the Secretary of State for Work and Pensions, not the Northern Ireland Executive. However, the Northern Ireland Social Security Agency (NISSA), an Executive Agency of the Department for Social Development (DSD), has overall responsibility for the delivery of most benefits. Of the DSD's 8,000 workforce, 91 per cent are involved in this agency and also the Child Support Agency (CSA), which deals with child maintenance payments. The DSD budget for 2009/2010 was £5.8 billion, of which £5 billion was allocated to social welfare.

The second form of entitlement is means-tested, non-contributory benefits which are available either for those who are not covered by NI contributions or for those on low incomes. Their value is again set by UK-wide legislation. NISSA handles a wide range of benefits such as Income Support which is designed to help the elderly, the long-term sick, disabled and unemployed. It provides a basic income, and possession of the Income Support Book entitles the holder to free prescriptions, dental treatment, opticians' services and free school meals. Housing benefit is also an entitlement of those on Income Support and is also available to those in employment but on low pay. Families on low pay with children can also take advantage of the Working Tax Credit (WTC) which is designed to increase the earnings of an employee. However, deciding on entitlement by assessing the means of applicants is only one aspect of the Agency's role. The other is investigating social security fraud which is one unintended effect of the complexity of the benefit system.

In line with the rest of the UK, the recent trend in Northern Ireland has been away from a focus on welfare payments to encouraging benefit claimants to return to work. The link between seeking work and benefits is reflected in the DSD's public offices which have been renamed Jobs and Benefit Offices. Jobseeker's Allowances encourage those actively looking for work. There is also a range of financial incentives to ease the transition from unemployment to work allowing some benefits, such as housing credit, to carry over in a transition period. The UK New Deal (in Northern Ireland after 2008 the Steps to Work programme) is run by the Department for Employment and Learning. It provides work experience, skills training for young people and retraining for those moving from one form of work to another.

The take-up of social security benefits in Northern Ireland is higher than the UK average. According to the Family Resources Survey in 2010, 74 per cent of all households in Northern Ireland were claiming some kind of welfare benefit compared with 70 per cent in the rest of the UK. Twenty-six per cent of families were in receipt of tax credits (UK 23 per cent) and 9 per cent of households were claiming Income Support (UK 6 per cent). However, the highest differential was in the category of disability allowance. Over a quarter of households in Northern Ireland were claiming, nearly twice the UK average.

As elsewhere, the main cause of poverty is unemployment. Recent prosperity in Northern Ireland has been a function of its falling unemployment rate. In the early 1980s, unemployment rose to just over 20 per cent. In 2004 it was 4.7 per cent. In 2010 it had risen again to 7 per cent (about 60,000), slightly below the UK rate but significantly lower than Ireland's (14 per cent). However, the Northern Ireland Labour Force Survey suggests that the current rate of economic inactivity – defined as those who are not in employment and not actively seeking work – is 26.5 per cent. This is 5 per cent higher than the UK average. In 2010, those in long-term unemployment (out of work for more than one year) numbered about 12,500 or over a quarter of the unemployed total. Using the measure of low income (60 per cent or less of the average income in the UK) it has been estimated that about 20 per cent of the population of Northern Ireland (350,000 people) live in low-income households. Comparatively, then, Northern Ireland tends to be less well-off than some other areas in the UK. Average annual earnings are the third lowest, with only Wales and the north-east of England being lower. In 2010, average earnings in Northern Ireland were about £23,500 compared with a UK average of about £26,000.

PLATE 10.5 Jobs and Benefits Office, Co. Antrim. This is one of 38 such offices throughout Northern Ireland which integrate the claiming of benefit with searching for work. © Stephen Barnes/Northern Ireland/ Alamy

The UK government pledged to halve child poverty by 2010 and to eradicate it by 2020. There has been progress on this issue in Northern Ireland. The charity Save the Children estimated that in 2010 1.7 million children in the UK (13 per cent) were living in severe poverty (defined as a couple with one child living on less than half of average earnings). In Northern Ireland the figure was 10 per cent or 43,000 children. Pensioners in Northern Ireland were also likely to be in the poverty risk category. According to research carried out for the Joseph Rowntree Trust, 20 per cent of pensioners in Northern Ireland are living in low-income households. Forty per cent of single pensioners and 20 per cent of pensioner couples in Northern Ireland had no income other than the state pension and benefits, twice the average in the rest of the UK. The Northern Ireland Executive has established a Central Anti-Poverty Unit in the Office of First and Deputy First Minister (OFMDFM) to set overall priorities and develop a National Action Plan against poverty and social exclusion.

Healthcare

Hospital and most medical treatment under the NHS in Northern Ireland – today called Health and Social Care – continues free at point of use for all citizens. There are charges for dental work and eye tests, subjected to a means test, and those with insufficient income or on Social Security benefits are exempt. Free prescriptions for medicines were reintroduced in April 2010. The distinction in the organization of healthcare in Northern Ireland compared with the rest of the UK has been its integration of health and social services. After 1974, the Department of Health and Social Services was responsible for the overall management of policy while the delivery of healthcare and personal social services became the responsibility of four Health and Social Services Boards. Both hospital management and GP services were covered by these Boards. Each was divided into Districts to provide teams of healthcare professionals. The justification for combining health and social services was twofold: that it provided coordination of related forms of need, for example, hospital treatment and home help for the elderly; and that it assisted with long-term planning, for example, matching medical developments with programmes of health promotion. This combination works well in most cases but not in others, since the priorities of doctors are not necessarily those of social workers.

The Conservative governments between 1979 and 1997 wanted to reform the NHS and make its use of public money more efficient (health expenditure accounts for about 9 per cent of the UK's GDP). They also wanted to provide more choice for patients. The main change was the introduction of an 'internal market' in the NHS. This meant a separation of the purchasing of healthcare and the provision of healthcare. In Northern Ireland the NHS Trust hospitals became providers, funded by contracts purchased by the Health and Social Services

Boards. Some GP practices also became 'fund holders' and were able to purchase services for their patients from either the Trusts or the private sector. However, all of the local Northern Ireland political parties were opposed to GP fund holding and critical of the operation of the internal market. This coincided with the policy of the Labour government elected in 1997. GP fund holding was abolished in 2002. Today there are over 1,200 GPs working in 350 practices in Northern Ireland. There are about the same number of dental practices. Dental care is free only for children, students and those who are either below a certain income threshold or in receipt of social welfare.

In 1999, following devolution to the new Northern Ireland Assembly, a Department of Health, Social Services and Public Safety (DHSSPS) was established to manage policy for hospitals, GP services, community health and personal social services; public health policy; and public safety (fire and rescue services). It is responsible for about 73,000 professionals working in health and social care, ambulance and fire services, and in 2010 had an annual budget of approximately £4 billion or about 45 per cent of Northern Ireland's assigned expenditure. Of this total, 97 per cent is allocated to health and social services. In 2005, the Review of Public Administration advised major reform of the administration of health and social services. An Independent Review of Health and Social Care Services, also reporting in 2005, came to the same conclusion. The result was that in 2007 the old structure of 19 Health Trusts was replaced by 5 integrated Health and Social Care (HSC) Trusts along with the existing Northern Ireland Ambulance Services HSC Trust. In 2009 a single Health and Social Care Board (HSCB) replaced the four Health and Social Services Boards.

The HSCB is charged with the execution of DHSSPS policy and is responsible for commissioning services through Local Commissioning Groups. It also manages contracts for family health provided by GPs, dentists and pharmacists. The actual delivery of healthcare is the business of the HSC Trusts. These five Trusts – Belfast, Northern, Southern, Western and South Eastern – provide what is known as integrated care. This involves acute (hospital) services and community services (home care and health centre-based). For example, the Belfast HSC Trust has an annual budget of about £1 billion (spending about £3 million each day), a staff of 20,000 serving 350,000 people and is one of the largest Trusts in the United Kingdom. Care is provided though four Service Groups. These are acute hospital-based services; social and primary care services such as mental health, nursing and residential care; children's health and maternity; cancer therapy and other specialist services such as occupational therapy and physiotherapy.

Life expectancy in Northern Ireland is slightly lower than the national average: 81.2 years for females (UK 81.6) and 76.3 years for males (UK 77.4). For Ireland the figures are 81.7 and 77.3 respectively. Cancer, heart disease and stroke are responsible for over half the deaths in Northern Ireland. According to Northern Ireland Executive figures, there were 14,400 deaths in 2009. Of these, cancer claimed 3,900, heart disease, 2,300 and stroke, 1,200. Survival rates are improving, especially for cancer patients. A modern cancer centre was opened in Belfast City Hospital in 2006. Half of all deaths take place in hospital and about one-fifth in nursing homes or hospices. As the population ages and life expectancy rises, so conditions such as dementia increase. Since 1999 there has been a 40 per cent increase in dementia-related deaths. The DHSSPS has target hospital waiting times of 9 weeks for outpatients and 13 weeks for inpatients and in 2010 the achievement rate was 90 per cent.

Since healthcare is free at the point of use and the standard high, the number covered by private insurance is small because it is neither essential nor required in Northern Ireland. Nevertheless, more people are now covered by private health insurance than ever before. For some, private health insurance is provided by their employer but for most people personal health plan premiums are paid to major companies like British United Providence Association (BUPA). Having private health insurance means that holders can avoid public hospital waiting lists and most people expect a better standard of care. The public sector may also use the private sector to treat its patients. About 6,000 operations of this sort take place each year at a cost of over £20 million. The main role played by the private sector in Northern Ireland is the provision of residential homes for the elderly. More than three-quarters of residential places are in the private or voluntary sector.

Between 1998 and 2008, expenditure on healthcare across the UK grew by 82 per cent and the most significant increase was in the five-year period after 2002, when it rose by an average of 7 per cent each year. Northern Ireland secured a fair share of this funding growth. Though the UK Coalition government which came into office in 2010 has promised to 'ring fence', or protect, spending on health, the budget of the DHSSPS – because it has wider responsibilities than health alone – has been earmarked for reduction. On the projections of the Northern Ireland Executive's budget 2011 to 2015, spending will be about £4.5 billion per year to 2015. However, on its own estimation, the DHSSPS calculates that this will mean a real, if small, reduction.

Housing

Housing conditions have shown the most dramatic improvement in Northern Ireland over the past 35 years. In the 1970s nearly one in five homes were designated unfit. By 1990 around 34,000 substandard houses had been demolished and few homes lacked one or more basic amenities like water supply. The Department for Social Development (DSD) has responsibility for public housing policy in Northern Ireland today and works closely with the Northern Ireland Housing Executive (NIHE) and Registered Housing Associations. According to the DSD's report on Northern Ireland Housing Statistics there were approximately 745,000 dwellings in Northern Ireland in 2010. Eighty-seven per cent of new house builds were in the private sector.

PLATE 10.6 An aerial view of new public housing in the Sandy Row area of Belfast. The redevelopment of such areas is intended to improve the standard of accommodation while keeping traditional communities together. © Elizabeth Leyden/Alamy

Over the past 40 years there has been a shift from public housing to home ownership. From under 50 per cent of all homes in the early 1970s home ownership is now over 70 per cent. Thirteen per cent rent houses from the NIHE and 13 per cent are in privately rented accommodation. One of the reasons for the growth in home ownership was the selling of public sector housing which began under UK Conservative governments in the 1980s. Though there was no 'right to buy' in Northern Ireland, the NIHE did introduce its own House Sales Scheme. This provided substantial discounts to sitting tenants. By 2009, the NIHE had sold 117,000 of its properties. Today it manages just over 100,000 dwellings. Eighty-seven per cent of NIHE tenants receive housing benefit. One of the legacies of the Troubles has been housing segregation as a result of either choice or fear. Nearly 75 per cent of all public housing estates are entirely segregated and the process has intensified rather than eased since the Belfast Agreement of 1998. This has been a factor in the waiting list problem since families are unwilling to move to houses not in 'their own' area. It is estimated that in 2009/2010 there were about 19,000 homeless, 6,000 of whom had dependent children. This is a substantial increase since 2000. Most commonly cited reasons were loss of accommodation with friends or relatives (24 per cent) and relationship breakdown (18 per cent).

Attitudes to social services

According to a Eurobarometer survey in 2008, people in Ireland placed health (53 per cent) as their top priority. In 2009, however, worries about unemployment (61 per cent) had displaced health (24 per cent). Social service issues, such as pensions and housing, were far down the list (both 3 per cent). Though a Eurobarometer survey in 2007 on health and long-term care found that 64 per cent of Irish respondents thought their hospitals were 'good' (UK 77 per cent) and 65 per cent found access to healthcare 'easy' (UK 80 per cent), 33 per cent believed that healthcare was not very affordable or not affordable at all (UK 8 per cent). However, GP services were looked on more favourably. Over 90 per cent thought that GP services were good and easy to access. By the end of the decade, opinion remained critical of Irish healthcare. In July 2010, the HIQA published *Opinions on Safer Better Care*. It revealed that people wanted better information, greater accountability and better quality in services. Forty-three per cent of people felt that healthcare is below expected standards. No one agreed *strongly* that money was spent wisely on healthcare in Ireland and only a quarter of those surveyed agreed *slightly* that money was spent wisely. Eighty-six per cent said they believed no one currently takes responsibility for the problems of health provision and nearly everyone wanted more information, especially when treatment goes wrong.

In Northern Ireland, attitudes to healthcare are more positive. Opinion surveys in the 1990s showed that 50 per cent of respondents, like their counterparts in Ireland, consistently rated health as the number one priority. Very few rated pensions, social security benefits or housing as major issues. The 1996 *Northern Ireland Social Attitudes Survey*, for example, found that the greatest sources of dissatisfaction with healthcare were waiting lists for hospital treatment (85 per cent) and staffing levels of hospital doctors and nurses (75 per cent). Time spent waiting for outpatient treatment (74 per cent) also rated as a major complaint. However, there was a general level of satisfaction with the actual standard of treatment by healthcare professionals. The higher the social class, the more critical was the attitude to public healthcare. This may account for the recent growth in private medical insurance.

Just over a decade later a similar survey conducted in 2009, *Public Attitudes to Health and Social Care Services in Northern Ireland*, found that 82 per cent were satisfied with healthcare overall; 79 per cent were satisfied with social work services and 90 per cent with community nursing. In 2010, research by the GP Patient Survey (102,214 respondents) found that 94 per cent of patients were satisfied with care received at their surgery, 97 per cent trusted their doctor and 84 per cent who needed to see a GP or healthcare professional were seen either on the same day or within the next two days. These figures are rather out of line with those in the rest of the UK, where polls have tended to find much lower satisfaction rates with healthcare. However, the *Northern Ireland Life and Times*

Survey in 2010 showed that respondents believed unemployment (26 per cent) was now the most important problem, a sign of the economic times.

Exercises

Explain and examine the following terms:

social insurance	leeway	Irish Poor Law
workhouse	less eligibility	TB
National Insurance	social inclusion	universal benefits
pay-related benefits	NHS	GP
poverty line	means test	long-term unemployment
tax base	medical card	Health Service Executive
risk equalization	waiting lists	owner occupation
long-term homelessness	NIHE	Working Tax Credit
hospital	outpatient	dependants
life expectancy	'excepted' matter	Child Support Agency

Write short essays on the following topics:

1   Describe the differences in healthcare organization and provision between Northern Ireland and Ireland.

2   Discuss the different types of housing in both parts of Ireland. How do you account for the rise in home ownership?

3   How effective is welfare policy at addressing problems of poverty and disadvantage? Discuss with reference to either Ireland or Northern Ireland.

Further reading

Birrell, D. (2009) *The Impact of Devolution on Social Policy* Bristol: Policy Press

Considine, M. and Dukelow, F. (2009) *Irish Social Policy* Dublin: Gill and Macmillan

Norris, M. and Redmond, D. (eds) (2007) *Housing Contemporary Ireland: Policy, Society and Shelter* Dordrecht: Springer

Websites

Citizens Advice Bureau Northern Ireland: http://www.citizensadvice.co.uk/

Citizens Information Ireland: http://www.citizensinformation.ie/en/

Department for Social Development (Northern Ireland): http://www.dsdni.gov.uk/

Department of Environment, Community and Local Government (Ireland): http://www.environ.ie/en/

Department of Health (Ireland): http://www.dohc.ie/

Department of Health, Social Services and Public Safety (Northern Ireland): http://www.dhsspsni.gov.uk/

Department of Social Protection (Ireland): http://www.welfare.ie/EN/Pages/default.aspx

Health and Social Care Northern Ireland: http://www.n-i.nhs.uk/

Northern Ireland Housing Executive: http://www.nihe.gov.uk/

11

Education

Education has historically been a significant (and controversial) religious and political force in Ireland, but the state did not accept a comprehensive responsibility for schools and higher and further instruction until the twentieth century. Education was for centuries organized by religious, charitable, private and royal bodies, which reflected social class and economic conditions, and reached a minority of students.

The earliest Irish education was based on oral teaching of ancient knowledge, which was used to train poets (bards), largely in bardic schools. Following the arrival of Christianity between AD 300 and 500, monks and missionaries founded monastic schools and spread religion, learning and writing in Ireland, Britain and the Continent in the early medieval period between AD 500 and 900. It is likely that most Irish people did not have access to formal teaching.

Various types of education became available in later centuries, but they were often socially divisive, politically contentious and a source of conflict between Protestant and Catholic churches. The influence and role of the churches in education and society was increasingly criticized in the modern period.

After partition in 1921, educational policies in the north and south of Ireland diverged. Northern Ireland reflected the English/Welsh system, although there are now significant differences, such as a grammar/secondary school division, Irish-medium schools, a distinct National Curriculum and segregated schooling. Ireland distanced itself from pre-independence British influences, developed its own educational models, emphasized Irish language, literature and history in the schools, and encouraged information technology (IT) and science.

Education history

In early Irish history, the primary oral language was Gaelic, and Ogham was the only form of writing. The latter was a runic script scored on stone and wood monuments in Ireland, Wales and Scotland between the third and sixth centuries AD. These contained lists of family and place names rather than extended texts and Ogham was probably not widely taught or used.

Education and training were based on the needs of a hierarchical society in Gaelic Ireland. Children were orally instructed in subjects appropriate to their social class in what were essentially agricultural communities. Sons of the local aristocracy learnt horsemanship, shooting, chess and swimming and their sisters practised sewing and embroidery. Lower class boys were taught kiln drying,

PLATE 11.1 Ogham inscriptions, such as this from Co. Kerry, were scored markings in stone or wood rather than conventional letters. They are the earliest written forms of Irish and date from the fifth to the seventh centuries in Ireland, Wales, Devon, Cornwall, the Isle of Man and Scotland. © Holmes Garden Photos/Alamy

woodcutting and animal herding, while the girls were instructed in domestic crafts such as grinding corn and making bread.

Bardic schools were apparently open only to the descendants of poets and reflected an oral Gaelic society. They were staffed by writers, artists and Brehon intellectuals who also travelled widely, passing on their knowledge and recruiting students. The later Christian conversion of Ireland associated education with the written word, Latin, scholarly learning and formal teaching. Monks and missionaries travelled the country teaching and selecting suitable students, who might join monastic schools and learn Latin and church traditions. Debate continues as to whether bardic and religious students were taught together by scholars in schools attached to monasteries or whether monastic and bardic schools developed separately. Scholars were also trained in (and taught) Irish law, history and literature, and entry to all schools required proficiency in Gaelic and memory skills. Bardic and monastic schools were respectively suppressed in the fourteenth and sixteenth centuries.

From AD 500 to 900, when Europe was largely illiterate and uneducated during the Dark Ages, Ireland was known as the Island of Saints and Scholars and its reputation was based on religious and classical studies. Irish scholars and missionaries travelled to Britain and Europe to spread Christianity and knowledge. They founded monasteries in Europe (such as Saint-Gall, Switzerland) in the seventh century, which made influential contributions to education and literature. Monasteries in Ireland itself produced rich art and illuminated manuscripts.

During this period, monastic Latin education and Irish oral teaching influenced each other. Students were trained to read and write, and the Latin model gradually embraced secular Irish law and history as monks began to operate more in the wider society. Monasteries attracted secular settlement and became bases of learning and defence as well as religious centres, and a basic schooling may have become available to more local people.

The relatively settled society was disturbed by Viking invasions in the tenth to twelfth centuries, which led to the sacking of monasteries, destruction or theft of manuscripts and art treasures, slaughter of clergy and educational decline. The Viking era was followed by the Anglo-Norman Conquest from 1167, which significantly affected the development of Irish education. The Anglo-Norman King Henry II was granted the overlordship of Ireland by Pope Adrian IV and Irish land was given to absentee landlords in England. This system created a poor and uneducated native peasant class. From the fourteenth century, the English suppressed Gaelic, the bardic schools and Irish culture, and the sixteenth-century English Protestant Reformation undercut Roman Catholicism and the monastic schools. Religious conflicts exacerbated social divisions, increased sectarian tension and produced political upheavals. It is argued that the competing allegiances and beliefs of Protestant and Catholic Churches prevented the potential development of a unified Irish educational system.

English rule influenced schooling in Ireland. The Protestant (Anglican) Church of Ireland became the state church in 1537 after the English Reformation (with the English monarch as Governor) and from 1539 monasteries were gradually dissolved. Although in the sixteenth century most areas of the country outside Dublin were Catholic, the Crown settled Protestant English and Scots in the north of Ireland and the Church of Ireland attempted to establish parishes in

PLATE 11.2 Glendalough monastic site, Wicklow Mountains, associated with the hermit St Kevin who died in 618 includes a cathedral and round tower and was an early focus for pilgrimages. © imagestopshop/Alamy

all counties. The growth of Protestantism led to non-Catholics having the best schools by the late 1500s. In 1570 the erection of free (diocesan) schools was permitted, and in 1592 the Anglican University of Dublin (Trinity College) was founded. James I in the 1600s authorized Church of Ireland bishops to establish Royal Schools (grammar schools) in the north of Ireland for Protestant settlers and the King's Hospital School in Dublin was created by Charles II.

Some schools were therefore well supported by the eighteenth century and trained the sons of the wealthy and aristocratic for leadership roles. However, although Protestant diocesan schools and Royal Schools benefited wealthier Protestants, there was a need for charity schools to be established to provide for the educational needs of poor Protestant children during the seventeenth and eighteenth centuries. Funding for these schools was provided by philanthropists, parishes, landlords, clergy, district governing boards and individuals, but the educational needs of most Catholic children were not met.

The introduction of Penal Laws at the end of the seventeenth century was intended to further restrict Catholic education. They prevented educational travel, forbade Catholics to teach in public or private schools and prohibited the building of Catholic schools. The laws resulted in illegal Catholic schools and some students were obliged to follow higher education in Catholic Spain, France and Italy. The inadequate school provision for poor students of all religions led to an unofficial system of mainly rural schools known as hedge schools or pay schools, which provided elementary instruction. Pupils (boys and girls) were taught in various premises (as well as in the open air) by local schoolmasters, clergymen, female teachers or families. Some schooling was therefore already available to Catholic children in towns and the countryside in the eighteenth century before the repeal of many of the Penal Laws at the end of the century, but most children had no formal or adequate schooling funded by the state.

More Catholic schools of various types were established by religious orders and individuals at the end of the eighteenth century. They were privately financed and intended for poor urban children. An early venture was the Presentation Congregation, founded by Nano Nagle in Cork in 1776. The first school and monastery of the Irish Christian Brothers were built by Edmund Rice in Waterford in 1802. The Sisters of Mercy was founded by Catherine McAuley in Dublin, and their teaching arm was recognized by the Catholic Church in 1830.

Model schools and missionary institutions were also set up by Protestant religious societies in the seventeenth and eighteenth centuries, and reflected the growing role and influence of religion in education. These included the Incorporated Society for Promoting English Protestant Schools in Ireland (Charter Schools) founded in the early eighteenth century by Archbishop Boulter; the Sunday School Society (Hibernian Sunday Society from 1809); the Bible Society; and the Society for Discountenancing Vice. Some received royal and parliamentary support. In 1811 the government gave funds to the Society for Promoting the Education of the Poor in Ireland (Kildare Place Society) to encourage the

Engraved by C. Turner.

MISS NANO NAGLE,

Foundress of the Ursuline

and Visitation Convents in Cork.

London Pub. as the Act directs, by the Proprietor, Oct 25 1809.

PLATE 11.3 Nano Nagle (1728–1784) was an educationalist, who established seven schools for poor Catholic children. She founded her own teaching congregation, the Presentation Order, which became an important teaching organization in Ireland. Private Collection/The Bridgeman Art Library

establishment of mixed-religion schools in the country. This represented an attempt by government to prevent segregated religious schooling, alleviate tension between Catholics and Protestants and encourage integration.

The Kildare Place Society tried to organize schooling by producing reading material, employing school inspectors and providing teacher training. The Society was initially supported by all Christian churches, but by 1820 tension between the faiths grew. The Society lost its financial support when a national school system was established in 1831.

By 1824 there were some 11,000 schools in Ireland. Most were hedge or pay schools, which catered for both Catholic and Protestant children. Few schools received financial aid from public authorities until 1831, when primary National Schools under a Board of Commissioners of National Education were founded. The Board provided textbooks and school materials for these schools, which catered for children of all Christian denominations. The children were taught together for most subjects in a non-denominational structure, but were separated into their individual faiths for religious instruction. Although the state was not prepared to fund all school education, the national school system expanded and by 1850 there were 4,500 schools catering for about 250,000 pupils.

Two Protestant churches (the Church of Ireland and the Presbyterian Church) were opposed to the national system of mixed-religion schools. Campaigns in the late 1830s gave school managers greater control over religious instruction; the Roman Catholic, Church of Ireland and Presbyterian churches obtained large concessions; and the system became denominational, with many schools owned by different churches. This situation largely continues today in Ireland, where most national schools are organized or managed by either the Catholic or Protestant churches or by management boards. Segregated schools are also a majority in Northern Ireland, although there have been attempts at desegregation.

The Intermediate Education (Ireland) Act, 1878 provided that secondary education would be partly supported by the state through national taxation. Although the principle of state funding for all types of schools was accepted, secondary schools remained mostly private religious institutions. Catholic schools were under clerical control and managed by nuns, brothers or priests; Protestant schools were usually governed by a mixed board of clergy and laymen; and there were a number of private schools owned and controlled by laymen. Unlike England/Wales, schools did not receive local support through the rates system before partition; there was no public control or political involvement of local citizens in the schools; and the influence of the churches continued.

Irish school history illustrates that educational opportunities existed for the sons of the rich and powerful; some pupils enrolled in monastic and bardic schools; and a few were able to pay for the remaining schools. But most children received, at best, a basic education. Primary national school opportunities grew in the nine-teenth and early twentieth centuries, prior to the partition of Ireland. Secondary (intermediate) education, although restricted by social class and financial access to some 10 per cent of children, was developed with a common syllabus. At partition, north and south had a network of schools and an inspection system; education was expanding; and more children were attending school. Newspapers and printed works were gradually finding a wider market as literacy and numeracy expanded.

Following partition in 1921, systems of education developed separately. Ireland established its own educational institutions, structures and policies, and Northern Ireland moved initially towards the English/Welsh system. In both cases, education involved conflicts about religious and pedagogic principles.

Ireland: education after 1921

There were significant educational developments following the creation of the Irish Free State in 1921. Government policies influenced schooling and promoted national identity. The Irish language was compulsory in the educational system; Irish history teaching emphasized the campaign for independence from Britain; and images of Irishness were mediated through rural life, an agricultural economy and Catholicism.

In 1924 a new two-level school examination system was introduced for intermediate (secondary) schools. The Intermediate Certificate was awarded after two or three years and the Leaving Certificate after a further two years. Compulsory school attendance for all children between ages 6 and 14 was introduced in 1926. The 1929 Primary Certificate Examination was abolished and replaced by a school record card. Continuing or vocational education for students aged 14 to 16 was added in 1930 and the Day Group Certificate examination was introduced in 1947 for children in vocational schools.

Major educational changes occurred in the 1960s. In 1966, comprehensive schools at post-primary level were opened, where children of all abilities were educated under one roof at local schools with no academic entry selection. Free post-primary education was introduced from 1967 for all children; facilities were expanded; transport was provided for pupils living over three miles from the nearest school; and school catchment areas were established.

Ireland's educational system is administered by the Department of Education and Skills (2010), which has responsibility for policy, funding and planning. Government spending on education in 2009 to 2010 was 4.9 per cent of GDP. The Higher Education Authority was established in 1972 to deal with the financing and organization of higher education.

Schooling is now compulsory from 6 to 16 years of age, or until students have completed three years of second-level (secondary) education. Over 50 per cent of 4-year-olds and most 5-year-olds are in fact enrolled in infant classes in primary schools and the average age for starting school is 4. This is due to increased numbers of single- (often working female/male) parent families and the growth of two-income families. Private pre-schools for children between ages 3 and 4 are available. Parents pay for this service out of their income/capital or state child allowance, and since 2009 children have been eligible for one year of free schooling prior to starting primary school.

The *primary* (or *first-level*) education stage served 505,998 children between ages 4 and 12 in 2009 to 2010 and consists of 3,165 primary schools, 130 special schools and 64 private non-aided primary schools. Irish-medium schools (with Irish as the medium of instruction) and integrated multi-denominational schools for students of all religions and backgrounds have recently been developed. Primary schools provide the education of 98 per cent of children at this level. Most receive funding from the state, supplemented by local contributions. There are funding arrangements for schools and programmes in disadvantaged areas and for children with special needs and the children of travellers.

The primary curriculum (revised in 1999) is divided into language (including foreign languages), arts and mathematics. Most schools are denominational (with clerical input in religious studies). Boards of management with mixed social membership are responsible for the organization of the schools. Ninety-two per cent of denominational primary schools in 2010 were Catholic, 2 per cent were inter- or multi-denominational and 6 per cent were Church of Ireland, Presbyterian, Muslim, Methodist, Jewish, Jehovah's Witnesses and Quaker.

The *secondary* (or *second-level*) education stage consists of secondary, vocational, community, comprehensive and Irish-medium schools with students following junior and senior cycles. In 2009 to 2010, there were 313,136 students between the ages of 12 and 18 attending a total of 739 schools at this level. Of these, some 384 are secondary schools and 254 vocational schools. Most second-level schools are owned by religious denominations or private bodies and are state funded in terms of teachers' salaries and other costs. They are managed by boards of governors or by private individuals (Table 11.1).

Vocational schools educate about 28 per cent of second-level students and are owned and administered by Vocational Education Committees. They are mostly denominational; 93 per cent of fees and costs are paid by the state; and they are designed to provide school leavers with practical apprenticeship training and courses leading to vocational qualifications in architecture, accountancy, engineering and similar professions, and also include art, music, domestic science and hotel training.

Comprehensive (community) schools developed in the 1960s, are privately owned and educate about 15 per cent of second-level students. Most are organized by local Boards of Management and the state meets the cost of teachers' salaries and individual budgets. Irish-medium stand-alone schools, in which the language of instruction is Irish, attract about 3 per cent of secondary students.

A significant independent or voluntary secondary school sector for students aged 14 to 18 consists of fee-paying schools, such as Blackrock and Belvedere

TABLE 11.1 Number of students attending first- and second-level schools, Ireland (2009–2010)

School	Number of students
First level (primary)	
National schools (mainstream classes)	490,010
Special classes in mainstream national schools	9,083
Special schools	6,905
Second level (secondary)	
Junior cycle	172,648
Senior cycle	139,511
Other departments	977
Total	*819,134*

Source: adapted from Department of Education and Skills statistics, Ireland, 2009–2010

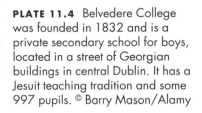

PLATE 11.4 Belvedere College was founded in 1832 and is a private secondary school for boys, located in a street of Georgian buildings in central Dublin. It has a Jesuit teaching tradition and some 997 pupils. © Barry Mason/Alamy

Colleges, with boarding facilities. They are denominational (mainly Catholic) foundations, but are now often organized by lay trusts. Although small in number, they play a significant role in Ireland's social hierarchy and have traditionally been the training grounds for politicians, lawyers, academics and businesspeople. They have become increasingly controversial because, although they have private status, their staff are paid from state funds. Some associated primary schools act as feeder schools for the larger colleges.

Secondary education is based on breadth and depth of learning. It is divided into a three-year junior cycle from the age of 12 and a two- or three-year senior cycle, which finishes between the ages of 17 and 19. The Junior Certificate examination is taken in up to 10 subjects after completing the three-year course and is a preparation for employment or further study. In the senior cycle there is a one-year optional Transition Year Programme, which allows experience outside examination structures and the choice of additional forms of study. This is followed by a choice of three two-year Leaving Certificate programmes (the Established Leaving Certificate, the Leaving Certificate Vocational Programme or the Leaving Certificate Applied) in which, depending on university entrance requirements, subjects such as English/Irish, maths, a modern foreign language and science subjects are taken. Most students continue from junior to senior cycle, and only 12.3 per cent leave after the Junior Certificate, which was lower than the EU school-leaving average of 15.2 per cent in 2007.

Further education and training

Further education and training courses are a vocational stage which follows second-level schooling, but is outside the third level of higher education. It is provided by the Department of Education and Skills and includes education opportunities for the unemployed, early school leavers and travellers, and includes adult literacy classes and community education (47,338 students in 2009 to 2010). Broad and flexible provisions give opportunities for adult learners, educationally disadvantaged groups, trade apprentices who have achieved Leaving Certificate standard and those who need further education, technology skills and the opportunity to combine family demands and education.

Further education vocational and training courses provide skills for the information technology (IT) industries and apprenticeship training in trades such as engineering, printing, construction and furniture making. The quality of further education has improved and expanded, confidence has grown, and the Department of Education and Skills has developed new approaches to adult and continuing education.

The *higher education* (or *third-level*) stage consists of 7 universities, 14 institutes of technology and 5 colleges of education. All are mainly funded by the state, but are autonomous and self-governing. Recently, several independent private colleges have opened, offering mainly business-related courses. There were 157,946 students at this level in 2009 to 2010; more students were entering higher education; and 50 per cent took degree-level programmes.

Higher education in Ireland has experienced religious and political conflict, although this has decreased in recent years. In 1592, the oldest university (the University of Dublin) was established, with Trinity College as its only college. Trinity's agenda and curriculum have historically had a Protestant (Church of Ireland) orientation and some Catholics and Presbyterians avoided enrolment at Trinity. But since the 1700s it has been a leading academic institution and the student population became more diverse in the twentieth century.

The Roman Catholic Church in Ireland became involved in higher education in 1854, when the Catholic University was created with John Henry Newman as rector. It was not successful, and after various name changes it became inactive in 1909 and was re-established as the National University of Ireland (NUI). Today the NUI has constituent university colleges with varied histories in Cork, Dublin, Galway and Maynooth. The college in Galway, for example, evolved from Saint Patrick's College, founded in 1795 as Ireland's main Roman Catholic seminary. There are other associated colleges, such as the Royal College of Surgeons, the National College of Art and Design and the Institute of Public Administration. The university system was further extended in 1989 when the national institutes for higher education in Limerick and Dublin were given university status and respectively became the University of Limerick and the Dublin City University

PLATE 11.5 Trinity is the only college of the University of Dublin, was founded by Elizabeth I in 1592 and is the oldest seat of learning in Ireland, with an Anglican orientation. © Associated Sports Photography/Alamy

(DCU). Both institutions specialize in technical subjects and emphasize applied studies in flexible course structures.

Ireland also has state-subsidized teachers' colleges (which train primary teachers and teachers of home economics and religious education, and are religiously segregated at initial teacher education level); technical colleges in larger communities; and Institutes of Technology. The last offer education and training, full-time and part-time, for trade and industry in business studies, engineering, technology, science and paramedicine. The Dublin Institute of Technology, for example, is the country's largest third-level institution with some 22,000 students. It has constituent colleges specializing in technology, catering, marketing, design, commerce and music, and emphasizes career-focused learning.

The universities and colleges offer degrees at Bachelor, Master and Doctorate levels. A range of diplomas and continuing and distance education programmes are also offered. Some universities have recently introduced semesters as the basis for the academic year and modularization of courses and course work which is supposed to give students greater flexibility of work and choice. Undergraduate teaching is through lectures supplemented by tutorials, and practical demonstration and laboratory work in some subjects.

Research in disciplines such as sciences, social sciences, humanities, engineering and technology is undertaken and the Irish Council for Science, Engineering and Technology stresses the importance of these areas for Ireland. In 1997, the government established a fund to develop information technology education at all levels, including the schools. The state-owned telecommunications service provider, Telecom Éireann, aims to link every school in the country to the internet and a special schools internet, Scoilnet, was established in 2000 with links to other international networks. But research on island-wide education by Roger Austin and others suggests that IT education in schools in Ireland is lagging behind that in Northern Ireland. In 2006, the government published a *Strategy for Science, Technology and Innovation*, which was intended to support Ireland's growth as a knowledge economy.

Student entry to higher education through the Central Applications Office (CAO) is competitive and depends upon grades achieved in the Leaving Certificate Examination. In 2010, 65 per cent or 43,000 school leavers and mature students transferred to third-level education. Among adults aged 25 to 34, 41.6 per cent have attained third-level degrees, the second highest number in the EU after Cyprus and above the EU average of 29.1 per cent.

The student grant is the main source of financial assistance for students in further and higher education (subject to complex regulations). In 2011, it was reduced by 4 per cent for mature students and those studying close to home. There are qualifying conditions relating to nationality and immigration status, residence, means and attendance at an approved course in an approved institution. Family and personal income is a factor when assessing the amount of the grant, which is divided into maintenance grant and fee grant. A maintenance grant is a contribution towards the student's living costs and, if awarded, the student will also qualify for relevant elements of a fee grant, which means that tuition fees are paid by the Exchequer for students who meet requirements. But students pay a registration charge on entry to their courses to cover costs such as examinations, insurance, registration, administration expenses and exam fees. Such charges for the 2009/2010 academic year amounted to €1,500 per student and have been called unofficial fees to protect university funding. Formal tuition fees payable by students may be introduced. Some students cannot afford the total costs and there are alternative sources of funds to which they may apply, such as the Fund for Students with Disabilities, Student Assistance Fund and institutions' Bursaries and Scholarship schemes.

Fourth-level education builds on the third-level base and most research is carried out in Higher Education Institutions (HEIs). They cover most of the colleges above as well as other higher education institutions, such as the Royal College of Surgeons Ireland and the National College of Art and Design. Much HEI funding comes from the Higher Education Authority's Programme for Research and research initiatives are funded by Science Foundation Ireland. It was intended that government research support would increase under the National Development Plan, 2007 to 2013, but this may be affected by the 2007/2008 recession and cuts.

Significant features of education in Ireland

In the mid-1970s, some democratization was injected into school organization when boards of management were established in primary schools to counterbalance denominational ownership. A greater recognition of the rights of parents in education (including the choice of school for their children) was reflected in the demand in Ireland and Northern Ireland from the 1970s for Irish-medium schools and multi-denominational or integrated schools. In 2006, there were 400 Irish-medium schools mostly at pre-school and primary level providing education to 34,500 children outside the Irish-speaking Gaeltacht. They were located in the border counties between the north and south of Ireland, Northern Ireland and other locations in Ireland. By 2010 there were 58 integrated primary schools in Ireland (27 in Greater Dublin) with continuing campaigns for integrated secondary schools. However, integrated schooling for Catholic and Protestant children is not supported by all parents.

From the late 1960s, enrolment at all educational levels grew and the numbers taking the secondary Leaving Certificate had increased to more than 80 per cent in the mid-1990s. But second-level enrolments started to fall in the late 1990s; the numbers of school leavers going on to third-level education stabilized; and there was a low rate of mature student representation. These trends improved up until 2010, but the 2007/2008 recession slowed expansion and employment possibilities. Larger numbers of young people left Ireland in 2010 to 2011 (out of a total emigration rate of 42,000), raising fears of substantial emigration.

Compared with other Western countries, Ireland has a high proportion of single-sex schools. It is estimated that one-third of second-level schools are single sex and 17 per cent of primary age children attend single-sex schools. An OECD PISA report in 2003 found that at age 15, 18 per cent of all pupils were in single-sex boys' schools and 26 per cent of all pupils were in single-sex girls' schools. But a majority of schools are coeducational, such as most primary, secondary, vocational, community and comprehensive schools, and most single-sex schools are voluntary or independent. Coeducational education has become more usual, due partly to the amalgamation of small, rural, single-sex schools into coeducational schools.

There are opposed views about the effects of single-sex education on academic performance. It is argued that girls do better academically in single-sex than in coeducational schools, while the effect on boys is more neutral, but a 2011 study in *Science* found that single-sex schooling does not benefit students more than coeducational systems. A review of existing research by Buckingham University (UK) in 2006 also suggested that single-sex education in itself seems to make no difference to students' (girls' and boys') achievements.

However, Ireland does appear to have differences in actual examination results, irrespective of the type of school attended. A gender gap appeared in Junior and Leaving Certificate points scores in 2011 when girls consistently outscored boys with higher points results and a higher proportion of top grades.

Northern Ireland: education after 1921

Education in Ireland before partition was administered from Dublin Castle. Ulster Unionist MPs in the Westminster Parliament campaigned for educational reforms prior to 1921, such as the creation of a Ministry of Education in the north; local control of schools; and local funding for primary, intermediate and technical education through the council rates. These reforms were opposed by the Catholic Church and Irish Nationalist MPs and defeated in Parliament, but were presented again in the new Northern Ireland Parliament in 1921.

Although many in the Catholic minority in Northern Ireland looked to the independent Irish Free State (IFS) and the Catholic Church as their Irish models, the Protestant majority inclined towards Britain and opposed the influence of the Catholic Church in government and education. After 1945, Britain's Welfare State developed quickly under both Labour and Conservative parties, but the Northern Ireland government had a gradualist approach to modernization and educational reform.

Changes in the Northern Ireland education system after 1921 can be conveniently examined according to the periods of the Northern Ireland Parliament

1921 to 1972; direct rule from 1972 to 1999; and legislation of the Northern Ireland Assembly from 1999 to the present.

The Northern Ireland Parliament 1921 to 1972

Following the creation of Northern Ireland, a Ministry of Education in Belfast was established to organize local schooling. It had a three-level school system: primary, secondary and technical. The Commissioners of National Education in Dublin had controlled the primary National Schools, which were managed mainly by denominational clergy. The Commissioners paid teachers' salaries and awarded grants for the construction of new schools. Secondary (intermediate) schools were owned by religious bodies, which received grants from the Intermediate Education Board. Technical schools were the responsibility of the Department of Agriculture and Technical Instruction, and were controlled by committees of local people.

Northern Ireland took over the existing institutions in the province, such as 2,040 National Schools, 75 intermediate schools, 12 model schools, 45 technical schools, one teacher training college (St Mary's), Queen's University, Belfast and Magee College.

The Education Act (Northern Ireland), 1923 controversially established a centralized, non-denominational administration. The churches opposed the Act, arguing that it would replace their educational roles, such as curriculum policy and appointment of teachers. The Education Act (Northern Ireland), 1930 reversed the 1923 Act, a move which reflected the influence of the churches, and created new administrative and management procedures.

However, the Protestant churches in Northern Ireland subsequently transferred their schools to state control under a local authority framework, while retaining a religious voice on the governing boards. The Catholic churches opposed local authority control, maintained ownership of their schools and remained autonomous. The state schools became 'controlled schools' and the Catholic schools were 'maintained schools'. Both types had their annual costs, such as teachers' salaries, paid by the state. Capital costs in controlled schools were met by the state, while maintained schools paid 50 per cent of these expenses. However, the state share for maintained schools increased to 100 per cent if they waived their right to a majority on the Board of Governors.

Northern Ireland was next influenced by a radical Education Act, 1944 which created a new English/Welsh education model. It set up a unified system of free, compulsory schooling from the ages of 5 to 15. Northern Ireland introduced a similar Education Act in 1947, which provided free secondary and university education for students (earlier than in Ireland).

The 1947 Act established a three-stage system: primary, secondary and higher education. Local government authorities were responsible for providing education for the population of their area at these levels. Selective criteria based on an 11-Plus examination taken at the age of 11 assessed academic ability and determined a student's future career. Those who passed the 11-Plus went to grammar schools, the rest to secondary schools.

This procedure was similar to that in England and Wales, which was criticized as elitist, socially divisive and weak as a diagnostic tool. After much debate, the 11-Plus was abolished in most of England and Wales. It was replaced by a comprehensive non-selective school system to which all students would transfer at the age of 11. Such policies were not adopted in most of Northern Ireland and the grammar/secondary school system remained.

Direct rule 1972 to 1999

In 1972, the Northern Ireland Parliament was abolished owing to unrest in the province and primary legislation for Northern Ireland on many matters (including education) was carried out from Westminster (direct rule). Generally, this meant that educational reforms already in place in Great Britain were later implemented in Northern Ireland.

Changes in English/Welsh education, such as open enrolment (approved number of pupils admitted to schools and parental preference), special education needs, the statutory National Curriculum, reform of governing bodies and LMS (Local Management of Schools) were applied in Northern Ireland. Legislation could be amended to reflect political and cultural contexts, such as mutual understanding clauses in the Northern Ireland Curriculum.

The Northern Ireland Assembly 1999 to 2002

Direct rule from Westminster ceased with the establishment of the Northern Ireland Assembly and Executive in 1999; devolution was reintroduced; and a Minister of Education had legislative responsibility for education. Some changes were initiated, such as the abolition of league tables and the planned removal of the 11-Plus examination. However, conflict in the province resulted in the dissolution of the Assembly in 2002 and direct rule returned. After some false starts, the Assembly eventually became operative again in 2007.

The education system today

Northern Ireland generally has a high standard of education, when measured by national examination results, but there is concern that some children underachieve and experience social and educational deprivation, and child (and adult) illiteracy occurs. School education is compulsory for all children between the ages of 4 and 16. Students may choose to stay on at school or an equivalent college until the age of 18 and the official age for leaving school or training may rise to 18 from 2013 (as is planned for England/Wales). Over 50 per cent of young people regularly progress from secondary school education to university or college.

The complex structure of education in Northern Ireland was previously reflected in 10 Statutory Bodies, which organized the school system. These were replaced in 2011 by the Northern Ireland Executive, and the Department of Education (DE) is responsible for the central administration of education, services, funding and policy formulation, and priorities for school and youth services. It is intended that a new Education and Skills Authority (ESA) will replace the previous Education and Library Boards by April 2013. It will improve administration, savings and operational delivery, and take over the Council for the Curriculum, Examinations and Assessment (CCEA) and the Regional Training Unit (RTU).

The ESA will also take on the educational services and front-line support of the Council for Catholic Maintained Schools (CCMS), the Northern Ireland Council for Integrated Education (NICIE) and Comhairle na Gaelscolaiochta (Irish-medium schools). It will act as the employing authority for teachers and non-teaching staff in all schools. But Boards of Governors in the schools will still make decisions about transport, curricula, school attendance, recreation and the appointment and management of staff. Ownership of maintained and voluntary schools will remain with trustees, while the ownership of controlled schools will be transferred to the ESA. State funding, services and support supplied to a school will be provided, irrespective of the ownership of the school. It seems that two statutory organizations, the Transferor Representatives Council (consisting of the Church of Ireland and the Presbyterian and Methodist churches) and the Association of Governing Bodies, which represents voluntary grammar schools, will remain.

In Northern Ireland, pupils compulsorily start school at the age of 4 (compared with 5 in England/Wales and 6 in Ireland), with nursery provision offered to 3-year-olds. There were 330,147 students in full- and part-time education in 2010 to 2011. They attend schools at pre-school (free education for one year), nursery, primary, secondary and technical levels, which are now largely financed from public funds. The DE has an annual budget of some £1.3 billion; there are over 20,000 teachers; and the pupil:teacher ratio is about 17:1. Northern Ireland has more schools with smaller numbers of pupils than the rest of the UK. Northern Irish schools today are divided into six categories (see Table 11.2):

1   *Controlled schools* are state-funded nursery, primary, special, secondary and grammar schools, which are mostly Protestant schools under the management of Boards of Governors with Protestant church representation. The ESA is the employing and owning authority.
2   *Maintained schools* are nursery, primary, special and secondary schools. They are mostly Catholic-owned schools; the Church is represented on their management Board of Governors; annual costs and employment of teachers and non-teaching staff are funded by the state; and the overall service and support authority will be the ESA.

TABLE 11.2 Number of students attending schools (by type), Northern Ireland (February 2011)

School type	Number of students
Voluntary and private pre-school	7,599
Nursery	5,906
Primary school – nursery	8,502
Primary school – reception	497
Primary school (years 1–7)	154,452
Total primary students	163,451
Secondary (non-grammar) schools	85,769
Secondary grammar schools	62,133
Total secondary students	147,902
Special schools	4,458
Hospital schools	200
Independent schools	631
(Students in total schools)	322,548
(Students in total schools and pre-school education)	330,147

Source: adapted from Department of Education statistics, Northern Ireland, February 2011

3   *Other maintained schools* are primary, special and secondary schools. They are mainly Protestant church owned, are managed by Boards of Governors and receive funding for recurrent costs from the state.

4   *Voluntary schools (grammar) and integrated schools (primary and secondary).* These are mixed schools for Catholic, Protestant and other-faith children; partially owned by trustees; managed by Boards of Governors, and grant maintained for recurrent costs by the state.

5   *Independent schools.* There are some 16 privately owned and run independent schools which mostly tend to be Christian foundations.

6   *Irish-medium schools.* The DE has a statutory duty to encourage and assist the development of Irish-medium education. There are some 21 stand-alone grant-aided voluntary schools in which teaching is in Irish in more than half the compulsory subjects and 12 Irish-medium units (where teaching is in Irish) attached to English-medium host schools.

Features of education in Northern Ireland

The majority of Protestant children in Northern Ireland attend state-controlled schools, while the majority of Catholic children attend maintained schools. The state did not fund Catholic schools until the 1970s and currently more than half the children in Northern Ireland attend Catholic schools. Some Catholic children attend non-Catholic schools and a small minority of non-Catholic children attend Catholic schools. According to Department of Education revised figures in February 2011, the reported religion and number of students in schools in Northern Ireland are: Catholic, 163,693; Protestant, 120,415; other Christian, 8,282; non-Christian, 1,726; and other/no religion/not recorded, 27,601.

There have often been attempts to reform the segregated system of schooling in the province. The first integrated school, Lagan College, opened in 1981 with 28 pupils under the auspices of All Children Together. The 1989 Education Reform (Northern Ireland) Order officially introduced this new category of school, which provides a religiously mixed schooling for Catholic and Protestant pupils and a common curriculum for children of both religious traditions. Managed by a Board of Governors, there has been a steady increase in the numbers of these schools. The Northern Ireland Council for Integrated Education (NICIE) is a voluntary organization, established in 1992, which promotes integrated education. The Integrated Education Fund (IEF) is a financial foundation which bridges the financial gap between starting integrated schools and securing full government funding. According to NICIE there are currently 61 grant-aided integrated schools in Northern Ireland (2011) at primary and secondary levels, educating over 18,000 pupils. This represents 5 per cent of the total school population and numbers and parental interest are increasing, but the majority of children still attend non-integrated schools and many parents are opposed to integration. There is the potential for all schools to transform to integrated status, but only state (controlled) schools (not Catholic maintained schools) have followed this option.

At present, the majority of maintained schools are managed by the Catholic Church. In order to improve management of these schools, the Education Reform (Northern Ireland) Order, 1989 transferred responsibility for all Catholic main-tained schools to a statutory body, the Council for Catholic Maintained Schools (CCMS). The CCMS had responsibility for Catholic maintained schools, provided advice, employed teaching staff and was the largest employer of teachers (about 8,500) in Northern Ireland. It seems that the CCMS will be taken over by the ESA.

A confused grammar–secondary school divide still exists in Northern Ireland. At the age of 11, pupils used to take an 11-Plus examination in English, maths and science, which selected which children would attend grammar or secondary schools. This system was due to be abolished in 2008 and schools would not be able to select pupils on the basis of academic ability. The 11-Plus would be replaced by a transfer procedure, which would be based on parental choice of school in consultation with the staff of the child's primary school. However, there was opposition from grammar schools and parents to the proposed changes, and the grammar–secondary divide continues. Grammar schools commission their own entrance examinations in English and maths and fall into two groups: the Association for Quality Education (AQE) and the Post Primary Transfer

Consortium (PPTC). While both tests are based on the Northern Ireland Key Stage 2 Revised Curriculum, they are different in style, structure and format. Students (who may choose to sit a number of tests) and parents find it difficult and confusing to navigate the new procedures. The Executive is opposed to testing, insists on its own policy, and an acceptable solution to the impasse has not yet been achieved.

The Education (Northern Ireland) Order, 1998 placed a duty on the Department of Education 'to encourage and facilitate the development of Irish-medium education'. Irish-medium schools may apply for voluntary maintained status and become grant aided. They may operate as free-standing schools where Irish is the language medium or as self-contained Irish units in existing English-medium schools. The aim is to improve diversity, choice, identity, integration and linguistic ability, and the number of pupils attending such schools is growing. In 2010/2011, 2,745 pupils attended these schools at nursery, primary and secondary levels.

School curriculum and national examinations

Most schools in Northern Ireland follow the Revised Northern Ireland Curriculum which was introduced in the 2007/2008 school year. It covers the 12 years of compulsory education from a primary Foundation Stage and through post-primary Key Stages. Independent schools are not obliged to adhere to it. The aim of the curriculum is to develop literacy, numeracy, awareness, understanding and skills, improve children's prospects and raise standards in schools.

The primary curriculum comprises religious education, language and literacy; mathematics and numeracy; the arts; the world around us; personal development and mutual understanding; and physical education. The post-primary curriculum covers learning for life and work; religious education; areas of learning such as language and literacy; mathematics and numeracy; modern languages; the arts; environment and society; physical education; and science and technology. At each area of learning, pupils are expected to learn life and work skills.

The large majority of examinations sat, and education plans followed, in Northern Irish schools were previously set and marked by the Council for the Curriculum, Examinations and Assessment (CCEA), which will be taken over by the ESA, but other awarding bodies in England/Wales may also be used. The system covers age groups and examinations, mainly at General Certificate of Secondary Education (GCSE) and General Certificate of Education (GCE) Advanced Level .

On entering secondary education at age 12, all pupils study a mixture of traditional subjects and new areas under the Revised Curriculum. At age 14 pupils select which single subjects, such as English or mathematics, to study over two years for General Certificate of Secondary Education (GCSE) examinations which are marked by independent examination boards. Pupils may study up to 10 or 11 subjects. GCSEs mark the end at age 16 of compulsory schooling in Northern Ireland. According to Department of Education statistics, in 2009/2010, 74.3 per cent of Year 12 (16 years) pupils gained five or more GCSEs (including equivalents) at grades A*(starred) to C, an increase of 3.1 per cent over 71.2 per cent in 2008/2009. But the important and more demanding results, with subjects such as English and mathematics, showed 58.6 per cent of Year 12 pupils gaining five or more GCSEs (including equivalents) at grades A* to C. Females generally perform better than males; 79.9 per cent of females achieved five or more GCSEs (including equivalents) at grades A* to C compared with 68.7 per cent of males, a difference of 11.2 percentage points.

After taking GCSEs, some pupils may leave secondary schooling. Alternatively, they may choose to continue their education at vocational or technical colleges, or stay at school to study Advanced Level AS- and A2-level subjects or more vocational qualifications such as the Advanced Vocational Certificate of Education (AVCE). Those choosing AS and A levels normally pick three or four subjects, and success in these can determine acceptance into higher education courses. AS levels may be taken after one year of study. Following two years of total study, students usually take four A-level (Advanced-level) examinations. In 2009/2010, 97.9 per cent of Year 14 (age 18) pupils gained two or more A levels (including equivalents) at grades A* to E, an increase of 0.1 percentage points over 97.8 per cent in 2008/2009. In a more demanding statistic, 65.3 per cent of Year 14 pupils gained three or more A levels (including equiv-alents) at grades A* to C, an increase of 1.4 percentage points over 2008/2009. Schools can develop curriculum elements to express their particular ethos and meet pupils' individual needs and circumstances. The curriculum also includes Irish in Irish-speaking schools.

Girls in Northern Ireland at both GCSE and A level have traditionally achieved better results than boys. Students in Catholic schools tend to perform better in arts subjects and languages than pupils in Protestant schools, while pupils in Protestant schools tend to do better in science subjects. School-leaver figures from the 1980s and 1990s reveal that fewer school leavers go directly into employment, and a greater percentage go on to further and higher educa-tion. A higher proportion of Catholic pupils tend to progress to further and higher education on leaving school than their counterparts in Protestant schools and a higher proportion of pupils from Protestant schools go directly into employment.

Despite variations, the general standard of education in Northern Ireland is considered to be relatively high. A low proportion of students in their final year of compulsory schooling do not achieve a graded examination result (reduced to 3 per cent from some 17 per cent in the mid-1980s); a high proportion of students in post-compulsory schooling achieve two or more passes at GCE A level; secondary school leavers have higher educational attainments than the UK average; and these students are generally associated with the grammar schools.

Grammar schools in Northern Ireland have traditionally attracted students capable of an academic education, while non-selective schools offer more general and vocational training.

Nevertheless, although the results of many students are good, a minority, such as Protestant males, underachieve. It is argued that reform and improvements are often hindered by historic inertia, a segregated society and denominational control of education. Although formally open to all, state-controlled schools tend to attract Protestant children, and pupils from nationalist backgrounds attend schools effectively under Catholic Church control. Few schools recruit from both communities.

Further and higher education

The further and higher education sectors offer full-time and part-time study opportunities for students aged 16 to 18, mature students and adults. Further education (FE) colleges provide vocational, recreational and training courses. In 2007, Northern Ireland's 16 FE colleges formed six area-based or regional colleges, such as the North West Regional College (NWRC) and the large urban Belfast Metropolitan College (BMC).

Degree-level study in the higher education sector is provided by two universities. Queen's University, Belfast, established in 1845, has had a charter since

PLATE 11.6 Founded by Queen Victoria in 1845, Queen's, Belfast was intended as a non-denominational alternative to Trinity College, Dublin and joined other Queen's Colleges in Cork and Galway. It became a university in its own right in 1908. © Stephen Saks Photography/Alamy

1908 and has two University Colleges affiliated to it (Stranmillis for Education and the Catholic St Mary's). The University of Ulster was established in 1968 and restructured in 1984 by the merger of the New University of Ulster (at Coleraine) and the Ulster Polytechnic. It now has campuses at Coleraine, Jordanstown, Londonderry and Belfast. The Open University provides degree courses for external, part-time students over long periods of study by distance learning. Students also study at university or college in Great Britain, Ireland, the USA and Europe.

The number of students entering full-time higher education in Northern Ireland has increased. In 2009 to 2010 there were 50,990 students at higher education institutions (HEIs), which was a 6 per cent increase from 48,240 in 2008/2009. Eighty-six per cent of students were from Northern Ireland, 7 per cent from Ireland, 3 per cent from Great Britain, 1 per cent from other EU countries and 3 per cent from non-EU countries. The most popular subjects taken by students were 'subjects allied to medicine' (9,470 students) and 'business and administrative studies' (8,530). The proportion of students in Northern Ireland who go to university is higher than in any other country in the EU and undergraduate degrees take three years to complete. The number of Northern Ireland-domiciled first-year students at UK HEIs increased by 3 per cent to 14,080 in 2008/2009, but there was a 7.4 decrease in total applications for entry to English, Welsh and Northern Irish universities in 2012, due partly to increased tuition fees.

Students studying at universities and colleges of higher education in Northern Ireland, Wales and England no longer receive grants to cover expenses, but must apply for student loans. Loans from Student Finance NI for Northern Irish students help with living costs such as course materials, accommodation, food, clothes and travel. They are dependent on where the student lives/studies and the annual maximum in 2011/2012 was £6,780 in London, £4,840 outside London, £5,770 overseas and £3,750 for those staying with parents. Extra help, bursaries and loans may be available to those with disabilities, special needs or family commitments. Universities and colleges of higher education in Northern Ireland now also charge up to £3,500 tuition fees for courses for Northern Irish students (2011), which are paid by the student. Help towards the cost of tuition fees is available in the form of tuition fee loans while the student is studying.

These loans are repaid over time after graduation when the student reaches an income of £15,000 (2011) and payment is made on 9 per cent of income over £15,000. It is estimated that a student may have to repay up to £30,000 over time for maintenance and tuition costs.

Attitudes to education

A *European Values Survey*, 1999 to 2000 asked how much confidence there was in the educational systems of the 33 European nations covered. Thirty-five per cent of respondents from Ireland had 'a great deal of confidence'; 56 per cent had 'quite a lot'; 8 per cent had 'not very much'; and 1 per cent had 'none at all'. The corresponding figures for Northern Ireland were 28 per cent; 57 per cent; 3 per cent and 2 per cent. These figures suggest a greater degree of scepticism at the top end of the scale ('great deal of confidence') by the Northern Irish, but overall the statistics on confidence ('great deal' combined with 'quite a lot') were considerable in both Ireland and Northern Ireland.

A *European Quality of Life Survey, 2003* suggested a similar approval rating. When respondents in the former 15 EU member states were asked to rate education in their own countries on a scale of 1 ('very dissatisfied') to 10 ('very satisfied'), a high mean value of 7 was achieved for Ireland and the UK (including Northern Ireland).

Northern Ireland

Contemporary educational debates in Northern Ireland are particularly concerned with the selective system of secondary/grammar schools, integrated education and Irish-medium schooling. These topics are connected to questions about Northern Irish society and how it could become more inclusive following the Good Friday (Belfast) Agreement.

Integrated education of different faiths is increasing slowly in Northern Ireland, but most pupils still attend either a maintained (Catholic) school or a controlled (Protestant) school. An Ipsos MORI poll for the Integrated Education Fund (IEF) in April 2011 found that 9 out of 10 respondents were in favour of integrated education; two-thirds would support the transformation of their local school to integrated status; and there was support for the idea that schools which received state funding should be open to children of all faiths and none. Some critics argue that integrated education in Northern Ireland has a positive impact on social identity, intergroup attitudes, social cohesion and reconciliation, but this view is opposed by faith-based and other groups.

Respondents to the IEF poll also associated integration with concerns about the educational system and the role of government. A majority of respondents would reduce spending on schools by combining premises and resources rather than cutting maintenance and jobs. They wanted an independent commission to rethink educational delivery as a whole. There was support for holding a referendum on any proposed educational system if the Education Minister and the Executive did not accept the commission's recommendations. These views indicate considerable concerns about the state of education in the region.

Northern Ireland still uses grammar schools, although there is little consensus about academic selection or changes to it. It was decided to abolish selection by 11-Plus examination in 2001, but the matter is not resolved and transfer tests are set by grammar schools, which supposedly determine entry for students from primary school.

The *Belfast Telegraph* (25 June 2009) reported that grammar schools were in fact selecting children with a wide variety of grades (and not solely the best). The then Minister of Education queried why the schools therefore needed to continue with academic testing to select pupils and maintained that there was no need to test 10-year-old children. Opponents argued that the grade intake was caused by a temporary downturn in the school population and was no reason to adopt the comprehensive system. The earlier decision to allow open enrolment in grammar schools enabled them to trawl down during a demographic slowdown.

Respondents to polls are divided in their attitudes to transfer tests, academic selection, grammar schools and comprehensive schooling. A BBC Newsline poll in 2004 found that while 55 per cent of respondents in Northern Ireland said that the 11-Plus should be abolished, 67 per cent thought that academic selection for grammar school should stay in some form. A majority thought that transfer decisions should be delayed beyond the age of 11. Similarly, an ARK *Social and Political Archive* poll in 2003 found that while three out of five respondents believed that change to the system was needed, 'the most favoured alternative' was for all pupils to attend the same school until the age of 14.

There are also polarized attitudes on Irish-medium schools. The Department of Education has a statutory duty to organize the development of such education. New schools are being created at primary and secondary levels to meet demand for education in Irish, even though there are empty places in existing schools and unequal provision in some areas. Some Unionists regard the use of the Irish language as a political weapon and the spread of such schools as support for Catholicism, Ireland and reunification, although there is now more tolerance and some Protestants are learning Irish to revive their cultural roots. Despite adaptation problems and slow progress, it is argued that Irish-medium education encourages cultural diversity, inclusivity, linguistic proficiency and educational benefits.

Ireland

Attitudes to education in Ireland have historically been associated with the roles of the state and the Catholic Church, and how education should respond to Ireland's wider needs. Article 42 of the 1937 Constitution states that the primary educator of the child is 'the family', with inalienable rights and duties to provide, 'according to their means, for the religious and moral, intellectual, physical and social education of their children'. The state had a lesser role and 'shall endeavour to supplement, and give reasonable aid to private and corporate educational initiative . . . with due regard for the rights of parents, especially in the matter of religious and moral formation'. Parents could choose the schooling that they thought suitable for their children and the state interfered minimally with the educational system. Nevertheless, the churches (particularly the Catholic Church) recognized the importance of schools, colleges and curricula. Their policies and particular attitudes fundamentally conditioned Irish education. The state funded educational institutions to provide schooling on its behalf and it avoided closer involvement in educational policy and action until the 1950s.

However, the 1960s brought more prosperity, openness and economic planning to Ireland as the world economy changed. Education became an inevitable policy concern of the state and an OECD/Irish government-funded report in 1965, *Investment in Education*, examined the relationship between education and an industrializing society. Social class, regional differences, educational participation rates and any shortage of trained and educated manpower in the 1970s were central concerns for the national economy. New types of schools and subjects, curricula and regional technical colleges were introduced. All children from 1967 entered second-level education free of charge, participation rates increased and the education system expanded as Ireland competed more equally with other European countries.

It is argued that Irish education today has retained much of its traditional quality schooling, with good discipline and academic strength in higher education, the professions, the Civil Service and management and financial services. However, the debate and attitudes in the 1990s and the twenty-first century have centred on the alleged conflict between such an education system and the technological and entrepreneurial needs of modern Ireland. There is also concern that the system has failed some young people. The National Adult Literacy Agency, 2011 reported that up to 30 per cent of children from disadvantaged areas in Ireland leave primary school with literacy difficulties. In international terms, 25 per cent of Irish adults have literacy problems (compared with 3 per cent in Sweden and 5 per cent in Germany).

Internationally, Ireland was placed eighth and 16 per cent above average in an OECD Programme for International Student Assessment (PISA) in 2000, which assessed combined scores in reading, mathematics and science for 15-year-olds. PISA rankings in 2006 showed Ireland in sixteenth place in mathematics, fourteenth in science and sixth in reading. By 2009, Ireland had dropped out of the top 30 in mathematics and fallen to twentieth place in sciences and twenty-first in reading.

Critics therefore suggest that Ireland's place in international education is faltering and that its educational system needs change and modernization. There is criticism of the shorter time students spend in school each day; a shorter secondary cycle; and a shorter school year than international norms. Comparative statistics have promoted a debate about educational quality, encouraged parents to ask critical questions and raised demands that governments spend more on the educationally disadvantaged.

Exercises

Explain and examine the following terms:

Queen's University	National Curriculum	Penal Laws
A levels	Unionist	Presentation Congregation
hedge schools	segregated schooling	Kildare Place Society
Ogham	integrated schools	National Schools
transfer tests	bardic schools	denominational
Royal Schools	monastic	maintained schools
grammar schools	Trinity College	NICIE
vocational schools	autonomous	the Leaving Certificate
Dublin City University	comprehensives	Department of Education and Skills
controlled schools	GCSE	Education (NI) Act, 1947
Irish-medium schools	CCEA	ESA

Write short essays on the following topics:

1   Analyse the growth of schools in Ireland until 1921.

2   Examine the effects (if any) of single-sex and coeducational schooling.

3   Consider the arguments for and against segregated and integrated schools.

4   Discuss the validity of Irish-medium schooling in the globalized economy.

5   Examine selection, testing and grammar schools in Northern Ireland.

Further reading

Austin, R. (2010) 'Dissolving Boundaries in North–South Education', *Journal of Cross Border Studies in Ireland*, 5: 57–70

Austin, R. (2011) 'ICT, Enterprise Education and Intercultural Learning', *International Journal of Information and Communication Technology Education*, 7(4): 60–71, October–December

Clancy, P., Hughes, I. and Brannick, T. (2005) *Public Perspectives on Democracy in Ireland* Dublin: TASC

Coohill, J. (2000) *Ireland: A Short History* Oxford: Oneworld Publications

Coolahan, J. (2000) *Irish Education: Its History and Structure* Dublin: Institute of Public Administration

Fahey, T., Hayes, B.C. and Sinnott, R. (2005) *Conflict and Consensus: A Study of Values and Attitudes in the Republic of Ireland and Northern Ireland* Dublin: Institute of Public Administration

Gallagher, T. (2004) *Education in Divided Societies* London: Palgrave Macmillan

Gallagher, T. and Smith, A. (2002) 'Attitudes to Academic Selection, Integrated Education and Diversity within the Curriculum', in A.M. Gray *et al. Social Attitudes in Northern Ireland: The Eighth Report* London: Pluto Press (pp. 120–137)

Gallagher, T. and Smith, A. (2003) *Attitudes to Academic Selection in Northern Ireland* ARK Northern Ireland Social and Political Archive, Research Update, Number 16, January

Halpem, D.F. *et al.* (2011) 'The Pseudoscience of Single-Sex Schooling', *Science*, 23 September

Hussey, G. (1993) *Ireland Today: An Anatomy of a Changing State* Dublin: Town House Viking

McGlynn, C., Niens, U., Cairns, E. and Hewstone, M. (2004) 'Moving Out of Conflict: The Contribution of Integrated Schools in Northern Ireland to Identity, Attitudes, Forgiveness and Reconciliation', *Journal of Peace Education*, 1(2): 147–163, January

McWilliams, D. (2006) *The Pope's Children: The Irish Economic Triumph and the Rise of Ireland's New Elite* Dublin: Gill and Macmillan

Murray, D., Smith, A. and Birthistle, U. (1997) *Education in Ireland* University of Limerick: Irish Peace Institute Research Centre

Pritchard, R.M.O. (2004) 'Protestants and the Irish Language: Historical Heritage and Current Attitudes in Northern Ireland,' *Journal of Multilingual and Multicultural Development*, 25(1): 62–82

Renehan, C. (2006) *Different Planets? Gender Attitudes and Classroom Practice in Post-Primary Teaching* Dublin: Liffey Press

Wright, M. and Scullion, P. (2007) 'Quality of School Life and Attitudes to Irish in the Irish-Medium and English-Medium Primary School', *Irish Educational Studies*, 26(1): 57–77

Websites

Department of Education (DE) (NI): www.deni.gov.uk/

Department of Education and Skills, Ireland: http://www.education.ie/home

Department for Employment and Learning (NI): www.delni.gov.uk/

Higher Education Authority, Ireland: http://www.hea.ie

Integrated education, Northern Ireland: www.nicie.org

Multi-denominational Schools, Ireland: http://educatetogether.ie

National Council for Curriculum and Assessment, Ireland: http://www.ncca.ie

National Qualifications Authority of Ireland: http://www.nqai.ie

Northern Ireland Curriculum: www.nicurriculum.org.uk/

Northern Ireland Transfer Test: www.nitransfertest.co.uk/

12

The media

Some writers believe that the development of the print media was the condition for the emergence of nationhood. The communication of ideas, opinions and news throughout a territory helped generate a sense of common belonging. People began to feel that they were participating in a national culture. If this sort of national identity emerged from below, states were also conscious of promoting national identity from above. In Ireland, both forms of nation-building are detectable from the late eighteenth century onwards. Governments, of course, have been concerned to regulate the views expressed in the media – especially the broadcast media – owing to their possible political impact. This has become increasingly difficult in recent years owing to technological changes affecting the circulation of information. Internet access and satellite reception, for example, make it difficult for governments to manage news 'in the national interest'. Contemporary media are a dynamic part of the electronic or information economy. Their interconnection has promoted multi-media enterprises that combine, for example, television, radio and the print editions of newspapers along with simultaneous online versions. This has opened up new perspectives on the world that were unimaginable only a generation ago.

Media history

The first newspapers in Ireland began to appear in Dublin in the 1660s, printing reports of English and Irish events. Circulation was extremely limited in terms of both geography and readership. One incentive for the development of an Irish print industry was that there was no government tax on either paper or advertisements until 1774. Before that date about 165 newspapers had been launched in Dublin, most of which were short-lived. In the same period, newspapers also began to appear in towns like Belfast, Cork and Kilkenny. The *Belfast News Letter*, founded in 1737, is the oldest surviving daily newspaper in the UK and Ireland. The authorities in Dublin Castle were suspicious of the potential of newspapers to spread political subversion and publishers faced the threat of imprisonment for libel or sedition. The government also used its own funds to influence what was printed. Though the purchase of newspapers remained small their circulation was much greater. In the early nineteenth century, those campaigning for the repeal of the Act of Union, for instance, used reading rooms to spread the message. The practice of reading aloud to an often illiterate audience multiplied many times the significance of the printed word. Today, the readership of newspapers is also greater than the circulation figures suggest in that a single newspaper may be read, for example, by members of a family, or by people in libraries, offices and universities.

By the mid-nineteenth century a number of developments promoted the popularity of the newspaper. The Liberal government in London had abolished taxes on paper and advertisements. Literacy rates were steadily improving and this widened the market for sales. More efficient modes of transport, like the railway, allowed for a reliable system of distribution. English newspapers became more readily available in Ireland, new titles were established in Dublin and Belfast, and a flourishing provincial press emerged. The rise of democratic politics and divisions over the Union also encouraged this development. Some of the newspapers established in this era have continued to the present day. The *Irish Times* (founded in 1859) was initially the voice of southern Unionism and later liberal Nationalism; the *Irish Independent* (founded in 1905) promoted the Nationalist cause and emerged as the largest-selling daily newspaper in Ireland; the *Belfast Evening Telegraph* (founded in 1870) expressed the view of northern liberal Unionism; and the *Irish News* (founded in 1891) expressed the view of northern Nationalism. By the 1920s, the morning editions of newspapers (the 'dailies') had a circulation of about 500,000. This meant that about two-thirds of households were buying a daily newspaper. In Ulster, over half the newspapers were English editions like the popular *Daily Mail*, a percentage slightly higher than in the rest of Ireland. These figures do not include the market in weekly newspapers or magazines like the former *Illustrated London News*. There was no mass market for an Irish-language newspaper, though most of the Nationalist press did carry either an Irish-language section or feature. The penetration of the Irish market by English news and views was not welcomed by cultural Nationalists.

Ireland: media structures after 1921

If the print media was well-established by 1921, the foundation of the Irish Free State coincided with the beginnings of new broadcasting technology. In 1919, the Marconi Wireless Telegraph Company had transmitted a message from Ballybunion in the south-west of Ireland to North America, the first instance of transatlantic communication. For those who could afford radio sets, it was now possible to receive programmes from the new British Broadcasting Corporation (BBC) in London. The Irish government also decided to establish radio broadcasting as a state service, paid for by licence fee and supplemented by advertising, under the control of the Department of Posts and Telegraphs. Its primary purpose was to be the dissemination of national culture. The new station used the call sign 2RN (a play on the word *Erin*, or Ireland) and it began broadcasting on 1 January 1926. The reach of the signal was restricted to the area around Dublin. It was not until 1933 that national reception was possible through a new high-power transmitter sited in Athlone. The programming of Radio Athlone (later named Radio Éireann) consisted mainly of Irish traditional music and news bulletins. By the mid-1930s about 105,000 households held radio licences. That was not a true sign of radio's popularity since licence evasion was common. By 1939 the number of licence holders had risen to 140,000 and by 1961, to just over 500,000. That figure meant that nearly every household was in possession of a radio by the mid-twentieth century.

A significant change in the structure of radio services occurred following the Broadcasting Act of 1960. The Act set up the Radio Éireann Authority, later replaced in 1966 by the Raidió Teilifís Éireann (RTÉ) Authority which assumed control of both public service radio and television. Like public service broadcasters elsewhere, Irish radio was slow to adapt to important popular musical trends in the late 1950s and early 1960s. As a consequence, so-called 'pirate radio' stations, catering to a young audience and playing contemporary music, responded more effectively. By the beginning of the 1980s there were at least 70 pirate stations in Ireland. Some of them had larger audiences than RTÉ's own new pop radio channel, Radio 2 (now 2FM), which was launched in 1978 to complement the main public service channel, RTÉ Radio 1. Unofficially, commercial radio had entered the Irish broadcasting mainstream. The government accommodated this new reality and ended RTÉ's broadcasting monopoly. The Radio and Television Act of 1988 established the Independent Radio and Television Commission (IRTC) to regulate the now legitimized commercial sector. The IRTC considered applications for commercial licences and two licences were granted for Dublin and 24 for local stations in the rest of Ireland. One further licence was awarded for an all-Ireland commercial station. Commercial radio began transmitting officially in July 1989.

An Irish television service began on 31 December 1961. BBC TV and UK Independent Television (ITV) were already available to about one-third of the population. Those on the east coast could receive these broadcasts from Great Britain and those in the northern counties could receive similar broadcasts from Northern Ireland. RTÉ television was controlled by the RTÉ Authority (after 1966) and was financed by a mix of licence fee and advertising. Originally the licence fee contributed 70 per cent of RTÉ's income and advertising 30 per cent. These figures were to be reversed in the course of the next two decades. Though the government generally accepted a 'hands-off' approach to most programming issues, RTÉ remained accountable to the Minister for Posts and Telegraph. When political violence erupted in Northern Ireland in 1969, the question of broadcasting freedom created difficulties in that relationship. In 1972 the RTÉ Authority was dismissed by the government following a TV news interview with a member of the Provisional IRA. Under Section 31 of the 1976 Broadcasting Amendment Act, the government banned all interviews with named terrorist organizations and their sympathizers. This ban was removed only in 1994 to assist the course of the Northern Ireland peace process.

Within two years of the launch of Ireland's national TV service, one-third of households possessed television licences and two decades later almost every household possessed at least one television set. A second TV channel, RTÉ 2, began broadcasting in 1978. These channels were in competition with better resourced British television. Competition became even stiffer in the 1980s with the arrival of cable and satellite television (even though RTÉ provided most of the cabling service and all independent providers had to carry the two RTÉ channels). By the mid-1990s, though 70 per cent of homes had access to multi-channel viewing, RTÉ continued to secure at least 50 per cent of TV viewers. In October 1996, a third public service network, the Irish language Telefís na Gaeilge (TG4), was established and in September 1998 the first Irish commercial channel, TV3, began broadcasting. The contract for a commercial channel had been available since 1989 but it took almost a decade for it to come on air.

It is a similar story with print media. In 1932, the Fianna Fáil government imposed tariffs on British newspapers. Protectionism reduced the circulation of British newspapers and boosted the Irish press. These tariffs remained in place until 1971. Thereafter, British titles have become more popular and competitive in the Irish market, partly as a result of efficient air services between London and Dublin. There have also been changes in the fortunes of the major Irish newspapers. In 1931 Éamon de Valera helped found the *Irish Press* in order to support his party, Fianna Fáil. It was intended to challenge the dominant *Irish Independent*, the sympathies of which tended to be with Fianna Fáil's political rivals, Cumann na nGaedheal (later called Fine Gael). By the 1950s the two major titles, the *Irish Independent* and *Irish Press*, had readerships of about 200,000 each while the *Irish Times* had about 40,000. By the 1990s, the *Irish Press* was struggling in the circulation war and it went out of business in 1995, leaving the *Irish Independent* and the *Irish Times* as the two largest domestic morning papers. Of concern to newspaper managements was the fact that an MRBI poll in 1983 found that only 17 per cent looked to newspapers as their prime source of news compared with 53 per cent and 20 per cent respectively for TV and radio. The National Newspapers of Ireland (NNI), consisting of the proprietors of the major Irish titles, was established in 1985 to promote newspaper readership and to win back advertising income from TV and radio. In the 1990s, and for most of the next decade, revenues for Irish newspapers were buoyant owing to rapid economic growth. The prosperity of the national press was also reflected in the prosperity of the Irish provincial press.

The print media in Ireland today

A JNRS/Lansdowne survey in 2003/2004 found that slightly more than 90 per cent of Irish adults claimed to read a daily or Sunday newspaper. Of the newspapers purchased, the majority are Irish titles. British newspapers account for

TABLE 12.1 Daily newspaper circulation in Ireland (2011)

Irish Independent	135,000
Irish Times	100,000
Irish Star	87,000
Irish Sun	80,000
Irish Daily Mirror	62,000
Irish Examiner	44,000

Source: NNI, 2011

about a quarter of the market in the sale of 'dailies' and for about one-third of Sunday newspapers. Most of the British titles have special Irish editions such as the *Irish Daily Mail* and *Irish Mail on Sunday* (launched in 2006), and distinctive Irish content such as the *Sunday Times*.

According to NNI figures for 2011 (Table 12.1), the largest-selling daily newspaper in Ireland remains the *Irish Independent*, with 20 per cent of the market. The circulation of the *Irish Independent* is about 135,000. The newspaper is owned by Independent News and Media PLC (formerly Independent Newspapers), which is Ireland's major publishing company and which also has an international presence. It publishes over 180 titles (including the *Belfast Telegraph* in Northern Ireland), runs over 70 online sites and employs about 10,000 people worldwide. Its former chairman, Sir Anthony O'Reilly, has been the dominant personality in the Irish media industry for a generation. The *Irish Independent* is pro-business, socially liberal, centrist in its political outlook and appeals to a 'middle-of-the-road', cross-class readership. Like all other major media concerns, the current strategy of Independent News and Media has been to integrate traditional news in new multimedia formats. In January 2001 it launched *Unison.ie*, a popular online service that brings together access to the *Irish Independent* as well as the company's regional titles.

The *Irish Times* is the second-largest-selling daily with a circulation of just over 100,000. It is internationally recognized as the premier paper of record for Ireland. In October 2006, the editorial offices were moved from D'Olier Street in Dublin (the *Irish Times* used to be known as the 'old lady of D'Olier Street') to Tara Street. Since 1974, the newspaper has been controlled by a Trust designed to maintain its commercial and political independence. The *Irish Times* prides itself on the distinctive character of its readership. Surveys show that it is the favoured newspaper of business executives and that it is also read by a large proportion of the country's academics and professionals. Its status as a quality newspaper also makes it popular with professionals outside Ireland. In 1994, the *Irish Times* was the first newspaper in Ireland and the UK to be published on the internet. Sixty-four per cent of the readers of its so-called Irish 'lifestyle portal', *Ireland.com*, which offers access to information on events in Ireland, live overseas. A quarter

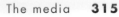

PLATE 12.1 A display of Irish newspapers outside a newsagent shop in Limerick. It includes both national and local newspapers. Such newsagents will also sell most British titles. © Andrew Michael/Alamy

live in the United States. The *Irish Examiner* has the smallest daily circulation of the quality newspapers and is the only daily that is not published in Dublin. It used to be called the *Cork Examiner* but dropped that name in 1996 and in 2000 relaunched itself with its current title. This national label did increase circulation but the *Examiner* has found it difficult competing with both the *Irish Independent* and the *Irish Times*. Currently it has a circulation of about 44,000.

The best-selling of the popular or tabloid dailies in Ireland is the *Irish Daily Star*, the readership of which is mainly working class. It is also partly owned by Independent News and Media. It was first published in 1988 and tried to capture the same sort of readership as the *Daily Star* in the UK. Similar in content to the British format, the emphasis has been on popular entertainment, celebrities and sport. In the UK that appeal has tended to be predominantly male but the readership of the *Irish Daily Star* is evenly balanced between men and women. Its circulation is about 87,000. It competes closely with the Irish editions of two popular British tabloids, the *Irish Sun* (owned by Rupert Murdoch's News International) with a circulation of about 80,000 and the *Irish Daily Mirror* (owned by Trinity Mirror) with a circulation of about 62,000. The *Evening Herald*, also owned by Independent News and Media, is the only surviving evening title in Ireland and it has a circulation of 62,000. One-third of its readership live in the Dublin area. *Herald.ie* is an online daily version of the same paper. The weekly *Irish Farmers Journal*, established in 1948, continues to have a strong market identity, with a circulation of 71,000. Managed by the Agricultural Trust, it exists to promote the interests of the rural community.

The Sunday print market in Ireland is even more competitive than the daily market because the challenge from British titles is even stronger (Table 12.2). Two Sunday papers with more or less the same circulation jostle for market leadership. The companion to the daily *Irish Independent*, the *Sunday Independent*, has a circulation of 256,000. Its close rival is the *Sunday World*, launched in 1973, which has a circulation of about 247,000. It is also owned by Independent News and Media but it is targeted at a different, and more working-class, readership. The *Sunday World* has adopted the style of the British Sunday tabloids with a mix

TABLE 12.2 Sunday newspaper readership in Ireland (2011)	
Sunday Independent	256,000
Sunday World	247,000
Irish Mail on Sunday	113,000
Sunday Times	111,000
Sunday Business Post	48,000
Irish Sunday Mirror	41,000
Source: NNI, 2011	

of populist campaigning journalism and stories of crime, sex and celebrity. *Ireland on Sunday* (founded in 1997) was retitled the *Irish Mail on Sunday* in February 2006 and has a circulation of 113,000. The *Sunday Business Post* has a circulation of around 50,000 and takes a strongly nationalist position on Northern Ireland. The largest circulation of a British Sunday used to be the *Irish News of the World* (owned by News International) which had a readership of 116,000 but it was closed in July 2011 because of public outrage and withdrawal of advertising which accompanied revelations of widespread 'phone hacking' by its journalists in the UK. The *Sunday Times* (also owned by News International) is the best-selling British quality Sunday with 111,000 readers. The *Irish Sunday Mirror* has a readership of 41,000.

In a JNRS readership survey in 2003/2004, 75 per cent of adults outside the main urban areas of Dublin and Cork claimed to read a regional newspaper, though sales have fallen by about one-third in the past five years. Nearly all of these newspapers are published weekly. The 1990s witnessed a series of mergers and take-overs in the regional press but it is still a vibrant market. There remain over 60 regional and local titles and about 600,000 copies are bought every week. Because of the proximity of the British market, many of the periodicals and magazines published in the UK are readily available in Ireland. For example, since most Irish football supporters follow teams in the English Premier League, English football magazines are popular. The best-selling magazine of all, however, is the *RTÉ Guide* (radio and television schedule) with a circulation of over 100,000 and an estimated readership of 487,000 per week. The best-selling British title is *Hello!* magazine (which covers celebrity events) with a circulation of 40,000.

Newspapers are regulated by the Press Council of Ireland and the Office of the Press Ombudsman, which were established on 1 January 2008. These new institutions have arisen to meet public concerns about possible invasions of privacy and the potential abuse by journalists of press freedom. The objective of the Press Council is to provide a forum for resolving public complaints free of charge according to a commonly agreed Code of Practice. The role of the Ombudsman in the first instance is to resolve individual complaints by a process of conciliation and, if that is not possible, to make a decision case by case. More difficult and contentious issues will be referred to the Press Council. The Ombudsman has no authority to monitor press behaviour and no power to impose fines. There has been an average of one complaint per day since the establishment of the Council and most of these have to do with accuracy and fairness of reporting rather than with issues of privacy. The majority of complaints are not proceeded with.

The representative body of the major Irish newspapers, NNI, identified two issues affecting the press today. The first is the competitive practice of large British publishers. Their economies of scale permit the selling of newspapers at a price below that of the Irish print media. Though the European Commission dismissed this complaint, NNI believes that the Irish government should act against publishers selling newspapers below cost price. The second is the high rate of value-added tax (VAT) on newspaper sales. While the UK press enjoys a zero rating in its own market, the Irish press pay 13.5 per cent. NNI has proposed a zero rate of VAT for Ireland. One further issue has been that of press ownership. Concern has been expressed, first, about the ownership of major Irish titles by Independent News and Media. According to the Irish Competition Authority, however, the market is sufficiently diverse and competitive because of the sales of UK newspapers. Second, there is concern about the acquisition of Irish titles by British companies. Some believe this could, if unchecked, undermine altogether the idea of a distinctively Irish *national* press.

The broadcast media in Ireland today

The current regulatory framework for broadcasting in Ireland was established by the comprehensive Broadcasting Act of 2009. The Broadcasting Authority of Ireland (BAI) was set up, replacing both the Broadcasting Commission of Ireland and the Broadcasting Complaints Commission. The BCI had been established originally in 2003 as the regulatory body for the commercial sector, charged with licensing independent broadcasting services to ensure choice and diversity. It also oversaw the introduction of digital terrestrial television (DTT) which will eventually replace traditional, analogue television. Digital provides more broadcasting space for more channels. Since the UK had already committed itself to digital television, the Irish government needed to do so as well. In addition to these inherited roles, the BAI was also given oversight of the operation of public service broadcasters, RTÉ and TG4. It is funded by a levy on all broadcasters licensed in the state. Apart from regulatory duties, its statutory responsibilities are to stimulate high-quality programming; facilitate public service broadcasting objectives; and promote diversity in the commercial and community sectors. Currently, it licenses 14 television services, 4 national, 5 regional and 26 local radio stations as well as 21 community channels. The RTÉ Board was also established by the 2009 Act as the new governing authority for public service radio and television, replacing the RTÉ Authority. Article 114 of that Act requires RTÉ to operate a national television and radio broadcasting service which should be 'free-to-air' in Ireland. RTÉ must provide a comprehensive range of programmes in both English and Irish that reflect the cultural diversity of the whole island of Ireland, including Northern Ireland. The Broadcasting Act specified the public service remit of RTÉ to be: entertain, inform and educate. The same words were also used to define the original remit of public service broadcasting in the UK. TG4, the Irish-language television channel, became an independent statutory entity on 1 April 2007. The channel has been on air since late 1996 and is charged with similar public service responsibilities as RTÉ.

Nearly every household in Ireland has a television licence (costing €160 but free for those aged over 70). In the public service network, RTÉ provides two national channels. RTÉ 1 is the flagship channel, providing general programming such as news, documentaries, drama, comedy, quiz shows and films. From figures supplied by the European Commission-funded MAVISE database of TV companies and TV channels in the European Union, RTÉ 1 has just under a quarter of viewers with slightly more in the prime-time, early evening period. RTÉ Network 2 aims to cater for younger viewers and broadcasts much of RTÉ's sports coverage. It has a 10 per cent share of viewers. TG4 provides an Irish-language channel – although it also carries programmes in English – and claims about 2.5 per cent of the market. The national commercial station TV3 shares much of its programming, especially soap operas, with the Independent Television (ITV) network in the UK. Indeed, one of the largest investors in TV3 is ITV. The channel now has around 14 per cent of Irish viewers.

Most television viewers in Ireland also have access to the UK networks of the BBC (public service) and ITV (commercial). BBC 1 (Northern Ireland) is available throughout most of the island though some areas in the south and east receive BBC 1 (Wales). BBC 1 is a popular entertainment and news channel. BBC 2 produces more serious programming of news analysis, documentaries and minority-appeal shows. New BBC digital channels, such as BBC News 24, are also available on cable or via satellite. ITV programming in Ireland is mainly provided by Ulster Television (UTV), although some Irish regions receive ITV (Wales). UTV provides strong competition to BBC (Northern Ireland) as a popular entertainment and news channel. It has marketed itself strongly in Ireland, especially lobbying cable networks to carry it rather than ITV (Wales). UTV now has a share of the viewing public on a par with RTÉ Network 2 (around 10 per cent). The other major UK channel available in Ireland is Channel 4. It was originally designed as a commercial alternative to BBC 2 and its digital version E4 may also be received. As yet, Ireland does not receive the other major UK broadcaster, Channel 5.

It is estimated that over 60 per cent of Irish households receive digital television which provides not only multi-channel viewing but also telephone, interactive and internet services, either by cable or by satellite. The ambitious plans for digitalization in Ireland have been hit by the economic crisis of 2008 and some of the new companies, like Setanta, have experienced financial difficulties. Cable and satellite provide households with packages of television channels such as movies, sports, cartoons and music, paid for by individual subscription. The cable market is controlled by one provider, UPC Ireland, which claims 450,000 subscribers or about one in four of all households. Satellite provider Sky: Ireland, a part of British Sky Broadcasting (BSkyB), permits a choice of over 200 channels. Ninety-eight per cent of these channels are not Irish and most of the programming is either American or British. Sky has about 580,000 subscribers or about one in three households.

Something like 85 per cent of Irish people claim to listen to the radio at some time every day. There are four public service radio channels provided by RTÉ.

According to the Joint National Listenership Survey in 2011, RTÉ Radio 1, RTÉ's 'premier' station which broadcasts music, drama, news, entertainment and features, has a market share of 25 per cent. RTÉ 2 fm (11 per cent) is a pop and rock music channel and Lyric fm (3 per cent) is a classical music channel. Raidió na Gaeltachta is the Irish-language broadcaster with programming similar to Radio 1. Since 2002, the four RTÉ radio channels have been carried on Sky Digital network and this makes them available to subscribers throughout the UK. The nationwide commercial station, Today FM, with its mix of talk and music, has about a 10 per cent share of listeners with the current affairs channel, Newstalk, on about 5 per cent. Local commercial radio, appealing to more specific tastes, has developed a strong presence in the market. This is especially so in Dublin where FM104 and Q102, both owned by UTV Media, have a strong market share and also in Cork where 96FM and C103 (again owned by UTV Media) are also dominant.

The other major media form in Ireland is film. The Irish Film Board (IFB) is the national development agency for the film industry, and through its Film Commission and Location Services Unit it promotes Ireland as a setting for international productions. In 2010 it had a budget of €16.5 million. According to the IFB, the industry in Ireland is worth more than €557 million, employs over 6,000 people in 560 enterprises and represents 0.3 per cent of GDP. In the past 20 years films such as *Braveheart*, *Saving Private Ryan* and *Harry Potter* have been partly made on location in Ireland. Irish-made films like *The Magdalene Sisters* have won international awards. According to the IFB, 18 per cent of all tourists in 2008 visited as a result of having watched an Irish film, contributing about €369 million to Ireland's economy. Raising awareness of the importance of film-making has the support of the national agency for the promotion of Irish arts abroad, Culture Ireland.

The role and influence of broadcasting in Ireland

Public service radio and television were originally conceived to serve and support a distinctive national culture and to promote the country's identity against its powerful UK neighbour. The political and religious establishment in the 1950s and early 1960s wanted to use the media to sustain Irish cultural (Gaelic) and religious (Catholic) values which had hitherto been enforced, when necessary, by the Censorship of Publications Board (which still exists, though without the extensive power it once had). It may be argued that television and radio both helped to transform those cultural and religious values and to portray the extent to which Ireland was changing.

One illustration is perhaps the most famous Irish television programme, the *Late Late Show*, a chat show which began in 1962 and which was hosted for 37 years by Ireland's most celebrated presenter, Gay Byrne. For critics, the *Late Late*

PLATE 12.2 The famous Irish TV presenter Gay Byrne arriving at the Annual Irish Film and Television Awards in Dublin in 2009. Byrne presented the iconic *Late, Late Show* for 37 years. © ni press photos/Alamy

Show contributed to a decline in Ireland's public morality but for most people it became a measure of Ireland's changing identity, discussing formerly taboo issues such as contraception and homosexuality. What is certain is that the programme remained unmistakably and distinctively Irish in form and content.

Since most contemporary programming today is made outside Ireland, it is difficult to sustain the old ideal of exclusively national broadcasting. The content of twenty-first-century broadcasting – as well as what is available on the internet – has become global. One concern shared with the print media is that ownership is becoming concentrated in the hands of a few powerful, multinational and multi-media organizations. This concentration, some suggest, brings with it too much political as well as cultural influence. There is also unease about the effect of the broadcast media on public life and behaviour, what some have called 'dumbing down'. People now watch game shows, celebrity talk shows, reality shows and soap operas; they read about them in the tabloid press; and they listen to reports about them on popular radio channels. If that is partly true of Ireland's experience, it is far from unique. However, it is also the case that technological changes have helped democratize the media by providing greater access to the public sphere for ordinary people. According to International Telecommunication figures, internet usage in Ireland has risen from 20 per cent of the population in 2000 to 66 per cent in 2010 and this provides citizens with access to a range of information (however reliable) unimaginable until very recently. The phenomenon of 'blogging' also challenges the authority of older media formats.

Northern Ireland: media structures after 1921

In Northern Ireland the print media has always reflected the religious and political divisions in society. Of the morning dailies, the *Belfast News Letter* (after 1962 the *News Letter*) serviced the Protestant and Unionist community as did the *Northern Whig* (1824–1963). The former was more conservative in its political sympathies than the latter. At this time both newspapers claimed to be the largest selling. The *News Letter* gained in popularity throughout the 1920s and soon overtook its rival. The estimated circulation for each was around 30,000 to 35,000. The *Irish News*, also printed in Belfast, serviced the Catholic and Nationalist community and had a circulation of about 20,000. The *Belfast Telegraph* (it had dropped *Evening* from its title in 1918) remains the only evening newspaper in Northern Ireland and, despite its mainly mainstream Unionist sympathies, is read by both communities. Its circulation in the 1920s and 1930s was over 70,000. With the exception of the *Northern Whig*, which ceased publication in 1963, these newspapers have remained the popular local daily newspapers in Northern Ireland. Because the *News Letter* and the *Irish News* were clearly communal newspapers, this affected their ability to grow beyond a certain limit. The readership of the *News Letter* has remained more than 90 per cent Protestant and the readership of the *Irish News* has remained more than 90 per cent Catholic.

The *Belfast Telegraph* was not so constrained by either community or competition. Its readership was about two-thirds Protestant and one-third Catholic, matching the demographic divide within Northern Ireland. By the mid-1950s the *Belfast Telegraph* had become the largest-selling newspaper on the whole island. Its circulation then stood at about 195,000. Though its circulation has declined steadily since then, it remains the most popular of Northern Ireland's newspapers. In 1985, financial success allowed the *Belfast Telegraph* to be the first local press to use colour printing. During the Troubles, the two morning dailies

PLATE 12.3 BBC Broadcasting House in Ormeau Avenue in central Belfast was first opened in 1941. The Ulster Television Studios are about half a mile away on the Ormeau Road. © Stephen Barnes/Belfast/Alamy

struggled to maintain their circulation in an exceptionally competitive market. The *News Letter*, for example, experimented with free copy in Belfast in order to boost advertising revenue. The first exclusively Northern Ireland Sunday newspaper was the *Sunday News*, owned by the *News Letter*. Started in 1965, it lasted until 1993. By that time it had been overtaken by the *Sunday Life*, owned by the *Belfast Telegraph*, which began publication in 1988. The Dublin-based *Sunday World* also produced a popular Northern Ireland edition.

Radio broadcasting in Northern Ireland began two years ahead of Ireland. The BBC made its first broadcast in Northern Ireland in September 1924. However, reception was only available in the immediate Belfast area. A new transmitter was built in 1936 at Lisburn, just outside Belfast, and this extended the broadcasting range to most of Northern Ireland. In 1939 there were 124,000 radio licence holders or about 50 per cent of households. By the end of the 1950s this was nearly 100 per cent. Northern Ireland fitted into the regional structure of the BBC with its own Advisory Committee and regional Director. In 1979, Radio Foyle became the BBC channel for Londonderry/Derry and the north-west. Locally produced commercial radio began in 1976 with Downtown Radio. BBC television broadcasts in Northern Ireland started in 1955. Locally produced programming was extremely limited and local daily news bulletins did not begin until 1959. In that year the BBC's local commercial rival, Ulster Television (UTV), began broadcasting. UTV has held the commercial licence in Northern Ireland ever since. Competition between BBC Northern Ireland and UTV increased the number of locally produced programmes, though both channels mainly feature UK-wide entertainment. The popularity of television led to almost universal television ownership by the end of the 1960s. BBC (radio and television) is paid for by licence fee while UTV relies on advertising. Northern Ireland has access to all the new terrestrial channels as they began broadcasting in the rest of the UK – BBC 2, Channel 4 and Channel 5. Satellite television became available in 1989. Cable services were only slowly introduced in the Greater Belfast area and the north-west but became more competitive after 1996, providing as well telephone and internet services.

The print media in Northern Ireland today

Surveys consistently show that in Northern Ireland the local press is believed to be the most valuable medium for news and information. Around 20 per cent think this compared with 14 per cent for the national press. This is important since it makes newspaper space attractive for advertisers. To compete for advertising revenue as well as to make the newspaper more attractive, the local press publish regular supplements aimed at specific markets like business, farming, job recruitment and property. However, much of the content of Northern Ireland's newspapers continues to reflect its political and religious divisions (Table 12.3).

The *News Letter*, now published entirely as a tabloid, has a circulation of about 25,000. It was purchased in 1998 by the UK-based Mirror newspapers, now Trinity Mirror, which has large holdings throughout the UK and Ireland. In 2005 it was sold to the UK-wide media group Johnston Press (with other titles such as *The Scotsman* and the *Yorkshire Post*). The *News Letter*'s readership is more rural than urban and its circulation, like all local dailies, has been steadily declining in recent years. Though it does deal with national and international stories, the strength of the *News Letter* remains its appeal to the Unionist and Protestant community. From its coverage of political events and in its personal columns like births, deaths and marriages, the newspaper reflects a distinct way of life and contributes to sustaining it.

TABLE 12.3 Circulation of Northern Ireland daily and Sunday newspapers (2011)

Belfast Telegraph	59,000
Irish News	44,000
News Letter	25,000
Sunday Life	50,000
Sunday World	50,000

Source: adapted from ABC, 2011

The *Irish News* performs a similar function for Catholics. Its political coverage deals sympathetically with nationalist concerns, its sports reporting is heavily weighted towards Gaelic games, and its records of births, deaths and marriages are almost entirely inserted by Catholic families. Unlike the other dailies, it has not been absorbed into a large media corporation. The *Irish News* is independently owned and is a shareholder in the Northern Media Group. It also has an interest in River Media which owns a small number of weekly titles in the border counties of Ireland. Its circulation has declined less than its rivals and now stands at about 44,000. In 2002 it was the first regional or national newspaper to introduce subscription charges for its web edition. A short-lived competitor for the *Irish News* was *Daily Ireland*, founded in January 2005 as part of the Andersonstown News Group (renamed the Belfast Media Group) which articulated an Irish Republican perspective. Low circulation (estimated at about 10,000) forced its closure in September 2007. However, in June 2007 the Belfast Media Group bought a controlling stake in the *Irish Echo*, a New York-based weekly, to make it the only Irish newspaper group with operations on both sides of the Atlantic.

The *Belfast Telegraph* remains the most widely read (and the only evening) newspaper in Northern Ireland. In 2005 it also launched a new daily morning edition. The circulation of the *Belfast Telegraph* has also been declining steadily in recent years and is today about 59,000 (though this figure includes some copies distributed free). It was formerly owned by Trinity Holdings which, when it

PLATE 12.4 The three main Northern Ireland daily newspapers. They compete with both the Irish and major British daily newspapers. © JoeFox/Alamy

bought the Mirror Group (and so the *News Letter*) in 1999, could have controlled nearly 70 per cent of the Northern Ireland market. To secure the Mirror deal, Trinity was compelled to sell the *Belfast Telegraph* and it was bought in 2000 by the Irish-based Independent News and Media. It remains a very profitable title, partly because it has maintained a cross-community appeal.

Northern Ireland newspapers compete with the English tabloids such as *The Sun*, the *Daily Mail*, *Daily Mirror* (which has a separate Northern Ireland edition) and 'qualities' such as the *Daily Telegraph* and *Guardian*. They also compete with Irish titles like the *Irish Times* and the *Irish Independent*. These newspapers are bought as alternatives, but sometimes as complements, to the local dailies. Northern Ireland also has its own Sunday editions. The *Sunday Life* and the *Sunday World* both have circulations of about 55,000. Like the local dailies they compete with English editions such as the *Observer* and the *Sunday Telegraph* and Irish editions such as the *Sunday Independent*. Northern Ireland has a diverse range of newspapers which reflects well the overlapping cultural influences: Northern Irish, British and Irish. It continues to be well served too by newspapers that cater for local readerships. There are about 50 such titles in circulation today, both daily and weekly. In some areas, these newspapers replicate the roles of the Northern Ireland-wide newspapers. For example, in the north-west, the *Londonderry Sentinel* is read mainly by Protestants while the *Derry Journal* is read mostly by Catholics.

The press in Northern Ireland, as elsewhere in the UK, comes under the Editors' Code of Practice or press standards designed to balance individual rights and the public's right to know. The Press Complaints Commission (PCC), based in London, handles grievances made under the provisions of the Code and the main complaints dealt with are those of inaccuracy and invasion of privacy. As in the Irish case, the process of self-regulation attempts to resolve complaints in the first instance between complainant and newspaper editor. Only when that fails does the PCC take up a particular case.

The broadcast media in Northern Ireland today

The broadcasting framework for Northern Ireland was established by the Communications Act, 2003. It created a single UK regulatory body, the Office of Communications (Ofcom), replacing five pre-existing bodies: the Broadcasting Standards Commission, the Independent Television Commission, Office of Telecommunications (Oftel), the Radio Authority and the Radiocommunications Agency. Like its predecessors, Ofcom is mainly concerned with commercial providers but it has a remit to cover standards in public service broadcasting as well. It has an executive office in each of the UK nations. The Director (Northern Ireland) coordinates Ofcom's responsibilities and consults with a Northern Ireland advisory committee.

The BBC is responsible for public sector broadcasting, radio and television, throughout the UK and is funded by licence fee (currently £145.50). BBC Northern Ireland (BBCNI) is an integral regional component of the Corporation. At the UK level, 12 non-executive Trustees are charged with ensuring that the BBC is run in the interest of viewers and listeners. The Trust sets the BBC's strategy and appoints the Director-General who is responsible for running the day-to-day business of broadcasting. Northern Ireland has one Trustee who represents local viewer and listener interests at the UK level as well as within BBCNI. There is an advisory Audience Council, made up of local appointees and chaired by the National Trustee. The role of the Council is to assess audience reaction to programming; to assess whether BBCNI is meeting its objectives; and to advise on local programming. The day-to-day management of radio and television for BBCNI is the responsibility of the local BBC Executive.

The network's premier television channel is BBC1 NI. Apart from daily news coverage, locally produced programmes are also screened on BBC1 NI. It provides input into UK news services and UK-wide television events. Sometimes locally produced or commissioned programmes are broadcast nationwide. BBC1 NI has a peak-time audience of 23 per cent, most of which is accounted for by nationally networked entertainment, while BBC2 has a peak-time audience share of 8 per cent. BBC NI radio programming is provided by Radio Ulster and Radio Foyle. Radio Ulster delivers a mix of music, news, talk shows, documentary features and outside broadcasts (mainly sports events). Radio Foyle delivers a dedicated broadcasting service for the north-west. The two share programmes and presenters and form part of the wider UK BBC network which is listened to throughout Northern Ireland. Radio Ulster/Foyle has about 37 per cent of the weekly listening public, the highest reach for any of the regional radio services in the UK. BBC UK-wide radio channels such as Radio 1 (pop music), Radio 2 (pop music and discussion), Radio 3 (classical music) and Radio 4 (news, drama, documentaries and current affairs) are freely available. In 2008/2009 according to Ofcom figures, the BBC spent £18.4 million on radio services for Northern Ireland listeners which was the highest 'spend per head' for any region of the UK. Digital radio still has a low take-up in Northern Ireland. At 20 per cent it is half the UK average, though a new digital transmitter, installed at Armagh in 2009, will extend the range of service.

Commercial television in Northern Ireland is provided by UTV. Its peak-time share of television viewers in Northern Ireland is between 35 and 37 per cent which makes it the most popular of the two channels. The key competitive slot for local viewers remains the evening news programme. According to research by Ofcom, Northern Ireland viewers watch more hours of early evening news than anywhere else in the UK (probably a legacy of the Troubles). Here UTV has consistently outperformed its BBC rival and registers a 45 per cent higher audience rating. Like BBC NI, much of the air time on UTV is accounted for by UK-network programming. UTV is required by Ofcom to produce an Annual

Programme Statement outlining its commitment to promoting local broadcasting. UTV broadcasts about 650 hours of locally produced programmes each year, including news, current affairs, documentaries and entertainment, as well as local sporting events. In recent years, UTV has developed into a multi-media group with interests in commercial radio in the rest of Ireland and in Great Britain. In 2000, it also launched an internet service (UTV Internet). The five terrestrial channels – BBC 1 and 2, UTV, Channel 4 and Channel 5 (also UK-wide) – together have a viewing figure of 66 per cent in Northern Ireland, a figure which replicates figures elsewhere in the UK.

PLATE 12.5 One of Northern Ireland's most familiar media personalities, the UTV news presenter Paul Clarke, at a St Patrick's Day Celebration in Belfast, 2011. © J Orr/Alamy

The television market in Northern Ireland, like the newspaper market, provides a wide variety of choice and is very competitive. Seventy-five per cent of households can receive both RTÉ 1 and RTÉ 2. The border areas and the west (both with 90 per cent coverage) have better reception than the east, though RTÉ channels are also available on satellite. According to an Ofcom survey in 2007, about one-third of respondents claimed to watch RTÉ on a daily basis. An agreement in 2010 between the British and Irish governments paved the way for the RTÉ channels, as well as TG4, to be available throughout Northern Ireland by the end of 2012. Over 50 per cent of households subscribe to Sky satellite television which is a growing sector of the market. Cable (Virgin Media) and satellite broadcasts now have about 25 per cent of peak time viewing. In 2009, 65 per cent of households had a broadband connection, higher than either Scotland or Wales but slightly lower than England.

There has been a growth in the commercial radio sector as well. In 1976, Downtown Radio initially served the Belfast and east coast area only but it became more widely available in the mid-1980s. Downtown provides mainly popular music programming. In 1990 it created a second station, Cool FM, directed at a younger audience. Together, Downtown and Cool FM have a 29 per cent market share in this sector. Two further commercial stations developed in the 1990s, Belfast Citybeat and Q102 in Londonderry. Citybeat has a 9 per cent market share and Q102 3.5 per cent (in its own transmission area of the north-west it can

PLATE 12.6 The Paint Hall is situated in the newly named Titanic Quarter of Belfast. It was once used to paint components for ships but is now a fully functioning commercial film studio. © Stephen Barnes/Belfast/Alamy

rise to 20 per cent). U105, launched in 2005, is part of the UTV group, and has 6 per cent of listeners.

Northern Ireland Screen is the agency which, like the Irish Film Board, promotes both Northern Ireland's small film industry and Northern Ireland as a major production location. It rents out the large Paint Hall in the Titanic Quarter of Belfast (formerly part of Harland and Wolff shipbuilders) as a film studio. Broadcasting of all kinds employs about 1,200 people directly but also depends on freelance workers. A recent report of the House of Commons Northern Ireland Committee recommended that television companies should raise their level of production in Northern Ireland to encourage creative industries.

The role and influence of the media in Northern Ireland

In Northern Ireland the Troubles directly affected the print media. For example, the *Belfast Telegraph*'s presses were bombed twice by the IRA in the 1970s. Northern Ireland's daily newspapers are recognizably partisan. As one would expect, the *News Letter* supports the Unionist position and the *Irish News* supports the Nationalist position. The *Belfast Telegraph*, while not identified with any Unionist political party, supports Northern Ireland remaining a part of the UK. All of the dailies, however, maintain an editorial line that opposes violence and supports constitutional politics. Though they do reflect in their pages the passions of the communities they serve, the print media is collectively a force for moderation. All three were supportive of the Northern Ireland peace process in the 1990s and all gave their backing to the Good Friday (Belfast) Agreement of 1998. Throughout the Troubles journalists often faced threats from terrorists. In 1989, Martin O'Hagan of the *Sunday World* was abducted, threatened but released by the IRA. In 2001 he was murdered by Loyalist paramilitaries.

The Troubles also had an important effect upon the broadcast media. In the course of the past 30 years they provided an important source of information for citizens about the conditions of political violence. People listened to news bulletins regularly because bombings or bomb scares would affect travel and work. They also conveyed details about security arrangements in the aftermath of violent events. One long-running Radio Ulster programme, *Talkback*, has provided a daily forum in which people can express their own views on Northern Ireland issues. The significance of the broadcast media is their duty, unlike the print media, to be impartial and to report the news in an even-handed manner. Critics thought that they failed to do so. Some argued that they were too receptive to the UK government's interpretation of events. Others argued that they were often too willing to broadcast the views of terrorists. In 1976 the Irish government banned all interviews with spokespersons for terrorist organizations. In October 1988 the British government introduced similar restrictions in Northern Ireland under the terms of the 1981 Broadcasting Act. However, BBC and UTV got around this restriction with the device of having the words of these representatives spoken by actors. The ban was lifted in September 1994 following ceasefires by the IRA and loyalist paramilitaries.

In 2010 a House of Commons Northern Ireland Affairs Committee Report argued that there was insufficient portrayal of ordinary life in Northern Ireland in the media. The Report said that news and current affairs coverage had in the past concentrated largely on the Troubles and that drama, documentary or film about Northern Ireland continued to be mainly concerned with violence and conflict. Moreover, Northern Ireland has never produced a long-running series for UK network television. The Committee recommended that the government encourage broadcasters to reflect more accurately everyday life in Northern Ireland. In particular, it thought that programmes on its people, geography, wildlife, history and culture should replace a fixation on the Troubles.

Attitudes to the media

A Eurobarometer survey published by the European Commission in 2002 confirmed that the majority of Irish people preferred television as their main source of news. Sixty-eight per cent watched television news bulletins every day while 91 per cent watched them several times a week. They also tend to trust the news reports they hear on television. Seventy-eight per cent thought television news trustworthy, one of the highest rates of trust in the EU. That same survey found that 63 per cent of Irish people listened to news on the radio every day while 82 per cent listened to it at some time during the week. This was much higher than the EU average. Radio news reports had the same high level of trust as television bulletins with 77 per cent of respondents finding them believable. There is less trust, however, in what people read in newspapers.

One reason is that people expect radio and television news to have a public service ethos because they are broadcasting to everyone and so need to present a reasonably balanced report. Newspapers, on the other hand, are thought to appeal to a more limited section of opinion and to have a distinct view on political and socio-economic affairs. This distinction is reinforced in Ireland where people perceive a different emphasis not only between Irish newspapers but also between UK and Irish newspapers. Indeed, Irish people tend to be quite sensitive to what they feel are misrepresentations of their country in the UK media. A British Council survey in 2003 found that many were concerned about the attitude of the UK media, especially the tabloid press, towards Ireland and the Irish.

These attitudes are replicated in Northern Ireland. In 2005, the *Northern Ireland Life and Times Survey* asked people if they believed the media had a large impact on their lives. Forty-five per cent said yes but 55 per cent said no. People are more sceptical of all forms of news reporting mainly because of the intensity of the political divisions. The partisan character of Northern Ireland's newspapers means that Unionists will tend to be sceptical of the political bias in the Nationalist press. Nationalists will tend to be sceptical of the political bias in the Unionist press. The common view is that radio and television bulletins are more objective but this will not apply to documentaries that criticize one community or the other. Many believe that the media pursues its own agendas. For example, the same *Northern Ireland Life and Times Survey* found that 66 per cent of respondents felt that people's perceptions of migrant workers had been tainted by the media. That is why there is a very strongly held view that everything one reads, sees or hears about Northern Ireland needs to be taken with a 'large pinch of salt'.

Exercises

Explain and examine the following terms:

media	press	circulation
public service broadcasting	censorship	RTÉ
BBC NI	UTV	network
media balance	*Irish Times*	*Irish Independent*
tabloid	*Irish News*	*News Letter*
Press Council of Ireland	cable	Broadcasting Authority of Ireland
satellite broadcasting	Ofcom	digital switch-over
soap operas	pirate radio	terrestrial broadcasting

Write short essays on the following topics:

1   Explain and describe the differences between the *Irish News* and the *News Letter* in Northern Ireland.

2   Discuss how far one can have a 'national' media in Ireland given the availability of British newspapers, radio and television channels.

3   What challenges did the Troubles pose for the media in both parts of Ireland and how did governments respond?

4   Describe the structures of media regulation in either Ireland or Northern Ireland.

Further reading

Horgan, J. (2001) *Irish Media: A Critical History since 1922* London: Routledge.

Horgan, J. (2004) *Broadcasting and Public Life: RTÉ News and Current Affairs* Dublin: Four Courts Press

McLoone, M. (1996) *Broadcasting in a Divided Community: Seventy Years of the BBC in Northern Ireland* Belfast: Institute of Irish Studies

Morash, C. (2009) *A History of the Media in Ireland* Cambridge: Cambridge University Press

Websites

BBC NI: http://www.bbc.co.uk/northernireland/
Irish newspapers online: http://www.onlinenewspapers.com/ireland.htm
Ofcom Northern Ireland: http://www.ofcom.org.uk/about/ofcom-in-the-nations-and-regions/
    ofcom-in-northern-ireland/
Press Association Ireland: http://www.presscouncil.ie/reland
Press Council of Ireland – Office of the Press Ombudsman:
http://www.pressassociation.com/ireland.html
RTÉ: http://www.RTÉ.ie/
Ulster Television: http://www.u.tv/

Index

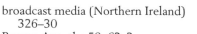

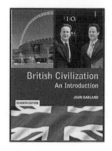

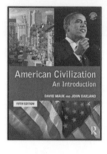

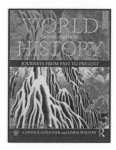